MAKING A MANTRA

CLASS 200 | NEW STUDIES IN RELIGION

Edited by Kathryn Lofton and John Lardas Modern

The Privilege of Being Banal: Art, Secularism, and Catholicism in Paris
by Elayne Oliphant

Experiments with Power: Obeah and the Remaking of Religion in Trinidad
by J. Brent Crosson

The Lives of Objects: Material Culture, Experience, and the Real in the History of Early Christianity
by Maia Kotrosits

Make Yourselves Gods: Mormons and the Unfinished Business of American Secularism
by Peter Coviello

Hunted: Predation and Pentecostalism in Guatemala
by Kevin Lewis O'Neill

The Aliites: Race and Law in the Religions of Noble Drew Ali
by Spencer Dew

Faking Liberties: Religious Freedom in American-Occupied Japan
by Jolyon Baraka Thomas

Credulity: A Cultural History of US Mesmerism
by Emily Ogden

Consuming Religion
by Kathryn Lofton

Death Be Not Proud: The Art of Holy Attention
by David Marno

MAKING A MANTRA

Tantric Ritual and Renunciation on the Jain Path to Liberation

ELLEN GOUGH

The University of Chicago Press
Chicago and London

The University of Chicago Press, Chicago 60637
The University of Chicago Press, Ltd., London

Published 2021
Printed in the United States of America

30 29 28 27 26 25 24 23 22 21   1 2 3 4 5

ISBN-13: 978-0-226-76690-4 (cloth)
ISBN-13: 978-0-226-76706-2 (paper)
ISBN-13: 978-0-226-76723-9 (e-book)
DOI: https://doi.org/10.7208/chicago/9780226767239.001.0001

Library of Congress Cataloging-in-Publication Data

Names: Gough, Ellen, author.
Title: Making a mantra : tantric ritual and renunciation on the Jain path to liberation / Ellen Gough.
Other titles: Class 200, new studies in religion.
Description: Chicago : University of Chicago Press, 2021. | Series: Class 200 | Includes bibliographical references and index.
Identifiers: LCCN 2020053125 | ISBN 9780226766904 (cloth) | ISBN 9780226767062 (paperback) | ISBN 9780226767239 (ebook)
Subjects: LCSH: Jaina mantras. | Jainism—Rituals.
Classification: LCC BL1377.3 .G68 2021 | DDC 294.4/37—dc23
LC record available at https://lccn.loc.gov/2020053125

For my parents

CONTENTS

A Note on Transliteration and Translation ix
List of Abbreviations xi
Preface xiii

PART ONE: SETTING THE SCENE

Introduction. Tantra, Asceticism, and the Life of a Mantra 3
1 From *Maṅgala* to Mantra: Destroying Karma with Sound 20

PART TWO: THE TANTRICIZATION OF MENDICANT INITIATION

2 *Maṇḍala*s and Mantras: The Jina's Preaching Assembly as a Tantric Initiation Diagram 45
3 Sects and Secrecy: Comparing the Mantras of the Levels of Initiation 69

PART THREE: THE TANTRICIZATION OF DAILY WORSHIP

4 Tantric Meditation as a Means of Liberation 111
5 The Tantric Rituals of Modern Monks 144
Conclusion: The Past Lives of Modern Mantras 197

Acknowledgments 215 *Notes* 219 *Bibliography* 273 *Index* 295

A NOTE ON TRANSLITERATION AND TRANSLATION

THIS BOOK ENGAGES WITH SOURCES IN Sanskrit, different Prakrits, Gujarati, and Hindi. Unless noted otherwise, for consistency, I have transcribed all terms and titles of texts into Sanskrit (*vidhāna* instead of the Hindi *vidhān*, Prince Megha instead of the Prakrit Meha). This means that terms in parentheses in translations of Prakrit texts are, unless otherwise noted, in Sanskrit. I have used the Sanskrit version of the names of prominent premodern laypeople (e.g., Paṇḍita Āśādhara) and mendicants of all time periods, including for Śvetāmbaras of the highest rank of mendicancy the suffix *sūri* that indicates their rank as an *ācārya* (e.g., Hemacandrasūri).

There are only a few exceptions to this rule of prioritizing Sanskritized transliteration. In these cases, I transcribe the vernacular pronunciations of a word, removing the medial and final "*a*" sounds that are not pronounced in Hindi and Gujarati. One of these exceptions is the vernacular "Jain," which I use instead of the Sanskrit "Jaina" simply because it has become the standard spelling in academic literature on Jainism in the United States. Another exception is the names of modern lay scholars and their Gujarati and Hindi texts and publishers. I follow the scholars' own romanized versions of their names, if given in the publication (Shrichand instead of Śrīcanda), but if not provided, I transcribe the vernacular spelling of Hindi and Gujarati names and titles (Dhīrajlāl instead of Dhīrajalāla, *Bṛhad Yog Vidhi* instead of *Bṛhadyogavidhi*) because I want to represent the way these names and titles are pronounced today. The Sanskrit titles of modern compilations and multilingual books are replicated as published. I also use the English versions of the names of modern places (e.g., Kekri instead of Kekaḍī). A few common English loanwords—for example, "guru," "karma," "mantra"—are styled roman.

Unless otherwise noted, all translations are my own.

ABBREVIATIONS

ĀP	*Ādipurāṇa* of Jinasena
ĀS	*Ācārāṅgasūtra*
AV	*Aṅgavidyā*
Aup	*Aupapātikasūtra*
Bh	*Bhagavatīsūtra*
Bhāv	*Bhāvasaṅgraha* of Devasena
BYV	*Bṛhad Yog Vidhi* of Pūrṇacandrasāgarasūri
Dh	*Dhavalā* of Vīrasena
JñA	*Jñānārṇava* of Śubhacandra
JñS	*Jñānasāra* of Padmasiṃha
MRR	*Mantrarājarahasya* of Siṃhatilakasūri
Mūl	*Mūlācāra*
NĀV	*Nitya Ārādhanāvidhi* of Somacandrasūri
PP	*Pañcāśakaprakaraṇa* of Haribhadrasūri
PrT	*Pratiṣṭhātilaka* of Nemicandra
SBE	*Sacred Books of the East*
ṢKhĀ	*Ṣaṭkhaṇḍāgama*
SMKS	*Sūrimantrakalpasamuccayaḥ*
Śrā	*Śrāvakācāra* of Amitagati
Śrī	*Śrīsūrimantrapañcaprasthānaprārambhavidhi* of Somacandrasūri
TA	*Tattvānuśāsana* of Rāmasena
TP	*Trilokaprajñapti*
TS	*Tattvārthasūtra*
VMP	*Vidhimārgaprapā* of Jinaprabhasūri
VVK	*Vardhamāna Vidyā Kalpaḥ*
YŚ	*Yogaśāstra* of Hemacandrasūri

PREFACE

IN APRIL 2018, I SPOKE AT Florida International University on "Jain Tantric Meditation." The talk was funded by the local Jain community and was attended mostly by Jains—about fifty local families and a few nuns (*samaṇī*) from the Śvetāmbara Terāpanthī order who were teaching at the university. I was initially nervous about using the term "tantric" in a talk for a Jain audience, since in both English and in Indian vernaculars, it is linked to transgressive acts such as ritualized sex, black magic, and the consumption of meat and intoxicants. In addition, the topic of my talk—a Jain monk's ritual transformation into an enlightened being through visualization practices, the showing of hand gestures (*mudrā*), the recitation and placement on his body of mantras, and the making of offerings of sandalwood powder to a cloth diagram inscribed with mantras—is not often called "tantric" in relevant texts or by modern monks who practice these rites. I anticipated pushback on the use of a word with such unsavory connotations to describe Jain practices, since the Jain path to liberation requires nonviolence, celibacy, adherence to truth, and the rejection of intoxicating substances. I feared that the Jain community would see only harm in the use of this term.

The title of my talk was motivated not by malice, however, but by a desire for academic inclusion. The last few centuries have marked a huge increase in the production of scholarship on "Tantra" and so-called "tantric traditions." Just a few of the many sources of this scholarship include the yearly conference of the American Academy of Religion, which hosts multiple panels in its "Tantric Studies" unit; the academic press Routledge, which publishes the series Studies in Tantric Traditions; and the Society for Tantric Studies, which holds a conference in Arizona every year. But scholarship on Jainism is rarely present in these forums.

By using the term "tantric" as a second-order category to explain some rituals of modern Jain monks, then, I showed the many ways in which the mantra-based practices scholars have defined as tantric form an important part of the path to liberation in some sects of Jainism. And to my relief, my talk was well received. Afterward, a master's student studying Jainism—a devout Jain himself—approached me to recommend a YouTube video of the influential Jain monk Ācārya Mahāprajñā (1920–2010) explaining that the Sanskrit term *tantra* simply means a "system," so *tantra* can mean a systematic ritual use of powerful invocations, or mantras.

This student's understanding of *tantra* as a system of mantras recalls other Jain discussions of the Sanskrit term. The modern monk Ācārya Somacandrasūri, in a Gujarati explanation of monks' daily use of mantras, has explained that a teaching (*śāstra*) on the ritual use of diagrams that contain mantras (*yantra*) is called a *tantra* (*NĀV*, 11–12). The fourteenth-century Jain monk Ācārya Jinaprabhasūri, in a Sanskrit praise poem, declared that the use of the most popular Jain mantra, the Fivefold Praise (*pañcanamaskāra*), should be understood as *tantra* combined with devotion (*bhakti*).[1] And Sagarmal Jain, the important scholar of Jainism and the author of the Hindi study "Jainism and Tantric Ritual Practice," *Jaindharm aur Tāntrik Sādhnā* (1997), chose a Sanskrit verse from the medieval Śaiva text the *Kāmikāgama* to provide a definition of Tantra that can apply to Jainism. This verse has been cited in other academic introductions to Tantra—most famously in *Shakti and Shâkta* (1918) by the pioneer of tantric studies, the British Orientalist John Woodroffe, alias Arthur Avalon—and draws upon an etymology of *tantra* as deriving from the Sanskrit root *tan*, to "spread" or "propagate," and the termination *tra*, "protecting."[2] Summarizing this verse, Sagarmal Jain explains that something is called *tantra* when it is connected to mantras and the components of reality (*tattva*) and it propagates an abundant amount of knowledge of a variety of topics. By means of that knowledge, oneself and others are protected (*Kāmikāgama, Pūrvabhāga* 1.29).[3]

Not all uses of mantras are tantric, however, and these sources do not present a coherent, consistent definition of how mantras are used in *tantra*. In different ways, these Jains gesture at larger dialogues taking place in South Asia among various religious communities—Buddhist, Hindu, and Jain. Therefore, my talk at Florida International University, like Sagarmal Jain's study, highlighted this dialogue by engaging with existing scholarship on tantric traditions. That talk asked the question: What if we apply scholarly definitions of what constitutes a "tantric tradition" to Jainism, which is itself a tradition that has been characterized as ascetic (*śrāmaṇika*), not tantric (*tāntrika*)? How might that complicate our understandings of asceticism, Jainism, and scholarly uses of the term "tantric"?

The student who recommended the video recognized parallels between some scholarly and Jain definitions of the term "*tantra*." He also recognized that Jains perform and discuss many of the worldly and soteriological mantra-based practices that scholars posit as defining components of tantric traditions. Including Jainism in the conversations about tantric traditions, then, can help wrest the term "tantric" from popular connotations involving transgressive acts and the appropriation of material powers, thereby enriching and clarifying the term.

A year after my talk, when I attempted to reach out to the student, I learned that he no longer had email access because he had renounced the world, joining Mahāprajñā's Śvetāmbara Terāpanthī mendicant order. He had become a monk (*muni*), what early Buddhist and Jain scriptures call in Pali and Prakrit a *nigganṭha*, literally meaning "the one without ties," or more broadly, "the unattached one." This foundational practice of detachment remains essential to the continuation of the Jain tradition.

Jains have not, however, remained frozen in time as the unattached ones of the early Jain scriptures, adverse to an engagement with innovations in Indian religiosity. They have contributed profoundly to every major religious development in India, so any rigorous historical or theoretical analysis of Indian religions must, by necessity, engage with Jainism. In one way, then, this book continues the conversation from Florida and reattaches the unattached ones to a larger discussion of the history of ritual development on the Indian subcontinent.

I
SETTING THE SCENE

INTRODUCTION

Tantra, Asceticism, and the Life of a Mantra

IN 2011, MANJU JAIN, A BUSINESSWOMAN and counselor at the Spiritual Healing Center in Nagpur, Maharashtra, published *Jaina Method of Curing*, a study that documents how certain acts of Jain worship can cure various ailments, from headaches to cancer. *Jaina Method of Curing* describes the creation of forty-eight different geometric diagrams (*yantra*) that can be made out of foodstuffs, painted on cloth or paper, or inscribed on metal. These diagrams are composed mainly of words: they contain different incantations (mantra) and praises to people Jains regard as being spiritually advanced and having superhuman powers (*ṛddhi*). In the pages of Manju Jain's book, readers encounter stories from premodern literature and letters from doctors in India and abroad describing how people's lives have been transformed through the ritual use of the *yantra*s along with the recitation of verses from the medieval Jain Sanskrit praise poem the "Hymn of the Devoted Gods," the *Bhaktāmarastotra*. One of the many case studies in the book tells the story of a fourteen-year-old girl who was being treated for leukemia at the Central India Cancer Research Institute, Nagpur. When doctors told Manju Jain that the patient's platelet count had dropped to 4,000, she introduced the girl to a Jain understanding of the power of sound (*mantraśāstra*):

> I advised her to continuously chant [the] 45th Shloka [verse]—a Cure for incurable diseases [—] which she followed sincerely. Her mother & her father were told to do Abhishek [ritual ablution] of this yantra daily and put this holy water on her forehead, eyes & neck. This was followed

> by them sincerely in the mornings and in the evenings. Within 15 days (24 September to 9 October), her platelet count per cu mm reached 37,000 and her Haemoglobin increased from 3.4gm%hb to 11.1 gm.[1]

Just over a month later—on November 16, 2009—the girl was cancer free.

Skeptics who attribute the healed livers, thwarted miscarriages, and cured cancers described in *Jaina Method of Curing* to nonritual causes may see the monograph not only as a laughable bit of superstition, but also as a dangerous message for the millions of uneducated Indians who should be looking to modern medicine, not charms or magical diagrams, to cure deadly diseases like leukemia. Indeed, in December 2013, the government of Manju Jain's home state of Maharashtra passed the Anti-superstition and Black Magic Act, which outlaws the "display of so-called miracles by a person and thereby earning money" and prevents "a person from taking medical treatment in case of dog, snake or scorpion bite and instead giving him treatment like *mantra-tantra* . . . or such other things."[2]

But while *Jaina Method of Curing* does offer mantra-based relief for snake and dog bites, Manju Jain has repeatedly insisted in interviews and talks that she encourages patients to use Jain *mantraśāstra* not in place of but in concert with allopathic medical treatment. Proponents of Manju Jain's teachings would also deny that following her methods is practicing *tantra*—a term that in modern Indian vernaculars often signifies activities like "black magic, illicit sexuality, and immoral behavior"[3] and that scholarship often uses to describe Asian religious traditions that encourage practitioners to adopt transgressive rites. Indeed, *Jaina Method of Curing* never uses the term "tantric" or *tantra*. Instead, Manju Jain recommends using the mantras and *yantra*s described in the book in combination with ascetic activities such as maintaining a strict vegetarian diet, avoiding salt, remaining celibate, and not eating after sunset. These acts of asceticism ostensibly contradict the desire-embracing practices associated with Tantra, and align more with the world-renouncing ethos of Jainism, a tradition established in north India around the fifth century BCE by Mahāvīra, an ascetic and rough contemporary of the Buddha. For many Jain practitioners and scholars of Asian religions, a "Jain tantric" would appear at first a contradiction in terms.

As we will see in the following pages, however, Jain practices can be tantric. Indeed, some of the incantations Manju Jain uses for healing initially rose to prominence because medieval Jains employed them in ways that scholars have defined as "tantric": as the mantras of initiation ceremonies and daily rituals of purification and divinization. One component of *Jaina*

Method of Curing's regimen in particular—a set of Prakrit praises to ascetics who have achieved superhuman powers (*labdhi*, *ṛddhi*, or *siddhi*)[4]—has played an especially important role in these rituals, and its history reveals how "tantric" practices can emerge naturally from and complement ascetic ones.

The evolving interpretations of this litany—called the *ṛddhi-maṅgala* in this book—chart the progression from early Jain ascetic practices to medieval tantric rituals to a modern engagement with European scholarship and scientific developments. The Prakrit praises were first composed as a forty-four-line benediction (*maṅgala*) for a chapter of a Jain text on karma theory. The first five praises of the benediction honor the founders of Jainism, the twenty-four enlightened teachers who reestablish the Jain teachings on Earth in each time period—the *jinas*—and recognize their clairvoyance (*avadhi*). The beginning of the *maṅgala* reads: *ṇamo jiṇāṇaṃ, ṇamo ohijiṇāṇaṃ, ṇamo paramohijiṇāṇaṃ*, meaning "praise to the *jinas*, praise to the *jinas* with clairvoyant knowledge, praise to the *jinas* with supreme clairvoyant knowledge." The remaining praises of the benediction, then, honor practitioners who have achieved other powers, such as the ability to fly (*ṇamo āgāsagāmīṇaṃ*, "praise to those who can travel in the sky") or to cure with one's touch (*ṇamo āmosahipa*, "praise to those whose touch is medicinal"). In the medieval period, Digambaras and Śvetāmbaras—members of the two main sects of Jainism—began to understand this Prakrit litany as a mantra that should be inscribed on geometric diagrams[5] made on cloth, metal, or other materials and used in rites scholars have called "tantric": initiation ceremonies and divinization practices said to engender the attainment of special powers and eventual liberation. These practices continue to this day, and they have become so influential that the *ṛddhi-maṅgala* has become a common component of lay ritual culture, eventually becoming associated with the *Bhaktāmarastotra* and the healing practices of Manju Jain.

This book examines the connections between these diverse practices. How, when, and why did this litany, rather than one of the thousands of other Indian invocations, acquire the authority to grant superhuman powers and liberation, initiate Jain ascetics, enliven temple images, and cure diseases? And what does the evolving use of these praises say about the beliefs and practices of Jain communities over this period of almost two thousand years? The answers to these questions have as much to do with the philosophies, narratives, art, and ritual practices of Jains as it does with their interactions with the larger religious landscape of South Asia and Asia more broadly.

As highlighted in the example of *Jaina Method of Curing*, however, the topic of this book is not without controversy. Both superhuman powers and the use of mantras are contested aspects of Jainism; some people herald the worldly and soteriological results of their use, while others dismiss their use as superstition and the antithesis of "true Jainism." During my eighteen months of field research for this project in 2013, 2016, and 2019 in various cities in India—with the most time spent in Jaipur, Ahmedabad, and Mumbai—Jain laypeople and mendicants offered a variety of opinions about my topic. One layman in Ahmedabad, an esteemed scholar I visited seeking help with my research, took no interest in my questions, claiming that mendicants who meditate on this mantra "are literate but uneducated," as they perform rituals that are forbidden in the earliest Jain texts. "The most fundamental thing in Jainism," another layman in Mumbai explained to me, "is that there are no spiritual powers." Other practitioners of Jainism disagreed, and their testimonies, combined with hundreds of manuals like *Jaina Method of Curing*, form a vast body of material promoting the potency of these phrases. One monk recounted a time when he was able to cure a layman's seriously injured shoulder by sprinkling it with sandalwood powder sanctified with this mantra. Other mendicants refused to speak to me about the invocation, fearing that its great power would be wrongfully manipulated. When I asked one monk why he could not explain to me the contents of the mantra, he replied, "Why can't just anyone go into the Pentagon?"

These varied responses both reflect and shape the state of academic research on Jain tantric practices. The long-standing secrecy surrounding many aspects of Jain *mantraśāstra* has limited scholarly access to the topic,[6] while literature on both Tantra and Jainism far too often aligns with the sentiments of the practitioners who see the belief in superhuman powers and particular uses of mantras as "non-Jain" and antithetical to the ascetic essence of "authentic" scriptures. Scholarship on Asian religions would define many of the worldly and soteriological uses of Jain mantras discussed in this book as "tantric," yet the Jain and tantric paths to liberation are often seen as separate. Jainism is consistently characterized as a celibate, ascetic path to liberation in which one destroys karma through austerities. Most scholarly discussions of Jainism agree with the *Tattvārthasūtra* (*TS*; ca. fourth/fifth century CE[7]), an important Sanskrit text that codifies earlier Jain teachings into a systematic presentation of the Jain path to liberation. The *Tattvārthasūtra*, accepted as orthodox by both Digambaras and Śvetāmbaras, outlines the seven ontological categories (*tattva*) that make up the contents of the universe: (1) soul (*jīva*), (2) nonsoul (*ajīva*), (3) influx of karma to the soul (*āśrava*), (4) bondage of karma to the soul (*bandha*), (5) stopping karma from binding to the soul (*saṃvara*), (6) shedding karma from the soul (*nirjarā*), and (7) liberation of the soul (*mokṣa*) from the cycle of rebirth through "the elimination of all types of karma" that have been bound to the soul (*TS* 10.3).

The text makes it clear that becoming a mendicant and performing ascetic practices constitute the path to liberation. A householder—someone who has not taken the five mendicant vows (*mahāvrata*) of nonviolence (*ahiṃsā*), adherence to the truth (*satya*), not taking what is not given (*asteya*), celibacy (*brahmacarya*), and nonpossession (*aparigraha*)—cannot achieve liberation. Karma is destroyed through asceticism—*tapas*—which is defined as the performance of six external and six internal acts. The external acts are fasting (*anaśana*), limiting one's food (*avamaudarya*), restricting one's food (*vṛttiparisaṅkhyāna*), abstaining from eating tasty food (*rasaparityāga*), sleeping alone (*viviktaśayyāsana*), and bodily suffering (*kāyakleśa*) (*TS* 9.19). The internal practices are atonement (*prāyaścitta*); respecting spiritual leaders, especially mendicants (*vinaya*); serving these spiritual leaders (*vaiyāvṛttya*); study (*svādhyāya*); ignoring the needs of the body (*vyutsarga*); and meditation (*dhyāna*) (*TS* 9.20). Both this influential Jain text and scholarship on Jainism emphasize variations of these twelve practices as the path to liberation.[8]

The tantric path to liberation, however, is characterized as one that requires the ritual use of mantras, not necessarily asceticism, to destroy karma. To achieve liberation, so-called tantric traditions require initiation into the ritual practice of the mantras of the cult; they do not require a monastic initiation. Some tantric traditions can consequently include transgressive rites such as ritualized sex and wine drinking, and many introductions to tantric traditions emphasize tantric practitioners' appropriations of worldly, material powers. Therefore, because of its world-rejecting ethos and requirement that *tapas* destroys karma, Jain texts and practices are rarely cited in any substantial way in scholarship on tantric traditions, despite Jains' longstanding, common use of mantras in tantric ways.

To overcome these scholarly limitations, this book proposes that scholars move beyond the framework of defining entire systems, worldviews, traditions, time periods, texts, or religious practitioners as "tantric" and instead use the term primarily to refer to ritual components. To show how these tantric ritual components developed in Jainism, and thus to shed light on how they developed in India more broadly, this book focuses on the "tantricization" of one Prakrit litany. It looks at this litany's evolution from an auspicious invocation that honors Jain ascetics into a mantra used in tantric rites of initiation and daily worship. This approach sheds light on the dynamics of ritual change on the Indian subcontinent (and in Asia more widely) over a period of nearly two thousand years and illustrates that Jainism includes tantric practices not because it became an instance of a larger medieval tantric paradigm developed by Hindus and Buddhists, but because tantric practices are a logical extension of the ascetic path to liberation.

TANTRA

Tantra is one of the few Sanskrit terms, like *svastika*, that has gained wide recognition in the English language according to definitions only tangentially related to its original uses. "Roughly translated, Tantra means the science of ecstasy. . . . In Tantra, orgasm is not the goal. Pleasure is," Judith Bennett explains in *Sex Signs*, while Gavin Flood more accurately outlines the term's etymology from the Sanskrit root *tan*, "to weave," explaining that *tantra*'s meaning—"the warp of a loom"—metaphorically designates it as a type of system or model.[9] In India, texts have been conceived as woven together like fabrics, so in the medieval period, beginning around the sixth century, *tantra*, like other Sanskrit terms related to stitching, such as *grantha* (knot) and *sūtra* (thread), became a term for a kind of Buddhist or Hindu scripture. *Tantra* began its journey into the English language around 1800,[10] when Indologists used the term to refer to the antinomian, secretive rites involving meat eating, ritualized sex, and consumption of alcohol that some (but certainly not all) of the texts called *tantra* promote. These scholars began to discuss a type of religiosity called Tantrism based on these texts. But because of the diversity of gods, ideologies, and practices promoted in the Tantras, no coherent definition of the term could emerge.

Robert Brown has therefore noted that "almost every study of Tantrism begins by apologizing,"[11] as researchers seem required to show that they do, indeed, understand that Tantra or Tantrism is a problematic category "created out of the scholarly imagination."[12] Many scholars have written on the historiography of Tantra, more or less blaming Westerners from the nineteenth century onward for the construction of this category, which, as Donald Lopez explains, has "zero symbolic value."[13]

The term "tantric" is here to stay, however, and for good reason: scholars of religion need second-order terms to designate different types of beliefs and practices. Scholars thus continue to posit definitions of Tantra, many of which emphasize how it is in one way or another separate from the ascetic path to liberation. The divide between asceticism and Tantrism in scholarship is summed up well by André Padoux's often-quoted definition of Tantra as "an attempt to place kama, desire, in every sense of the word, in the service of liberation . . . not to sacrifice this world for liberation's sake, but to reinstate it, in varying ways, within the perspective of salvation."[14] Scholarship posits Tantra as a way to remain partly in the world—at least, to avoid mendicancy—and still achieve liberation.

In recent decades, the most useful employment of the term "tantric" has also distinguished between ascetic and tantric paths to liberation. This scholarship establishes a distinction between Vedic, ascetic and tantric traditions, and it identifies the Vaiṣṇava Pāñcarātra, different forms of medieval Śaivism grouped under the heading the Śaiva Mantramārga, and forms of Buddhism grouped under the term "Vajrayāna," among other names, as representative of these "tantric traditions." Using the scholarly category tantric to group together these different traditions has been helpful, as scholars have for decades recognized the "shared ritual syntax" of these Vaiṣṇavas, Śaivas, and Buddhists.[15] One key component of this syntax is a liberating initiation into the tradition involving the imparting of karma-destroying mantras and the construction of a *maṇḍala*, defined succinctly by Gudrun Bühnemann as "a space with a special structure that is enclosed and delimited by a circumferential line and into which a deity or deities are invited by means of mantras."[16] These initiations are required in order to perform the liberating rituals of the cult in which practitioners "divinize" themselves—becoming identical to the main deity of the cult—by inscribing mantras on their bodies, chanting and visualizing mantras, and performing certain hand gestures, or *mudrās*.[17]

THE ASCETIC-TANTRIC DIVIDE IN SCHOLARSHIP ON HINDUISM

Alexis Sanderson was the first scholar to promote the use of the Sanskrit term *mantramārga* (path of mantras) for Tantric Śaivism, arguing that scholars should follow the classification of different Śaiva groups found in the *Niśvāsamukha* (ca. seventh century), a text that identifies itself as belonging to the Mantramārga. The *Niśvāsamukha* identifies two forms of Śaivism that require an initiation: the Atimārga and the Mantramārga.[18]

Sanderson argues that the *Niśvāsamukha* understands the Mantramārga in the same way as scholars have understood Tantric Śaivism so modern scholars should use the *Niśvāsamukha*'s distinction between Atimārga and Mantramārga to distinguish between ascetic and tantric Śaivism.[19]

The ascetic worshipers of Śiva belonging to the traditions of the Atimārga understood themselves to be beyond (*ati*) the path (*mārga*) of the Brahmanical life stages (*āśrama*) of student, householder, hermit, and renunciant. Practitioners of the earliest and best-known Atimārga tradition to emerge, the Śaiva Pāśupatas, were brahmin males who had undergone a Vedic initiation required to perform the Vedic fire sacrifice (*upanayana*). They then went on to take the non-Vedic, Pāñcārthika initiation, becoming celibate ascetics in the "'fifth' life-stage, that of the Perfect (*siddha-āśrama*)."[20] Pāśupatas have been documented as early as the second century CE, and thus can be understood as "the earliest organized Hindu ascetic response to the *śramaṇa* [ascetic, renunciant] systems of Buddhism, Jainism, and cognate traditions" that emerged in the early centuries BCE.[21]

The so-called Śaiva Mantramārga developed from the Atimārga, and its rites are first outlined in the *Mūlasūtra* of the *Niśvāsatattvasaṃhitā*, which was likely was composed between 450 and 550 CE.[22] Scholars have laid out some key differences between the practices of the ascetic Atimārga and the tantric Mantramārga. Firstly, all initiates in the Atimārga are male, brahmin ascetics, while initiates into the Mantramārga can be married, come from all castes, and sometimes can be female.[23] Secondly, the Mantramārga puts more emphasis on the ritual pursuit of superhuman powers (*siddhi*).[24] And finally, in the Atimārga, liberation occurs through post-initiatory ascetic practices, while in the Mantramārga, liberation occurs at the time of initiation, when the guru, using mantras, becomes Śiva in order to destroy the karma and impurities of the initiate.[25]

The Mantramārga is thus appropriately named the path of mantras. It constitutes a path to liberation—a path to omniscience, infinite power, and the release of the soul from karma and the cycle of rebirth—that is predicated not on ascetic acts or on one's status as a brahmin male, but on the use of mantras developed by these Śaiva cults. At the time of initiation, mantras are used in a variety of ways, with a key difference between the initiation rites in known texts of the ascetic Pāñcārthika system and in the earliest text of the Śaiva Mantramārga being the inclusion of a *maṇḍala* the initiate must honor to gain entrance into the cult.[26]

Just before the eighth century, Śaiva texts begin to describe how the practitioner who has been initiated into the Mantramārga should perform daily rites involving the placement of mantras on the body to ensure that the karmic bonds that have been loosened at the time of initiation do not rebind.[27] Gavin Flood has compared these rituals of the Śaiva Mantramārga with those of the Vaiṣṇava Pāñcarātra soteriological system of initiation and daily rites, arguing that a "general ritual structure is found in all tantric traditions": it begins with "purificatory ablutions (*snāna*)" and moves on to "the purification of the elements within the body (*bhūtaśuddhi* or *dehaśuddhi*), the divinization of the body through imposing mantras on it (*nyāsa*), internal worship of the deity (*antara/mānasa-yāga*) performed purely in the imagination, followed by external worship (*bahya-yāga*) with offerings of flowers, incense and so on to the deity."[28]

Within the Mantramārga, Śaivas developed the more transgressive practices and worship of fierce goddesses (*śakti*) that many people today associate with the term "tantric."[29] The Kūlamārga—the nondual cults of Śiva and Śakti that developed even more antinomian practices, such as sex with a consort, as a key component of initiation and daily rites—emerged later, with the earliest evidence of their practices dating to the ninth century. While the orgies with lower-class women and consumption of wine and menstrual blood described in the texts of the Kūlamārga may have gained much attention and allowed the term "tantric" to be associated with black magic and sex, these cults were simply a continuation of what scholarship has identified as "tantric traditions." Initiation into a *maṇḍala* and daily rites of purification and divinization using mantras, *mudrās*, and *maṇḍalas*—not transgressive practices—distinguish a tantric tradition from an ascetic one in scholarship on Hinduism.

THE ASCETIC-TANTRIC DIVIDE IN SCHOLARSHIP ON BUDDHISM

Buddhist sources, like Śaiva ones, mark a progression from ascetic Buddhism, to forms of Buddhism that forgo ascetic/monastic initiation in favor of an initiation into a cult of mantras and *maṇḍalas*, to forms of Buddhism that are increasingly antinomian and transgressive. Early Buddhist texts dating from the first few centuries BCE describe only one type of initiation: monastic. These texts—specifically, the *Vinaya* of the Pali Canon—describe how the renunciant, for the ceremony of "going forth" (*pravrajyā*), must approach a senior monk (*upādhyāya, ācārya*); have his hair shaved;

don ochre robes; verbally take refuge in the Buddha, the teachings of the Buddha (*dharma*), and the community of Buddhists (*saṅgha*); and adopt the ten monastic vows, among them nonviolence, celibacy, and refraining from handling gold and silver.[30] To achieve liberation from the cycle of rebirth, this monk or nun (*bhikṣu, bhikṣuṇī*) must follow the monastic rules of conduct outlined in the *Vinaya*, upholding complete chastity.[31] In this way, early Buddhists, like the Śaivas of the Atimārga, saw the rejection of the life of the householder as the path to liberation.

By at least the seventh century, however, new Buddhist texts emerged that outlined a different path to liberation, one that required an initiation (ritual ablution—*abhiṣeka*) into a *maṇḍala* and regular divinization rites involving mantras and *mudrās*. Because the original Sanskrit versions of nearly all these texts have been lost, seventh-century Chinese translations provide us with the most evidence of this new Buddhist system of *maṇḍalas*, *mudrās*, and mantras. The most influential texts, the *Mahāvairocanābhisambodhitantra* (*Mahāvairocanatantra*) and the *Sarvatathāgatatattvasaṃgraha*, date from the end of the seventh century and were translated into Chinese at the outset of the eighth century by the Indian monks Śubhākarasiṃha (637–735), Vajrabodhi (669–741), and Amoghavajra (705–74) and the Chinese monk Yixing (683–727). These translators used various names to refer to this new soteriological system. Śubhakarasiṃha preferred "mantra vehicle" (Skt. *mantrayāna*; Chinese *zhenyan sheng*) and "mantra basket" (Skt. *mantrapiṭaka*; Chinese *zhenyan zang*), while Vajrabodhi and Amoghavajra more often used "path of the adamantine diamond" (Skt. *vajrayāna*; Chinese *jingang cheng*).[32]

In these texts, the initiation rite—*abhiṣeka*—is not a monastic ordination.[33] It does not require vows of celibacy but instead entails the construction out of organic substances such as flowers a large *maṇḍala* into which deities of the cult are be invited by means of mantras.[34] The candidate for initiation will enter this *maṇḍala*, and his guru will pour consecrated water over his head, sanctifying him so that the new initiate has been granted the authority to perform the secret rituals of the cult.[35]

These post-initiatory rituals are said to engender superhuman powers (*siddhi*) and eventual enlightenment and liberation.[36] Buddhists' mantra-based rites of divinization, which are often referred to in English scholarship as "deity yoga," use the same tantric syntax as their Hindu counterparts and likely also developed in the seventh century.[37] The *Mahāvairocanatantra* outlines multiple rites that, like the *dehaśuddhi* rites of Vaiṣṇavas and Śaivas, involve the visualization of the elements for the purification of the body.[38] It also outlines rites that transform the worshiper's body into the body of his chosen deity through mantra repetition (*japa*), visualization, *nyāsa*, and offerings of scents, flowers, lamps, and water to *buddhas* and *bodhisattvas* invoked into a *maṇḍala* via mantras and *mudrās*.[39] In this new system, achieving enlightenment—buddhahood—did not require initiates to become celibate ascetics; instead, initiates practiced mantra-based rites. It is likely no coincidence that the Buddhist *Mañjuśriyamūlakalpa* refers to this system as *mantramārga*, the same term used by Śaivas.[40]

Most modern scholars of Buddhism, however, do not use the term "*mantramārga*." Scholars of East Asia prefer to designate this mantra-based path to liberation as "esoteric Buddhism," because tenth-century Chinese scholars influenced later Korean and Japanese scholars to use a word meaning "secret teaching"—Chinese *mijiao*, Korean *milgyo*, and Japanese *mikkyō*—to refer to a coherent system of Buddhist practices centered around the teachings of the *Mahāvairocanatantra* and the *Sarvatathāgatatattvasaṃgraha*.[41] Scholars of India and Tibet more often use the term "tantric" to refer to these same texts, following Tibetan twelfth-century scholiasts who developed the taxonomy of four classes of texts called tantra: action (*kriyātantra*), practice (*caryātantra*), yoga (*yogatantra*), and supreme yoga (*anuttarayoga*), identifying the *Mahāvairocana* as the principle *caryātantra*, and the *Sarvatathāgatatattvasaṃgraha* as a *yogatantra*.[42]

Other texts identified as *yogatantras* in this scheme, *mahāyogatantras*, developed in the second half of the eighth century and, like contemporaneous texts of the Śaiva Mantramārga, promoted transgressive practices such as visualizing *maṇḍalas* while performing sex. An often-cited quotation from one of these *mahāyogatantras*, the *Guhyasamājatantra*, embodies the antinomian stance of these texts, rejecting the five precepts that a mendicant must accept in order to achieve liberation:

> Those beings who take life,
> Who delight in telling lies,
> Those who covet others' possessions,
> And always delight in [sexual] passion,
> Those who consume faeces and urine as food,
> They are indeed suitable for meditative practice (*sādhana*).[43]

It is this final transgressive development—an inversion of monasticism—that scholars often posit as the defining feature of "Tantric Buddhism."[44] However, as in Hinduism, these cults were simply the latest evolution of the mantra-based tantric paths to liberation.

A variety of Hindu and Buddhist traditions thus have different names but very similar soteriologies of ritual action, thereby establishing a framework for scholars to think in terms of separate ascetic and tantric soteriological systems or traditions.[45] Ascetic traditions such as early Buddhism and the Śaiva Atimārga require an initiation into a life of celibacy and austerities, while tantric systems require an initiation into a *maṇḍala* and mantra-based divinization practices. This division does not mean that scholars do not recognize continuities between early Buddhism and tantric Buddhism, or the Śaiva Atimārga and tantric Śaivism. Scholars also recognize the many ascetic practices tantric initiates undertake. Nevertheless, this division has limited understandings of the historical developments of so-called ascetic traditions and has obscured the extent to which "ascetic systems" such as Jainism have been innovators in the soteriological use of mantras and *maṇḍalas*.[46]

JAINISM: AN ASCETIC TRADITION

In 1879, in the introduction to the Jain canonical text (*āgama*) the *Kalpasūtra*, the great German scholar Hermann Jacobi transformed the field of Indology and the burgeoning study of world religions by arguing that Jainism should be categorized as a distinct religion from Hinduism and Buddhism because early Hindu and Buddhist scriptures referred to Jains, then known as the *nigganṭhas* (Skt. *nirgrantha*)—"the ones without knots" or "the unattached ones"—as heretics (*tīrthika*)."[47] Since this formative period at the end of the nineteenth century when German scholars developed the field of Jain studies,[48] academic introductions to Jainism have, by and large, focused on this idea of Jains as "unattached" and somehow immune to tantric developments that affected Buddhists and Hindus. Padmanabh Jaini's pioneering textbook, *The Jaina Path of Purification* (1979), for example, explains that "Jainism has remained for the most part untouched by the sort of tantric practices which typified many Śaivite cults and eventually permeated the Buddhist community as well."[49] More recently, Jeffery D. Long's *Jainism: An Introduction* (2009) claims that "the tantric approach to the spiritual path was particularly difficult for Jains to assimilate, given the centrality of the ascetic ethos to a Jain understanding and the tradition's metaphysical realism."[50]

It should be no surprise, then, that Jainism is not characterized as a "tantric tradition" or a "tantric system." Scholars present the Jain path to liberation as devoid of the use of esoteric mantras and as involving mendicancy and *tapas* alone.[51] Jains might use mantras and *maṇḍala*s, but do so only for mundane rather than soteriological benefits.[52] In this understanding, *tapas* destroys karma and helps one progress toward liberation, while the ritual use of *maṇḍala*s is a strictly worldly affair, destined to cause repeated rebirth.

Scholarship has sidelined Jainism as an ascetic tradition in this way for a number of reasons. Firstly, the idea that Jainism is a separate religion from Hinduism requires a defining characteristic of the religion. This characteristic became the teachings of the earliest texts: asceticism. Hinduism, conversely, has been understood as an amalgamation of such an enormous variety of beliefs and practices that virtually every Indian act relating to immaterial powers—from the worship of rocks to monistic philosophies—can be part of this tradition.[53] Therefore, if texts or practices suggest that both Hindus and Jains perform a non-ascetic act, Jains must have borrowed the practice.[54] In this formulation, Jains were influenced by their "Hindu"—especially Śaiva—neighbors to use mantras and *maṇḍala*s, but their worship remained a "popular" practice unrelated to "true" Jainism.[55] "There are also Jain Tantric texts, but they are not important or original enough to be described here," André Padoux claims in *The Hindu Tantric World*.[56]

Scholars could label Jain tantric practices as derivative in part because Hindus and Buddhists, unlike Jains, had a category of scripture called Tantra. The preference for textual studies in the early stages of Indology meant that in structuring their understandings of traditions around the "canons" of Buddhism, Hinduism, and Jainism, Orientalist scholars could not overlook an entire category of scripture, regardless of their disdain for the texts' teachings. Despite presenting a more nuanced understanding of the Tantras than "mere manuals of mysticism, magic, and superstition of the worst and most silly kind," introductions to Hinduism used in college classrooms today essentially follow the organization of the first survey of Hinduism in English, Monier-Williams's *Hinduism* (1877).[57] Eugène Burnouf's *Introduction à l'histoire du Buddhism indien* (1844) has similarly set the template for modern introductions to Buddhism.[58] Despite wanting to highlight the "series of entirely human events" in the early *sūtra*s and downplay "the most puerile practices and the most exaggerated superstitions" of the Tantras, Burnouf recognizes the latter's existence.

In Jain studies, late nineteenth-century German Indologists set the template for future studies by declaring that the "Jain canon" included the scriptures that Jains of one sect had classified into groups: the forty-five *āgama*s of some image-worshiping Śvetāmbaras.[59] Though some of these texts contain tantric material, and tantric practices emerge from the teachings in these texts, explicit discussions of mantra-based rituals do not dominate discussions in the *āgamas*; so early surveys of Jainism such as Albrecht Weber's "Über Die Heiligen Schriften der Jaina" (1883, 1885) and Georg Bühler's *Über die Indische Secte der Jaina* (1887) make no mention of mantras or *maṇḍalas*.[60] English-language introductions to Jainism from within the tradition from the early twentieth century emphasized Jain philosophy, not often recognizing lived forms of religiosity as an area of academic study.[61] Specialized studies exist—and will be cited throughout this book—but Jains and non-Jains were aligned from the beginning of Jain studies in excluding *mantraśāstra* from introductions to the tradition.[62]

An examination of the contents of Jains' impressive manuscript libraries highlights, however, the extent to which *mantraśāstra* has influenced Jainism.[63] In a Gujarati study, Dhīrajlāl Ṭokarśī Śāh has listed 148 unpublished Jain ritual manuals that he would consider tantric (Guj. *tantragrantho*),[64] and works that focus on mantras and *yantra*s rival *āgama*s and philosophical works in popularity in Jain manuscript collections throughout India. The collection of Śvetāmbara manuscripts in Patan, Gujarat, for example, contains twenty-four manuscripts of the *Tattvārthasūtra*. In contrast, the same library holds 1,004 manuscripts of the *Bhaktāmarastotra*, the Sanskrit poem associated with the *yantra*s Manju Jain uses in her healing practices.[65] It is thus impossible in one book to properly address the vast scope of the topic of Jain *mantraśāstra*; but framing my study in terms of a single litany that eventually makes its way into the *yantra*s of the *Bhaktāmarastotra* can be one effective strategy for introducing the tantricization of parts of Jainism.[66]

TANTRICIZATION AND THE LIFE OF A MANTRA

In examining the evolution of one litany from the early centuries CE to the present day, I have adopted for this book what David Germano has called a "non-traditional developmental history," whereby the structuring element of a historical study is not a category commonly found in scholarly literature such as a text, a particular individual, place, or time period, or a thematic conceit such as "modernity" or "magic," but is instead a single ritual component.[67] Undertaking Germano's nontraditional developmental history allows me to combine historical and ethnographic methodologies and to compare the practices of Śvetāmbaras and Digambaras. Following the "developmental track of a given element across several different traditions"—in this case, the use of a set of Prakrit praises in Śvetāmbara and Digambara traditions—is one way to see lasting, significant conversations between time periods and sects that have not been previously recognized in scholarship on Jainism.

Focusing on the life of a single incantation can also bring new perspectives to existing understandings of the term "tantric."[68] Rather than beginning with a philosophy, practice, time period, or tradition that scholarship already deems tantric, we begin with a ritual component outside the category and examine how the use of that component changes when it begins to function in ways scholars would identify as tantric. Following Catherine Bell's understanding of "ritualization,"[69] I look at the "tantricization" of the Prakrit praises at the focus of this book.

I use "*tantricization*" instead of "esotericization" or another synonym because "tantric" is consistently used interchangeably with other terms offered in studies of Hinduism and Buddhism. It therefore can become a useful comparative analytical category that does not privilege one tradition over the other, as the term "*esoteric*" privileges Buddhism and Mantramārga privileges Śaivism. The word "tantric" becomes especially useful for distinguishing some ritual practices from others in Jainism, because Jains saw the development of a mantra-based soteriology as fitting seamlessly into their existing ascetic path to liberation and did not coin a term like *mantramārga*, *mijiao*, *mantrayāna*, or *vajrayāna* to distinguish these practices from earlier ascetic soteriologies. Scholarship on Jainism needs the term "tantric" to recognize the different ritual systems Jains have developed over time; indeed, many Jain scholars and practitioners themselves use the terms "*tantra*" or "*tāntrika*" to describe specific uses of mantras.[70]

The Prakrit praises on which this book focuses (the *ṛddhi-maṅgala*) were not originally related to ritual diagrams used in the initiation and promotion of mendicants, but they developed this association during the medieval period.[71] This use of the *ṛddhi-maṅgala* in initiations is one type of tantricization of these praises. Another key ritual of tantric traditions is the mantra-based divinization of the body via visualization rites of purification (*dehaśuddhi*), the imposition of mantras on the body (*nyāsa*), the making of offerings to a *maṇḍala* via *mudrā*s, and the completion of the ritual with a fire offering (*homa*). The *ṛddhi-maṅgala* has also been included in ritual diagrams, both physical and imagined, used in these types of rites, offering another type of tantricization of these praises. These rituals show how the performance of initiations and daily divinization practices involving mantras, as in traditions termed "tantric," are central to the image-worshiping Jain's path to liberation.

Jains seamlessly integrated the tantric use of mantras and *maṇḍala*s into their ascetic path to liberation because the components of tantric traditions were part of the ascetic Jain tradition from an early period: the use of utterances to destroy karma and progress toward liberation, the fostering of superhuman powers, the formation of a non-Vedic lineage of gurus and disciples, the creation of a hierarchical representation of the tradition in the form a *maṇḍala*-like ritual diagram, and the recognition of the identical nature of a worshiper's soul and the object of worship, the enlightened *jina*. Ascetic and tantric practices are not, then, in opposition to each other. Instead, in many ways, the mantra-based path to liberation emerged out of an ascetic model in which one must separate oneself from the material world, reject societal norms, and connect oneself to a non-Vedic lineage in order to achieve liberation.[72] This is not to say that tantric practices emerged solely from ascetic practices,[73] but that Jain sources can encourage scholars to examine the ways in which they did. Tantric practices did not arise from a nondual vision of the cosmos in which practitioners seeking liberation embrace the pleasures of the material world to realize the ultimate reality. The movement from asceticism to antinomian tantric practices is not a leap from a path of rejecting the world (celibacy) to a separate route that embraces it (sex). Rather, it is a gradual development in ideas about *how* to renounce the life of a brahmin householder.

In this way, the term "tantric" helps us understand what Jains do, and Jainism helps us understand the productive uses of the term. If celibate, vegetarian Jain mendicants perform rituals that have been called "tantric," then the word cannot be defined in terms of antinomian elements such as sex and meat eating. It also cannot define entire traditions or philosophies; it can only relate to ritual elements. As Robert Sharf notes, "If it makes sense to talk about a pan-Asian phenomenon of Tantra at all . . . then I believe it is better approached not in terms of thought ['meanings'] but of practice ['actions']."[74] Here, we can follow the claims of one of the most influential Hindu texts, the *Bhāgavatapurāṇa* (ca. tenth century), which has the god Kṛṣṇa explicitly claim, "My worship is threefold—Vedic, Tāntric, and a synthesis of these two. But of these three modes, one should offer me worship according to the method of his choice".[75] Kṛṣṇa recognizes that tantric rituals are distinct in some ways from other types of ritual action, but he does not argue that the term "tantric" (*tāntrika*) defines an entire soteriology or tradition.

Indeed, it is too simplistic to designate people or religious traditions as wholly tantric, because religious actors and communities are composites of many layers of history and therefore extend into multiple analytic categories. While the ritual lives of Jain laypeople and mendicants include acts that have been consistently labeled tantric in wider scholarship, it would be too reductive to claim that they belong to a tantric community or to argue that Jainism is a tantric tradition or a tantric system. This book does not make assumptions about all of Jainism. Only image-worshiping (Guj. *derāvāsī*, Skt. *mūrtipūjaka*, *mandiramārgin*) Śvetāmbara and Digambara Jains, not the followers of the anti-iconic sects, Terāpanthīs and Sthānakavāsīs, perform tantric practices using *yantras*; and, as noted, many image-worshiping Jains reject these practices.[76] Therefore, rather than thinking in terms of "tantric traditions," it is better to think in terms of tantric ritual components that are used to create traditions.

By combining fieldwork, textual studies, and the study of material culture to tell a very specific story—the life of one set of praises—this book will show that many of the ritual practices Jains perform today arose in the medieval period when earlier ascetic Jain practices were tantricized. The book begins with the birth of the mantra, before it was tantricized—and before it was called a mantra. In the earliest formulation of the praises, they constituted an auspicious benediction of forty-four lines in the Prakrit Digambara text the *Ṣaṭkhaṇḍāgama* (ca. first half of the first millennium CE). The praises had no name and were called a *maṅgala*, not a mantra, but the interpretations of how *maṅgala*s work to destroy karma set the basis for the litany's later development into a mantra used in tantric practices. The book then turns to the tantricization of mendicant initiation and daily worship practices, exploring the historical development and persistence of these practices to this day, as observed during fieldwork in Rajasthan, Gujarat, Madhya Pradesh, and Maharashtra in 2013, 2016, and 2019.

01

FROM *MAṄGALA* TO MANTRA

Destroying Karma with Sound

SINCE THE EARLIEST KNOWN STAGES OF religious thought on the Indian subcontinent, a wide range of sources has posited the idea that sound, properly manipulated, can profoundly affect the universe, bringing practitioners everything from material wealth to the ultimate religious goal, variously conceived. Sanskrit hymns of the early Vedic texts such as the *Ṛgveda Saṃhitā* (ca. 1200 BCE) praise deities to garner their favors of well-being and rebirth in heaven. Later Brahmanical texts such as the *Chāndogya Upaniṣad* (ca. seventh-sixth centuries BCE) famously posit the syllable *oṃ* as embodying eternal life, and texts such as the *Kaṭha Upaniṣad* (ca. fifth century BCE) name *oṃ* as the ultimate principle (*brahman*) to which liberated souls (*ātman*) return.[1] Building on these earlier speculations, Sanskrit grammarians and Brahmanical philosophers at the beginning of the first millennium posited that the only language to have power to change the universe is Sanskrit, the root of all languages (*mūlabhāṣya*) that constitutes the eternal essence of the cosmos (*brahman*).[2]

With the emergence of the early so-called tantric traditions, however, sound began to play a different role in the liberation of the soul from transmigratory existence. The Upaniṣads of the late Vedic period, claim that Sanskrit utterances, as truth and the ultimate principle itself, allow reciters who know this truth to become it. Early tantric traditions, on the other hand, focused on the ability of mantras to destroy the impurities (*mala*) that bind the soul to rebirth. Texts of the Śaiva Mantramārga outline four fetters (*pāśa*) that bind the soul to the material world: impurity (*mala*), confusion about the reality of existence (*māyā*), previous actions (*karman*), and Śiva's will that controls the previous three (*rodhaśakti*). In the Śaiva initiation and subsequent daily rituals of an initiate, at the bequest of Śiva's will, "mantras . . . are the immediate agents by which the fetters are destroyed."[3] For Śaivas of the Mantramārga, then, language is a tool of destruction.

Jains, since their earliest speculations on the nature of sound in the first half of the first millennium, have agreed with these Śaivas. Like Buddhists and many Śaivas of the Mantramārga, Jains rejected the Vedas as an eternal source of truth, and they rejected any language's primacy in the realm of ritual.[4] They did not, for example, develop sophisticated theories about the relationship between the language of their earliest scriptures, Prakrit, the essence of the universe, and ultimate liberation. Jain texts from the first half of the first millennium, both Digambara and Śvetāmbara, envisage sound not as an eternal entity synonymous with *brahman*, but as a modification (*paryaya*/*paryāya*) of matter. Language (*bhāṣā*) has been classified, along with karma, as being caused by one of the eight types of *vargaṇās*, or clusters of matter.[5] Like the Śaivas of the Mantramārga, Jains believe that each living being is an omniscient soul (*jīva*) that is bound to the world through a physical substance, karma. Unlike Śaivas, however, who posit the soul as passive, Jains believe that the soul is active, and every time it does act, it attracts karma, forcing it to act further and to eventually reincarnate.[6] According to the Śvetāmbara canonical text the *Prajñāpanāsūtra*, the karmically bound soul, when it undergoes certain types of action (*yoga*), causes vibrations in the air to drive particles to cluster together to form sound matter.[7] These same actions also cause karma to bind to or fall away from the soul. Therefore, because karma and sound are both material substances that interact with each other and the soul, when Jain texts of the early centuries CE began to discuss the importance of mantras and verbal spells (*vidyā*), they framed the discussion of utterances' power in terms of how sound can modify karma.[8]

To date, little research has been done on how Jains have built on these connections between mantras and karma to develop a philosophy of *mantraśāstra*, with André Padoux claiming that "Jain Mantraśāstra, in fact, does not differ in its essentials from the Hindu version and is not very developed."[9] More recently, Phyllis Granoff has shown how the Digambara Prabhācandra (ninth century), like the Buddhist Dharmakīrti (ca. seventh century),[10] countered the Mīmāṃsakas by stressing that "the power of a mantra does not lie in the language; it lies with the special characteristics of the mantra's author" or reciter.[11] The later Digambara commentator Amṛtacandra (eleventh century?) also adopted this stance.[12] Much more can be said, however, about Jain discussions of how mantras work.

This chapter therefore examines an important source for Jain understandings of the power of sound: commentaries on *maṅgalas*—auspicious preambles, or benedictions, whose placement at the outset of a text remove obstacles to successful reading. Many Jain *vidyās* and mantras used today are made up of Prakrit praises that were originally understood as *maṅgalas*. By far the most popular Jain mantra—which is today recited in nearly every Jain ritual, by Jains of all sects, mendicant and lay—is first found as a *maṅgala* at the start of a Digambara Prakrit text on karma theory dated to the first half of the first millennium, the "Scripture of Six Parts," the *Ṣaṭkhaṇḍāgama*. This mantra today has many names, including the Ṇamokār, Navkār, and Nokār, but in the earliest texts, it is named the "Fivefold Praise," in Prakrit the *paṃcanamokkāra* or *paṃcaṇamoyāra* (Skt. *pañcanamaskāra*), since it honors the Five Supreme Beings (*pañcaparameṣṭhin*) of Jainism: enlightened souls (*arhat*), liberated souls (*siddha*), mendicant leaders (*ācārya*), mendicant teachers (*upādhyāya*), and ordinary mendicants (*sādhu*). This *maṅgala* of the first chapter of the *Ṣaṭkhaṇḍāgama* reads as follows:

> *ṇamo arihaṃtāṇam, ṇamo siddhāṇaṃ, ṇamo āiriyāṇaṃ* |
> *ṇamo uvajjhāyāṇaṃ, ṇamo loe savvasāhūṇaṃ* || (*ṢKhĀ* 1.1)
> Praise to the omniscient beings, praise to the liberated souls,
> praise to the mendicant leaders, praise to the mendicant teachers,
> praise to all mendicants in this world.

By the medieval period, Jain texts begin to call these praises a mantra and encourage its recitation, often affixed with combinations of seed syllables (*bījamantra*), in an impressive variety of rites that could cure diseases, defeat enemies, purify initiands, and so on.

At first blush, these practices seem to contradict the teachings of the earliest Jain texts from the first few centuries BCE, which ban monks from using magical spells and mantras. For example, the *Sūtrakṛtāṅgasūtra*, a Śvetāmbara *āgama*, declares that people who perform "the spells for making somebody fall down, rise, yawn; for making him immovable, or cling to something; for making him sick, or sound, for making somebody go forth, disappear, (or come)" will be reborn as demons (*asura*), evildoers, and those who are blind, deaf, and dumb.[13] And the original text of a Śvetāmbara canonical text, the Praśnavyākaraṇa, that details divination rites and magical spells, was even replaced with a the five mendicant vows, perhaps because of early Jain ideological discomfort over the promotion of magical arts.[14]

Examining the earliest discussions of the *pañcanamaskāra* from the early centuries CE, however, shows why Jains approved of the use of the Fivefold Praise in such a variety of rites. The earliest discussions of the *pañcanamaskāra* essentially argue that its use constitutes one of the six kinds of internal *tapas*—respecting mendicants (*vinaya*). Therefore, its pronunciation destroys karma, effecting material changes in the world.

We thus have found one answer to the question Christopher Minkowski poses in a study of Buddhist and Brahmanical auspicious preambles: "Why should we read the *maṅgala* verses?"[15] Early Jain *maṅgalas* form components of the most important Jain mantras and *vidyās*, so the commentaries on these *maṅgalas* provide a Jain philosophy of *mantraśāstra*. Jains denied the authority of the Vedas, so in the middle of the first millennium when they began to develop an increasing number of rituals centered around the pronunciation of mantras, they did not develop their mantras from the Vedas, nor did they simply appropriate the non-Vedic mantras of "tantric systems" or non-tantric Buddhists. Instead, they looked to their own literature for components of texts that could be used as mantras. The auspicious beginnings to texts from the first few centuries CE were ideally suited to be used in a variety of rituals because scholiasts from the first half of the first millennium had already established that to pronounce them could determine the outcome of certain actions. These Prakrit pronouncements rose to prominence as mantras not because they represented the ultimate reality or were linked to the Vedas or certain deities, but because they praised spiritually advanced souls and modified karma.

This chapter focuses on one *maṅgala* in particular. It introduces the ritual utterance at the focus of this book, a set of Prakrit praises I have termed the *ṛddhi-maṅgala* because it is made up of forty-four praises, most of which are offered to Jain practitioners who have achieved certain superhuman powers (*ṛddhi*), such as the ability to fly or to generate an unlimited amount of food.[16] This *maṅgala* is also first found in the *Ṣaṭkhaṇḍāgama*; while the *pañcanamaskāra* opens the first chapter of this text, the *ṛddhi-maṅgala* opens the fourth and sixth chapters. Both the *pañcanamaskāra* and the *ṛddhi-maṅgala* would eventually become two of the most important

Jain mantras. But while a great deal of literature has been devoted to the *pañcanamaskāra*,[17] few Jains know the meaning and history of the *ṛddhi-maṅgala*, even if they recite it daily. Looking at early Jain texts' discussions of the acquisition of superhuman powers and the only known commentary on the *ṛddhi-maṅgala*, Vīrasena's ninth-century Prakrit text the *Dhavalā*, provides the foundation for understanding the *ṛddhi-maṅgala*'s later emergence in rites of initiation and divination.

SUPERHUMAN POWERS IN EARLY ŚVETĀMBARA AND DIGAMBARA TEXTS

By the early centuries of the Common Era, Brahmanical, Jain, and Buddhist traditions were all in agreement that particularly adept ascetics could generate special powers (*labdhi*, *ṛddhi*, *siddhi*) by practicing different types of austerities.[18] Suzuko Ohira has estimated that Jain texts began to discuss these powers around the fourth century CE,[19] though Sonya Rhie Mace (formerly Quintanilla) has documented "sculptures from as early as the beginning of the first century BCE. . . . [that represent] . . . Jaina monks as *cāraṇamunis* who have achieved the ability to fly through the sky."[20] Early Jain texts maintain that these *labdhi*s or *ṛddhi*s are manifestations of the different qualities (*guṇa*) of the souls present in all living beings—gods, hell beings, plants, animals, humans, and even the elements of earth, water, fire, and air. By the end of the first half of the first millennium, the soul was understood to possess infinite power (*vīrya*), infinite knowledge (*jñāna*), and infinite perception (*darśana*).[21] Superhuman powers, then, can occur when the karmas suppressing this innate power (*vīryāntarāyakarma*) or infinite knowledge and perception (*āvaraṇakarma*) undergo destruction, suppression, or destruction-cum-suppression. In early Jain texts, this destruction and suppression of karma occurs through austerities such as the fasting and bodily suffering.

Both Śvetāmbara and Digambara texts provide lists of these powers. Digambaras often classify these powers into seven or eight different categories. The longest list of extraordinary powers is found in the Digambara Prakrit text the *Trilokaprajñapti* (*TP*), a text on the cosmos and the Jain version of the history of the universe whose core has been dated to between the fifth and seventh centuries CE, though it has additions that date as late as the tenth century.[22] Among other topics, the *Trilokaprajñapti* outlines the makeup of the cosmos and the biographies of each of the founders of Jainism, the "victors," *jinas*, or "fordmakers," *tīrthaṅkaras*: the twenty-four ascetics of our time period who were born on Earth to achieve victory over the senses, become enlightened, and ford the waters of reincarnation for their followers by teaching the truths of Jainism. The fourth chapter of the *Trilokaprajñapti* confirms that, in total, there were 1,452 disciples (*gaṇadhara*) of the twenty-four *tīrthaṅkaras*, with, for example, the first *tīrthaṅkara*, Ṛṣabha, who lived millions of years ago, having eighty-four chief disciples, and the final *tīrthaṅkara* of our time period, Mahāvīra, a historical contemporary of the Buddha, having eleven (*TP* 4.961–63). These 1,452 disciples, the *Trilokaprajñapti* contends, possessed sixty-four different types of special powers, organized into eight categories: (1) power of the intellect (*buddhi*), (2) power to change bodily form (*vikriyā*), (3) the power to perform special actions like flying or moving without bending one's knees (*kriyā*), (4) the power to undertake extreme austerities (*tapas*), (5) physical strength (*bala*), (6) the power of healing (*auṣadhi*), (7) the power to transform speech or food from ordinary to sweet (*rasa*), and (8) the power over certain places (*kṣetra*) (*TP* 4.767–68).

Though Śvetāmbara discussions of these powers are never as long as the list of sixty-four different *ṛddhis* in the *Trilokaprajñapti*, they name similar powers and also associate the powers with ascetics, especially the disciples of the *tīrthaṅkaras*. The canonical *Aupapātikasūtra*, for example, associates twenty-eight different powers with the disciples of Mahāvīra.[23] And in one well-known story from the Śvetāmbara *Bhagavatīsūtra*, Mahāvīra himself shows his soul's power to some competing ascetics. According to the *Bhagavatīsūtra*, one day when wandering outside the town of Vaiśyāyana, Mahāvīra and Gośāla, a follower of the fatalistic ascetic sect the Ājīvikas, came across an ascetic under the heat of the midday sun performing strange austerities. From his long hair, insects kept dropping to the ground, and the ascetic would pick them up and place them back in his dreads. Gośāla laughed and made fun of the ascetic, asking him if he was an ascetic or a home for insects. The ascetic, angered at the disrespect, used his *tejoleśya* power to shoot fire at Gośāla. Mahāvīra, then, out of great compassion, used his power to shoot streams of cool air (*śītaleśya*) to extinguish the fire, saving Gośāla from immanent death.[24] These types of stories about the miraculous powers of the *tīrthaṅkaras* and their disciples are common in Jain texts from the first half of the first millennium CE.

EARLY LITANIES TO PRACTITIONERS WITH SUPERHUMAN POWERS

Digambaras and Śvetāmbaras not only discussed superhuman powers in narratives about famous monks, they also composed litanies to practitioners who have achieved these powers. The lengthiest of these litanies is the *ṛddhi-maṅgala* at the outset of the fourth and sixth chapters of the *Ṣaṭkhaṇḍāgama*. Scholars, using *paṭṭāvali*s, or lists of successions of disciples of Mahāvīra, have placed the composition of the text in the second century—in 156 CE[25]—but these traditional accounts have been challenged.[26] If Ohira is right to date discussions about extraordinary powers to the fourth century and beyond, then the *ṛddhi-maṅgala* could be dated to that time period. In any case, the *Ṣaṭkhaṇḍāgama* likely belongs to the first half of the first millennium CE.

The Ṛddhi-maṅgala of the Ṣaṭkhaṇḍāgama

The so-called *ṛddhi-maṅgala* begins by honoring the enlightened founders of Jainism, the *jina*s, and ends with praises to *jina* shrines and the final and twenty-fourth *jina*, Mahāvīra. In between, it contains seven different groups of praises honoring, in order, practitioners who have achieved (1) powers of intellect, (2) powers of transformation, (3) powers of austerities, (4) powers of healing, (5) powers of physical strength, (6) powers to transform speech or food from ordinary to sweet, and (7) powers to make food and dwellings inexhaustible (*akṣīṇa*).

The *Ṣaṭkhaṇḍāgama* 4.1–44 and 6.1–44 (*Mahābandha* 1–44) both read:

1. *ṇamo jiṇāṇaṃ*
Praise to the *jina*s.

2. *ṇamo ohijiṇāṇaṃ*
Praise to the *jina*s who have clairvoyant knowledge (*avadhi*).

3. *ṇamo paramohijiṇāṇaṃ*
Praise to the *jina*s who have supreme clairvoyant knowledge.

4. *ṇamo savvohijiṇāṇaṃ*
Praise to the *jina*s who have complete clairvoyant knowledge.

5. *ṇamo aṇaṃtohijiṇāṇaṃ*
Praise to the *jina*s who have infinite clairvoyant knowledge.[27]

6. *ṇamo koṭṭhabuddhīṇaṃ*

Praise to those whose intellects are like granaries that store the seeds of teachings.[28]

7. *ṇamo bījabuddhīṇaṃ*

Praise to those who can understand entire teachings from a single word.[29]

8. *ṇamo padāṇusārīṇaṃ*

Praise to those who can have complete knowledge of a text after knowing just one word.[30]

9. *ṇamo saṃbhiṇṇasodārāṇaṃ*

Praise to those who can hear sounds beyond the range of normal hearing.[31]

10. *ṇamo ujumadīṇaṃ*

Praise to those who have limited mind-reading capabilities (*ṛjumati*).

11. *ṇamo viulamadīṇaṃ*

Praise to the *jina*s who have extensive mind-reading capabilities (*vipulamati*).[32]

12. *ṇamo dasapuvviyāṇaṃ*

Praise to those who know ten *pūrva*s.

13. *ṇamo coddasapuvviyāṇaṃ*

Praise to those who know the fourteen *pūrvas*.[33]

14. *ṇamo aṭṭhaṃgamahāṇimittakusalāṇaṃ*

Praise to those who have eight different types of prognostic abilities (*naimittika*).[34]

15. *ṇamo viuvvaṇapattāṇaṃ*

Praise to those who have the power of shape transformation (*vikriyārddhi*).[35]

16. *ṇamo vijjāharaṇaṃ*

Praise to the *vidyādharas*—those who have knowledge of magical spells.

17. *ṇamo cāraṇāṇaṃ*

Praise to those who have extraordinary powers of movement (*cāraṇarddhi*).[36]

18. *ṇamo paṇṇasamaṇāṇaṃ*

Praise to those who have ascetic wisdom (*prajñāśramaṇa*).[37]

19. *ṇamo āgāsagāmīṇaṃ*

Praise to those who can travel in the sky.

20. *ṇamo āsīvisāṇaṃ*

Praise to those who have poisonous speech.[38]

21. *ṇamo diṭṭhivisāṇaṃ*

Praise to those who havc a poisonous gaze.[39]

22. *ṇamo uggatavāṇaṃ*

Praise to those who can endure difficult fasts (*ugratapas*).[40]

23. *ṇamo dittatavāṇaṃ*

Praise to those who can glow from undertaking fasts (*dīptatapas*).[41]

24. *ṇamo tattatavāṇaṃ*
Praise to those who reduce food to its elements rather than to urine, excrement, or semen.[42]

25. *ṇamo mahātavāṇaṃ*
Praise to those mendicants who can undertake all types of fasts.[43]

26. *ṇamo ghoratavāṇaṃ*
Praise to those who can bear extreme (*ghora*) austerities and calamities.[44]

27. *ṇamo ghoraparakkamāṇaṃ*
Praise to those who can destroy the three worlds, make dangerous objects rain down, and dry up the sea.[45]

28. *ṇamo ghoraguṇāṇaṃ*
Praise to those who can perform fierce acts.[46]

29. *ṇamo ghoraguṇabaṃbacārīṇaṃ*
Praise to those whose celibacy ensures safety from disease, thieves, wars, etc.[47]

30. *ṇamo āmosahipattāṇaṃ*
Praise to those whose touch is medicinal.[48]

31. *ṇamo khelosahipattāṇaṃ*
Praise to those whose phlegm, saliva, etc. is medicinal.[49]

32. *ṇamo jallosahipattāṇaṃ*
Praise to those whose sweat is medicinal.[50]

33. *ṇamo viṭṭhosahipattāṇaṃ*
Praise to those whose urine and excrement is medicinal.[51]

34. *ṇamo savvosahipattāṇaṃ*
Praise to those who can heal with all parts of their bodies.[52]

35. *ṇamo maṇabalīṇaṃ*
Praise to those who have a powerful mind.[53]

36. *ṇamo vacibalīṇaṃ*
Praise to those who have powerful speech.[54]

37. *ṇamo kāyabalīṇaṃ*
Praise to those who have a powerful body.[55]

38. *ṇamo khīrasavīṇaṃ*
Praise to those who have milk-like speech or the power to transform rough food into milk.

39. *ṇamo sappisavīṇaṃ*
Praise to those who have ghee-like speech or the power to transform rough food into ghee.

40. *ṇamo mahusavīṇaṃ*
Praise to those who have honey-like speech or the power to transform rough food into honey.

41. *ṇamo amaḍasavīṇaṃ*
Praise to those who have nectar-like speech or the power to transform rough food into nectar.[56]

42. *ṇamo akkhīṇamahāṇasāṇaṃ*
Praise to those who can provide an inexhaustible supply of food.[57]

43. *ṇamo savvasiddhāyadaṇāṇaṃ*
Praise to all the Jain shrines.

44. *ṇamo vaḍḍhamāṇabuddharisissa*
Praise to the sage Vardhamāna Mahāvīra.

Magical Spells of the *Aṅgavidyā*

Some other early litanies to practitioners with superhuman powers are found in a Prakrit Śvetāmbara text, the "Knowledge of the Parts of the Body," the *Aṅgavidyā* (*AV*), which details how to divine outcomes based on a variety of sources, itemized in sixty chapters. In this text, signs shown by one's bodily limbs (*aṅga*), different types of dreams, and signs in the heavens such as rainbows and constellations can all be used to divine outcomes. The *Aṅgavidyā* has been dated to the fourth century CE based on coins and other objects described in the text, but this date has been debated. While some Śvetāmbaras include the text in the category of miscellaneous (*prakīrṇaka*) texts of the canon, others place it outside the canonical texts, in part because it includes many worldly topics such as sexual positions and warfare.[58]

Divination rites described in the first ten chapters of the *Aṅgavidyā* prescribe the pronunciation of several different *maṅgala*s and *vidyā*s that contain praises to practitioners with extraordinary powers. The text itself opens with a *maṅgala* that corresponds to the *pañcanamaskāra* plus the first five lines of the *ṛddhi-maṅgala* that praise the clairvoyant *jina*s (*AV*, 1). Chapter 8, then, is entitled "*Bhūmikarma*" (Pkt. *bhūmikamma*), or the "establishment of a foundation." The chapter outlines a series of rituals required as foundational for practicing divination through the examination of limbs of the body. In one rite, the practitioner should fast for three meals and then break the fast on the fourteenth day of the dark half of a month. Then, wearing unstitched garments, he should break the three-day fast seated on a mat made of *kuśa* grass and recite a ritual formula eight hundred times that opens with the *pañcanamaskāra* and praises to people with superhuman powers of healing, intellect, and an inexhaustible supply of food, among other praises of the *ṛddhi-maṅgala* (*AV*, ch. 8, p. 8, lines 7–13). Later in the same chapter, before a list of twenty-three different actions such as laughing and yawning that should be analyzed to predict the future, the text again records a series of praises that include lines similar to the *pañcanamaskāra* and *ṛddhi-maṅgala*. This time, the litany praises the mendicant leaders who possess the eight different types of prognostic abilities, ascetics who have the four types of discrimination, those who know magical spells, and those who have extraordinary powers of movement, such as flying (*AV*, ch. 8, p. 9, lines 9–10).

The ninth chapter of the *Aṅgavidyā*, which describes a scene in which a client who wishes to portend the future arrives for analysis, also begins with a *maṅgala* that includes praises of the *ṛddhi-maṅgala*. Along with other praises, it praises the Śrutakevalins—the mendicants who knew the ancient, now-forgotten Jain scriptures the *pūrva*s and are known for their superhuman abilities and knowledge of spells. It also praises those people who know the eight types of prognostication (*AV*, ch. 9, p. 57, lines 1, 3).

A Spell of the *Mahāniśīthasūtra*

Another example of the ritual use of part of the *ṛddhi-maṅgala* is found in the *Mahāniśīthasūtra* (ca. eighth to ninth centuries), a text on mendicant conduct that is accepted as a canonical text on mendicant discipline (*chedasūtra*) by image-worshiping Śvetāmbaras but rejected by the anti-iconic Sthānakavāsī and Terāpanthī Śvetāmbaras because of its late composition and promotion of temple worship.[59] Along with describing the use of the *pañcanamaskāra* in a variety of contexts, the *Mahāniśīthasūtra* also describes an expiation rite that requires the recitation of a portion of the *ṛddhi-maṅgala*. The incantation is here termed the "Spell of Śrutadevatā," the embodiment of the scriptural teachings. The *vidyā* is outlined in the context of a lengthy ritual that mendicants should undertake on an auspicious day to rid themselves of a fault (*śalya*).

The *Mahāniśīthasūtra* instructs that for this ritual, a mendicant should undertake a series of fasts (*ācāmāmla*) over a period of 13.5 days, recite the *pañcanamaskāra*, praise the temple and mendicants, and confess to his wrongdoings.[60] Then the monk should fast for two and half more days and, in a temple, recite one hundred thousand times an incantation that includes praises to Mahāvīra and ascetics with powers of healing, intellect, mind reading, and the production of an inexhaustible amount of food, among other powers (*Mahāniśīthasūtra* 1.7–8). In this spell, as in the spells of the *Aṅgavidyā*, there is a connection between the superhuman powers invoked and the purpose of the spell. The chapters of the *Aṅgavidyā* show a link between honoring practitioners with superhuman powers that relate to divination and superhuman knowledge and the desire to cultivate these qualities in oneself in order to know the future. And in this spell in the *Mahāniśīthasūtra*, the superhuman powers of knowledge, memory, and listening relate directly to the deity of the scriptures the spell propitiates, Śrutadevatā, who in some Jain texts is identified as the goddess of knowledge, Sarasvatī.[61]

However, while it may make semantic sense to place praises to knowledge in the context of honoring scriptures, the *Mahāniśītha*, like the *Aṅgavidyā* and the *Ṣaṭkhaṇḍāgama*, never explains how exactly these praises operate in the universe. The *Ṣaṭkhaṇḍāgama* never explains why forty-four praises to practitioners with superhuman powers would be placed at the outset of two chapters on karma theory, the *Aṅgavidyā* never explains why reciting a praise to mendicants who can cure diseases with their bodily fluids should aid in divination practices, and the *Mahāniśītha* does not clarify why these praises should be recited in an expiation rite. Unfortunately, while Jain texts from the first half of the first millennium make plenty of references to the power of verbal spells and mantras,[62] we have few detailed prescriptions of how they work. There are, however, early Jain discussions of how *maṅgala*s operate in the universe that can be used to explain the power of these spells.

DEFINING *MAṄGALA*

By the middle of the first millennium, it had become standard practice for authors of Sanskrit and Prakrit texts to place *maṅgala*s at the beginning of texts to ensure readers' unhindered completion of the text at hand. The origins of this practice are unclear, though Minkowski has suggested, among other hypotheses, that they were first formed because of the "rise of the personal deity [*iṣṭadevatā*]" and/or "the advent of astrology on the subcontinent in the first few centuries CE."[63] The idea that unfavorable events can be offset by reciting certain praises to deities, Minkowski suggests, perhaps emerged only after astrological traditions had established that people can determine and ritually change the outcomes of future events. In fact, the oldest Brahmanical text with a *maṅgala* Minkowski has found is a fourth-century text on astrology, Mīnarāja's *Vṛddhayavanajātaka*.[64]

However, the theory that astrology influenced the composition of *maṅgala*s requires more research to substantiate. Even earlier *maṅgala*s than

Mīnarāja's are found in Jain and Buddhist sources: Minkowski notes, for example, that the earliest *maṅgala* he has found comes from a Buddhist text from the second century CE, Nāgārjuna's *Mūlamadhyakakārikā*.[65] In addition, inscriptions as early as the third-century-BCE Aśokan rock edicts 1 and 2 at Jaugaḍa in modern-day Odisha contain symbols like the *svastika* at the outset of the inscription that appear to have functioned as auspicious openings to the declarations of the inscriptions.[66]

One of these inscriptions that certainly predates the emergence of astrology on the subcontinent around the second century CE—King Khāravela's lengthy inscription from the second century BCE at the monastic caves in Kalinga, in modern-day Odisha—opens with Jain praises that could be understood as a *maṅgala*. Before the inscription that describes King Khāravela's excavation of the caves and other events in his life, two lines are inscribed that praise the enlightened and liberated souls: *namo arahaṃtānaṃ* | *namo savvasiddhānaṃ*.[67] These two lines are reminiscent of the most famous Jain *maṅgala*, the *pañcanamaskāra*, which opens the first chapter of the *Ṣaṭkhaṇḍāgama*.

The *Mūlācāra*'s Discussion of *Maṅgalas*

Another early Jain source for *maṅgalas* is the *Mūlācāra*, an important Digambara Prakrit text on mendicant conduct attributed to Vaṭṭakera; the text contains *maṅgala* verses at the outset of each of its twelve chapters. While the *Mūlācāra* is difficult to date, evidence suggests that it is quite old. The seventh chapter is understood to be an earlier version of the Śvetāmbara *Āvaśyakaniryukti*, which was codified between the first and fifth centuries CE.[68] We can thus safely place the *Mūlācāra* in the first half of the first millennium.

It is important to note that the seventh chapter of the *Mūlācāra* opens with a Prakrit benediction with the same meaning as the *pañcanamaskāra* of the *Ṣaṭkhaṇḍāgama*, though the wording differs slightly:

> *kāūṇa ṇamokkāraṃ arahaṃtāṇaṃ taheva siddhāṇam* |
> *āiriyauvajjhāe logammi ya savvasāhūṇaṃ* ||
> *āvāsayaṇijjuttī vocchāmi jahākamaṃ samāseṇa* |
> *āyariparaṃparāe jahāgadā āṇupuvvīe* || (*Mūl*, vv. 502–3)

> Having praised the enlightened beings, the liberated beings, the mendicant leaders, the mendicant teachers, and all the mendicants in the world,

> I will pronounce, in order, a condensed commentary on the essential daily duties of a mendicant (*āvaśyaka*) in an orderly manner according to the tradition of the mendicant leaders.

The text then provides several verses of commentary on the nature and purpose of this *maṅgala*, suggesting that its utterance is not simply about gaining the favor of the advanced practitioners invoked to prevent obstacles that might hinder the completion of a text; it is also about more general goals related to happiness, the destruction of karma, and ultimate liberation. In this text, benedictions are effective because of a supplicant's proper sentiment (*bhāva*) and devotion to the correct ideals. Commenting on this *maṅgala*, the *Mūlācāra* claims:

> Whoever is intent on devotion and praises the enlightened one with the proper sentiment quickly achieves freedom from all suffering. Whoever, with pure speech, body, and mind, praises the five teachers who have the qualities [discussed in previous verses] quickly achieves liberation (*nirvṛti*). This five-fold praise destroys all bad karma and is the foremost *maṅgala* of all the *maṅgalas* (*Mūl*, vv. 506, 513, 514).[69]

Even if it was not yet termed a mantra, the *Mūlācāra* sees this fivefold praise not simply as affirming the power of Jain ideology, but as possessing power to modify karma and thus effect a variety of changes in this world. The *Mūlācāra* may be the earliest discussion of the nature and fruits of *maṅgalas*. It is certainly the earliest Jain discussion, and later analyses build on its claims. In Digambara sources, the two lengthiest discussions of the function of a *maṅgala* are found at the beginning of the *Trilokaprajñapti* and Vīrasena's *Dhavalā*, a Prakrit commentary on the *Ṣaṭkhaṇḍāgama* that was composed in modern-day Karnataka, in 816 CE, during the reign of the Rāṣṭrakūṭa king Amoghavarṣa (r. 814–77 CE).[70] Since the *Dhavalā* builds on both the *Mūlācāra* and the *Trilokaprajñapti*, looking at the text's analysis of how both the *pañcanamaskāra* and the *ṛddhi-maṅgala* function in terms of the laws of karma will provide a type of Jain philosophy of mantras that developed between the early centuries CE and the early ninth century.

The Sole Commentary on the Ṛddhi-Maṅgala

Vīrasena's *Dhavalā* provides lengthy commentaries on both the *pañcanamaskāra* and the *ṛddhi-maṅgala*. In his discussion of the *pañcanamaskāra*,

Vīrasena first provides the history of the composition of the two *maṅgalas*. He describes how in the second century CE, when the entirety of the teachings of Mahāvīra was on the brink of being forgotten, Dharasena, the monk who possessed the remaining memory of these teachings, knew he had to preserve these fractions of the scriptures, so he called for two exemplary monks he could task with recording the teachings. Upon meeting two monks, Puṣpadanta and Bhūtabali, Dharasena put them to a test, giving one monk a magical spell with an extra syllable, and the other monk a spell lacking a syllable. He told his two pupils to meditate on these formulas for a period of six fasts. Puṣpadanta and Bhūtabali followed his orders, and eventually a goddess with huge teeth revealed herself to the monk with the lengthened formula, and a goddess with a missing eye materialized before the monk with the shortened formula. Realizing they had been put to a test, Puṣpadanta and Bhūtabali examined their spells, located the problems, and added a syllable to one and removed one from the other. These two monks then again meditated on the formulas, this time conjuring up two beautiful goddesses. When their guru Dharasena saw their deep understanding of the correct combination of sounds and the power of certain syllables, he knew these two monks were worthy of being taught the scriptures. Before his death, Puṣpadanta is said to have recorded the text's first 20 sūtras, placing at the outset a Prakrit benediction praising the Five Supreme Beings of Jainism, the *pañcanamaskāra*. Bhūtabali, then, is said to have completed the remainder of the text, opening the fourth chapter, the *Vedanākhaṇḍa*, and the sixth chapter, the *Mahābandha*, with another Prakrit benediction of forty-four lines, the *ṛddhi-maṅgala* (*Dh* 1.1.1, in *ṢKhĀ*, pt. 1, book 1, ch. 1, pp. 71–72).

Vīrasena explains that these two benedictions represent two different two types of *maṅgalas*: those that have been composed (*nibandha*) for the text at hand, and those that have not (*anibandha*) (*Dh* 1.1.1, p. 42). Contemporary Jains might immediately think that the *pañcanamaskāra* has not been composed, as they often describe this mantra as eternal.[71] Vīrasena insists, however, that Puṣpadanta himself composed the five lines of this *maṅgala* for the *Ṣaṭkhaṇḍāgama* (*Dh* 1.1.1, p. 42).

The *ṛddhi-maṅgala*, on the other hand, was not composed specifically for the *Ṣaṭkhaṇḍāgama*. Instead, Bhūtabali took his *maṅgala* from a *pūrva*, or one of the fourteen Jain scriptures composed during the lifetime of the twenty-third *tīrthaṅkara* Pārśva. Vīrasena explains that Gautama, Mahāvīra's chief disciple, originally placed the *ṛddhi-maṅgala* at the outset of the *Mahākarmaprakṛtiprābhṛta*, the fourth chapter of the second *pūrva*, the *Agrāyaṇīya*.[72]

By the time of Bhūtabali in the second century CE, Jain monks remembered only pieces of these scriptures, which all were eventually forgotten, so when Bhūtabali placed the *ṛddhi-maṅgala* in the *Ṣaṭkhaṇḍāgama*, he thankfully preserved for all time one of the few parts of the ancient Jain scriptures.[73]

While this account cannot be historically verified, as scholars cannot confirm the existence or contents of the *pūrva*s, it is possible that at least a portion of the *ṛddhi-maṅgala* had a life before the *Ṣaṭkhaṇḍāgama*. In any case, it is important to note that Vīrasena does not attempt to claim these praises as timeless. While a mantra like *oṃ* in the Upaniṣads, for example, derives its power because it is eternal and the essence of the cosmos, Vīrasena makes no such claim about these two Jain invocations. Instead, for Vīrasena, these *maṅgala*s are powerful because they praise ideal Jain practitioners, and this devotion and respect destroys karma, thus creating real changes in one's circumstances.

In his analysis of the *pañcanamaskāra*, Vīrasena answers six primary questions related to a *maṅgala*: (1) what is a *maṅgala*, (2) who is the composer (*kartā*) of a *maṅgala*, (3) who is worthy of pronouncing a *maṅgala* (*karaṇīya*), (4) what is the means (*upāya*) of a *maṅgala*, (5) what are the types of *maṅgala*s, and (6) what are the effects (*phala*) of a *maṅgala* (*Dh* 1.1.1, p. 40). He provides a number of different answers to the first question, about the definition of a *maṅgala*. He quotes a few lines of Sanskrit from an unknown text that defines a *maṅgala* as that which dissolves, destroys, slaughters, burns, kills, purifies, and crushes both mental and physical impurities (*mala*) (*Dh* 1.1.1, p. 33). This exact same claim, word for word, is made in the *Trilokaprajñapti* in Prakrit,[74] so it must have been popular. Continuing to quote Sanskrit equivalents of Prakrit verses in the *Trilokaprajñapti*, Vīrasena also glosses the term "*maṅgala*" as that which brings happiness, or the means by which one moves (√*maṅg* = √*gam*) toward accomplishing one's task (*Dh* 1.1.1, pp. 34–35).[75] All these understandings align with the earlier claims in the *Mūlācāra*: *maṅgala*s burn karma so practitioners can advance toward particular goals.

To give us a sense of what, or who, could be praised in a *maṅgala*, Vīrasena further identifies *maṅgala* as the *jīva*, or soul, and states that it contains qualities like infinite knowledge (*Dh* 1.1.1, pp. 35–37). Still using Sanskrit and thus drawing upon an earlier unknown source, he emphasizes that the essence of a soul (*jīvatva*) does not exist in false views (*mithyā*), noncessation of bad behavior (*avirati*), or carelessness (*pramāda*), so wrong-believers cannot be auspicious (*Dh* 1.1.1, p. 37). This argument seems to contradict the Jain understanding that all *jīva*s contain auspicious qualities like infinite knowledge, and it is only karma that causes wrong faith. To circumvent this objection, Vīrasena emphasizes that one must understand *jīva* not just as the substance, which inherently contains auspicious qualities, but also as the particular modification the substance has undergone.[76] By the time of Vīrasena, a key component of Jain ontology had become the idea that the six permanent substances (*dravya*) of the universe—the soul (*jīva*), matter (*pudgala*), motion (*dharma*), rest (*adharma*), space (*ākāśa*), and time (*kāla*)—all contain inherent qualities (*guṇa*) that undergo modifications (*paryāya*). Keeping this in mind, Vīrasena insists that only *jīva*s that have undergone auspicious modifications should be considered *maṅgala* (*Dh* 1.1.1, p. 35). Ultimately, the purpose of these complicated discussions is to draw upon Jain ontology to ensure that praises to non-Jains will not be considered as effective *maṅgala*s.

Vīrasena then answers the second and third questions: who is the composer of a *maṅgala*, and who is worthy of pronouncing a *maṅgala*. He claims that an *ācārya* who has knowledge beyond the fourteen areas of Brahmanical knowledge—the four Vedas, the six limbs of the Veda (Vedāṅga), Nyāya, Mīmāṃsa, the Dharmaśāstras, and the Purāṇas—can compose *maṅgala*s, and only souls that have the ability to achieve liberation (*bhavya*) can pronounce or engage with them (*Dh* 1.1.1, p. 40).[77] He then answers the fourth question, about the means of a *maṅgala*, or what is needed for *maṅgala*s to work. He describes the means of the success a *maṅgala* as whatever leads to the accomplishment of the three jewels that the *Tattvārthasūtra* 1.1 claims constitute the Jain path to liberation: right vision (*darśana*), knowledge, and conduct (*Dh* 1.1.1, p. 40). Here it is clear that the composer of a successful *maṅgala* must be more than a knowledgeable brahmin conversant with the fourteen areas of Vedic study—he must be a Jain ascetic of the highest rank, an *ācārya*. In addition, *maṅgala*s are effective only if the reciter is capable of liberation and the recitation encourages right vision, knowledge, and conduct.

Vīrasena's answer to the fifth question, about the different types of *maṅgala*s, is more elaborate than these previous answers, because he employs a Jain hermeneutical tool whereby a word is analyzed in terms of at least four different categories (*nikṣepa*).[78] According to texts on *nikṣepa*, humans cannot fully understand a word unless they examine how it can be used in different ways. In this case, Vīrasena analyzes the word "*maṅgala*" in light of the categories of name (*nāman*), establishment (*sthāpanā*), substance (*dravya*), place (*kṣetra*), time (*kāla*), and mode (*bhāva*). While Vīrasena's discussion here is interesting—especially since it promotes the important idea that the context of a concept determines its meaning—it is not necessary to get into the weeds of his argument to understand his general claim.[79] Suffice to say that in this analysis, after listing, among other things, particular dates of festivals and pilgrimage sites as auspicious times (*maṅgalakāla*) and places (*maṅgalakṣetra*), he eventually defines the *pañcanamaskāra* as a *bhāvamaṅgala*, or a mode (*bhāva*) of a substance that at the present moment has undergone an auspicious modification (*paryāya*) (*Dh* 1.1.1, pp. 30–31). Ultimately, in this application of *nikṣepa*, Vīrasena's discussion of *maṅgala* stretches far beyond the understanding of a *maṅgala* as a praise-cum-ritual act at the outset of a text. The synonyms he provides of *maṅgala* such as merit (*puṇya*), purified (*pūta*), sacred (*pavitra*), praised (*praśasta*), auspicious (*śiva*), and so on demonstrate that he is not specifically discussing the *pañcanamaskāra*, but rather the idea of auspiciousness in general (*Dh* 1.1.1, p. 33).

When Vīrasena answers the sixth question, about the fruits of a *maṅgala*, he draws upon the *Mūlācāra* and the *Trilokaprajñapti* to emphasize the wide-ranging worldly and soteriological effects of these lines of praise. After claiming that the fruits of a *maṅgala* are the happiness of liberation and prosperity (*abhyudaya*) (*Dh* 1.1.1, p. 40), he then quotes some Prakrit verses similar to ones in the *Trilokaprajñapti* (*TP* 1.29–31) to provide some specific examples of these fruits. He confirms that praising the excellent *jina*s destroys obstacles and fear, ensures that malevolent deities do not cause harm, and guarantees that one will always achieve one's desires (*Dh* 1.1.1, p. 42).

Along with answering these six questions, Vīrasena also engages with an imagined objector. At the conclusion of the commentary on the *pañcanamaskāra* of the first chapter of the *Ṣaṭkhaṇḍāgama*, the objector asks whether or not the *sūtra*, or the scripture itself, should be considered a *maṅgala* (*Dh* 1.1.1, p. 42). If a text is not a *maṅgala*, the objector reasons, then it should not be understood as a scripture (*sūtra*), because as something inauspicious, it would cause bad karma to attach to one's soul. On the other hand, if it is understood as a *maṅgala*, then there is no use in the auspicious invocation, because one could, by means of the scripture alone, achieve one's goals (*Dh* 1.1.1, pp. 42–43). Vīrasena responds to this objector by asserting that the *maṅgala* is necessary because the scripture and the auspicious invocation destroy bad karmas in different ways. The *maṅgala* prevents obstacles in reading, while the *sūtra* at all times destroys innumerable forms of bad karma, and then eventually is the cause of the destruction of all karma. Refuting the objector's comment that the *namaskāra* also will destroy all karmas in the end, Vīrasena counters that this is not the case because without understanding the subjects of the scriptures, praising Jain holy beings does not destroy karma (*Dh* 1.1.1, p. 43). Karma attaches to one's soul with every action, so pure meditation (*śukladhyāna*), which culminates in the cessation of all activity, mental and physical, is the means of the destruction of all karma. *Namaskāras* alone are not pure meditation, Vīrasena confirms (*Dh* 1.1.1, p. 43).[80] In this way, he promotes the use of invocations for destroying karma and making progress on the path to liberation, but he does not undermine the Jain ascetic path to liberation, which requires the cessation of activity for complete liberation.

And in his commentary on the *ṛddhi-maṅgala* of the fourth chapter of the *Ṣaṭkhaṇḍāgama*, Vīrasena continues his engagement with the imagined objector to further discuss the nature and fruits of a *maṅgala*. After concisely defining a *maṅgala* as that which destroys previously accumulated karmas (*Dh* 4.1.1, p. 2), he addresses an important critique related to how, and in which contexts, the praises of the *ṛddhi-maṅgala* operate. The objector notes that if these praises destroy only karmas that hinder the study of scripture, then recitation at the time of death would be useless (*Dh* 4.1.1, p. 3). Vīrasena responds that no rule declares that *maṅgalas* destroy only karmas that hinder the study of scripture (*Dh* 4.1.1, p. 4). This means that while Vīrasena does not specify when, where, and how one should recite or study the *ṛddhi-maṅgala* outside the context of reading the *Ṣaṭkhaṇḍāgama*, he accepts the recitation of *maṅgalas* as a legitimate way to destroy different types of karmas in a variety of contexts, including at the time of death. To show these diverse ways in which a *maṅgala* can be used, he quotes the *Mūlācāra*'s verse on how the *pañcanamaskāra* destroys *all* bad karma, not just karma related to reading scripture, and another Prakrit verse similar to *Trilokaprajñapti* 1.29 that insists that a *maṅgala* must be placed at the beginning, middle, and end of a text so students can complete the text easily, have uninterrupted study, and retain knowledge (*Dh* 4.1.1, p. 4). A *maṅgala*, according to this commentary, should not simply be understood as a text's benediction; it operates in different parts of a text, and even outside the context of a text, in the same way as a spell or a mantra, producing distinct results depending on which type of setting, action, knowledge, and devotion accompanies its study or recitation.

The *Dhavalā*, therefore, sheds light on how Jains of that time conceptualized the workings of mantras and *vidyās*. According to Vīrasena, mantras are effective only if paired with right vision, knowledge, and conduct learned from the Jain scriptures; they should be composed by knowledgeable mendicant leaders; they should be recited by souls who have the ability to achieve liberation; they are not effective if they praise wrong-believers; their results differ based on context and can relate to mundane and supramundane goals; and they function in this universe because their recitation modifies different types of karma. Vīrasena's silence on how, exactly, one should use these praises in ritual should not be taken for this *maṅgala*'s lack of ritual use among Digambaras at that time, since Vīrasena was much more interested in analyzing karma theory than in outlining ritual. His mention that the *maṅgala* can be recited at the time of death to destroy karma and presumably bring about a better rebirth suggests that Digambaras used it in this way by the outset of the ninth century.

Indeed, Vīrasena may have even known about geometric diagrams on which the *ṛddhi-maṅgala* were inscribed, since he references the name of one of these diagrams, the Ring of Disciples (*gaṇadharavalaya*). Throughout his commentary on the *ṛddhi-maṅgala*, Vīrasena repeatedly refers to the disciples (*gaṇadhara*) of the *jinas* as the people who have obtained these powers.[81] For example, *Dhavalā* 4.1.7 notes that the disciples must possess the power of "seed intellect" (*koṣṭhabuddhi*) because without the ability to store various teachings and texts in their intellects like seeds in a granary, the disciples could not have compiled the twelve limbs (*aṅga*) of the canon from the words of the *tīrthaṅkaras* (*Dh* 4.1.7, pp. 58–59). Later in the commentary, he lists all the superhuman powers that are associated with the disciples, citing a Prakrit verse from an unknown source whose full meaning remains a bit obscure:[82]

> *buddhitavaviuvaṇosahirasabalakkhīṇasussarattādī* |
> *ohimaṇapajjavehi ya havaṃti gaṇabālayā sahiyā* || (*Dh* 4.1.44, p. 128)

> The powers of intellect, austerities, bodily transformation, liquids, strength, imperishability of food and space, beautiful speech, etc., along with the powers of clairvoyance, and mind-reading, are the *gaṇabālayas*.

This verse could have important implications for the history of Jain *mantraśāstra*. While the meaning of the term "*gaṇabālaya*" is not entirely clear, it likely refers to a ring (*vālaka*) of the *tīrthaṅkaras*' disciples (*gaṇa*[*dhara*]). The ritual diagrams we will look at in the next three chapters, termed exactly that—"Ring of Disciples"—were likely so named because these powers associated with the disciples are inscribed in rings. In using this term, Vīrasena's *Dhavalā* thus not only presents a sophisticated Jain understanding of the power of certain invocations, it also suggests that by at least the eighth century, the *ṛddhi-maṅgala* was inscribed on ritual diagrams and used as a powerful invocation that could manipulate a variety of situations unrelated to reading scripture.

THE POWER OF A PRAISE

The *Dhavalā* is not the first Jain text to discuss ritual diagrams, however. Indeed, the ca. seventh-century Śvetāmbara Prakrit text the *Āvaśyakacūrṇi* of Jinadāsa records a story of a miraculous recovery from illness via the propitiation of a ritual diagram that perfectly encapsulates the Jain understandings of invocations analyzed in this chapter.[83] In this tale, a merchant, Jinadatta, wishes to marry the daughter of a man named Dhana, but the daughter, Harāprabhā, is beset by illness. Jinadatta confides to the father, Dhana, that he knows a spell that can cure the girl, but if someone other than a celibate ascetic (*brahmacārin*) undertakes the spell, not only will the spell not work, but the one who recites the spell will die. Dhana thus calls for four different non-Jain celibates. They, as instructed, stand as guardians of the directions of a *maṇḍala* and pronounce *huṃ phaḍu*, but upon pronunciation, they die. Dhana, having lost faith in these non-Jain ascetics, asks some Jain renunciants to participate in the ritual, but they, as pious monks who do not take part in such spells, refuse. Thus, in place of their participation, another *maṇḍala* is made, the names of these Jain monks are written on it, and the diagram is honored. This is the trick! Harāprabhā is cured.

In discussing the early history of praises to Jains with superhuman powers, this chapter has examined some reasons Jains supply for the success of Dhana's second attempt at the spell. The power of a praise, Vīrasena explains in the ninth-century *Dhavalā*, does not come from the language in which the admiration is written, but instead is dependent on proper religious belief and practice.[84] The most powerful Jain invocations therefore include praises to the true celibates who are the embodiments of right vision, knowledge, and conduct: Jain ascetics.[85] Because these praises are essentially a form of *tapas*—praising mendicants—they destroy the karma that blocks the infinite knowledge and power of one's soul.

The *ṛddhi-maṅgala* became an ideal component of the ritual diagrams used in tantric rites of initiation and meditation because of this idea that its pronunciation destroys karma. Because early Jain texts are so difficult to date, it is impossible to argue that Jains were the first to claim that utterances are soteriological tools because they destroy karma. It is clear, however, that karma-destroying utterances, a key component of "tantric traditions," are also present from an early stage of the "ascetic" tradition of Jainism.

Another dominant concern of tantric traditions the obtainment of superhuman powers, is also present in the early stages of Jainism. In Jain texts from the first half of the first millennium, the idea that the destruction of karma allows for the manifestation of the soul's inherent powers developed from an ascetic rejection of material bondage. Jains in the early centuries CE promoted the acquisition of superhuman powers as a natural part of the ascetic path to liberation. With the rise of tantric practices on the subcontinent in the medieval period, they were able build on these ascetic ideas to tantricize their mendicant initiations and daily worship practices.

2
THE TANTRICIZATION OF MENDICANT INITIATION

02

MAṆḌALAS AND MANTRAS

The Jina's Preaching Assembly as a Tantric Initiation Diagram

IN SUKETU MEHTA'S 2004 PULITZER PRIZE–nominated *Maximum City: Bombay Lost and Found*, the journalist returns to the city of his youth after twenty-one years abroad and chronicles his time spent with right-wing militants, corrupt cops, dancing girls, poets, gangsters, and Bollywood directors. Then, in the penultimate chapter, "Goodbye World," Mehta describes the renunciation (*dīkṣā*) of a Śvetāmbara Gujarati family—a wealthy diamond merchant, his wife, and their three teenage children. He zooms in on the "fantastic privations" the family undertakes, describing how the husband and wife will never touch again, how they take vows of nonpossession, shave their heads, don white robes, and "literally [throw] money away" by "[flinging] out their arms, scattering rice mixed with gold and silver coins and currency notes" to throbbing crowds that surround the family as they parade through the streets on a palanquin on the way to take their mendicant vows.[1] By the end of the ceremony, "they have left behind everything from their former world; all traces of Sevantibhai the diamond merchant, Rakshaben the housewife, and their Bombay-bred teenagers, Vicky and Chiku and Karishma. At long last, they have abandoned all their possessions."[2] With this moment, after dedicating five hundred pages to Mumbai's dreams and devastations, excesses and disparities, Mehta provides a way out.

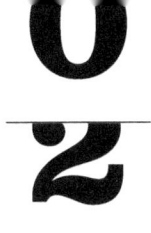

And this is exactly what Jain mendicant initiation is in literature and film: a self-abnegating departure from the world. Writers of popular nonfiction and scholars of Jainism have agreed that Jain initiation is primarily an ascetic undertaking.[3] Michael Carrithers's ethnography of Digambara Jains in south India, for example, highlights the ascetic core of modern Digambara initiations by focusing on how the initiate severs ties with all worldly connections upon initiation, including connections to mendicants. He explains that "the form of the ceremony . . . gives no place to the notion of the *muni saṅgha* [mendicant community]. Unlike the Buddhists, the Digambar Jains do not enshrine the collectivity of ascetics in their initiation. . . . Nor is anything passed on which might form a bond, such as the mantra which is part of many Hindu ascetics' *dīkṣā*."[4] Carrithers emphasizes that modern Digambaras reject ties to a worldly community and thus uphold the "original project of Jainism, which stressed *tapas*," not collectivity.[5] In this view, the Jain path to liberation is about cutting ties with one's community.

A tantric initiation, on the other hand, is seen as a separate enterprise from an ascetic initiation. Hindu and Buddhist tantric initiations are not monastic ordinations—they do not require vows of celibacy, since mantras, not asceticism, are the key to destroying karma. In Buddhism, the ceremony in which one takes the vows of a Buddhist monk (*pravrajyā*) and a tantric ordination (*abhiṣeka*) are separate rituals. Buddhist monks can undergo a tantric initiation, but they do not have to undertake this ordination involving the construction of a *maṇḍala* and a ritual ablution in order to become monks. Similarly, texts of the Pāñcarātra and the Śaiva Mantramārga encourage married householders to initiate. The tantric path to liberation in early tantric traditions, therefore, is separate from the ascetic path and cannot be achieved on one's own. One can receive the karma-destroying mantra used in meditative rites from a guru only after gaining acceptance into the community by honoring the deities of the tradition as represented in the *maṇḍala*.

Because a Jain initiation is not a tantric initiation in this way, Jainism has not been classified as a tantric tradition. Modern Jain initiations are monastic, and they contain many ascetic components that are modeled on descriptions of renunciation in early Jain texts such as the description of Mahāvīra's renunciation of his life as a prince as found in the Śvetāmbara canonical text the *Ācārāṅgasūtra* II (first few centuries BCE).[6] In this account, the king of the gods, Indra, anoints Mahāvīra with oil, perfume, fine robes, and jewelry, and the prince is then seated on a throne on a palanquin and paraded around the streets. The moment of renunciation follows:

> There, just at the beginning of night, [Mahāvīra] caused the palanquin Candraprabhā to stop quietly on a slightly raised untouched ground, quietly descended from it, sat quietly down on a throne with the face towards the east, and took off all his ornaments and finery.

> . . . After the Venerable Ascetic Mahāvīra had plucked out . . . his hair in five handfuls he paid obeisance to all liberated souls, and vowing to do no sinful act, he adopted equanimity (Pkt. *sāmāiyaṃ carittaṃ*).
>
> . . . . When the Venerable Ascetic Mahāvīra had adopted equanimity, which produced a state of the soul in which the reward of former actions is temporarily counteracted . . . he formed the following resolution: I shall for twelve years neglect my body and abandon the care of it; I shall with equanimity bear, undergo, and suffer all calamities arising from divine powers, men or animals.[7]

This text parallels Mehta's account of modern renunciation in many ways. Both accounts describe the flaunting of wealth before it is rejected through the removal of clothes, the pulling out of hair, and the adoption of a lifestyle of extreme abnegation. The *Ācārāṅgasūtra*'s account of Mahāvīra's ascetic initiation also emphasizes that his adoption of a vow of equanimity (*sāmāyika*) halts the karma he has previously accrued from coming to fruition. In early Jain literature, the passions (*kaṣaya*) of pride, anger, deceit, and greed attract karma to the soul, so removal of these passions through equanimity—developing a detached disposition in which one is unconcerned with both the good and the bad—ensures the disassociation of karma from the soul.[8] To this day, Śvetāmbara and Digambara monks must take vows of equanimity upon their initiations, and this understanding that karma is destroyed in the process contrasts the tantric perspective in which mantras destroy karmic bonds built up over previous lifetimes.

Looking further at modern Jain ceremonies of renunciation, however, shows that these ascetic initiations also give great importance to mantras and *maṇḍalas*. At the end of 2013, I participated in two of these ceremonies, one Digambara and one Śvetāmbara.[9] In November, in a small city ninety miles southwest of Jaipur, in Kekri, Rajasthan, I joined hundreds of Digambara laypeople in watching a man and his wife decide to sever their vows of marriage, take the lifelong vows of a Jain monk (*muni*) and nun (*āryikā*), and join the mendicant community of Ācārya Vairāgyanandi.[10] They, like Mahāvīra, made the transition from the comforts of the wealthy to a life of nonposession. The evening before their renunciation, they were paraded around town, seated on a throne under a parasol wearing garlands and royal headwear, and pulled in a chariot by horses following a brass band. The next morning, the chariot took them to a large pavilion (*maṇḍapa*) where they climbed atop a stage in front of hundreds of lay Jains and undertook the acts of asceticism associated with Jain renunciation. The initiands took vows to fast all day, and the monks and nuns of their to-be mendicant community spent hours pulling out their hair, strand by strand, displaying to the crowd the initiands' apathy to the pains and pleasures of the body and their focus on the source of eternal, true pleasure: the soul. The initiating guru Ācārya Vairāgyanandī recited Prakrit verses to impart to the man becoming a monk the twenty-eight root qualities of a mendicant, the first of which are the five mendicant vows: nonviolence, adherence to the truth, not taking what is not given, celibacy, and nonpossession. At the end of the ceremony, members of the lay community presented the initiands the insignia of a Digambara mendicant: a water pot (*kamaṇḍalu*) used to clean after relieving oneself, a broom (*picchikā*) used to nonviolently sweep away living beings on one's path, and a scripture (*śāstra*)—the *Mūlācāra*, which outlines the duties of a Digambara mendicant.[11] And in the climactic moment of the renunciation, the soon-to-be monk stood at the edge of the stage in front of the cheering laypeople, removed his clothes, and adopted the meditative posture of abandoning the body (*kāyotsarga*) by standing, legs shoulder-width apart, hands at his sides. The most memorable moments of the ceremony, therefore, promoted the absolute renunciation of any conformity to societal norms and the embracement of the dualistic ascetic ideal that rejects the body and focuses on the soul.

This ceremony also, however, included the imparting of mantras and the construction of a ritual diagram. While the *muni* initiand's hair was being pulled out, the initiating guru Ācārya Vairāgyanandī dropped cloves on top of his head and recited the key mantra of modern Digambara mendicant initiation, the *vardhamānamantra*, which can be translated as the "mantra of Mahāvīra," or the "mantra of prosperity," as it reflects Mahāvīra's birth name, Vardhamāna, which means "increasing," or "thriving." Ācārya Vairāgyanandī also completed the rite of pulling out the initiand's hair by pronouncing a Sanskrit version of the *pañcanamaskāra*. Then he used sandalwood paste to write the seed-syllable signifying prosperity, *śrī*, thirty-four times on the forehead of the initiand (fig. 2.1) and recited 108 times into a microphone a mantra made up of the first syllables of the names of the Five Supreme Beings of the *pañcanamaskāra*: *a si ā u sā*.

In addition, the husband and wife, along with another man initiating into a lower rank of mendicancy (*kṣullaka*), spent the eight days leading up to the initiation proper making offerings of coconuts to the "Ring of Disciples" (*gaṇadharavalaya*), a large diagram of three rings made from colored synthetic powder at the center of which sat an icon of the *jina* and a metal *yantra* on which the *ṛddhi-maṅgala* was inscribed. Ācārya Vairāgyanandī

FIGURE 2.1. Ācārya Vairāgyanandī (left) uses sandalwood paste to paint mantras on the head of the initiand, who has removed his clothes and has had his hair pulled out. Kekri, Rajasthan, November 2013.

confirmed to me that this diagram of three rings surrounding the *jina* represents the Jina's Preaching Assembly (*samavasaraṇa*)—a common image in Jain art and literature that represents the gathering of humans, gods, and animals in three concentric circles around a *jina* to hear him give his first sermon. For eight days, the initiands recited an expanded version of the *ṛddhi-maṅgala* and praises to the disciples of the *tīrthaṅkaras*, offering 1,452 coconuts to the Ring of Disciples: one for each disciple. In this way, they used the *ṛddhi-maṅgala* to call the disciples into the diagram and then symbolically joined these disciples in gathering around the *jina* to hear his teachings. To complete the ceremony on the final day, they undertook a *homa*, making offerings to a fire as they repeated a Hindi/Sanskrit mantra praising the 1,452 disciples (fig. 2.2).[12]

The Śvetāmbara ceremony of mendicant promotion I witnessed also involved the recitation of the *ṛddhi-maṅgala*, the construction of a model of the Jina's Preaching Assembly, the imparting of an invocation named after Mahāvīra, and the promotion of monastic ideals. In October 2013, I traveled to Surat, Gujarat, to observe the promotion (*padapradāna*) of two image-worshiping (*mūrtipūjaka*) Śvetāmbara monks, first to the rank of mendicant teacher (*upādhyāya*) and then to the highest rank of mendicancy (*ācārya*/*sūri*).[13] The initiating gurus—Aśokasāgarasūri, Jinacandrasāgarasūri, and Hemacandrasāgarasūri—oversaw both these ceremonies in a single day, and

FIGURE 2.2. Above, the three crowned initiands offer 1,452 coconuts to the Ring of Disciples diagram. Below, they make offerings to a fire to complete the ceremony. Rajasthan, November 2013. Photos courtesy of Paras Jain and Jitendra Jain for Khushbu Films.

the monks to be promoted—Nayacandrasāgara and Pūrṇacandrasāgara—took a vow to fast all day and had their hair pulled out in preparation for the rites. The shorter ceremony of promotion to mendicant teacher happened early in the morning, in the worship hall attached to the temple, and was attended only by a few dozen lay devotees and the mendicant community. To become *upādhyāyas*, the monks to be promoted received from their gurus the Prakrit recitation the Spell of Mahāvīra, the *vardhamānavidyā*. Seated on small white platforms, the gurus decorated the two monks' right ears with sandalwood powder, oil, and silver foil (Guj. *bādlā*) and whispered the spell three times into their ears.

In the late morning, the two monks, along with the few dozen monks and nuns of their mendicant community, processed onto the stage in an initiation pavilion established near a temple to undertake a much grander ceremony of promotion to the rank of *ācārya*. Onstage, in the presence of hundreds of lay Jains and a three-tiered model of the Jina's Preaching Assembly, the monks engaged in a series of questions, answers, and recitations with their gurus. The disciples received the symbol of the mendicant leader, the *sthāpanācārya*—the tripod made of three wooden sticks and a white cloth bundle of five shells (symbolizing the Five Supreme Beings) that represents the Jain mendicants of the past whose lineage mendicant leaders preserve.[14] A monk took forty-five minutes to recite all seven hundred verses of the *Nandīsūtra*, an appendix of the Śvetāmbara canon that contains instructions on the study of all the canonical texts and thus symbolizes the *ācārya*'s mastery of the scriptures and his authority to interpret them. Then, in the key moment of promotion, after the monks had circumambulated the model of the Jina's Preaching Assembly while pronouncing the *pañcanamaskāra* (fig. 2.3), the gurus whispered three times into the ritually decorated ears of the candidates the Mantra of the Mendicant Leader, the *sūrimantra*, which contains a version of the *ṛddhi-maṅgala*. They also received cloth diagrams on which the *sūrimantra* is inscribed, the *sūrimantrapaṭa* (see chapter 5).

From one perspective, every component of these Śvetāmbara and Digambara ceremonies upholds the ascetic ideal of the destruction of karma through austerities. These mendicant initiations and promotions promote the twelve acts that constitute *tapas* according to the *Tattvārthasūtra*, including limiting one's food, ignoring the needs of the body, respecting mendicants, and scriptural study. Honoring a model of the Jina's Preaching Assembly and reciting invocations like the *pañcanamaskāra*, the *ṛddhi-maṅgala*, and the Mantra/Spell of Mahāvīra can be understood as the ascetic act of respecting mendicants. However, when we compare these ceremonies with their counterparts in Hindu and Buddhist tantric traditions, we also see that these modern Digambaras and Śvetāmbaras impart mantras and honor diagrams in ways that closely resemble the rites of Hindu and Buddhist tantric initiations and promotions. The "tantric" and "ascetic" components of these modern Jain rituals are difficult to disassemble from each other

FIGURE 2.3. The monk Nayacandrasāgara, with face shield and cloth broom in his hands, his upper garment removed, and his head sprinkled with sanctified scented sandalwood powder (*vāsakṣepa*), circumambulates the model of the Jina's Preaching Assembly established for his promotion to the rank of mendicant leader. Surat, Gujarat, October 2013.

only because Jains have developed their *maṇḍalas* and mantras from earlier Jain understandings: the image of the Jina's Preaching Assembly and the idea that praising mendicants destroys karma. Moving chronologically through Jain texts on mendicant initiation reveals that medieval Jains drew upon early ascetic models to insert key "tantric" components of initiation—mantras and *maṇḍalas*—into existing monastic ordinations.

MENDICANT INITIATION IN EARLY JAIN LITERATURE

Jain texts from the first half of the first millennium contain few discussions of the ritual of renunciation, but those that do exist shed some light on early understandings of the actions required to initiate as a Jain monk. The earliest account of Digambara initiation may be found in Kundakunda's Prakrit text the *Pravacanasāra*, which likely dates to the first half of the first millennium and must have been composed by the eighth century.[15] The beginning of the third chapter dedicated to mendicant duties briefly describes the process of renouncing the world:

> Having again and again honored the liberated souls (*siddha*), the mighty, supreme *jinas*, and the monks (*muni*), if he desires release from suffering, may he become a monk, having taken leave of all his relatives, having been let go by elders, his wife and children, and being intent on the cultivation of knowledge, faith, conduct, austerities, and power.
>
> He prostrates himself before a monk who is the head of a mendicant group (*gaṇin*), fixed in virtues, endowed with distinctive family, form, and age, and honored by mendicants, saying "Admit me," and he is accepted into the mendicant order.
>
> I do not belong to others, nor do others belong to me; there is nothing that is mine here: thus determined and conquering his senses, he adopts a form similar to that in which he was born [i.e., nudity].
>
> The [external] mark [of a Jain monk] consists in possessing a form in which one is born (being nude), in pulling out the hair on one's head and face, in being pure, in being devoid of violence, etc., and in not attending to the body (*apratikarman*). The [internal] mark [of a Jain monk], which is the cause of freedom from rebirth, consists in being free from infatuation (*mūrcchā*) and intentional activity (*ārambha*), in being endowed

with purity of consciousness (*upayoga*) and action (*yoga*), and in having no desire for anything else.[16]

Having adopted [these] mark[s] at the hands of an excellent guru, having bowed before him, and having heard the course of duties consisting of vows, when one begins to practice [these vows], he becomes a monk (*śramaṇa*).[17]

In modern Digambara initiation ceremonies, in order to become a *muni*, initiates must recite the next two verses—*Pravacanasāra* 3.6–7—that outline the twenty-eight root qualities (*mūlaguṇa*) of a male mendicant (*śramaṇa*). These root qualities are:

(1–5) The five mendicant vows:
- nonviolence (*ahiṃsā*)
- truth (*satya*)
- not taking what is not given (*asteya*)
- celibacy (*brahmacarya*)
- nonpossession (*aparigraha*)

(6–10) The five restraints (*samiti*):[18]
- care in walking
- care in speaking
- care in accepting alms
- care in picking things up and putting them down
- care in relieving oneself

(11–15) Restraining the five senses

(16–21) The six essential actions that must be performed daily (*āvaśyaka*):[19]
- equanimity (*sāmāyika*), or lack of attachment and aversion
- recitation of the Prakrit hymn of praise to the twenty-four *jina*s (*caturviṃśatistava*),
- veneration of mendicants (*vandana*), the ritualized honoring of one's gurus
- repentance (*pratikramaṇa*), the standardized Prakrit recitation of repentance for faults performed, knowingly or unknowingly
- abandoning negative acts (*pratyākhyāna*), the adoption of temporary vows to restrict food and other worldly pleasures
- abandoning the body (*kāyotsarga*), the adoption of the meditative posture in which on stands, feet shoulder-width apart, hands dangling at one's sides

(22) Pulling out one's hair

(23) Nudity
(24) Not bathing
(25) Sleeping on the ground
(26) Not brushing one's teeth
(27) Eating standing
(28) Taking meals once a day

These twenty-eight mendicant requirements were likely formulated quite early, with one of the earliest Digambara texts on mendicant conduct, the *Mūlācāra*, also identifying the same twenty-eight qualities (*Mūl*, vv. 2–3).

Narrative accounts of the initial entrance into a mendicant group (*pravrajyā*) from Śvetāmbara canonical texts from the first half of the first millennium such as the *Bhagavatīsūtra* (*Bh*) and the *Jñātādharmakathā* (*Jñā*) provide a bit more information about the rituals surrounding initiation. The majority of these accounts describe how the initiands face the northeast, ritually pull out their hair, remove their clothes and ornaments, and approach a senior mendicant, circumambulating him three times and expressing an intent to renounce using a standard formula found in multiple texts. The *Jñātādharmakathā* contains a lengthy description of the renunciation of Prince Megha, who decides to renounce into the mendicant order of Mahāvīra.[20] In this account, Prince Megha has his hair cut to the length of four fingers, is ritually bathed with gold and silver pots, and then parades through the city on a palanquin. Facing east, the prince sits on the palanquin with his mother and his nurse, who carries two symbols of a Śvetāmbara monk—a broom and an alms bowl—that she bought from a shop so that she could gift them to the prince upon his renunciation (*Jñā* 1.143). After reaching a temple outside the north Indian city of Rājagṛha, the prince stands to the northeast of Mahāvīra, removes his clothes and ornaments, pulls out his hair in five fistfuls, and makes three circumambulations of Mahāvīra while reciting an intention to renounce that includes a description of the state of the world as ablaze with the fire of decay and death, a statement of faith in the Jain teachings, and a declared desire to have one's hair pulled out and to accept the ascetic way of life (*Jñā* 1.140–59).[21] In these early accounts, the pulling out of one's hair seems to constitute the key rite of renunciation.[22] While the general Prakrit term for pulling out one's hair is *muṃḍāvaṇa*, the specific rite performed at renunciation is known as "pulling out of five fistfuls of hair," and this phrase often appears as shorthand for renunciation.

The Śvetāmbara *Jñātādharmakathā* and the Digambara *Pravacanasāra* thus provide some clues about what early Jains were required to do in order to renounce the world. In these texts, we can see the celebratory and ascetic components of modern Jain initiations. We see the procession around town of the initiand that promotes these Jain ideals to the larger community, proclaiming renunciation as the ideal undertaking. We also see the ascetic core of the rite: the removal of clothes for Digambaras; and for initiates of both sects, the pulling out of one's hair, the adoption of mendicant vows, the gifting of the insignia of a mendicant, and an *ācārya*'s acceptance of a disciple. The Digambara *Pravacanasāra*'s account in particular emphasizes the life of extreme abnegation a mendicant must accept, sleeping on the ground, not brushing one's teeth, and eating only once a day while standing. Just as in the narrative of Mahāvīra's renunciation from the *Ācārāṅgasūtra*—in which his adoption of the vow of equanimity halts the inflow of karma—in this account as well, "freedom from rebirth" requires that the mendicant have "no desire." This ascetic core of Jain renunciation belongs to the earliest layer of the rite, found in texts from the first few centuries of the first millennium.

THE JINA'S PREACHING ASSEMBLY IN EARLY JAIN LITERATURE

Texts from the first half of the first millennium also describe another component of modern mendicant initiations and promotions: the Jina's Preaching Assembly. Both Digambara and Śvetāmbara narratives of the lives of the twenty-four *tīrthaṅkara*s confirm that when a *tīrthaṅkara* achieves enlightenment, the gods construct this assembly hall for him to give his first sermon to members of all classes of living beings, and this image of a *tīrthaṅkara* seated at the center of three concentric rings of living beings has become one of the most popular Jain temple images, with Digambaras and Śvetāmbaras from the medieval period onward commonly constructing two- and three-dimensional models of the assembly.[23] The most influential early account of this assembly is found in the *Āvaśyakaniryukti*, a Prakrit commentary on the Śvetāmbara canonical text the *Āvaśyakasūtra* that contains narratives of heroes and discussions of doctrine. Because it was compiled over a long period of time, it is difficult to date the sections of the *Āvaśyakaniryukti*, but its final compilation likely occurred in the fourth to fifth centuries CE.[24]

The *Āvaśyakaniryukti* explains that after Mahāvīra achieved omniscience (*kevalajñāna*), the gods rushed to the scene to construct an assembly hall where he could give his first teaching. The animal vehicles of the gods (the *abhiyoga* deities) and one of the four classes of gods (the *vyantara* gods who inhabit the uppermost region of the underworld) first readied the space by sprinkling water and flowers and establishing in the four directions gateways decorated with ornaments and banners. The three other classes of gods then arrived on the scene to construct three zones where audience members could sit to hear the *jina* preach at the center of the assembly.[25] The *vaimānika* gods, who live in traveling palaces in the heavens, constructed a wall (*vapra*) of jewels and gems protecting the area closest to the *jina*. The *jyotiṣka* gods, the celestial bodies of the middle world, made a wall of gold and jewels protecting the middle section, and the *bhavanavāsin* gods, who inhabit the palaces of uppermost region of the heavens, made the outermost wall out of silver and gold. Then, at the center of the assembly, on a platform ornamented with jewels, other gods prepared Mahāvīra's seat, placing a throne and a canopied stool beneath a tree. The assembly was ready for the *jina*. Mahāvīra entered from the east and sat on his throne under three parasols, flanked by fly whisks. The *vyantara* gods then made three identical images of Mahāvīra to face the other directions so that he would appear simultaneously to everyone in the assembly.

After a full circumambulation of the assembly, gods, humans, and animals took their places in the three zones surrounding Mahāvīra, with movement toward him marking a progression from a lower to higher spiritual status. In the innermost zone of the assembly, the gods and humans were situated in a strict hierarchy. Mahāvīra's disciples, for example, as the most spiritually advanced humans, sat closest to their guru, with the eldest disciple seated the closest. In the middle zone, animals took their places, while the outermost zone was saved for the vehicles of the gods.[26] With the audience members thus arranged, Mahāvīra was able to impart the truths of life and death to all the living beings in the universe simultaneously, with the Prakrit prose commentary, the *Āvaśyakacūrṇi*, explaining that the *jina*'s teachings, upon arrival at the listeners' ears, were translated into their own languages.[27] In the assembly, the *Āvaśyakaniryukti* explains, "there is neither oppression, nor wrong talk, nor mutual hate, nor fear" (562). Nalini Balbir has thus argued that the Jina's Preaching Assembly manifests equanimity, "ability to consider all beings as having as much importance as oneself."[28] In this way, the Jina's Preaching Assembly represents the ascetic path to liberation. It contains the teachings of right vision, knowledge, and conduct; it embodies equanimity; and movement from the border to the center of the assembly—from animals, to laypeople, to ascetics, to the *jina*—maps the levels of existence through which one must progress to destroy one's karma, realize the infinite knowledge, bliss, and power of one's soul, and never reincarnate again.

Though no extant image of a *samavasaraṇa* predates the medieval period, they may well have existed by the time these textual accounts were composed. The eighth-century Śvetāmbara monk Haribhadrasūri, author of the *Āvaśyaka*, a Sanskrit commentary on the *Āvaśyakaniryukti*, references diagrams (*paṭa*) of the assembly mentioned by previous monks.[29] In addition, between the first century BCE and first century CE, Jains had developed diagrams with a seated image of a *jina* surrounded by a symmetrical design. These diagrams were carved into stone "tablets of homage" (*āyagapaṭa*), which have been found in Mathura, in north India, and may have been used as objects of worship "within a monastic or temple setting." The so-called Dhanamitra *āyagapaṭa* at the State Museum, Lucknow, for example, which is dated to ca. 20 BCE, contains a circular diagram at the center of which sits a *jina* in front of a lotus. Three zones surround the *jina*, and four three-pronged symbols (*nandipada*) emerge out of the *jina* in each of the four directions.[30] Though this does not necessarily represent the Jina's Preaching Assembly and we cannot be certain what exactly these images represented at this early period, *āyagapaṭa*s like this show that the representation of a *jina* seated at the center of three concentric rings, or zones, can be traced back to the earliest known Jain images.

Thus, when medieval Jains, in conversation with non-Jains, wanted to develop an image representing their tradition to be constructed during initiations, they did not need to appropriate a *maṇḍala* from another tradition—they had for centuries been using a perfectly symmetrical representation of their tradition with their main object of reverence at the center. Medieval Jains tantricized their mendicant initiation ceremonies by building on early speculations about language's ability to destroy karma to develop initiation mantras. They also built on these earlier depictions of the Jina's Preaching Assembly to develop an initiation *maṇḍala*.

THE TANTRICIZATION OF ŚVETĀMBARA INITIATION

Throwing a Flower onto a *Maṇḍala*

The eighth-century Haribhadrasūri composed an important early Śvetāmbara account of these tantric components of initiation. Haribhadrasūri was one of the most prolific and important Śvetāmbara monks of the medieval period, and several hagiographies have been written about him; but little is known about his actual life. From the contents of the texts attributed to him, however, it is clear that he was well versed in a wide array of non-Jain practices, including Śaiva and Buddhist tantric traditions.[31]

Haribhadrasūri's Prakrit manual on lay and mendicant conduct, the *Pañcāśakaprakaraṇa* (*PP*), which contains one of the earliest known prescriptive accounts of a Śvetāmbara mendicant initiation, engages with these non-Jain tantric traditions.[32] At the outset of the chapter on renunciation, Haribhadrasūri emphasizes the ascetic component of renunciation found in earlier Śvetāmbara texts by defining renunciation as "pulling out one's hair" (*PP* 2.2). He also, however, shows his acceptance of certain tantric elements of initiation. He refers to Jain scriptures as *tantra*s in the final verse of the chapter on initiation,[33] and he devotes almost half of the text's discussion of initiation to the description of the construction and ritual use of a model of the Jina's Preaching Assembly in a way that resembles the tantric use of *maṇḍalas*.

Haribhadrasūri's description of the creation of the Jina's Preaching Assembly corresponds exactly to the account of the assembly in the *Āvaśyakaniryukti*, which makes sense, since he composed a commentary on this text. He first describes how the gods should be invited to purify the ritual space by means of the "opened oyster shell" (*muktāśukti*) *mudrā* (*PP* 2.12–13). He does not specify who should make this hand gesture, but in the ceremony in Surat, a mendicant leader showed this gesture and recited mantras inviting the inhabitants of the assembly while laypeople made offerings of water and flowers. According to Haribhadrasūri, the gods of the clouds should be invited by the sprinkling of scented water, the goddesses of the seasons with the sprinkling of flowers and water, and the gods of the fire with the offering of incense (*PP* 2.13–14). The *vaimānika*, *jyotiṣka*, *bhavanavāsin*, and *vyantara* deities are then invited so that the assembly can be constructed. Three ramparts dividing the three sections of the *samavasaraṇa* should be constructed out of jewels, gold, and silver, respectively, the gates of the assembly should be established in the four directions, and the banner, wheel, parasols, sacred tree, throne, and so forth should be placed at the center of the assembly (*PP* 2.15–16). Then the inhabitants of the assembly should be invited. A *jina* icon should be placed at the center of the *samavasaraṇa* atop a supreme color (*PP* 2.17). The *jina*'s disciples, monks, *vaimānika* goddesses, and nuns should be invited into the southeast section of the assembly (*PP* 2.20). The *bhavanavāsin*, *vyantara*, and *jyotiṣka* goddesses should be established in the southeast section of the assembly, while their male counterparts should be in the western section (*PP* 2.21). The *vaimānika* gods, men, and women should be established in the northeastern section of the innermost zone of the assembly, inside the first wall (*PP* 2.21). Animals such as serpents and deer should take their places in the zone inside the second wall, and the animal vehicles of the gods should be situated inside the third wall, in the zone farthest from the *jina* (*PP* 2.22). It is not clear whether physical representations of all these beings should be created or whether they should simply be called into the model by means of mantras, but the text declares that the *jina* should be placed on a color, and the *vaimānika* gods, along with men and women, should be represented in their respective colors (*PP* 2.21), suggesting a vibrant, ornately decorated, three-dimensional representation of this assembly that aligns perfectly with earlier scriptural accounts.

After the construction of the preaching assembly, the guru should blindfold the initiand with a white cloth and give him a flower, which the initiand should throw onto the replica of the assembly. Where the flower falls determines the birth placement from which the disciple has come and into which he will be born in his next life (*PP* 2.25). If, after three attempts, the aspirant cannot land the flower within the Jina's Preaching Assembly, he is deemed unfit to initiate (*PP* 2.27). A candidate determined suitable for initiation by landing a flower on the assembly, however, should circumambulate the guru three times, dedicating himself to his teacher (*PP* 2.29).

Haribhadrasūri concedes that not all monks accept this flower-throwing ritual, and he explains alternate ways of divining an aspirant's eligibility to renounce. Some monks claim that a disciple's birth placement should be determined by certain utterances; others believe that the appearance of the guru's actions should be an indication; others believe that the brightness of a lamp is determinative; and still others insist that the purity of the initiand's actions establishes birth placement (*PP* 2.26). This recognition of diverging views suggests that the flower-throwing rite was a contested component of Jain initiation, perhaps introduced to Jain ritual culture only shortly before Haribhadrasūri's time.

Indeed, in developing this rite, Haribhadrasūri was likely in conversation with non-Jain tantric traditions, since a blindfolded candidate's throwing of a flower onto a *maṇḍala* is a common component of non-Jain tantric initiations.[34] While Buddhists, Vaiṣṇavas, and Śaivas all eventually interpreted the rite to be a determination of the disciple's initiation name, early textual formulations of initiation rites do not provide clear reasons why a *maṇḍala* would have to be constructed for the ceremony, and different texts provide a range of ritual purposes for the flower throwing beyond simply naming the candidate. The earliest surviving text of the Śaiva Mantramārga, the *Mūlasūtra* of the *Niśvāsatattvasaṃhitā* (ca. 450–550 CE), indicates that the initial initiation (*vidyādīkṣā*) requires the drawing of a round or square *maṇḍala* with a lotus at its center that the initiand must view the morning of his initiation.[35] It does not, however, mention the flower-throwing rite, instead simply stating that upon seeing the *maṇḍala*, the initiand "is released from all the bonds that bind bound souls."[36] Only later Śaiva texts, beginning with the seventh-century *Svāyambhuvasūtrasaṅgraha*, declare that a blindfolded initiand must throw a flower onto this *maṇḍala* to determine his initiatory name:

> He should bring [the initiand], whose face should be covered by a cloth, into the presence of Śiva. He should tell him "Throw this garland, my dear (*aṅga*), onto [the *maṇḍala* in which resides] Śiva." The name made known by the fall of that [garland] should be proclaimed [to the initiand as his initiatory name], followed by the word—śiva.[37]

Vaiṣṇava Pāñcarātrikas also may have taken time to develop this idea that the landing place of the flower should determine the initiate's name. While most later Pāñcarātra texts claim that where the initiand throws his flower onto a *maṇḍala* determines his initiation name and the mantra he should use in later rituals, two earlier texts, the *Jayākhyasaṃhitā* and the *Sātvatasaṃhitā*, outline separate naming rites and do not specify the purpose of the flower-throwing rite. According to the *Sātvatasaṃhitā*, the guru should take the disciple "by the hand," blindfold him, and have him "toss *arghya* [from] the *añjali*. [Then the disciple] may see the mantra's highest abode, which bestows [the fulfillment of every] wish."[38]

Esoteric Buddhists in China, as well, first inserted the construction of a *mandala* into their initiation ceremonies and only later developed the flower-throwing rite to determine the initiate's name. Among the multiple discussions of initiation collected in the earliest Buddhist text to outline the flower-throwing rite, Atikūṭa's *Dhāraṇīsaṅgraha* (654 CE), the earlier-developed rituals do not mention a flower-throwing rite and involve a simpler *maṇḍala* dedicated to a single deity at the center surrounded by mantras; later rites have the initiand throw a flower onto a more elaborate *maṇḍala*.[39] In the *Dhāraṇīsaṅgraha*, the landing place of the initiand's flower on a *maṇḍala* of Buddhist divinities, called the All-Gathering Maṇḍala, determines the deity with whom the aspirant will be associated and the invocation (*dhāraṇī*) he will use for esoteric rituals.[40] Later developments of this ritual would also have the landing place of the flower determine part of the initiand's name. The throwing of a flower onto the diagram constituted a way to combine and systematize earlier "*maṇḍala* initiation rituals associated with individual deities."[41] The All-Gathering Maṇḍala could subsume a variety of cults of deities under a single "self-aware Esoteric tradition,"[42] with initiates linked to one deity via the flower.

Thus, while the ritual function of the initiation *maṇḍala* does not remain static through time and from tradition to tradition, all these *maṇḍala*s have consistently served as powerful representations of the tradition to which the practitioner is dedicating himself. Unlike an icon, which embodies a single divinity, these diagrams can become the loci of many divinities and represent the hierarchy of deities and mantras the tradition upholds.[43] Jain initiation diagrams can thus complicate the idea that the tantric *maṇḍala* represents a nondualistic vision of the world—"the mesocosmic template through which the Tantric practitioner transacts with and appropriates the myriad energies that course through every level of the cosmos."[44] Initiation *maṇḍala*s do not necessarily contain the energies of the universe the practitioner wishes to manipulate. Jain mendicants to not want to transact with the animals who have come to hear the *jina* preach. Rather, initiation *maṇḍala*s show the hierarchy of deities, ideals, and living beings of the tradition, with the focus of worship at the center of the diagram.

The Jain version of this ritual, then, highlights the ideological primacy of the *jina*s and the laws of karma. Just as a Śaiva or Vaiṣṇava *maṇḍala* contains a particular form of Śiva or Viṣṇu at its center and surrounds this deity with lower-level divinities, protector deities, and mantras, the Jina's Preaching Assembly creates a hierarchy of souls in the universe, claiming that all living beings are ultimately less spiritually advanced than the enlightened, supreme soul that is a *jina*. And instead of having the flower-throwing rite determine the initiate's name or chosen mantra, Haribhadrasūri's version of the rite determines the candidate's eligibility to renounce and karmic status.[45] The Jina's Preaching Assembly should not always be considered to be a tantric diagram, since the ritual use of components of worship, not their content or iconography, should determine whether or not they are tantric.[46] In the *Pañcāśakaprakaraṇa*, however, Haribhadrasūri has made this diagram tantric by using it for the flower-throwing rite, thus providing an important account of how Jains drew upon earlier concepts and Jain ideology to tantricize part of the ritual of renunciation.

Imparting a Mantra

The Śvetāmbara text on mendicant conduct the *Mahāniśīthasūtra* (ca. eighth to ninth century) provides a discussion of another key component of a tantric initiation—the imparting of liberating mantras—in its outline of the rituals required to take the five mendicant vows (*upasthāpanā*) or to be promoted to the rank of *gaṇin*, the head of a mendicant group (*gaṇa*). Though, as we saw last chapter, the anti-iconic Śvetāmbara sects do not accept the *Mahāniśīthasūtra* as a canonical text because of its late composition and promotion of image worship, image-worshiping Śvetāmbaras to this day follow the prescriptions of this text when initiating and promoting their mendicants. In the text, Mahāvīra explains to his disciple, Gautama, the rules of renunciation. He describes how the aspirant should bow before his guru, gifting him clothes, and then listen to him deliver a sermon that arouses repulsion at worldly pursuits (*saṃvega*). The guru then should impart a lifelong vow to the disciple that he must honor temple images thrice a day.[47] Mahāvīra continues:

> After [the disciple] has adopted the vow for life, then, Gautama, the guru, pronouncing, "May you be liberated, may you reach the other shore" shall place on the head [of the disciple] seven handfuls of a fragrant substance consecrated by this spell: "*oṃ namo bhagavao arahao! sijjhaü me bhagavatī mahāvijjā! vīre mahāvīre jayavīre seṇavīre vaddhamāṇavīre jayante aparājie! svāhā!*" The ceremony is completed with a fast of a day and a half. By this spell, he, in every respect, will become liberated; he will reach the other shore; when a novice is confirmed as a full mendicant or when a mendicant is promoted to the rank of *gaṇin*, [this spell] must be pronounced seven times.[48]

While earlier accounts of initiation focus on the pulling out of hair and the adoption of monastic vows, this account focuses on the imparting of an invocation that is understood to guarantee liberation.

Scholars of Śaiva traditions have identified this imparting of liberation-granting mantras at the time of initiation as a key way to distinguish between the Atimārga (earlier ascetic Śaiva sects) and the Mantramārga (later tantric Śaiva sects).[49] Jains should not be split into ascetic and tantric sects in this way, since they never developed a wholly tantric soteriology—a quick path to liberation through mantras that is separate from the monastic path.

However, comparing the initiation of Mahāvīra in the *Ācārāṅgasūtra* with this passage shows that medieval Jains also introduced the pronunciation of certain spells as a component of their initiations, thereby introducing a "tantric" component of monastic initiation. While the account of Mahāvīra's renunciation in the *Ācārāṅga* maintains that the vow of equanimity stops the inflow of karma, this passage claims that liberation comes by means of the spell: the *vardhamānavidyā* that we saw was imparted to the modern Śvetāmbara monks in their promotion to the rank of mendicant teacher. The content of this spell also suggests a conversation between Jains and tantric Śaivas, since the *vardhamānavidyā* invokes masculine forms of the four principle goddesses of the cult of Tumburu, a form of Śiva, and his sisters, Jayā, Vijayā, Jayantī, and Aparājitā (see chapter 5).

Another text that has been attributed to the eighth-century Haribhadrasūri—a Sanskrit treatise on the path to liberation, the *Brahmasiddhāntasamuccaya*—provides evidence of the tantricization of the promotion of mendicant leaders. This text may be the earliest to describe the promotion of a mendicant leader using the *sūrimantra* that we saw is imparted to mendicant leaders to this day. In this ceremony, "a pupil, on the appropriate day and in a suitable state of purity, should be given the *sūri*-mantra by his teacher along with sprinkling of the head with sandalwood powder (*abhivāsanā*)."[50] The text also hints at a similar ceremony to the one described in the *Pañcāśakaprakaraṇa* wherein the throwing of a flower onto a model of the Jina's Preaching Assembly determines the candidate's rank, since it says that the "station and so on" (*sthānādi*) of the pupil should be known by means of the fall of flowers and other offerings onto the Jina's Preaching Assembly.[51] With this account, we can piece together the clues we have from the *Pañcāśakaprakaraṇa*, the *Mahāniśīthasūtra*, and the *Brahmasiddhāntasamuccaya* to confirm that by around the eighth century, at least some Śvetāmbaras had adopted two key components of tantric initiation: the construction of a ritual diagram preceding the promotion to different ranks of mendicancy, and the guru's imparting of a mantra on the day of the initiation or promotion, with different invocations imparted for different ranks of mendicancy.

THE TANTRICIZATION OF DIGAMBARA INITIATION

Fewer Digambara texts chart the tantricization of initiation. No known medieval Digambara text provides a full account of the rituals involved in mendicant initiation, but a few descriptions of rituals modeled on mendicant initiations offer some insight. The earliest of these accounts, the initiation rites of a dedicated layperson (*upāsakadīkṣā*), is found in the *Ādipurāṇa* (*ĀP*), which tells the life story of the first *tīrthaṅkara*, Ṛṣabha. Ācārya Jinasena—a disciple of Vīrasena, the composer of the *Dhavalā* whom we met last chapter—composed the *Ādipurāṇa* in forty two chapters in Sanskrit, and the text features the inclusion of mantras in Jain rituals, in particular the fortieth chapter, which outlines sixteen life-cycle rites (*saṃskāra*) for "Jain Brahmins."[52] Jinasena likely had access to knowledge about non-Jain tantric traditions, since he was employed in modern-day Karnataka in the court of the Rāṣṭrakūṭa king Amoghavarṣa (r. 814–80), where kings before, during, and after Amoghavarṣa's time supported non-Jain, especially Śaiva, tantric sects.[53]

Chapter 38 of the *Ādipurāṇa* describes how Bharata, Ṛṣabha's son and the emperor of the universe (*cakravartin*), having established himself in his capital in north India, Ayodhya, lectures his subjects on the proper ritual actions of a lay Jain. Bharata insists that a twice-born (brahmin) has two births: one from his mother and another from ritual actions. A true twice-born performs 108 rites: fifty-three rituals related to birth (*garbhānvaya*), forty-eight rituals leading to initiation (*dīkṣānvaya*), and the seven acts that occur only because of the fruition of meritorious acts (*kartranvaya*), from birth as a human male to initiating as a monk and gaining liberation (*ĀP* 38.51–53; see chapter 4). Here, the verses on initiating as a monk (*pārivrājya*) recall Kundakunda's *Pravacanasāra* in describing the rite as adopting one's appearance at birth (*jātarūpa*) (*ĀP* 39.78), but initiation is also glossed as a *nirvāṇadīkṣā* (liberating initiation; *ĀP* 39.156), suggesting knowledge of non-Jain tantric traditions, since this term is used for the highest level of initiation in non-Jain tantric texts (see chapter 3).

Other parts of chapter 39, which outlines nineteen of the forty-eight rituals leading to initiation, also hint at knowledge of non-Jain tantric initiations into a *maṇḍala*. While Jinasena does not give the particulars of the rites involved in the initiation of a monk, his brief outline of the rituals for an initiation of a layperson is likely modeled on contemporaneous mendicant initiations. This lay initiation, "gaining a place [in the Jain community]" (*sthānalābha*), is listed as the third ritual leading to renunciation, following "descent [into the right path]" (*avatāra*), in which a worthy teacher's sermon compels the aspirant to follow the true teaching and reject false teachings, and "adopting right conduct" (*vṛttalābha*), in which the aspirant bows before the guru (*ĀP* 39.36). Jinasena prescribes that after a person accepts a guru and the Jain teachings in this way, experts should construct one of two types of colored diagrams inside a pure Jain temple (*jinālaya*) using finely ground powder (*cūrṇa*) mixed with either water or sandalwood paste. They should construct either an eight-petaled lotus or a circular diagram where the *jina* is established (*jinasthānamaṇḍala*), which likely refers to a representation of the Jina's Preaching Assembly. The diagram should be worshiped, and the mendicant leader (*sūri*) should have the initiand enter the *maṇḍala* facing the icon of the *jina* (presumably at the center of the diagram). Touching the head of the disciple, the guru should pronounce, "This is your lay initiation." Having touched the initiand's head according to the procedure of the rite of "pulling out five fistfuls of hair" and having said, "You are purified by means of this *dīkṣā*," the guru should announce, "By this mantra, all of your bad karma (*pāpa*) is purified" and teach the initiand the *pañcanamaskāra* (*ĀP* 39.40–43). Having been taught this mantra, the initiate is then allowed to break his fast and return home (*ĀP* 39.44), where he should expel the icons of false gods from his house (*ĀP* 39.45–48). He should then perform Jain rites such as fasting, temple worship, and listening to the meanings of the Jain scriptures (*ĀP* 39.49).

While the *Ādipurāṇa* lacks a detailed description of a monk's renunciation, this discussion of lay initiation hints at the tantricization of Digambara initiation. Jinasena has expertly combined early Jain teachings with medieval ritual developments. The initiation is still ascetic—the initiate has his hair pulled out—but the ceremony also includes a mantra and a *maṇḍala*. Like Haribhadrasūri, Jinasena likely also used the Jina's Preaching Assembly as a *maṇḍala* that the initiand should honor in a similar manner to non-Jain tantric initiation rituals. Jinasena also has the guru impart a karma-destroying mantra at the time of the hair-pulling ceremony, having the guru remind the initiand that the mantra destroys all bad karma. The *pañcanamaskāra* here becomes the perfect Jain initiatory mantra because of the understanding first formulated in the *Mūlācāra* that "this fivefold praise destroys all bad karma and is the foremost *maṅgala* of all *maṅgalas*" (*Mūl*, v. 514). Jinasena thus relies on an old Jain understanding of the power of praising spiritually advanced souls to develop a "tantric" component of initiation, and we saw that Digambaras continue to this day to recite the *pañcanamaskāra* at the time of the guru's pulling out of the initiand's hair. Kundakunda's *Pravacanasāra* and early narratives of the renunciation of the *tīrthaṅkaras*—including the description of Mahāvīra's renunciation in the *Ācārāṅgasūtra*—document the praising of souls (*siddha*) as a crucial component of renunciation.[54] The insertion of the *pañcanamaskāra* into the ceremony of initiation, then, maintains this practice by using a mantra whose second line praises the *siddhas*.

ASCETIC INITIATION AS INEXTRICABLY SOCIAL

The history of Jain monastic initiations from the eighth century to the present day, therefore, displays a gradual integration of tantric and ascetic components. However, for many non-Jain, especially Buddhist, traditions that distinguish between a monastic and tantric initiation, initiating into a *maṇḍala* in order to become a mendicant combines two paths to liberation that have been separated. A narrative at the outset of Amoghavajra's early eighth-century translation of the foundational Buddhist esoteric scripture the *Sarvatathāgatatattvasaṃgraha*, for example, establishes a key difference between tantric and ascetic means of achieving enlightenment. In this story, the Tathāgatas, the deities dedicated to the Buddha Vairocana, approach Sarvārthasiddha, an ascetic in meditation, and reject the idea of using "ascetic practices to achieve unsurpassed *bodhi* [enlightenment]." The Tathāgatas tell Sarvārthasiddha that instead of performing austerities, he "should dwell in the *samādhi* [meditation] contemplating the self and employ the mantra of accomplishing the self-nature."[55] In this tantric tradition, enlightenment is accomplished through the ritual use of a mantra. And in Charles Orzech's analysis of this account, he explains that "the story of Sarvārthasiddha's conversion from solitary asceticism to esoteric initiation in *abhiṣeka* seems intended to make an important point about tantric practice: . . . Enlightenment, in this model, is inextricably social."[56] Sarvārthasiddha cannot achieve enlightenment on his own; he needs to receive a mantra from his guru in a tantric initiation into a *maṇḍala* that represents the deities of the tradition. We thus could establish the "ascetic" path to liberation as solitary and the "tantric" as social.

However, the ease with which medieval Jains integrated "tantric" *maṇḍalas* and mantras into Jain ascetic initiations in the medieval period shows that the ascetic Jain path to liberation was never a solitary undertaking. The earliest accounts of renunciation in Digambara and Śvetāmbara sources require that a disciple initiate into the lineage of an *ācārya*. Indeed, Śvetāmbaras maintain that after the death of Jambū (the last mendicant to achieve liberation), sixty-four years after the death of Mahāvīra, the time period became so degraded that wandering alone was no longer allowed by the tradition, since disciples could easily fall off course without the guidance of gurus.[57] Similarly, the Digambara *Mūlācāra* has harsh words for anyone who considers becoming a solitary ascetic. Leaving one's mendicant group (*gaṇa*) to wander alone brings insult to one's guru, the tearing apart of the scriptural tradition, the soiling of the Jain community (*tīrtha*), stupidity, confusion, lack of virtue, and fatalism (*Mūl*, v. 151).

Indeed, one of the main components of Jain asceticism—celibacy—developed not in order to create solitary renunciants, but in order to establish guru-disciple relationships and lineages that would be antithetical to the dominant Brahmanical hereditary orders. Buddhism, Jainism, and other ascetic movements that arose in the early centuries BCE emphasized celibacy not only as a key ascetic practice but also as a social institution that rejected Brahmanical orthodoxy, in which fathers pass Vedic rituals on to their sons. "As a social institution . . . celibacy can have social and ideological dimensions different from simple chastity, such as negating the religious value of the institution of marriage and of procreating children," Patrick Olivelle explains.[58] These ascetic movements were the first in the subcontinent to develop the idea that in order to achieve liberation, one must join a community linked not by blood, but by vows.

Therefore, because Jainism has always been communal and concerned with proper lineage, adding to initiation ceremonies the transmission of a lineage's mantra and the worship of a diagrammatic representation of the Jain community—the Jina's Preaching Assembly—was a natural development of an *ācārya*'s acceptance of a disciple into a mendicant community. Texts confirm that by at least the eighth century, Jain ascetic initiations had been tantricized in this way to include *maṇḍala*s and mantras. Texts from the following centuries, then, confirm that the pronunciation and inscription of the *ṛddhi-maṅgala* became a key component of the construction of these tantric initiation diagrams for Śvetāmbaras and Digambaras of different ranks.

03

SECTS AND SECRECY

Comparing the Mantras of the Levels of Initiation

THE RESEARCH FOR THIS BOOK BEGAN with a mystery. In June 2008, a Digambara family from Delhi took me to visit one of the most influential living Digambara nuns, Āryikā Jñānamatī (b. 1934), who spends most of her time in Hastinapur, about ninety miles northeast of Delhi, where she has established a research center and pilgrimage site dedicated to the study of the Jain cosmos. At the pilgrimage site's bookshop, I purchased about a dozen short Sanskrit ritual manuals edited with Hindi explanations by Jñānamatī and her disciples. One of these manuals describes the construction and worship of the multicolored, circular Ring of Disciples diagram that Digambaras today honor in the days leading up to their mendicant initiations. In this manual, the description of the ritual begins with five Sanskrit verses outlining the contents of this diagram. According to these verses, at the center of a circular *yantra* sits a hexagram. Inside the six corners of this figure sit six syllables: *a pra ti ca kre phaṭ*. Between the six corners of the central figure sit six more syllables: *vi ca krā ya svā hā*. In circles surrounding this central figure, what's called the *ṛddhimantra*—the forty-four lines of the *ṛddhi-maṅgala* plus four additional Prakrit praises—are inscribed.[1] By honoring these forty-eight *ṛddhi*s through the ritual propitiation of the *yantra*, the introduction to Jñānamatī's manual confirms, worshipers themselves can obtain these superhuman powers.[2]

When I purchased this manual, I knew nothing about the contents or use of this *yantra*. I did not know that modern Digambaras require the propitiation of this diagram for the initiations and promotions of mendicants (fig. 3.1),

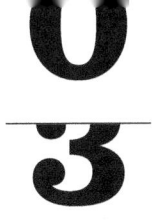

FIGURE 3.1. On the day before her initiation to become a lower-level nun (*kṣullikā*), an initiand follows the instructions of a lay ritual specialist to offer a coconut and an orange to the Ring of Disciples diagram modeled according to Āryikā Jñānamatī's manual. A metal *yantra* sits atop a throne above the hexagram at the center of the diagram. Forty-eight *svastikas* representing each line of an expanded *ṛddhi-maṅgala* surround the central image. Pushpagiri, Madhya Pradesh, November 2019.

and I had little idea what the *apraticakrā*-mantra inscribed in the central six-cornered figure could mean. However, I had seen the diagram's name—the Ring of Disciples (*gaṇadharavalaya*)—before. For Śvetāmbaras, the *sūrimantrapaṭa*—the Cloth Diagram of the Mantra of the Mendicant Leader gifted to *ācāryas* upon their promotions—is also sometimes called the Ring of Disciples, and it too contains variants of the *ṛddhi-maṅgala* in rings around a central image.[3]

With these similarities in mind, I asked Jñānamatī about the meaning of the mantra at the center of the Digambara Ring of Disciples and the historical connections between these Digambara and Śvetāmbara diagrams. But she gave me no clear understanding of the mantra's meaning and simply emphasized the power of these particular consonant combinations. She was also unaware of the Śvetāmbara diagram of the *sūrimantra*. She confirmed that Digambaras have different mantras called the *sūrimantra*, but none of them contain the *ṛddhi-maṅgala* and they are not inscribed on cloth diagrams that are gifted to mendicants. Instead, Digambara ritual specialists or mendicants use a variety of different Prakrit and Sanskrit mantras that they call *sūrimantra* to consecrate temple images.[4] The historical relationship between the Digambara Ring of Disciples and the Śvetāmbara Cloth Diagram of the Mantra of the Mendicant Leader thus became a mystery I had to solve.[5]

To date, scholars and practitioners have overlooked the historical connections between these Digambara and Śvetāmbara initiation mantras and ritual diagrams, in part because Śvetāmbaras have published dozens of medieval texts on the initiation and promotion of monks, but Digambara have published only a few brief discussions of premodern mendicant initiation and promotion.[6] In addition, Jain scholars and practitioners often pay little attention to the meanings of the contents of *yantras*. *Yantras*, as Jñānamatī explained, find their power not necessarily in the meaning of their mantras but in the assumption that the sounds of the recitations themselves are powerful through their association with particular traditions and mendicants. Not surprisingly, then, when I asked more than a dozen Digambara monks about the *apraticakrā*-mantra at the center of the Ring of Disciples, they also did not know its exact meaning or provenance. And scholars are in the same boat as these mendicants, since they too have not closely examined the contents of *yantras*—perhaps because these *yantras* are difficult to read in the way scholars typically read religious texts. *Yantras* have no explicit narratives, codes of conduct, or philosophical puzzles about which to make arguments. Many of the manuals outlining the contents of these diagrams read like cookbooks, filled with recipes involving the inscription of "nonsense" syllables such as *hrīṃ*, *hrūṃ*, *hrauṃ*, and so on. It is easy to overlook these diagrams as essentially pan-Asian amulet-like miracle workers that do not necessarily tell us much about the tradition of Jainism as a soteriological system or anything else.

Scholars have also overlooked the connections between these Digambara and Śvetāmbara initiation diagrams because research projects on Jainism often focus solely on one sect, reinforcing the existing divides in modern Jain communities that Jñānamatī's lack of knowledge about the Śvetāmbara *sūrimantra* highlighted. Despite her erudition, Jñānamatī did not know the Śvetāmbara understanding of the *ṛddhi-maṅgala*. This is not unusual: many Śvetāmbaras and Digambaras today are unaware of the practices of members of the other sect. On my 2008 trip to Hastinapur, for example, the Digambara family who drove me from Delhi spent days at Jñānamatī's Digambara temple compound, Jambudweep, but never visited the Śvetāmbara temples next door. This is common—Śvetāmbara and Digambara temples often sit side by side at pilgrimage sites or in cities, yet worshipers of one sect rarely if ever visit the temples of the other sect.

This does not mean, however, that Jains are uninterested in the beliefs and practices of members of other sects. In the past hundred years, important Jain mendicants have organized many intersectarian gatherings, and 1974 saw the publication of the Prakrit-and-English text *Samaṇ Suttaṁ*, which seeks to reconcile the teachings of the sects and received approval from leaders from diverse Jain communities.[7] During my fieldwork in 2013, 2016, and 2019, Śvetāmbara and Digambara monks familiar with my comparative project regularly asked about the texts of the other sect. Because Śvetāmbara and Digambara mendicants rarely interact, my visits with them often became more about me telling the mendicants about the practices of the other sect than them answering my questions. In 2013, during the rainy-season retreat (*cāturmāsa*), when mendicants of both sects reside in one location for four months, one Śvetāmbara monk residing just outside of Mumbai even walked with me from the Śvetāmbara temple where he was staying to the neighboring Digambara temple so that he could discuss the Ring of Disciples diagram with a Digambara monk (fig. 3.2).

Examining the manuals of the other sect, the mendicants became intrigued. Digambara monks confirmed what Jñānamatī had told me: when they are promoted to the rank of mendicant leader, neither are they imparted the *sūrimantra* nor are they gifted cloth diagrams on which it is inscribed. Indeed, in November 2019, at the newly built Digambara pilgrimage site Pushpagiri, twenty-five miles northeast of Indore, Madhya Pradesh, I attended the promotion of three Digambara monks—Pulakasāgara, Pramukhasāgara, and Praṇāmasāgara—to the rank of *ācārya*, and for their promotion, their guru Ācārya Puṣpadantasāgara imparted to each of them what the modern manual *Vimal Bhakti Saṅgrah* terms the *ācāryamantra*. At the promotion ceremony, the three monks sat on wooden thrones onstage in front of thousands of lay devotees gathered in a ritual pavilion, and Ācārya Puṣpadantasāgara, dropping cloves on their heads, repeated into a microphone: "*oṃ hrīṃ śrīṃ arhaṃ haṃ saḥ ācāryāya namaḥ*" (*Vimal Bhakti Saṅgrah*, 452). This Sanskrit mantra is quite different from the Śvetāmbara *sūrimantra* that is whispered into the ears of monks to make them *ācārya*s. It is in Sanskrit, not Prakrit, and it contains seed syllables, *arhaṃ*, the mantra for an omniscient soul, and a praise to the *ācārya*, not the *ṛddhi-maṅgala*.

FIGURE 3.2. The Digambara Ācārya Kuśāgranandī (left) and Śvetāmbara Pannyāsa Aruṇavijaya (right) discuss the Ring of Disciples (the book in front of them). Mumbai, September 2013.

Digambara monks today do, however, whisper *sūrimantras* into the ears of temple images when consecrating them. They also construct diagrams of the Ring of Disciples for image consecration ceremonies, and I was able to participate in a few of these ceremonies in Hastinapur and Jaipur in 2013. Through these observations of ritual, discussions with mendicants and lay ritual specialists, examinations of Digambara manuscripts, and comparisons with Śvetāmbara texts, it became clear to me that present-day Digambara image-installation ceremonies contain vestiges of the tantricization of medieval mendicant promotion, in which Digambara *ācāryas were* imparted a *sūrimantra* upon their promotions and used this mantra in parts of temple image consecration rites that imitate their own promotions. While no published premodern manuals on Digambara mendicant initiation exist, several medieval Digambara manuals on the consecration of temple images have been published. These manuals provide some of the best clues about the details of medieval Digambara mendicant initiations because they not only embed the initiation of a monk into the consecration of a temple image but also model parts of the consecration ceremony on the promotion of a monk to the rank of *ācārya*.

Comparing these Digambara accounts with medieval Śvetāmbara sources on mendicant initiation and promotion confirms that even though modern Digambara and Śvetāmbara monks know little of the other sect's practices and their initiation diagrams have evolved to look quite different, medieval Digambaras and Śvetāmbaras were in conversation with each other when tantricizing their rites of renunciation. Śvetāmbara texts on mendicant conduct from the thirteenth to fifteenth centuries and roughly contemporaneous Digambara image consecration manuals confirm that medieval Jains developed the Digambara Ring of Disciples and the Śvetāmbara Cloth Diagram of the Mantra of the Mendicant Leader in collaboration, modeling their initiation diagrams on the Jina's Preaching Assembly. For mendicants of both of these sects, the *ṛddhi-maṅgala* of these diagrams became an ideal mantra of initiation and promotion because of its connection to the superhuman powers of the disciples of the *tīrthaṅkara*s. By reciting this litany, mendicants could not only promote themselves as true ascetics who are connected to the founders of the Jain tradition, they could also destroy karma and develop themselves as superhuman protectors of the lay community.

Simply comparing the practices of Jain sects does not, however, provide a full understanding of how these mendicant ceremonies developed. To understand the development of different levels of ordination within Jain monasticism based on the use of different mantras and *yantra*s, Śvetāmbara and Digambara mendicant initiations and promotions must also be examined in the context of non-Jain tantric traditions. Both Śvetāmbaras and Digambaras used the *ṛddhi-maṅgala* to develop rites of promotion to various ranks of mendicancy that in some ways parallel the levels of promotion in the traditions of the Śaiva Mantramārga, Vaiṣṇava Pāñcarātra, and tantric Buddhism. In the medieval period, Jains seamlessly tantricized their existing levels of monasticism by associating a different mantra with each of these ranks. Higher levels of initiates within the Śvetāmbara tradition, then, were gifted cloth diagrams on which these mantras were inscribed to use in daily rituals (see chapter 5). Thus, on the one hand, ascetics rose up the ranks of mendicancy by performing the twelve acts that constitute *tapas* in the *Tattvārthasūtra*, including fasting, honoring mendicants, and the progressive study of Jain scriptures. On the other hand, monks also rose in station through "tantric" ordinations, by receiving different esoteric mantras and ritual diagrams (*paṭa*) from their gurus.

EARLY RANKS OF JAIN MENDICANCY

Śvetāmbara and Digambara texts from the first half of the first millennium discuss many different ranks of mendicancy. We have already seen that the most famous Jain invocation, the *pañcanamaskāra* that is found in the *Ṣaṭkhaṇḍāgama*, praises three different types of mendicants: mendicant leaders (*ācārya*), mendicant teachers (*upādhyāya*), and ordinary mendicants (*sādhu*). Early Śvetāmbara texts outline other mendicant ranks as well. The Śvetāmbara canonical text the *Sthānāṅgasūtra*, for example, confirms that after the ceremony of renunciation (*pravrajyā*), a mendicant becomes a novice (*śaikṣa*) or *antevāsin* for a period of a week, four months, or six months, after which he undergoes confirmation (*upasthāpana/upasthāpanā*), becoming a full mendicant, often called a *sthavira*.[8] Higher-level male mendicants include the *pravartin*, who perhaps looked after "the administrative aspect of the group of monks," and the *vācaka*, who may have been responsible for giving lectures.[9] Another position, the *upādhyāya*, was designated as the scholar within a group of monks whose "chief duty was to give proper reading of the *sūtra* to the junior monks."[10] The Śvetāmbara canonical text on mendicant conduct the *Vyavahārasūtra*, which has been dated to the first few centuries BCE, confirms that the *upādhyāya* must have knowledge of monastic discipline and have been a monk for at least three years before confirmation.[11] The highest level of mendicant, then, is the leader of a mendicant group, the *ācārya*, who is in charge of initiating new disciples.[12] The *Vyavahārasūtra* 3.7 maintains that the *ācārya* must be morally outstanding, have been a monk for eight years, and have studied two key Śvetāmbara "limbs" (*aṅga*) of the canon, the *Sthānāṅgasūtra* and *Samavāyāṅgasūtra*.[13] At this point in Śvetāmbara literature, the term "*gaṇin*" (leader of a group of mendicants, *gaṇa*) is sometimes used interchangeably with *ācārya*, but other sources consider them separate posts.[14] In addition, female Śvetāmbara initiates had similar ranks. The *gaṇinī* was the highest level of female initiate, or the female equivalent of an *ācārya* or *gaṇin* who led a group of nuns. The *pravartinī* was "responsible for the moral discipline of nuns under her care," while the *sthavirī* was the equivalent of a *sthavira*.[15]

Early Digambara texts on monastic conduct also describe different levels of promotion within mendicancy. The *Mūlācāra* provides some understanding of the members of a mendicant group when it claims that a mendicant should not reside without an *ācārya*, *upādhyāya*, *pravartin*, *sthavira*, and *gaṇadhara* (leader of a smaller group). According to the *Mūlācāra*, the *ācārya* is skilled in instructing his disciples, the *upādhyāya* teaches the *dharma*, the *pravartin* runs the monastic community, the *sthavira* teaches propriety of conduct, and the *gaṇadhara* protects the *gaṇa*.[16] The *ācārya*, according to another verse, is skilled in instructing his initiates and maintaining their unity, is a master in the meaning of the texts, has achieved fame, is skilled in rituals and right action, and speaks properly.[17] The *Mūlācāra* suggests that the *ācārya* initiates disciples, but the description of renunciation from Kundakunda's *Pravacanasāra* indicates that a *gaṇin* also may initiate new disciples (see chapter 2).

Śvetāmbara and Digambara texts from the first half of the first millennium therefore agree that there are ordinary mendicants, mendicant teachers, mendicants who were perhaps in charge of bureaucratic matters within the mendicant group, and leaders of mendicant groups. These texts do not outline the rituals required for promotion to these different ranks, but it is clear that a mendicant's knowledge of scripture, moral conduct, teaching abilities, and standing in the mendicant group would determine his ability to rise up the ranks of Jain monasticism. The twelve internal and external acts that constitute *tapas* in the *Tattvārthasūtra*—the daily practices of mendicants such as expiation and study—advance Jain monks in the mendicant hierarchy.

TANTRIC LEVELS OF INITIATION

By the seventh century, tantric traditions had established a similar hierarchy for their initiates, using the same term, *ācārya*, for their leaders of the tradition.[18] In these traditions, however, one's promotion to various ranks determined not solely one's ability to instruct and initiate disciples, but also which ritual uses of mantras and *maṇḍala*s an initiate was allowed to perform to obtain superhuman powers and inch closer to liberation. In the Śaiva Mantramārga, by the time of the seventh-century *Svāyambhuvasūtrasaṅgraha*, a hierarchy of four initiates—*samayin*, *putraka*, *sādhaka*, and *ācārya*—had been established.[19] The initiate becomes a *samayin* after the general initiation (*samayadīkṣā*), which involves the acceptance of the rules of conduct for the tradition (*samaya*), a construction of a *maṇḍala*, and the imparting of impurity-destroying mantras from guru to disciple. Higher-level initiates, then, may undergo the liberating initiation (*nirvāṇadīkṣā*), in which the initiate becomes a *putraka* and is allowed to undergo either the "ablution of the ritual adept who meditates on a mantra to achieve superhuman powers" (*sādhakābhiṣeka*) or the "ablution of the officiant" (*ācāryābhiṣeka*), which promotes the disciple to the rank of *ācārya*, who has the right to initiate new disciples, perform public worship, and consecrate temple images.[20] Similar levels of initiation—which also involve the construction of a *maṇḍala* and the imparting of mantras to destroy karmic bonds—appear in texts of the Vaiṣṇava Pāñcarātra and in tantric Buddhist texts.[21]

In his seventh-century *Commentary on the Mahāvairocanatantra*, the Buddhist Śubhakarasiṃha outlines three levels of promotion, all of which require the candidate for promotion to stand inside a *maṇḍala* and undertake an *abhiṣeka*. In the "rudimentary *abhiṣeka* of 'binding karmic affinity' . . . between practitioners and the Esoteric Teaching," the initiates "are given particular mantras for the worship of the personal divinities they have obtained during the initiation." The second level of initiation, the "*abhiṣeka* of 'studying the Dharma' . . . qualifies participants to study the elaborate yogic exercises consisting of numerous combinations of mantras, mudrās, and visualizations aimed at ritually invoking the personal divinities of the initiates and attaining the meditative union with them." The highest level of promotion, then, is the *abhiṣeka* of "transmitting the teaching," in which one becomes an *ācārya*, or master of the tradition who is able to instruct and initiate disciples and consecrate temple images.[22]

Tantric traditions appear to have developed the idea that higher-level initiates who have received the authority to use esoteric mantras are responsible for leading image consecration ceremonies. Early Śaiva Saiddhāntika and Pāñcarātrika texts confirm that the *sādhaka* should lead the ceremony, while later texts of these traditions require the *ācārya* to do so.[23] Hélène Brunner has explained that later texts of the Śaiva Siddhānta prescribe that the guru at the conclusion of the consecration of the *ācārya* "enumerates the duties, or privileges," of an *ācārya* to his promoted disciple: "All these texts agree on three main prerogatives: *dīkṣā*, *pratiṣṭhā*, *vyākhyāna*: the *ācārya* (and he alone) will give initiations to those deserving, perform the installation of Śiva's images for those who ask for it, and comment on the Scriptures (the Āgamas)."[24]

These levels of initiation in many ways parallel the hierarchies of Jain and Buddhist monastic orders that developed in the first few centuries before the Common Era. However, while Buddhist tantric levels of ordination became separate from levels of monastic ordination, Jains from at least the eighth century onward tantricized their existing levels of monasticism.[25] Just as Haribhadrasūri's *Pañcāśakaprakaraṇa* and the *Mahāniśīthasūtra* require a

Jain to become a mendicant via the throwing of a flower on a model of the Jina's Preaching Assembly and the receiving of the liberating *vardhamānavidyā* with a sprinkling of powder, an initiate into the Śaiva Mantramārga would become a *samayin* after a general initiation that involves the throwing of a flower onto a *maṇḍala* and the imparting of mantras from guru to disciple. However, Śvetāmbara texts do not provide a complete description of the rites of mendicant promotion until the eleventh or twelfth century, and it was not until the centuries that followed that texts begin to outline in detail the contents and uses of mendicants' mantras.[26]

The period between the thirteenth and fifteenth centuries witnessed an explosion in the production of Śvetāmbara manuals on the mantras used in mendicant ritual. In the middle of the thirteenth century, the Śvetāmbara *ācārya* Siṃhatilakasūri composed in Sanskrit the earliest known manuals on the Śvetāmbara *sūrimantra* and *vardhamānavidyā*, the *Mantrarājarahasya* (*MRR*) and the *Vardhamānavidyākalpa*. Digambara image-consecration manuals from this period suggest they too had adopted the imparting of the *vardhamānavidyā* and *sūrimantra* to promote higher ranks of mendicants by this time.

From one perspective, the thirteenth century seems quite late for so many Jains to be promoting the ritual use of mantras and *maṇḍala*s. The thirteenth century marks the end of what scholars have called the Tantric Age or the Śaiva Age—the period in India beginning in the sixth century during which tantric traditions—especially those of the Śaiva Mantramārga—came to prominence through the patronage of kings who wished to gain the extraordinary powers and liberation-granting initiations these traditions offered.[27] Jains were certainly part of this Tantric Age, with monks such as the ninth-century Jinasena developing some tantric ritual practices in the courts of kings who also supported non-Jain tantric sects (see chapter 2).[28] But the influence of kingly patronage from the sixth to thirteenth centuries was only part of the story of why Jains began to use powerful mantras in mendicant promotions.[29]

As Paul Dundas has shown in his studies of medieval Śvetāmbara *sūrimantra* manuals and narratives, the establishment of monastic lineages also played an important role in linking different types of Jain monks to different mantras.[30] In the thirteenth century, when texts more frequently begin mentioning the importance of the *sūrimantra* and the *vardhamānavidyā*, Śvetāmbaras were reacting to the increased splintering of their mendicant communities. From the eleventh century onward, Śvetāmbaras divided into a number of different mendicant groups (*gaccha*, *gaṇa*), with the two most populous mendicant lineages that survive today, the Kharatara Gaccha and the Tapā Gaccha, emerging in the eleventh and thirteenth centuries, respectively.[31] The peripatetic mendicants of these lineages who were mostly unattached to courts needed the support of the wealthy Jain merchant community for food and shelter,[32] so in this period, a mendicant's mantra that was said to ensure the destruction of enemies, the curing of diseases, and eventual liberation could legitimate one's lineage, attract lay followers, and become "a magic weapon in the struggle for sectarian dominance" among Jains and non-Jains.[33] Therefore, while the *sūrimantra* and *vardhamānavidyā* were imparted to promote mendicants long before the thirteenth century, it was only in this period of the splintering of mendicant communities at the end of the Tantric Age that monks felt the need to specify their particular lineage's uses of these mantras in texts.

A FOURTEENTH-CENTURY ŚVETĀMBARA ACCOUNT OF THE RANKS OF MENDICANCY

Focusing on an important text from 1306 that has informed modern Śvetāmbara manuals—Jinaprabhasūri's *Vidhimārgaprapā* (*VMP*)—provides a sense of how the *ṛddhi-maṅgala* became a component of the esoteric mantras that were integrated into the monastic path to liberation. Ācārya Jinaprabhasūri (ca. 1261–1333) was a prolific monk of the Kharatara Gaccha who was born in Rajasthan and spent much of his monastic life in Delhi, where later chroniclers of his life claim he used his erudition and connections to convince the sultan Muḥammad bīn Tughluq (r. 1325–1351) to issue a series of imperial edicts to protect Jains and their sites of worship.[34] According to chroniclers of the lives of important Kharatara Gaccha monks, Jinaprabhasūri came from a tradition of miracle-working mantra adepts of the Kharatara Gaccha, which from its founding in 1024 to the present day has had its strongholds in north and western India.[35] These accounts of the lives of important Kharatara Gaccha monks show how the mantras of monks played key roles in attracting the attention of laypeople and in gaining control of contested sacred sites. An account from perhaps the sixteenth century, for example, describes how Jinapatisūri (1153–1220) was able to use powder consecrated through his recitation of the *sūrimantra* to immobilize a Nātha *yogin* in Delhi who had tried to sabotage the consecration of a Jain temple because he was angry that Jain laypeople refused to give Nātha *yogins* alms.[36]

Jinaprabhasūri was also the leader of a newly established branch (*śākhā*) of the Kharatara Gaccha, the Laghu Śākhā, and therefore felt a responsibility to "delineate proper Kharatara practices" in works such as the *Vidhimārgaprapā*.[37] The *Vidhimārgaprapā* thus contains forty-one chapters, in both Prakrit and Sanskrit, that outline key rites of mendicancy, including the practice of equanimity, the twice-daily recitation of the ritual formula of repentance (*pratikramaṇa*), the consecration of a temple image, and going on pilgrimage. The text provides instructions for several different types of mendicant initiations and promotions: the initial ceremony of renunciation (*pravrajyā*; chapter 16); the ordination ceremony when the initiate takes the five vows of a mendicant (*upasthāpanā*; chapter 20); and the promotions (*padasthāpanā*) to the ranks of mendicant (*vācanācārya*; chapter 26), mendicant teacher (*upādhyāya*; chapter 28), mendicant leader (*ācārya*; chapter 29), female mendicants who are in charge of larger groups of nuns (*mahattarā* and *pravartinī*; chapter 30), and a leader of a *gaccha*, or mendicant lineage (*gaṇānujñā*; chapter 31).

On the one hand, monks and nuns rise up these ranks of mendicancy by performing what the early texts require to be promoted: the twelve forms of austerities in the *Tattvārthasūtra*, including fasting and the study of Jain scriptures (*svādhyāya*). Mendicants undertake the study of the authoritative Prakrit scriptures of image-worshiping Śvetāmbara Jainism (*āgama*) in a structured, ritualized order that integrates obedience to the guru, fasting, and memorization of scripture. In Śvetāmbara manuals on monastic practice such as the *Vidhimārgaprapā*, this progressive study of scriptures is termed *anuyoga* (examination) or *yogavidhi*. In his chapters on *yogavidhi*, Jinaprabhasūri requires the study of the following scriptures: three foundational texts (*mūlasūtra*) on daily mendicant conduct that must be understood at the outset of one's mendicant career (the *Āvaśyaka*, *Daśavaikālika*, and *Uttarādhyayana sūtras*);[38] eleven limbs (*aṅga*) that are thought to have been compiled by the disciples of Mahāvīra from the teachings of the *jina* himself;[39] twelve subsidiary limbs that are supposed to complement the limbs (*upāṅga*); fourteen miscellaneous texts on various topics (*prakīrṇaka*);[40] a collection of "Sayings of Seers," the *Ṛṣibhāṣita*; seven *sūtras* on mendicant discipline (*chedasūtra*), including the text we have examined in earlier chapters, the *Mahāniśīthasūtra*; and the *Nandīsūtra* and the *Anuyogadvārasūtra*, today known as appendices of the *āgamas* because they describe their contents (*VMP*, 48–58).

Along with the mastery of scripture, however, mendicants also rise in station through the daily ritual use of mantras they are imparted upon their promotions. *Gurus* promote disciples by imparting to them different mantras through the sprinkling of sandalwood powder consecrated through the recitation of a particular mantra (*vāsakṣepa*) and the gifting of cloth diagrams (*paṭa*) on which the mantra is inscribed (table 3.1). As mendicants progress through the levels of hierarchy, they receive mantras that include more and more parts of the *ṛddhi-maṅgala*. An examination of the rites required to rise through the ranks of mendicancy in Jinaprabhasūri's *Vidhimārgaprapā* highlights how increased acts of asceticism and the progressive study of scriptures have been linked to the transmission of different mantras and diagrams to mark different categories of Śvetāmbara mendicants.

Renunciation (*Pravrajyā*) and Ordination (*Upasthāpanā*)

Jinaprabhasūri's Prakrit chapter on *pravrajyā* (the initial renunciation of a Jain mendicant) describes the communal rites required to renounce one's status as a householder, enter a mendicant community, and begin a regimen of fasting and scriptural study. This ceremony, like the initiation described in Haribhadrasūri's *Pañcāśakaprakaraṇa*, requires the gathering of the lay and mendicant community at a temple where a three-dimensional model of the Jina's Preaching Assembly has been constructed. This construction of the Jina's Preaching Assembly is called *nandīracanā*, which literally means "making joy," since it represents the moment when the truths of Jainism that allow practitioners to achieve the pure joy of liberation are first taught.[41] Jinaprabhasūri's description of the construction and worship of the Jina's Preaching Assembly corresponds exactly to Haribhadrasūri's, but it offers more details of the mantras to be recited and the performers of these rites. Laypeople, having purified themselves, should construct the three levels of the Jina's Preaching Assembly out of jewels, gold, and silver[42] and place an icon of a *jina* at the center, while the *ācārya* leading the initiation ceremony should invite the inhabitants of the assembly into their assigned sections by placing the tips of his cupped hand on his forehead (showing the *muktāśuktimudrā*) and reciting different Sanskrit mantras (*VMP*, pp. 29–30, lines 31–10).[43]

Then, on the morning of renunciation, the initiand should perform the flower-throwing test. Relatives of the initiand should ask the guru to accept the disciple, and the disciple should arrive at the temple on a vehicle pulled by horses and elephants. There, with a coconut and grains of uncooked rice (*akṣata*) in his folded hands, the disciple should circumambulate the model of the Jina's Preaching Assembly three times while remembering the *pañcanamaskāra*. He then should throw the flowers and rice onto the assembly to determine his eligibility to renounce (*VMP*, p. 34, para. 27, lines 1–15). In prescribing the same flower-throwing rite as Haribhadrasūri, Jinaprabhasūri explains that *ācārya*s of the past claimed that the blindfolded initiand of wrong faith who cannot land the offerings on the model must accept from the guru the vow of right vision (*samyaktvavrata*) and be instructed before proceeding to initiation. Jinaprabhasūri notes, however, that for initiates from Jain families, this test is not necessary (*VMP*, p. 30, lines 12–17). In this way, he provides a bridge between Haribhadrasūri's *Pañcāśakaprakaraṇa*, which requires the blindfolded flower-throwing test, and modern ceremonies of renunciation, which do not include this test but do require initiands to circumambulate a model of the Jina's Preaching Assembly, coconut in hand, and to place the coconut at the base of the assembly.[44]

The ceremony of renunciation proper follows this flower-throwing test, and it is structured around a series of Prakrit questions and answers between disciple and guru. The disciple, standing erect with his hands at his sides in the *kāyotsarga* meditative posture, recites various ritual formulas and is gifted the insignia of a mendicant (the broom and so forth). He has his hair pulled out, he removes his householder clothes and dons the white robes of a mendicant, and he takes a lifelong vow of equanimity. By the end of the ceremony, he has received a teaching on Jain doctrine from his guru and a new mendicant name (*VMP*, 34–35).

The novice monk then enters a period of austerities and study that can last up to six months during which he masters the two foundational Śvetāmbara texts on mendicant conduct (*mūlasūtra*): the *Āvaśyakasūtra*, which includes description of the six essential actions mendicants must perform every day, from equanimity to the regular adoption of the "abandoning the body" (*kāyotsarga*) posture (see chapter 2),[45] and the *Daśavaikālikasūtra* attributed to Ārya Śayyambhava, who is thought to have put in one scripture all the essential knowledge for a life of mendicancy (*VMP*, p. 40, line 8). The ritualized study of the *Āvaśyakasūtra* should last eight days, the study of the *Daśavaikālikasūtra* fifteen.[46]

To receive permission to study scriptures (*yoganikṣepa*), the disciple and guru undertake what Jinaprabhasūri calls *nandī*, which refers to both the recitation of the *Nandīsūtra*, an appendix of the Śvetāmbara canon, and *nandīracanā*, the construction of a model of the Jina's Preaching Assembly. In this rite, the guru stands next to a model of the Jina's Preaching Assembly with the disciple at his side in the *kāyotsarga* meditative posture and grants permission to read the scriptures through a recitation of a variety of Jain formulas and a series of questions and answers. The rite culminates in the guru's recitation of the *Nandīsūtra*, because mendicants should use the list of scriptures found in this text to structure their ritualized study of texts (for the entire *yoganikṣepa* rite, see *VMP*, 44–46).[47] The disciple undertakes the *ācāmāmla* (Pkt. *āyaṃbila*) fast on the day he receives permission to begin reading the scripture, eating only one unseasoned meal a day to encourage equanimity. From that day on until he completes his study of these two foundational texts, he should undertake a *nirvikṛtika* fast (Prk. *nivvīya*), in which he avoids modified foods that have a negative effect on one's disposition: "milk, curds, butter, ghee, oil, hardened molasses, alcohol, meat, honey, and food cooked in oil that has been used more than three times" (*VMP*, p. 49, line 1).[48]

After spending up to six months fasting in this way and completing the study of the *Āvaśyaka* and the *Daśavaikālika*, the initiate undergoes the ceremony of ordination (*upasthāpanā*),which also involves the gathering of the lay and mendicant community, the construction and circumambulation of a model of the Jina's Preaching Assembly, and the recitation of a series of Prakrit questions and answers between disciple and guru. On the day of the ceremony, the novice adopts the five vows of a Jain mendicant and the sixth vow of not eating after sunset. To finalize the adoption of the vows, the guru sprinkles consecrated scented sandalwood powder and rice on the disciple's head (*VMP*, 38–40).[49]

The ceremony of ordination gives the disciple the authority to undertake the ritualized study of the rest of the scriptures (*yogavidhi*). Jinaprabhasūri requires the mendicant to undertake a fast—either an *ācāmāmla* or a *nirvikṛtika*—for each day of scriptural study, and he follows the *Nandīsūtra* in dividing the texts to be studied into two types: those that have to be studied at particular times (*kālika*), and those that can be studied at any time (*utkālika*). To begin each text, the disciple and guru must perform *nandī* at the outset of each section of the text, and for *kālika* texts, they also must perform a ritual called *kālagrahaṇa* to determine that the time of study is auspicious. For this ritual, in the presence of the mendicant community, the guru and the disciple, each holding a small stick, should stand next to the guru's *sthāpanācārya*—the tripod that represents gurus who are not present (see fig. 5.4 for an example of two *sthāpanācāryas*). After reciting various formulas and the first two chapters of the *Daśavaikālikasūtra*, they then should ask the mendicants present if they saw anything impure like a dead body or heard anything impure like a sneeze from the disciple during the performance of the *kālagrahaṇa*. If not, the *sādhus* present announce that the time is determined to be pure (*VMP*, pp. 42–44, para. 36).

A mendicant's study of the Śvetāmbara canon that follows these ritual prescriptions should take years.[50] The first text the disciple should study, the *Uttarādhyayanasūtra*, which is an *utkālika* scripture and thus does not require *kālagrahaṇa*, should take thirty-six days to complete (*VMP*, 50–51), while the last scripture to complete and the largest scripture in the canon—the *Bhagavatīsūtra*, a *kālika* scripture that requires *kālagrahaṇa*—takes six months and six days to study (*VMP*, p. 53, lines 1–2).[51] Once the mendicant has mastered the *Bhagavatīsūtra*, he should have the term "*gaṇī*" appended to his name, signaling that he is now a *gaṇin*, or a leader of a smaller group of mendicants (*VMP*, p. 53, line 34).

Thus, while tantric Buddhists, Śaivas, and Vaiṣṇavas undertake the flower-throwing rite to receive permission to perform the mantra-based rites of their cults, Śvetāmbaras make offerings to the *maṇḍala*-like model of the Jina's Preaching Assembly to begin the study of scriptures and a life of austerities organized around the performance of the six essential actions and adherence to the five mendicant vows. In the ceremony that begins a monk's study of scripture, the model of the Jina's Preaching Assembly not only represents the path to liberation but also replicates the moment when the contents of the Jain scriptures were first taught. It thus makes visible the transmission of the teachings from a *jina*, to his disciples, to the modern guru, to his disciples. In these ceremonies of renunciation and ordination, the emphasis remains on asceticism as defined in the *Tattvārthasūtra*—study of scripture, fasting, pulling out one's hair, and adopting the mendicant vows.

Higher Levels of Mendicant Promotion: Imparting the *Vardhamānavidyā* and *Sūrimantra*

As a monk advances up the mendicant hierarchy, however, his life begins to look more like the life of a tantric Śaiva or Buddhist. He receives the authority—and indeed, the responsibility—to integrate the ritual use of certain esoteric mantras into his daily routine. As in non-Jain tantric initiations, the ritual use of different mantras becomes one of the defining features of promotion ceremonies described in the *Vidhimārgaprapā*, determining the difference between mendicants of various ranks and progressing Jains on the path to liberation.

In the *Vidhimārgaprapā*, a monk first receives the *vardhamānavidyā* when he becomes a scriptural authority who lectures on the Jain scriptures: a mendicant preacher (*vācanācārya*). This promotion can occur only after a mendicant has completed his study of all the scriptures of the *yogavidhi*: the two root scriptures (*mūlagrantha*: the *Āvaśyakasūtra* and *Daśavaikālikasūtra*), the *Nandīsūtra*, the *Anuyogadvārasūtra*, the *Uttarādhyayanasūtra*, the *Ṛṣibhāṣita*, the limbs (*aṅga*), the sub-limbs (*upāṅga*), the miscellaneous texts (*prakīrṇaka*), and the books on mendicant discipline (*chedasūtra*) (*VMP*, p. 64, lines 8–9). For the mendicant preacher's promotion, the fourfold community of monks, nuns, laymen, and laywomen

TABLE 3.1. The mantras and *maṇḍalas* of ascetic promotion in Jinaprabhasūri's *Vidhimārgaprapā*

Rank of mendicant	Mantra imparted upon ordination/ promotion	Three-dimensional diagram constructed upon ordination	Cloth diagram (*paṭa*) gifted upon ordination
Monk (*muni*)	None*	Jina's Preaching Assembly (*samavasaraṇa*)	None
Mendicant preacher (*vācanācārya*)	Spell of Mahāvīra (*vardhamānavidyā*)	Jina's Preaching Assembly	Cloth Diagram of the Spell of Mahāvīra (*vardhamānavidyāpaṭa*)
Mendicant teacher (*upādhyāya*)	Spell of Mahāvīra	Jina's Preaching Assembly	Cloth Diagram of the Spell of Mahāvīra
Female mendicant leader (*mahattarā* / *pravartinī*)	Spell of Mahāvīra	Jina's Preaching Assembly	Cloth Diagram of the Spell of Mahāvīra
Mendicant leader (*ācārya*)	Mantra of the Mendicant Leader (*sūrimantra*)	Jina's Preaching Assembly	Cloth Diagram of the Mantra of the Mendicant Leader (*sūrimantrapaṭa*)

* The *Mahāniśīthasūtra* prescribes the imparting of the *vardhamānavidyā* for the ordination (*upasthāpanā*) ceremony (see chapter 2), but Jinaprabhasūri does not. No mantra is imparted to the initiate upon his ordination, but unlike earlier accounts of Jain renunciation, medieval accounts prescribe the recitation of the *pañcanamaskāra* at every important moment in the ordination ceremony. For the use of the *pañcanamaskāra* in the ordination ceremony, see *VMP*, p. 34, para. 27, lines 23–24, 27–28, 34.

should again gather in the presence of a model of the Jina's Preaching Assembly, and the preacher-to-be should sit to the left of his *ācārya*, where, at an auspicious time, the guru should pronounce the *vardhamānavidyā* three times into the disciple's right ear, which has been decorated with sandalwood powder. The version of the *vidyā* in this text is similar to the one found in the *Mahāniśīthasūtra* (see chapter 2). The spell calls for the success of the tradition by including various terms associated with victory. It too invokes epithets of Mahāvīra and invokes masculine terms related to "victory" that correspond to the goddesses Jayā, Vijayā, Jayantā, Aparājitā, and Anihatā:

> *oṃ namo bhagavao arahao mahai mahāvīravaddhamānasāmissa sijjhaü me bhagavaī mahaï mahāvijjā oṃ vīre vīre mahāvīre jayavīre seṇavīre vaddhamāṇavīre jaye vijaye jayaṃte aparājie aṇihae oṃ hrīṃ svāhā* (*VMP*, p. 65, lines 15–20)

After whispering this invocation, the guru gives the new *vācanācārya* the Cloth Diagram of the Spell of Mahāvīra, which features an inscription of the spell (*VMP*, p. 65, line 22).[52]

Other mendicants are promoted to other levels by receiving different versions of the *vardhamānavidyā*. When a monk is promoted to the rank of male mendicant teacher (*upādhyāya*) or when a nun is promoted to the rank of female mendicant leader (*pravartinī* or *mahattarā*), the guru imparts slightly different versions of this invocation.[53] From this day onward, these mendicants must recite their version of the *vardhamānavidyā* 108 times and sanctify scented sandalwood powder by sprinkling it on the physical representation of the spell, their cloth diagram (see chapter 5).

After a monk of supreme conduct and knowledge has studied the scriptures and daily propitiated his cloth diagram of the *vardhamānavidyā* for twelve years, he is eligible to be promoted to the highest rank of mendicancy, the *ācārya*. At this point he should receive the *sūrimantra* in an elaborate ceremony of promotion that aligns remarkably well with the one I witnessed in Surat in 2013 (see chapter 2). On an auspicious date, in the presence of a model of the Jina's Preaching Assembly, the disciple, seated to the left of the guru, should ask the guru, in Prakrit, for the authority to disperse the meanings of the scriptures. To grant this permission, with the guru and the disciple standing in the *kāyotsarga* meditative posture, the guru should sprinkle scented sandalwood powder consecrated by the *sūrimantra* on a physical copy of the *Nandīsūtra* and recite the seven hundred Prakrit *sūtras* of the *Nandīsūtra* to the gathered community of monks, nuns, laymen, and laywomen, signifying the new *ācārya*'s authority to safeguard and interpret the canonical scriptures outlined in the text (*VMP*, p. 66, para. 70, lines 20–27). After the disciple is granted the authority to interpret the scriptures, the key moment of transformation into an *ācārya* occurs. The disciple should circumambulate the Jina's Preaching Assembly three times, and the guru should then recite the *sūrimantra* three times into the disciple's right ear (*VMP*, p. 67, para. 70, lines 1–9).[54] Jinaprabhasūri emphasizes the secrecy of this ceremony and therefore does not provide the contents of the *sūrimantra*, noting that it should not be written in a book, to avoid undermining the tradition (*VMP*, p. 67, para. 70, line 11). He does, however, reference another of his texts that we will examine later in this chapter: the manual on the *sūrimantra* that the newly minted *ācārya* should study to undertake the required daily ritual propitiation (*sādhana*) of the cloth diagram of the *sūrimantra* that he receives upon his promotion (*VMP*, p. 67, line 23). The *ācārya* is required to daily sprinkle scented sandalwood powder on his Cloth Diagram of the Mantra of the Mendicant Leader, consecrating the powder for use in initiating disciples, consecrating temple images, and performing miraculous feats (see chapter 5).

With these promotions, higher-level Śvetāmbara mendicants in many ways resemble the higher-level initiates in tantric traditions—the *sādhaka* and the *ācārya*—who have undergone ritual ablutions (*abhiṣeka*), receiving the authority to use mantras in daily worship, initiations, and temple consecrations.[55] The Śvetāmbara mendicants who receive the *vardhamānavidyā* are similar to the *sādhaka* of the Śaiva Mantramārga who uses the mantra that was imparted to him upon his promotion (*svamantra*, *sādhyamantra*)[56] to undertake daily rites to achieve superhuman powers and eventual liberation. In early Jain texts, the *vācanācārya* and the *upādhyāya* are responsible for teaching and lecturing, but by the medieval period, after the imparting of the *vardhamānavidyā* became part of their promotions, these Jain mendicants became involved in using *mantraśāstra* to consecrate temple images and to develop superhuman powers. In the *Vidhimārgaprapā* and in another Prakrit hymn of seventeen verses to the *vardhamānavidyā*, the *Vardhamānavidyāstavana*, Jinaprabhasūri confirms the worldly and soteriological power of the Spell of Mahāvīra. He maintains that in supreme, revered ceremonies such as renunciation, ordination, the promotion of a leader of a mendicant group, and the temple image-consecration ceremony, the worshiper who is sprinkled with a scented substance that has been sanctified through the recitation of this spell seven times will achieve liberation, and a temple icon imparted with the spell will become worthy of worship

(*VMP*, p. 65, lines 20–21). In addition, the spell can destroy faults, prevent sickness, and bring other people under one's control (*VVK*, 1–3).

Similarly, the Śvetāmbara mendicants who receive the *sūrimantra*—*ācārya*s—resemble the *ācārya*s of Śaiva, Vaiṣṇava, and Buddhist tantric traditions who have the right to initiate new disciples, comment on the scripture, perform public worship, and consecrate public temple images. Just as the Śaiva *ācārya* upon his promotion receives the universal mantra the *vyomavyāpin* to be used in public rites,[57] so too do Jain *ācārya*s receive the *sūrimantra*. In the *Vidhimārgaprapā*, the Śvetāmbara *ācārya* is not only responsible for teaching and initiating disciples, as in early Jain texts, but he also must consecrate temple images, imparting the *sūrimantra* to the right ear of the icon that has been decorated with sandalwood and other substances in a replication of his own promotion (*VMP*, p. 102, lines 16–17). Combining the tantric understanding that an *ācārya* must consecrate temple images with the Jain understanding that *ācārya*s are still mendicants who must avoid temple worship using physical substances (*dravyapūjā*) caused controversy in some Śvetāmbara mendicant lineages.[58] While some Jains were critical of mendicants' involvement in temple consecration, the use of different versions of the *sūrimantra* in temple consecrations did allow mendicant groups to lay claim to certain temples. Mendicants would argue that only their lineage's version of the *sūrimantra* could properly consecrate a temple image,[59] presumably so that laypeople would fund and frequent temples connected to their lineage, providing them food and shelter. From defeating Nātha *yogin*s to making temple icons powerful images worthy of worship, in this period of competition between mendicant lineages, the secret invocations of Śvetāmbara monks of higher rank became key to bringing lay monetary support to one's mendicant community. Jinaprabhasūri's *Vidhimārgaprapā* thus gives us a good idea of how medieval Śvetāmbaras' path to liberation required both austerities and mantra-based practices.

EARLY MODERN DIGAMBARA EVIDENCE FOR THE MANTRAS OF MENDICANT PROMOTION

Scholars have done much less research on the history of Digambara monasticism, though we do know that Digambara Jains became increasingly splintered into competing monastic lineages at the same time as their Śvetāmbara counterparts, especially after the thirteenth century. From the early medieval period, Digambaras were grouped into several *saṅgha*s, including the Drāviḍa, Kāṣṭhā, Māthura, Yāpanīya, and Mūla,[60] which were further divided into *gaccha*s and *gaṇa*s. The most influential of these monastic groupings in north India, the Sena Gaṇa and the Balātkāra Gaṇa, both belonging to the Mūla Saṅgha, are first documented in texts and inscriptions from Karnataka from the ninth and tenth centuries, respectively.[61] Within these lineages, from about the beginning of the thirteenth century, a new position—the *bhaṭṭāraka*—emerged as the highest rank of mendicancy, above the *ācārya*.[62] While some *bhaṭṭāraka*s practiced nudity, most wore orange robes, and they owned property such as monasteries (*maṭha*) attached to temple compounds throughout north, central, and south India.[63] Some of these *bhaṭṭāraka*s, like their Śvetāmbara *ācārya* counterparts, broke off from their lineages to establish new mendicant groups. While records suggest only one Balātkāra Gaṇa lineage was influential in the thirteenth century, "consecutive bifurcations" from the late fourteenth century onward led to the *gaṇa* eventually being split into about fifteenth branches (*śākhā*).[64]

There are no known medieval accounts of Digambara initiation and promotion within these lineages, but scholars in recent decades have published examinations of manuscripts on the promotions of Digambara mendicants that date to the early modern period, likely the seventeenth and eighteenth centuries. Tillo Detige has translated and transcribed three different manuals on the consecration of a *bhaṭṭāraka* found in the manuscript collections of two former *bhaṭṭāraka* seats of branches of the Balātkāra Gaṇa. Two manuscripts were found at the Chandranāth Digambar Mandir in Karanja, Maharashtra, and the other was found in the collection at the important pilgrimage site in Sonagiri, Madhya Pradesh.[65] In addition, Ratancandra Jain has provided Sanskrit prescriptions for the promotion of a Digambara *upādhyāya*, *ācārya*, and *bhaṭṭāraka* said to be taken from a manuscript found at the pilgrimage site Śri Atiśay Kṣetra in Bediya, Gujarat.[66] I unfortunately do not have access to premodern rites of initiation for the rank of a Digambara monk (*muni*), but a brief overview of the promotion of a mendicant teacher, mendicant leader, and *bhaṭṭāraka* in this text from Bediya confirms that Digambaras in the early modern period, like Śvetāmbaras, rose through the ranks of mendicancy through austerities and the use of *mantraśāstra*.

The instructions for the promotions of an *upādhyāya*, *ācārya*, and *bhaṭṭāraka* in the text from Bediya are bare-bones, each consisting of only a paragraph of printed text and not providing any sense of the atmosphere of these ceremonies, which were likely grand occasions for the lay and mendicant community to gather and celebrate the teachings of the tradition. The promotions always begin with the worship (*arcana*) of the Ring of Disciples diagram, though the specific components of these diagrams are not outlined. After the Ring of Disciples is worshiped, the ceremony of promotion begins with the ritual in which mantras physically transform the disciple into a supreme being—either an *upādhyāya*, an *ācārya*, or a new type of supreme being not found in the *pañcanamaskāra*, a *bhaṭṭāraka*. The person leading the ceremony—either the guru or a lay ritual specialist (*paṇḍita*)[67]—should recite three mantras while dropping cloves and flowers onto the disciple's head: a Sanskrit mantra inviting (*āvāhana*) the *ācārya*, *upādhyāya*, or *bhaṭṭāraka* into the body of the disciple; a Sanskrit mantra establishing (*sthāpanā*) the supreme being in the disciple; and a Sanskrit mantra asking for the supreme being to remain in the disciple (*sannidhīkaraṇa*).[68]

If the monk is being promoted to the rank of *ācārya* or *bhaṭṭāraka*, after he has been transformed into a supreme being, he should receive a ritual ablution (*abhiṣeka*). When he is promoted to the rank of *ācārya*, his feet should be bathed from five golden pots filled with fragrant water from pilgrimage places; and when he is promoted to the rank of *bhaṭṭāraka*, his feet should be bathed with the fragrant waters from 108 golden pots.[69] Therefore, while Śvetāmbaras used the sprinkling of powder, not an ablution of water (*abhiṣeka*), to promote their mendicants, Digambaras appear to have adopted the *abhiṣeka* rites common to tantric Śaiva, Vaiṣṇava, and Buddhist promotions of *ācārya*s, though these *abhiṣeka*s are not performed today to promote *ācārya*s.

Upon promotion to the rank of *bhaṭṭāraka*, the monk receives the *sūrimantra*. After the ritual ablution, the guru should give the soon-to-be-*bhaṭṭāraka* the *sūrimantra* directly or indirectly, depending on whether the existing *bhaṭṭāraka* has died or a living *bhaṭṭāraka* is passing his position to his disciple. To transmit the *sūrimantra* indirectly, the incumbent *bhaṭṭāraka* "ought to write down the *sūrimantra* on a piece of paper, which is then sealed and properly stored" and, according to a version of the rite in a manuscript from Karanja, "covered with stamped paper and deposited in a [box]."[70]

These *bhaṭṭāraka*s were not only powerful specialists of *mantraśāstra*, however; they were also mendicants. Several early modern songs of praise describing the festive promotions of *bhaṭṭāraka*s emphasize what is not found in ritual prescriptions: *upādhyāya*s, *ācārya*s, and *bhaṭṭāraka*s also upheld the twenty-eight root qualities of monks, including the five vows, the five restraints (*samiti*), and control of the five senses that are outlined in the earliest known Digambara account of initiation, Kundakunda's *Pravaca-*

nasāra, and adopted by monks to this day (see chapter 2).[71] In addition, just as the monk in the initiation I witnessed in Kekri received the mendicant paraphernalia of the broom (*picchī*), water pot (*kamaṇḍalu*), and scripture (chapter 2), *bhaṭṭāraka*s also received a broom and water pot, along with a lotus instead of a scripture. Nemacanda's song of praise from 1712/13 CE that honors Bhaṭṭāraka Devendrakīrti of the Mūla Saṅgha of Amer recounts the following of his consecration:

> One monk (*yati*) [and] five ritual specialists (*paṇḍita*) together poured the golden pitcher.
> As he poured the [offering], Sāha Ghāsīrāma brought fame to the [community].
> The king-like *muni* was seated on a throne, above his head a parasol spread.
> Taking a lotus, water-pot (*kamaṇḍalu*), and broom (*picchī*) as insignia of compassion.
> Taking the paraphernalia, he took renunciation, keeping the five great vows in mind.
> He observed the five restraints (*samiti*) and the . . . self-control [of mind, body, and speech] (*gupti*), bringing his five senses under control.[72]

Digambaras and Śvetāmbaras therefore both combined tantric and monastic promotions, honoring a ritual diagram and receiving a secret mantra in order to maintain one's monastic vows. And while these published accounts of Digambara monastic promotions are quite late, evidence from earlier texts on image consecration suggests that Digambaras developed this monastic promotion with tantric elements by at least the twelfth century.

EMBEDDING THE INITIATION OF A DIGAMBARA MONK IN IMAGE CONSECRATION RITES

Medieval Digambara manuals on the consecration of a temple image provide the closest-known analogue of medieval Śvetāmbara sources on the levels of mendicant promotion, since both the initiation of a Digambara mendicant and the promotion of an *ācārya* are embedded in these rituals. I have had access to four premodern published sources on Digambara image consecration, all in Sanskrit. The earliest, Vasunandin's *Pratiṣṭhāpāṭha*, was most likely composed in the twelfth century.[73] Nemicandra's *Pratiṣṭhātilaka* (*PrT*) was composed around 1200, in Kanchipuram, Tamil Nadu.[74] Paṇḍita Āśādhara, the prolific lay scholar of the thirteenth century who spent most of his life in the Mālava region of west-central India, also composed a manual on image consecration, the *Pratiṣṭhāsāroddhāra*,[75] and what is likely the latest published premodern manual, the *Pratiṣṭhāpāṭha* by Jayasena, alias Vasubindu, has been dated to around the fourteenth or fifteenth century.[76]

All these texts have influenced modern Digambara image consecration ceremonies. In Digambara Jainism today, many laypeople and mendicants understand themselves to follow one of two main traditions: either the Terāpantha that is thought to have arisen from the writings of lay intellectuals (*paṇḍita*) in north India in the seventeenth-eighteenth centuries, or the Bīsapantha.[77] In practical terms, this designation affects primarily how and what Digambaras worship, since Terāpanthīs have rejected the worship of some gods and goddesses and the use of flowers, milk, and other substances in temple worship, but both Bīsapanthīs and Terāpanthīs have used the same premodern manuals to develop their modern image consecration rites. Mendicants and ritual specialists who lead these ceremonies (*pratiṣṭhācārya*)—laymen who have received ritual training from their fathers or at special schools—often draw upon multiple premodern texts when composing modern ritual manuals. In January 2013 in Hastinapur, I witnessed a Bīsapanthī image consecration ceremony led by the nun Jñānamatī that followed her own edition of Nemicandra's *Pratiṣṭhātilaka*, which includes an extensive appendix, an introduction, and a Hindi translation and commentary that draw upon other texts.[78] In February 2013, in Jaipur, Rajasthan, I attended a Terāpanthī Digambara image-consecration festival led by Ācārya Vibhavasāgara that followed the *Pratiṣṭhā Ratnākar*, a late twentieth-century Hindi handbook compiled by the Terāpanthī ritual specialist Paṇḍit Gulābcandra, who claims that he based his text mostly on Jayasena's *Pratiṣṭhāpāṭha*, but that he also consulted about ninety-five texts in total, including Āśādhara's *Pratiṣṭhāsāroddhāra* and Nemicandra's *Pratiṣṭhātilaka*.[79]

The Mantras of Digambara Promotion

In these medieval texts on image consecration, transforming an inert stone into the physical presence of the *jina* requires ritual specialists to use the stone representations of the *tīrthaṅkara*s to reenact the five auspicious events (*pañcakalyāṇaka*) in the life of a *jina*: (1) conception (*garbha*), (2) birth (*janma*), (3) renunciation (*dīkṣā/tapas/niṣkrama*), (4) omniscience, or enlightenment (*kevalajñāna*), and (5) death and liberation (*mokṣa*). Since the third event of renunciation is modeled on the renunciation of a monk, it provides some evidence of the medieval Digambara rites of initiation.

The tenth chapter of Nemicandra's *Pratiṣṭhātilaka* outlines the rites required for the temple icon to renounce the world. These rites should occur on the ninth day of the image-consecration ceremony, after the lay and mendicant community has reenacted the first two auspicious events, replicating the conception and birth of a *jina*.[80] Singing praises, lay worshipers representing gods should take the icon of a *tīrthaṅkara* to a pavilion established for the initiation ceremony. They should set the icon below a representation of a tree, where it is bathed, worshiped, ornamented, and rubbed with ointments (*PrT* 10.1–4, p. 234). The *vardhamānamantra* should then be pronounced seven times, and auspicious laywomen should perform a lamp offering to the icon (*PrT* 10.5, p. 234).[81] After offerings are made to the icon, laypeople should place it on a palanquin and take it to a representation of a forest (*PrT* 10.5, p. 234). The *tīrthaṅkara* icon then should undertake his initiation: his hair should be pulled out and worshiped by laypeople representing gods (*PrT* 10.9, p. 234), his clothes should be removed and worshiped, and four lamps should be lit to symbolize the *jina*'s attainment of the fourth type of knowledge, mind reading (*PrT* 10.10–11, p. 234). To initiate the icon in this way in the 2013 image-consecration ceremony I witnessed in Jaipur, Ācārya Vibhavasāgara, standing onstage in front of the congregation, removed the clothes of the *jina* icon and picked cloves off its head to symbolize the removal of his hair (fig. 3.3).

Nemicandra's text thus suggests that medieval Digambaras, like Śvetāmbaras, required the sevenfold recitation of an invocation named after Mahāvīra to initiate mendicants. While we cannot be sure of the contents of this medieval mantra, Digambara initiands are still imparted a Prakrit invocation termed the *vardhamānamantra* upon their initiations (see chapter 2).[82] This mantra asks for protection, victory in the court of the king, the stopping of opponents in their tracks, and triumph in battle.

The next auspicious event—the attainment of omniscience—provides evidence that Digambara *ācāryas*, like Śvetāmbara *ācāryas*, were also imparted the *sūrimantra*. This fourth auspicious event occurs after the *tīrthaṅkara* has renounced the world, and it is described in the eleventh chapter of Nemicandra's *Pratiṣṭhātilaka*. During this ceremony, the icon becomes worthy of worship through a key performance that transforms stone into a *jina*: the eye-opening ceremony. According to Nemicandra, when the

FIGURE 3.3. Ācārya Vibhavasāgara initiates an icon of a *jina*. Jaipur, February 2013.

eye-opening rites are undertaken, the *jina* icon also obtains omniscience. The rites include a smearing of scented substances on the icon; the recitation of mantras to impart the qualities of a pure soul (infinite knowledge, perception, power, and happiness) (*PrT*, 261); the recitation of mantras to impart the fourteen miraculous signs (*atiśaya*), such as pleasant weather and a halo, that accompany the enlightenment and omniscience of the *jina*;[83] and, at the end of the ceremony, the placement of the icon in a model of the Jina's Preaching Assembly (*PrT* 11.6, p. 244). In addition, both Vasunandin's and Jayasena's texts on image consecration understand the recitation of the *sūrimantra* as one of the foundational rites to perform to summon the nature of the *jina* (*jinatva*) into the icon.[84] In Jayasena's text, the imparting of the *sūrimantra* occurs right after the eye-opening rite and bestows omniscience on the icon: "The [*ācārya*] should perform the eye opening. Then he should bestow omniscience [to the icon] by means of the *sūrimantra*," it explains (*Pratiṣṭhāpāṭha*, p. 117, vv. 378–79). It insists that the *ācārya* should impart the *sūrimantra*, suggesting that the Digambara *ācārya* was at one point imparted the *sūrimantra*, perhaps before the *bhaṭṭāraka* took over the role of the possessor of this secret invocation.[85]

The Ring of Disciples as a Diagram of Initiation and Promotion

These Digambara image-consecration manuals from the twelfth to fifteenth centuries also provide some of the earliest evidence for the contents of the Digambara initiation diagram, the Ring of Disciples. They confirm that to become sacred objects of worship, temple icons not only must reenact the life events of the *tīrthaṅkaras*, they also must be sacralized by being placed in the presence of ritual diagrams into which the beings the temple icons represent are invoked. The image being installed—be it a *jina* icon, a representation of an *ācārya*, the footprints of a monk, or another type of temple image—dictates the type of diagram to be constructed for its consecration.[86] For example, for the consecration of a *jina* image, a *yāgamaṇḍala*, which represents all the *tīrthaṅkaras* of the past, present, and future, should be worshiped at the outset of each day of the consecration ceremony (*PrT*, 118–22), and to this day, ritual specialists in Digambara image consecrations follow this prescription, offering coconuts to *yāgamaṇḍalas* made of colored power.[87]

In premodern texts, the consecration of a temple image of an *ācārya* or another type of mendicant requires the construction of the Ring of Disciples diagram, the *gaṇadharavalaya* (*PrT*, 328–29).[88] According to Nemicandra, the Ring of Disciples should be constructed on a ritual platform on the sixth day of the worship ceremony. The size of the diagram and the materials used to make it are not specified, but descriptions of other diagrams include colors, suggesting the construction of a large, impermanent diagram made out of colored powder.[89] The components of the Ring of Disciples in Nemicandra's manual correspond exactly to the ones described in Jñānamatī's ritual manual I purchased in Hastinapur in 2008. At the center of three concentric circles sits a hexagram with the seed syllable *kṣmā* at its center. Inside the six corners of this hexagram, the syllables *a pra ti ca kre phaṭ* are inscribed. In each external angle of the hexagram, sit the six syllables *vi ca krā ya svā hā*, ending with *jhrauṃ*. A circle of goddesses—Śrī, Hrī, Dhṛti, Kīrti, Buddhi, and Lakṣmī—are placed at the six tips of the hexagram. Surrounding this central figure are forty-eight petals containing the forty-four lines of the *ṛddhi-maṅgala* and four additional praises (*PrT*, 328–29). After the ninth praise of the *ṛddhi-maṅgala* (*ṇamo saṃbhiṇṇasodārāṇaṃ*), three praises to types of enlightened beings are added:

> *ṇamo sayaṃsaṃbuddhāṇaṃ*
> Praise to the self-enlightened *buddhas*.
> *ṇamo patteyabuddhāṇaṃ*
> Praise to the *buddhas* who were assisted in enlightenment.
> *ṇamo bohiyabuddhāṇaṃ*
> Praise to the enlightened *buddhas*.[90]

"Praise to the Mahāvīra" (*ṇamo vaḍḍhamāṇāṃ*) is then appended after the forty-second line of the *ṛddhi-maṅgala* (*ṇamo akkhīṇamahāṇasāṇaṃ*). The redundancy of this praise—which essentially repeats the final line of the *ṛddhi-maṅgala* that honors Mahāvīra—suggests that these praises were added less for their specific meanings and more so that the number of lines of praises could be a multiple of eight that would fit the common eight-petaled structure of initiation *maṇḍalas* in Hindu, Buddhist, and Jain traditions. Therefore, just as the *tīrthaṅkaras* of the past, present, and future

FIGURE 3.4. A folio from a late nineteenth-century manuscript of Vasubindu's *Pratiṣṭhāpāṭha* showing the Ring of Disciples diagram. The central mantra of Ring of Disciples diagrams is not consistent, though the *apraticakrā*-mantra is required. Here, a Sanskrit praise to the *arhat* sits at the center of the central hexagram. The *apraticakrā*-mantra, with *a pra ti ca kre phaṭ* beginning at the bottom of the hexagram moving clockwise, and *vi ca krā ya svā hā* moving counterclockwise, sits in the angles of the hexagram. Manuscript no. 486, Bābā Dulicandjī Baḍā Mandir Śāstra Bhaṇḍār, Jaipur.

TABLE 3.2. The mantras and *maṇḍalas* of premodern Digambara ascetic promotion

Rank of initiate	Mantra imparted upon ordination/promotion	Diagram constructed upon ordination
Mendicant (*muni*)	Mantra of Mahāvīra? (*vardhamānamantra*)	Ring of Disciples (*gaṇadharavalaya*)
Mendicant teacher (*upādhyāya*)	Unknown	Ring of Disciples
Mendicant leader (*ācārya*)	Mantra of the Mendicant Leader? (*sūrimantra*)	Ring of Disciples
bhaṭṭāraka	Mantra of the Mendicant Leader	Ring of Disciples

are invoked into the diagram required for the consecration of an image of a *tīrthaṅkara*, in the same way, the mendicants of the past, via the mantra associated with them and their superhuman powers (the *ṛddhi-maṅgala*) are invoked into the diagram used to consecrate an image of a monk. Since by the early modern period we have evidence that Digambaras constructed the Ring of Disciples in the initiations and promotions of living monks, these medieval texts' descriptions of the construction of the Ring of Disciples for the consecration of an icon of a monk were likely modeled on the diagram used for initiations and promotions of living monks.

Therefore, image-consecration manuals provide evidence that Digambaras, like Śvetāmbaras, had tantricized their levels of mendicant promotions by at least the thirteenth century, constructing an initiation diagram and imparting the *vardhamānamantra* to lower-level monks and the *sūrimantra* to *ācāryas* (table 3.2). At some point, the *bhaṭṭāraka* replaced the *ācārya* as the highest rank of Digambara mendicancy and the possessor of the *sūrimantra*. These mendicant leaders, then, like their Śvetāmbara and tantric Hindu and Buddhist counterparts, were responsible for leading key parts of the image-consecration ceremony, using the *sūrimantra* to consecrate a temple icon.

COMPARING THE RITUAL DIAGRAMS OF DIGAMBARA AND ŚVETĀMBARA MENDICANT PROMOTION

Other premodern Digambara and Śvetāmbara sources on mendicant ritual provide even more evidence that monks of these two sects developed diagrams of initiation and promotion in conversation with one another. Indeed, these texts begin to answer the question that initially motivated the research for this book: What is the relationship between the Digambara Ring of Disciples diagram and the Śvetāmbara Cloth Diagram of the Mantra of the Mendicant Leader? Several *bhaṭṭāraka*s in northwest and central India between the fourteenth and sixteenth centuries composed Sanskrit ritual manuals on the worship of the Ring of Disciples, likely to define these rites for their own lineages as the Digambara mendicant community became increasingly fragmented. One manual is attributed to Padmanandin, who became *bhaṭṭāraka* of the Uttara Śākhā of the Balātkāra Gaṇa[91] in 1328. A highly influential pupil of Padmanandin, Sakalakīrti (1386–1442), who established the branch of the Balātkāra Gaṇa that would later be known as the Iḍar Śākhā, also composed an important manual. A similar text on the Ring of Disciples is attributed to Prabhācandra, likely the *bhaṭṭāraka* who was given the seat of the Delhi-Jaipur branch of the Balātkāra Gaṇa in 1514.[92] And the most popular manual today—the one followed in the initiation I witnessed in Kekri—was composed by the *bhaṭṭāraka* Śubhacandra in 1549.[93] Śubhacandra, who held the post of *bhaṭṭāraka* of the Iḍar branch of the Balātkāra Gaṇa from ca. 1516 to 1556, was one of the most prolific and active *bhaṭṭāraka*s of north India, traveling widely to consecrate new temples and composing multiple ritual manuals that remain popular today.[94]

At the same time as these *bhaṭṭāraka*s were composing texts on the Ring of Disciples, Śvetāmbara *ācārya*s in northwest India were composing texts on the Cloth Diagram of the Mantra of the Mendicant Leader. The earliest known manual on the *sūrimantra*, the *Mantrarājarahasya* (*MRR*), was composed by Siṃhatilakasūri in the thirteenth century.[95] Essentially nothing is known about Siṃhatilakasūri, but he is today understood as one of the most prominent medieval Śvetāmbara composers of texts on *mantraśāstra*, with works on two other important ritual diagrams, the *ṛṣimaṇḍala* and the *vardhamānavidyāpaṭa*, attributed to him.[96] *Ācārya*s from competing Śvetāmbara mendicant lineages—Rājaśekharasūri of the Maladhārīya Gaccha and Merutuṅgasūri of the Añcala Gaccha—composed their own manuals on the mantra soon after Siṃhatilakasūri did, between the fourteenth and fifteenth centuries. Jinaprabhasūri's *Sūrimantrabṛhatkalpavivaraṇa* was composed in 1317.

Comparing these Digambara and Śvetāmbara manuals sheds light on the extensive, long-standing connections between the ritual lives of the mendicants of these communities, despite modern Jains' lack of awareness of the historical connections between the two sects.[97] By the thirteenth century, and likely well before that time, both Digambaras and Śvetāmbaras had begun to use the *apraticakrā*-mantra and the *ṛddhi-maṅgala* to create their mendicant initiation diagrams to call to mind the preaching assembly of the first *tīrthaṅkara*, Ṛṣabha.

The Śvetāmbara Cloth Diagram of the Mantra of the Mendicant Leader

Śvetāmbara texts on the *sūrimantra* focus on the contents and ritual uses of the different sections (*pīṭhas* or *prasthānas*) of the mantra over which different deities rule. The earliest text on the *sūrimantra*, the *Mantrarājarahasya*, is also the longest, containing more than six hundred verses that outline thirteen different recensions of the mantra that divide it into one, four, five, or six sections (*SMKS*, 305–39). The first recension of the mantra Siṃhatilakasūri lists in the *Mantrarājarahasya* (table 3.3) is representative of other versions.[98] It, like the majority of other versions, contains five sections. The first section is called the "section of superhuman powers" (*labdhipada*), and it always includes lines of the *ṛddhi-maṅgala*. The second section comprises the Prakrit *bāhubalividyā*, which praises the strength and ascetic virtues of the son of Ṛṣabha, Bāhubali, and the *saubhāgyavidyā*, "which appears to represent a string of adjectives expressing beauty and attractiveness in the feminine vocative case, addressed either to the presiding deity of this mantra or the power associated with her."[99] The final three sections of the mantra contain variant combinations of a few syllable clusters (*kiri*, *piri*, *siri*, *hiri*, and *āyari*) that are interpreted in different texts to represent various Jain teachings (see chapter 5).[100]

Medieval texts on the *sūrimantra* devote significant attention to the first section. The lists of superhuman powers in different *labdhipadas* of this section range between eight and fifty lines long, demonstrating that competing mendicant lineages distinguished themselves via these lists. The longest list is found in the *Mantrarājarahasya* (*MRR*, vv. 2–7), and according to Siṃhatilakasūri, these *labdhis* contain one thousand different spells whose ritual use can produce a variety of results, among them eloquence and healing leprosy (*MRR*, v. 9).

The *Mantrarājarahasya*'s discussion of the first section of the *sūrimantra* also outlines a variety of rites involving the construction of *yantras* on which the first section of the mantra is inscribed. These descriptions show a direct relationship between the Digambara Ring of Disciples and the Śvetāmbara Cloth Diagram of the Mantra of the Mendicant Leader. They also show that at least some Śvetāmbaras explicitly understood these diagrams to be

TABLE 3.3. The components of a Śvetāmbara *sūrimantra* outlined in the *Mantrarājarahasya*

Section of the *sūrimantra* (*pīṭha, prasthāna*)	Contents	Presiding deity (*adhiṣṭhāyaka*)
1. *vidyāpīṭha*	*namo jiṇāṇaṃ, namo ohijiṇāṇaṃ, namo paramohijiṇāṇaṃ, namo aṇaṃtohijiṇāṇaṃ, namo aṇaṃtāṇaṃtohijiṇāṇaṃ, namo sāmannakevalīṇaṃ, namo bhavatthakevalīṇaṃ, namo abhavatthakevalīṇaṃ, namo uggatavacaraṇacārīṇaṃ, namo caudasapuvvīṇaṃ, namo dasapuvvīṇaṃ, namo ikkārasaṃgīṇaṃ*	Goddess Brāhmī/Sarasvatī
	(praise to the *jinas*, praise to the *jinas* with supreme clairvoyance, with infinite clairvoyance, with supremely infinite clairvoyance; praise to the ordinary omniscient ones, to the omniscient ones who are still living, to the omniscient ones who are not living; praise to those who can endure difficult fasts; praise to those who know the fourteen *pūrvas*, the ten *pūrvas*, the eleven *aṅgas*) (*MRR*, vv. 144–46)	
2. *mahāvidyāpīṭha* (*bāhubalividyā* and *saubhāgyavidyā*)	*oṃ namo bhagavao bāhubalissa paṇhasamaṇassa* (*oṃ* praise to Bāhubali, the wise ascetic) (*MRR*, v. 161)	Goddess Tribhuvanasvāminī
	oṃ vaggu vaggu nivaggu sumaṇe somaṇase mahumahure (*MRR*, vv. 161–62)	
3. *upavidyāpīṭha*	*irikālī pirikālī sirikālī mahākālī kiriyāe hiriyāe* (*MRR*, vv. 162–63)	Goddess of wealth, Śrī/Lakṣmī
4. *mantrapīṭha*	*oṃ kirikirikālī piripirikālī sirisirikālī hirihirikālī āyariya āyariyakālī* (*MRR*, v. 164)	God of the scriptures, Gaṇipiṭaka Yakṣa
5. *mantrarājapīṭha*	*kirimeru pirimeru sirimeru hirimeru āyariyameru* (*MRR*, v. 165)	Mahāvīra's disciple Gautama

Source: *SMKS*, 17–20

models of the Jina's Preaching Assembly. Verse 69 of the *Mantrarājarahasya* describes a diagram identical to the Digambara Ring of Disciples diagram in Nemicandra's *Pratiṣṭhātilaka*, with the *apraticakrā*-mantra at its center:

> *ṣaṭkoṇe 'praticakrāyantraṃ ṣaḍadhikadaśadvyadhitriṃśat* |
> *antardalaṃ stutipadī digantare gaṇabhṛtāṃ valayam* ||
>
> Inside a six-cornered figure, there is the *apraticakrā yantra*, [and] on the outside of that, in forty-eight petals, are the praises of the Ring of Disciples. (*MRR*, v. 69)

Elsewhere, Siṃhatilakasūri describes how the *sūrimantrapaṭa* should be understood as a depiction of the Jina's Preaching Assembly made of jewels, gold, and silver, with the sections of the mantra situated in the different parts of the assembly (*MRR*, vv. 298–303).

Other texts on the *sūrimantra* describe the *sūrimantrapaṭa* using the same language as descriptions of the Digambara Ring of Disciples diagram with the *apraticakrā*-mantra at its center.[101] An anonymous Sanskrit manual on how to construct a cloth diagram of the *sūrimantra* and recite its mantras tells worshipers to place the seed syllables *oṃ*, *hrīṃ*, and *śrīṃ* in the pericarp of a lotus and surround it with five rings in which the five sections of the *sūrimantra* are inscribed. The contents of the first ring are exactly the same as the Ring of Disciples described in the medieval Digambara manuals of image consecration except that the mantra for an omniscient being, *arhaṃ*, has replaced *kṣmā* at the center of the figure:

> In the first ring, having drawn a hexagram, having placed an *arhaṃ* in the center of that [figure], having written in the six corners [of the figure] from right to left *a pra ti ca kre phaṭ*, having written *vi ca krā ya* from left to right, having written *śrī hrī dhṛti kṛti buddhi* and *lakṣmī* on the outside [of the six-sided figure], make a ring. (*SMKS*, 251)[102]

Another text—Jinaprabhasūri's *Sūrimantrabṛhatkalpavivaraṇa*—also lists several variants of the *labdhipada* and documents a range of ritual uses for this first section, including defeating an adversary, finding success in battle, and removing poison (*SMKS*, p. 85, lines 17–20). He outlines the construction of one *yantra* of the *labdhipada* by explaining that practitioners should use sandalwood paste to draw on copper a representation of the Jina's Preaching Assembly that has four doors at its exterior, three concentric rings in the middle, and the Sanskrit mantra to the first *tīrthaṅkara* Ṛṣabha, *oṃ arhaṃ śrī yugādināthāya svāhā*, at its center (*SMKS*, p. 85, lines 7–8). This circle with eight sections is filled with what he terms the *gaṇadhara-vidyā* (the spell of the disciples of the *tīrthaṅkaras*) (*SMKS*, p. 85, lines 22–24).[103] At least some manuscripts of this text then include instructions for meditation on this *yantra* that includes the recitation of the *apraticakrā*-mantra:

> Having meditated on the above-described *yantra*, standing motionless in the position of "abandoning the body" (*kāyotsarga*), recite "*oṃ namo arihaṃtāṇaṃ hrāṃ hrīṃ hrauṃ hrūṃ hraḥ apraticakre phaṭ vicakrāya hrīṃ*

arhaṃ a si ā u sā jhrauṃ jhrauṃ svāhā oṃ namo bhagavate arihaṃtāṇam namo ohijiṇāṇaṃ hrāṃ hrīṃ hrauṃ hrūṃ haḥ apraticakre phaṭ vicakrāya hrīṃ arhaṃ a si ā u sā jhrauṃ jhrauṃ svāhā" 108 times. This stops fevers (*SMKS*, 87).[104]

In understanding the diagram of the *sūrimantra* as Ṛṣabha's preaching assembly in this way, Jinaprabhasūri has helped solve part of the mystery I encountered in Hastinapur in 2008: the meaning of the *apraticakre phaṭ* and *vicakrāya svāhā* mantras. Apraticakrā is another name for Cakreśvarī, the *yakṣī*, or protector goddess, of Ṛṣabha. By the medieval period, a pair of male and female deities (*yakṣa*, *yakṣī*), the *śāsanadevatā* (deities of the teachings), had become associated with each of the twenty-four *tīrthaṅkaras* and were depicted in temple images at the sides of the *tīrthaṅkaras* as their protectors and devoted worshipers.[105] In this Sanskrit mantra, the name of this goddess is in the vocative, with worshipers calling out, "Oh, Apraticakrā," to invoke her presence. Apraticakrā sits in the six-cornered figure surrounding the center of this diagram, protecting her main object of reverence, Ṛṣabha, who is made present at the center of the diagram through seed syllables. *Vicakrāya svāha*, then—which is inscribed counterclockwise around the six-cornered figure—could be translated as "pervasive wheel" and could pay obeisance to the diagram itself.[106] Indeed, one Digambara ritual specialist confirmed to me that *vicakra* refers to the hexagram at the center of the Ring of Disciples.[107] With Ṛṣabha thus established at the center of the diagram, the *ṛddhi-maṅgala* inscribed in rings (*valaya*) around the central image invoke the disciples of the *jina*, who sit in concentric circles around their guru Ṛṣabha in his preaching assembly to hear him give his first teaching.

Digambara Sources on the Ring of Disciples

Digambara manuals from the fifteenth and sixteenth centuries on the construction and ritual use of the Ring of Disciples diagram also develop a new version of the diagram to make clear that it represents the Jina's Preaching Assembly. Catalogues of the texts composed by *bhaṭṭārakas* and inscriptions detailing their activities in the early modern period confirm that one of their primary roles was the performance of large public rituals (*vidhāna*) that garnered funds and visibility for Digambara communities and mendicant lineages. In this period, *bhaṭṭārakas* fully embraced the worldly and soteriological uses of mantras and expanded many of the ritual diagrams mentioned in earlier sources, composing elaborate rituals for these diagrams. Since the Ring of Disciples was erected for every mendicant initiation and promotion, it likely became the symbol of initiations in the premodern period. But the Ring of Disciples diagram that is filled with the expanded *ṛddhi-maṅgala* does not immediately bring to mind the Jina's Preaching Assembly and the disciples of the *jina*. The many *bhaṭṭārakas* who composed ritual manuals on the worship of the Ring of Disciples would have wanted to make the diagram's components relate more explicitly to the disciples of the *tīrthaṅkaras*, thus linking themselves to the founders of Jainism in the eyes of lay followers.

Therefore, early modern Digambara texts on the Ring of Disciples expand the *ṛddhi-maṅgala*-filled *apraticakrā-yantra* that Nemicandra, Siṃhatilakasūri, and other medieval monks describe into the diagram that was used in the modern initiation in Kekri: the Ring of Disciples with 1,452 dots, each representing a disciple. These manuals connect the earlier version of the diagram to the new one in a multiple ways. They maintain, for example, that initiands should place a metal *ṛddhi-maṅgala*-filled Ring of Disciples *yantra* at the center of the colored diagram and recite the *ṛddhi-maṅgala* at the outset of the ceremony to invite the disciples into the diagram. The most visible part of the new version of the diagram, however, remains the diagram of three colored rings filled with 1,452 dots that surrounds this *yantra*.[108] Therefore, by placing a metal *yantra* of the *ṛddhi-maṅgala*-filled Ring of Disciples at the center of an expanded colored diagram of 1,452 dots, Śubhacandra and other *bhaṭṭārakas* created an initiation diagram that drew upon earlier ideas in Jain texts—the idea that the disciples of the *tīrthaṅkaras* had superhuman powers—and unambiguously connected initiands to the original mendicants of Jainism.

MODERN MONKS AND A MYSTERIOUS MANUSCRIPT

Despite many modern Jains' lack of knowledge about the ritual objects and practices of members of the other sect, my instinct in 2008 to connect the Digambara Ring of Disciples diagram and the Śvetāmbara Cloth Diagram of the Mantra of the Mendicant Leader was correct. Śvetāmbara and Digambara texts on mendicant conduct and image consecration that date between the twelfth and eighteenth centuries confirm that both Digambaras and Śvetāmbaras, from at least the thirteenth century, used the *apraticakrā*-mantra and the *ṛddhi-maṅgala* to create mendicant initiation and promotion diagrams modeled on Ṛṣabha's Preaching Assembly. Instead of creating two separate ascetic and tantric paths to liberation, medieval Jains saw that tantric components could easily be integrated into their mendicant initiations, promotions, and daily rites. Indeed, the tantric hierarchy of initiates—*samayin*, *putraka*, *sādhaka*, and *ācārya*—in many ways parallels early Jain monastic levels of initiation. Medieval Jains saw the worship of the Jina's Preaching Assembly as a natural development of the rites of existing mendicant initiations, making it so that becoming a celibate, possessionless mendicant dedicated to a life of study and fasting required an initiation into a *maṇḍala*.

But while the similarities between the medieval initiation diagrams of Digambaras and Śvetāmbaras can be firmly established, the similarities between sects' mantras of promotion cannot. Śvetāmbaras composed many texts on the contents of their mantras of initiation and promotion—the *vardhamānavidyā* and the *sūrimantra*—but the contents of the equivalent premodern Digambara mantras remain unknown. Even though mentions of the Digambara *vardhamānavidyā* and *sūrimantra* are found in texts as early as Vasunandin's twelfth-century image-consecration manual the *Pratiṣṭhāpāṭha*, premodern Digambara texts do not provide the components of these mantras.

The contents of at least one of these mantras, the *sūrimantra*, appear to have been lost in the twentieth century, when the post of *bhaṭṭāraka*—and the mantra of his post—became extinct in north and central India. The gradual extinction of the north Indian *bhaṭṭāraka* began on November 25, 1913, on the hilltop of Kunthalgiri, in Maharashtra, when a forty-seven-year-old lay Jain named Śivgouḍā Pāṭil from Ankali, Maharashtra, stood in front of a temple icon of a *jina*, removed his clothes, pulled out his own hair, and, according to his followers, reinstated the order of naked Jain monks after a near-complete absence of the order for hundreds of years. This man, who became known as Muni Ādisāgara Aṅkalīkara after he renounced, chose to stand before an image of a *jina*—he chose the founder of Jainism as his initiatory guru—because he did not recognize the clothed *bhaṭṭāraka*s as proper initiatory monks. In rejecting these *bhaṭṭāraka*s and embracing nudity, Muni Ādisāgara made a radical departure from the Digambara Jainism of his day and an argument for a return to the practices of the first Jain monks. And this departure was extremely successful. In 1919, he became a mendicant leader, an *ācārya*, when he initiated his first disciple. By the time of his death in 1944, he had initiated thirty-two naked monks, many of whom would go on to establish mendicant lineages that persist to this day.[109]

Today, no *bhaṭṭāraka*s remain in north India; only fourteen remain in south India;[110] and successors of Ācārya Ādisāgara and his disciples number in the hundreds, including Ācārya Vairāgyanandī, the Digambara *ācārya* whom we met in the previous chapter who oversaw the initiation in Kekri.

When Ādisāgara cut ties to the *bhaṭṭāraka*s and initiated himself in front of a temple image, he lost access to some of the practices of Digambara mendicancy, including the Digambara *sūrimantra*. While evidence suggests that medieval Digambara *ācārya*s were imparted the *sūrimantra* upon their promotions, once the post of *bhaṭṭāraka* emerged as the highest rank of mendicancy, they became the proprietors of the *sūrimantra*, and with their demise went premodern Digambara *sūrimantra* traditions. Some earlier Digambara practices, such as the honoring of the Ring of Disciples, could be readopted in the twentieth century by following instructions in manuscripts. Indeed, Ādisāgara's immediate disciple, Muni Sanmatisāgara, copied the seventeenth- to eighteenth-century Bediya manuscript on the initiation and promotion of Digambara monks that we examined in this chapter.[111] *Sūrimantra* traditions, however, were held in strict secrecy, passed down only from *bhaṭṭāraka* to *bhaṭṭāraka*. For this reason, a variety of Digambara *sūrimantra*s circulate today for use in image-consecration ceremonies, but many of them are simply popular Jain recitations that were likely made up in the twentieth century to replace the *bhaṭṭāraka*s' lost mantras.[112]

To date, scholars have found only one premodern description of the contents of the Digambara *sūrimantra*, and it is in a Śvetāmbara text: Jinaprabhasūri's *Sūrimantrabṛhatkalpavivaraṇa*. At the outset of his text, when listing variants of the first section of the *sūrimantra*, Jinaprabhasūri attributes a litany of eight lines to the Digambara tradition (*digambarāmnaya*):

(1) [*oṃ namo*] *jiṇ*[*āṇaṃ*]
Praise to the *jina*s.

(2) [*oṃ namo*] *ohi*[*jiṇāṇaṃ*]
Praise to the *jina*s with clairvoyant knowledge.

(3) [*oṃ namo*] *para*[*mohijiṇāṇaṃ*]
Praise to the *jina*s with supreme clairvoyant knowledge.

(4) [*oṃ namo*] *aṇaṃtohi*[*jiṇāṇaṃ*]
Praise to the *jina*s with infinite clairvoyant knowledge.

(5) [*oṃ namo*] *sāmanna*[*kevalīṇaṃ*]
Praise to ordinary omniscient beings.

(6) [*oṃ namo*] *ugga*[*tavacaraṇacārīṇaṃ*]
Praise to those who can endure difficult fasts (*ugratapas*).

(7) [*oṃ namo*] *caudasa*[*puvvīṇaṃ*]
Praise to those who know the fourteen *pūrvas*.

(8) [*oṃ namo*] *egārasaṃga*[*dhārīṇaṃ*]
Praise to those who know the eleven *aṅgas*. (*SMKS*, 80–81)[113]

There may, however, be other examples of premodern Digambara *sūrimantras* in manuscript collections. In 2013, I stumbled across a *sūrimantra* recorded in a manuscript housed in the Śrī Digambar Jain Candraprabhujī Mandir, Aṅkroṃ kā Rāstā, Kiśanpol Bāzār, Jaipur. The manuscript itself is only a single folio, on paper, that clearly belonged to a larger document at some point. One side of the folio, numbered the sixth page of a text, contains a discussion of *savaiyā*, a type of meter of premodern Hindi poetry. The other side presents a Sanskrit discussion of what it calls the *sūrimantra*, outlined as *irimeru girimeru pirimeru sirimeru hirimeru āirimeru. Meru*, the manuscript declares, means "arhatship," or embodying enlightenment. *Iri*, it continues, provides the pleasures of this world (*saṃsāra*); it is the wish-fulfilling tree (*kalpadruma*), guaranteeing that one will not be blind or deaf and bringing about the success of worldly and otherworldly desires. *Giri* means kingship (*rājya*) and the ability to make others prosper, *piri* stands for renunciation (*dīkṣā*), *siri* means enlightenment (*kaivalya*) and omniscience (*sarvajñatā*), *hiri* means one commands great respect (*mahāpūjā*) and is never obstructed throughout the three worlds, and *āiri* stands for the mendicant community (*saṅgha*) and liberation (*mokṣa*). According to this manuscript, then, the six syllable clusters of this mantra represent the path to liberation: the first two syllable clusters (*iri* and *giri*) stand for pleasures in this world, *piri* represents abandoning these pleasures and renouncing, and the final two syllables stand for the fruit of renunciation, honor in the three worlds, and eventual liberation.[114]

Remarkably, this Digambara manuscript is word for word the same as the description of the fifth section of the *sūrimantra* in Jinaprabhasūri's *Sūrimantrabṛhatkalpavivaraṇa* (*SMKS*, 98). How this single folio of a text on the *sūrimantra*, written on the back of an entirely different text, found its way to this Digambara temple in Jaipur remains a mystery. It cannot confirm that Digambaras used the same *sūrimantra* as Śvetāmbaras, and the study of more manuscripts is needed to confirm that medieval Digambaras and Śvetāmbaras tantricized their levels of mendicant initiation using similar, if not identical, mantras. However, this manuscript does confirm at least some textual exchange or concordance between Śvetāmbaras and Digambaras regarding the *sūrimantra*. And in the description of the meaning of the final section of the *sūrimantra*, Jinaprabhasūri and this manuscript confirm that in these Jain traditions, *mantraśāstra* is an important part of the path to liberation. The *sūrimantra*, Jinaprabhasūri declares, destroys all karma and is liberation itself.[115]

3
THE TANTRICIZATION OF DAILY WORSHIP

4

TANTRIC MEDITATION AS A MEANS OF LIBERATION

THE "FESTIVAL OF EIGHT DAYS," AṢṬĀHNIKAPARVA, is one of the most popular festivals for Digambaras. It occurs three times a year, from the eighth day to the full-moon day of the months of Āṣādha (June–July), Kārttika (October–November), and Phālguṇa (February–March). Jain texts from as early as the fourth century CE confirm that at these three times of the year, all the gods in the universe converge on an island inaccessible to humans—the "Island of Rejoicing," Nandīśvaradvīpa—to worship for eight days straight in the eternal Jain temples located there. By the medieval period, Jains had begun to replicate these eight-day festivals on Earth by constructing cloth, metal, and stone representations of this island in their temples and "becoming" the gods themselves praying at the eternal shrines.[1] Today, not only models of Nandīśvaradvīpa, but upward of a dozen other different types of circular diagrams are constructed out of colored powder for these festivals in Digambara temples throughout India.

In March 2013, in the Cāksū Digambara Jain Temple in the old city of Jaipur, I joined about sixty Terāpanthī Digambara laymen and women in their performance of the "Worship Ceremony of the Wheel of the Liberated Soul," the *siddhacakravidhāna*, for the Festival of Eight Days. The participants in this worship ceremony followed the instructions of a nineteenth-century Hindi manual by Paṇḍit Santlāl, the *Siddhacakra Vidhān*, which is the Sanskrit *Siddhacakrapūjā* composed by Bhaṭṭāraka Śubhacandra in the sixteenth century. When I arrived at the temple around 8 a.m. on the first day of the ceremony, lay ritual specialists (*pratiṣṭhācārya*) had already spent hours constructing out of synthetic colored powder a circular diagram of eight concentric rings that filled the western end of the worship

FIGURE 4.1. While seated laywomen perform the eightfold *pūjā* in the background, a Digambara layman, crowned as an *indra*, a king of the gods, offers a coconut to the Wheel of the Liberated Soul diagram for the second day of worship for the Festival of Eight Days. Cāksū Digambara Jain Temple, Jaipur, Rajasthan, March 2013.

hall (*upāśraya*) (fig. 4.1). At the center of the circular diagram on a small platform, the ritual specialists established a small icon of a *jina* and a *siddhacakrayantra*, a small metal diagram of an eight-petaled lotus that contains the mantras *oṃ* and *arhaṃ* at its center and the letters of the Devanagari alphabet inscribed in its petals.

In each of the colored rings surrounding these central objects, the ritual specialists carefully traced over and over again in white powder the seed-syllable *śrī*. Each of these seed syllables, the ritual specialists explained, represents a different quality of a *siddha*, or a soul that has freed itself of karma and become liberated from the cycle of rebirth. The innermost ring with eight *śrī*s signifies the standard eight qualities of a *siddha*: (1) right vision (*samyaktva*), (2) infinite knowledge, (3) infinite perception, (4) infinite power, (5) lightness, (6) interpenetration, (7) subtlety, and (8) lack of obstruction.[2] In each successive ring, then, the number of qualities of the soul doubled. In the fourth ring from the inside, sixty-four *śrī*s were traced to represent the sixty-four special powers (*ṛddhi*) a soul obtains before liberation: an expanded form of the *ṛddhi-maṅgala.*

On the first day of the worship of the *siddhacakra*, worshipers undertook a number of preliminary rites. The ritual specialists purified the worshipers in attendance as well as the ritual space by sprinkling water sanctified with mantras, and the worshipers purified their bodies and clothes by reciting mantras. The worshipers then underwent a ritual procedure termed *sakalīkaraṇa*—"transforming (*karaṇa*) into the entire (*sakalī*) deity"—in which they effectively became kings of the gods (*indra*) and their wives (*indrāṇī*) by donning crowns and reciting certain mantras. They then tied a protective thread (*rakṣāsūtra*) on their wrists so that they would remain as deities until after the worship ceremony was over and the thread was removed.[3]

Each morning, these worshipers returned to the temple for about four hours to make offerings of coconuts to one of the rings of the diagram. Laypeople, seated on the ground behind rows of tables, would recite Hindi verses and Sanskrit mantras honoring the qualities of the *siddha* and transfer one of the eight substances of the eightfold Terāpanthī *pūjā* from one metal plate to another: (1) water, (2) sandalwood paste used to trace a *svastika* on the plate (*gandha*), (3) uncooked white rice (*akṣata*), (4) uncooked rice colored yellow with sandalwood (*puṣpa*), (5) white coconut pieces (*naivaidya*), (6) coconut pieces colored yellow with sandalwood (*dīpa*), (7) incense (*dhūpa*), and (8) nuts and dried fruits (*phala*).[4] At the end of each recitation, with the collective pronunciation of *svāhā*, one layperson would place a coconut on the diagram.

The devotees to whom I spoke during the eight days of the ceremony brought different interpretations to their worship. One layman who approached me, eager to explain the process to an outsider, simply said the ceremony was for, in English, "world peace." On multiple occasions outside the ceremony when I was casually talking to Digambara laypeople about the *siddhacakra*, they recited this opening verse of a devotional song (*bhajana*) to the diagram:

> Oh, creature, worship the *siddhacakra* for eight days with ease; Queen Mainā did so, and achieved her goal.[5]

Here, because of an easily memorizable song, a medieval story about a queen's ability to cure her husband's leprosy through the worship of the *siddhacakra* became foremost on the minds of worshipers.[6] Other worshipers, however, had become quite knowledgeable about the qualities of the *siddha* and the other Jain ideals they praised through years and years of reciting the mantras to the diagram that describe each quality. One middle-aged woman called me to sit next to her during the *pūjā* so that she could explain to me each quality. She and other worshipers would consistently remind me that this ritual diagram represents a *siddha*: by reflecting on its attributes, they claimed, they purified their souls of karma, inching closer to liberation.

This ritual, then, contains the idea that because the gods worship Jain shrines for eight days at certain periods in the year, these ceremonies should be replicated in earthly temples. This ritual can also be understood in terms of Jain devotion as well as narrative—the idea that a queen cured leprosy through her worship of the diagram. Asceticism also plays a role here; one woman told me that as long as the thread was tied to her wrist for the eight-day ceremony, she would keep celibate and eat only once a day. And on top of all these interpretations, the structure of this ceremony can be called tantric. This worship of the Wheel of the Liberated Soul has the "general ritual structure" of the daily worship practices of initiates of the Śaiva Siddhānta and Vaiṣṇava Pāñcarātra that comprises purifications with water (*snāna*) and mantras (*bhūtaśuddhi*), the deification of the worshiper (*sakalīkaraṇa*) via visualizations and the placement of mantras on his body (*nyāsa*), and the physical worship of a *yantra* or icon that becomes a receptacle of objects of worship of the tradition.[7]

Existing literature on Jainism does not accept this type of worship of ritual diagrams as an important component of the Jain path to liberation. Padmanabh Jaini has argued that because Jains never understood *yantra*s as a component of Jain soteriology, have played a minimal role in the tradition. He claims that even though "in the medieval period the Jainas did develop a large number of mystical diagrams (*yantra*s), as well as the rituals (*vidhāna*) associated with them," because they "lack[ed] the basic ingredient of the tantric cult—fusion of the mundane and the supermundane—such practices seem to have had little effect upon the development of Jainism."[8]

The worship of the Wheel of the Liberated Soul, however, suggests otherwise. A ritual that elsewhere would be labeled as tantric has become one of the most well-known lay Jain temple practices, and it is performed in part to advance on the path to liberation. A Sanskrit verse describing the *siddhacakra* even claims that "whoever meditates on this divinity will enjoy liberation" (*PrT*, 326).[9] Language like this in a variety of texts shows that Jains from the medieval period to the present day have maintained that the ritual use of *yantras* is as effective in destroying karma and advancing toward liberation as ascetic practices like fasting that are more commonly associated with the path to liberation. Indeed, Jains have claimed that these worship practices *are* a type of asceticism. From at least the tenth century onward, Jain monks have categorized the physical worship of diagrams as a type of meditation (*dhyāna*), which constitutes one of the six internal forms of *tapas* in the *Tattvārthasūtra*. In part because medieval monks accepted *yantras* as a soteriological tool in this way, Jain *yantras*, especially among Digambaras, have become one of the most popular components of modern Jain worship practices.

This chapter looks at the processes by which medieval Jain monks made these claims about the soteriological uses of *yantras*. It looks at Jain texts on lay ritual conduct dated from the tenth to twelfth centuries, focusing on texts that mention ritual diagrams that include the *ṛddhi-maṅgala*. In these texts, the *ṛddhi-maṅgala* expanded to forty-eight lines is called the Ring of Disciples, and the earliest known datable descriptions of ritual diagrams that include it are found in the sections on meditation in manuals on proper lay conduct (*śrāvakācāra*).

Scholars have done little research on these Jain discussions of meditation on ritual diagrams. The most influential study of Jains' texts on lay conduct, Robert Williams's *Jaina Yoga*, identifies meditation on *yantras* and *maṇḍalas* as essentially non-Jain.[10] He explains that "mantras intruded more and more into the continually enriched ritual, yogic techniques" of the once ascetic, anti-ritualistic Jainism because of "the great inroads of Hinduism."[11] Because these elements are not uniquely Jain, Williams seems to reason, they belong more to a study of Hinduism than to Jainism, so he gives them little attention. However, most of the fifty-six texts on lay conduct in Williams's study, from those of the Śvetāmbara Haribhadrasūri (eighth century) onward, note the importance of mantras and *yantras* in meditation practices. If even these "highly idealised, not to say at times verging on the theoretical" portraits of Jain religiosity recognize the worship of *yantras*, then their worship must have been of such influence that monks were compelled to integrate them into discussions of the path to liberation.[12] The process of arriving at a consensus on the classification of ritual diagrams into meditation schemes therefore can be taken to reflect the gradual acceptance of tantric practices into Jain orthodoxy.

REINTERPRETING THE COMPONENTS OF JAIN MEDITATION

Meditation on one's soul has been a foundational component of the Jain path to liberation since the earliest scriptures. According to the biography of Mahāvīra in the *Ācārāṅgasūtra* II (first few centuries BCE), in the twelve years he spent as a wandering ascetic, "neglecting his body, the Venerable Ascetic Mahāvīra meditated on his Self (*ātman*)."[13] Ultimately, Mahāvīra achieved omniscience through pure meditation (*śukladhyāna*):

> Not far from a Sāl tree, in a squatting position with joined heels exposing himself to the heat of the sun, with the knees high and the head low, in deep meditation, in the midst of abstract meditation [*śukladhyāna*], he reached *nīrvāṇa*, the complete and full, the unobstructed, unimpeded, infinite and supreme, best knowledge and intuition, called *kevala*.[14]

Texts from the first half of the first millennium such as the *Tattvārthasūtra* outline what this "abstract meditation," or pure meditation, entails.[15] The ninth and penultimate chapter of the *Tattvārthasūtra* is devoted to the topic of shedding of karma (*nirjarā*), and it focuses on the twelve external and internal acts that constitute *tapas*, paying particular attention to *dhyāna*. *Tattvārthasūtra* 9.26 defines *dhyāna* as "the concentration of thought on a single object."[16] As in other early Digambara and Śvetāmbara texts, *dhyāna* is then divided into four different types: mournful (*ārta*), cruel (*raudra*), virtuous (*dharma/dharmya*), and pure (*śukla*) (*TS* 9.27; *Sarvārthasiddhi* 9.28[17]). The first two inauspicious types are said to cause the influx of karma, while the latter two auspicious types cause the destruction, or shedding, of karma. The latter two forms of *dhyāna*, the *Tattvārthasūtra* insists, "are the causes of liberation" (*TS* 9.29–30).[18]

The *Tattvārthasūtra* gives four examples of each type of meditation, describing, for example, wanting physical pleasures as a type of mournful meditation, and "dwelling on violence" as cruel meditation (*TS* 9.34, SS 9.33; *TS* 9.36, SS 9.35). Pure meditation in the *Tattvārthasūtra* is limited to only the most spiritually advanced mendicants and culminates in the fourth category, complete cessation of all activity (*TS* 9.43; SS 9.40). The *Tattvārthasūtra* understands this type of meditation as impossible to undertake in this degraded time period, insisting that only those people who know the fourteen *pūrva*s can perform pure meditation (*TS* 9.40; SS 9.37).[19] According to this understanding, since the time of Bhadrabāhu I (ca. third century BCE), when the *pūrva*s are traditionally said to have been forgotten, virtuous meditation is the only available form of meditation that will aid in one's pursuit of liberation. The *Tattvārthasūtra*'s fourfold division of virtuous meditation is:

(a) discerning the command of the *jina* (*ājñāvicaya*);
(b) discerning the nature of what is calamitous (*apāyavicaya*)
(c) discerning the consequences of karma (*vipākavicaya*);
(d) discerning the structure of the universe (*saṃsthānavicaya*).[20]

These four categories of virtuous meditation are consistently found in Śvetāmbara and Digambara texts on meditation from the first half of the first millennium onward.

Some early texts further divide *dhyāna* into meditation with and without aids, or supports (*ālambana*). Three Śvetāmbara canonical texts dated between the third and fifth centuries CE, the *Sthānāṅgasūtra*, the *Bhagavatīsūtra*, and the *Aupapātikasūtra*, list recitation (*vācana*), questioning (*pṛcchanā*), repetition (*pravartana*), and reflection (*anuprekṣā*) as the four supports of virtuous meditation.[21]A Digambara text on mendicant conduct dated to the fifth to sixth centuries CE, the *Bhagavatī Ārādhanā*, also list these four activities as the supports of virtuous meditation (v. 1705), as does an important Śvetāmbara text on meditation dated to the seventh century, Jinabhadrasūri's *Dhyānaśataka* (v. 42).[22]

From the eighth century onward, however, Jain monks began to modify the definition of the support of meditation to include temple image worship. In the eighth-century texts of the Śvetāmbara monk Haribhadrasūri, the support of meditation is the form of a *jina*. Haribhadrasūri confirms in his *Ṣoḍaśaprakaraṇa*: "There is also another kind of twofold yoga that should be known: one with support and one without support. The former consists of meditation on the form of the *jina* while the latter is related to the intrinsic nature [of the *jina*]" (14.1). Similarly, in his *Yogaviṃśikā*, Haribhadrasūri defines meditation with support as focusing on something that has a physical form (*rūpa*), and meditation without support (*anālambana*) as focusing on immaterial objects, specifically a liberated soul (v. 19). This reinterpretation of the support of meditation likely developed because of the increasing importance given to the physical worship of temple images in the early medieval period, and it is significant because later Jain authors used these categories to integrate the worship of *yantras* into the path to liberation.

The specific path to liberation these medieval Śvetāmbara and Digambara texts follow is outlined in Jinasena's ninth-century *Ādipurāṇa* (see chapter 2). This text describes the seven "fruition acts" (*kartranvayakriyā*) that occur because of proper conduct and chart the progression of a soul from birth as a man to eventual liberation:

Birth as a man in a good family (*ĀP* 39.82–98)
Being an honorable householder (*ĀP* 39.99–154)
Initiating as a monk (*ĀP* 39.155–200)
Birth as a god (*ĀP* 39.201)
Birth as a universal emperor (*sāmrājya*; *ĀP* 39.202)
Achieving enlightenment, or omniscience (*ĀP* 39.203–4)
Achieving liberation (*ĀP* 39.205–6)

In this Jain vision of the path to liberation, a soul passes through all these births on the way to liberation, and in each birth, a soul must perform the proper conduct to progress on the path. It takes a long time to truly understand the teachings of Jainism and to act on them; the minimum lifespan of a *bhavanavāsin* god, for example, is ten thousand years (*TS* 4.45). Many Jain narratives document examples of this journey of a single soul moving through various births toward eventual renunciation, and they almost always focus on the lives of prominent laypeople. To show the influence of Jainism and the importance of rejecting wealth to achieve spiritual success, Jain narratives from the early period to the present day do not focus on the renunciation of poor people, who can easily give up their few possessions and have little influence on their community, but instead highlight the renunciation of kings, especially universal emperors (*cakravartin*), who are the ultimate symbols of worldly power. In narratives like the *Ādipurāṇa*, to place one's soul in the proper position to renounce, one should develop enough good karma to become a king—ideally, a universal emperor.[23] These narratives have influenced texts on proper lay conduct, which have adopted these steps to liberation, emphasizing how the third act, becoming a monk, comes not after one's birth as a noble householder, but after one's birth as a universal emperor. In these texts from the tenth century onward, Digambaras and Śvetāmbaras insist that a key component of the second step, being an honorable householder, involves meditation on *yantras*.

DEVASENA'S DEVELOPMENT OF TANTRIC MEDITATION IN THE TENTH CENTURY

The tenth century produced a number of important Digambara texts on meditation. With the practice of constructing *maṇḍalas* and *yantras* well established throughout the subcontinent, Digambara monks were inspired to cast increasingly complicated ritual uses of diagrams as aids in liberation. In known texts, medieval Digambaras in central and south India seem to have first integrated the physical worship of *yantras* into discussions of Jain meditation. One of the earliest manuals on lay and mendicant conduct to provide detailed descriptions of ritual diagrams is a Digambara text in Prakrit dated to the early tenth century, Devasena's *Bhāvasaṅgraha* (*Bhāv*). Another text attributed to Devasena, the *Darśanasāra*, declares that the monk composed the text in 933 CE in Dhārā, in modern-day Madhya Pradesh, which was at that time the young capital of the Paramāra dynasty.[24]

Dhārā and the surrounding Mālava region in the tenth century were major centers of Sanskrit learning and hubs of both Jain and Śaiva ritual and intellectual cultures.[25] An initiate of the Śaiva Saiddhāntika monastery Gorāṭika in Dhārā, for example, is thought to have initiated the Paramāra king Sīyaka II, who ruled during the middle of the tenth century, right when Devasena was composing his texts.[26] Devasena's specific motivations for promoting meditation on ritual diagrams cannot be known, but he certainly lived in a time and place where the use of *maṇḍalas* and *yantras* was widespread.

The *Bhāvasaṅgraha*, like other Digambara texts on lay and mendicant conduct, follows the progression of a soul through the fourteen stages of spiritual development (*guṇasthāna*) that chart the path from a state of ignorance and delusion to the ideal state: inactivity and eventual liberation (see table 4.1 for some key *guṇasthānas* as described in the ca. eighth-century *Sarvārthasiddhi*, Pūjyapāda's commentary on the *Tattvārthasūtra*).[27] Jain texts from the *Tattvārthasūtra* onward use these fourteen stages of spiritual progression to determine who is ready to perform certain types of meditation.[28] The Śvetāmbara version of the *Tattvārthasūtra* claims that only monks in the seventh *guṇasthāna*—advanced mendicants who have abandoned carelessness—can undertake virtuous meditation (*TS* 9.37). The Śvetāmbara Jinabhadrasūri in his ca. seventh-century *Dhyānaśataka* agrees (v. 63).[29]

As theories on meditation developed, however, some Digambaras became less strict in their requirements for performing virtuous meditation.

TABLE 4.1. Some important *guṇasthānas*, or stages of purification

Stage on the path to liberation (*guṇasthāna*)	Characteristics
First	State of delusion, or ignorance of the nature of one's soul
Fourth	Realization of *samyaktva*, or the correct view of reality, in which one understands that the nature of one's soul is infinite knowledge
Fifth	Acceptance of the lay vows: partial elimination of non-restraint (*avirati*)
Sixth	Acceptance of the mendicant vows: complete elimination of nonrestraint, though carelessness (*pramāda*) persists
Seventh	Adherence to the mendicant vows without carelessness
Twelfth	Destruction of the harming karmas (*ghātin*) that cause confusion about proper action (*cāritramohanīya*) and the subsequent complete elimination of the passions of pride, anger, deceit, and greed that attract new karmas to the soul
Thirteenth	Destruction of all four types of harming karmas that obstruct the innate qualities of the soul and the realization of omniscience; one becomes an *arhat*, an omniscient being with a body (*sayogakevalin*)
Fourteenth	State of the soul moments before liberation in which there is both omniscience and inactivity

The Digambara commentaries on the *Tattvārthasūtra* 9.36 by Pūjyapāda and Akalaṅka (ca. eighth century) maintain that even laypeople who have right perception (*samyaktva*)—people who have advanced to the fourth *guṇasthāna*—can perform virtuous meditation.[30] Not all later Digambara authors agreed that laypeople can perform virtuous meditation,[31] but the monks who did make this doctrinal shift appear to have done so to subsume popular lay practices—specifically temple worship (*pūjā*)—under the only available type of meditation that sheds karma, virtuous meditation.

In the *Bhāvasaṅgraha*, Devasena tries to respect both the earlier thinkers who argue that only mendicants can perform virtuous meditation and the later thinkers who name image worship as a type of virtuous meditation. He first claims that in the fifth stage of purification, when one has taken the vows of a layperson,[32] one can undertake only three types of meditation: mournful, cruel, and a third type of meditation not typically found in Jain texts, "auspicious" (*bhadra*) (*Bhāv*, v. 357).[33] Auspicious meditation entails temporarily abandoning worldly pleasures (*bhoga*) and thinking about *dharma*, Devasena explains (*Bhāv*, v. 365). Later in his discussion of meditation, however, he contradicts himself and encourages householders to regularly undertake virtuous meditation (*Bhāv*, v. 388). This contradiction arises because he wants to respect earlier theorists who claim that virtuous meditation is restricted to renunciants, but he also wishes to include the worship of temple icons and ritual diagrams in the category of meditation that can shed karma.

To insert ritual diagrams and temple icons into the path to liberation, Devasena, like Haribhadrasūri, reinterprets early Jain understandings of meditation "with support." Devasena defines the "support" of virtuous meditation as the form (*svarūpa*) of the Five Supreme Beings (*Bhāv*, v. 374). According to Devasena, only practitioners who have advanced to the seventh stage of spiritual development—Digambara monks who have abandoned carelessness—can undertake meditation without support (*Bhāv*, 381), but householders should regularly undertake meditation with support, concentrating on the form of the Five Supreme Beings. Not only can lay practitioners focus on the forms of the Five Supreme Beings, he claims, but they can also focus on the mantras and syllables of the alphabet (*akṣara*) that represent them (*Bhāv*, v. 388). Here, Devasena is able to understand Jain *yantras* as objects of meditation that destroy karma because he sees them as icons, or sites of divine presence, of the Five Supreme Beings. With this understanding established, he can then focus his discussion of virtuous meditation on the physical worship of several different *yantras*—both physical and imagined.

Worshiping the *Siddhacakra*

The first *yantra* Devasena outlines is the diagram that was worshiped in the Festival of Eight Days described at the outset of this chapter: the Wheel of the Liberated Soul, the *siddhacakra*. The steps of worshiping of this *yantra* are very similar to those found in descriptions of daily *pūjā* (*nityapūja*) in non-Jain tantric sources.[34] Devasena's account begins with a description of several preliminary rites—the purification of the worshiper's body, the transformation of the worshiper's body into a deity via the placement of mantras on it (*nyāsa*), and the purification and protection of the ritual space. The first purification rite is an elaborate visualization of a fire *maṇḍala* that burns away the impure karmic body of the worshiper. The worshiper, after taking a ritual bath, dressing in pure clothes, and going to the place of *pūjā*, should sit with crossed legs like a temple icon (*pratimā*) and recite the "Path of One's Movement" (*īryāpatha*), the Prakrit formula of confession (*pratikramaṇa*) for the unwitting killing of living beings while walking.[35] Then, having his *pūjā* offerings near him, he should take a mantra bath and perform the *ācamana* ceremony in which he sips from his hands water that has been consecrated by mantras (*Bhāv*, vv. 426–27). Sitting down, he should imagine his body blazing with one hundred flames inside a fire *maṇḍala*, which is typically understood as having a triangular shape (*Bhāv*, v. 428).[36] Thinking, "My body with my bad karma is burning," he should display a hand gesture for pacification (*śāntimudrā*) called the *pañcaparameṣṭimudrā* for the names of the Five Supreme Beings (*Bhāv*, v. 429).[37]

The worshiper should then place the five "eternal" syllables (*a*, *si*, *ā*, *u*, *sā*—the first syllables of the names of the Five Supreme Beings) on five parts of his body. With this mantra, he washes away the ash that has been produced from the body and the bad karma that has been burned in the previous visualization (*Bhāv*, vv. 430–31). The text declares that by performing this exercise, one can quickly destroy all the bad karma that one accrues daily (*Bhāv*, v. 432). Thus purified, the practitioner realizes that the pure soul does not accrue merit (*puṇya*) or demerit (*pāpa*). He imagines that his own body is an ocean of merit, as bright as ten million moons (*Bhāv*, vv. 432–34). Readers familiar with Vaiṣṇava, Śaiva, and Buddhist tantric worship practices will recognize this imagining of one's body as being burned and replaced with a pure body ready for worship as a *bhūtaśuddhi* rite, in which practitioners visualize the elements that constitute their gross bodies (*bhūta*)—earth, water, fire, air, and space—and complete the visualization with the burning of these elements to remove their bodies' impurities.[38]

The next section of the text describes the preliminary rite that typically follows the purification of the elements in texts of other tantric traditions: the "transformation," or *sakalīkaraṇa* rite. Practiced by Jains, Hindus, and Buddhists alike, *sakalīkaraṇa* rites are best known from their descriptions in tantric Śaiva texts, in which practitioners "become Śiva to worship Śiva," transforming into Śiva through the imposition of certain mantras on their bodies (*nyāsa*).[39] In Jain worship ceremonies, however, practitioners are most often transformed into a king of gods, an *indra*, the prototypical worshiper of a *jina*.[40] Early Jains looked to counteract the importance given to chief of the deities, Indra, in Vedic texts by claiming that a *jina*, not Indra, is the ideal object of worship. Along with the story of all the *indra*s in the universe worshiping in Jain temples on Nandīśvaradvīpa noted at the outset of this chapter, Jain texts are filled with other stories of the *indra*s' reverence for the *jinas*. When each *jina* is born, for example, the *indras* are said to take the newborn to Mount Meru and perform an *abhiṣeka*.[41]

The *Bhāvasaṅgraha* explains that the worshiper, to prevent obstacles, should perform *nyāsa* by using his left hand to touch his feet, naval, heart, mouth, and head, placing each of the Five Supreme Beings on his body (*Bhāv*, v. 434–35). After performing *nyāsa* in this way and having thought, "I am Indra," he should put on a bracelet, a crown, a ring, and a sacred thread (*Bhāv*, v. 436). A practitioner imagining himself as an *indra* in this way is emphasizing that even the gods worship the ideals represented in the Wheel of the Liberated Soul.

The subsequent verses describe the demarcation and purification of the ritual space, the ablution of a *jina* icon, and the construction of the ritual diagram. After the worshiper is purified and transformed into an *indra*, an icon of a *jina* should be established in the ritual space, four pots filled with auspicious substances should be placed in the four corners of the place of worship, offerings to the guardians of the eight directions (*dikpāla*) should be made, and a ritual ablution of a *jina* icon should be performed with water, ghee, milk, and yogurt sanctified with mantras (*Bhāv*, vv. 437–41). The icon should then be smeared with scented sandalwood paste and camphor from Kashmir (*Bhāv*, vv. 437–42), and the Wheel of the Liberated Soul should be traced with scented substances on a cloth that is established between the four pots (*Bhāv*, v. 443). According to the instructions of one's guru, the worshiper should trace a sixteen-petaled lotus and place at its center the mantra for an omniscient being, *arhaṃ*, surrounded by the seed syllable *oṃ* and situated underneath the seed syllable *hrīṃ* (*Bhāv*, v. 444). The syllables of the Devangari alphabet and the Prakrit phrase "praise to the enlightened ones," *ṇamo arihaṃtāṇaṃ*, should be inscribed on its petals. The seed syllable *hrīṃ* should circle three times around this lotus. All these components should be situated inside a four-sided enclosure, an earth *maṇḍala*, affixed on a goad (*Bhāv*, vv. 444–45).[42] According to Devasena, a person who regularly worships this diagram with scented substances, lamps, incense, and flowers and recites its mantras destroys all previously acquired bad karma (*Bhāv*, v. 447).

Devasena also outlines a larger version of this diagram called the Wheel of the Liberated Soul, the *bṛhatsiddhacakra*, which takes a form common to *maṇḍalas* of all Indic traditions,[43] a lotus in which the focus of worship resides in the lotus's pericarp and deities and ideals of lesser importance are positioned on the surrounding rings of petals in multiples of eight. At the center of the lotus sits the focus of the diagram, the *arhat*, the omniscient being, and the mantras that Devasena claims represent the Five Supreme Beings: *hrīṃ* and *oṃ* (*Bhāv*, v. 450).[44] The components of the center and the six surrounding rings, from innermost to outermost, are:

Pericarp: the *arhat* plus the seed syllables *oṃ* and *hrīṃ*, which represent the Five Supreme Beings
Eight goddesses
Sixteen spell goddesses (*vidyādevī*)[45]
Twenty-four *yakṣas* and *yakṣīs*, the tutelary deities of the *jinas*
Thirty-two kings of the gods (*indra*) and their mantras
Forty-eight praises of the Ring of Disciples (*gaṇadharavalaya*)
Border: four doors, seven *vajras* (the hourglass-shaped protective ritual implement)[46] (*Bhāv*, vv. 449–53)

Due to the number of petals, it is likely that the Ring of Disciples mentioned here is the *ṛddhi-maṅgala* with four additional praises we saw last chapter in Nemicandra's *Pratiṣṭhātilaka* (*PrT*, 328–29).

Devasena confirms that worshipers should recite whatever root spell (*mūlavidyā*) is imparted for the worship at hand 108 times (*Bhāv*, vv. 478) and offer to the divinities of the diagram the following eight substances, which confer the following results:

Water—cleans the dust of karma
Scented sandalwood—grants reincarnation in heaven as a god with a metamorphic (*vaikriya*) body
Rice—grants the nine treasures (*navanidhi*) and reincarnation as a universal emperor[47]
Flowers—grant reincarnation as an *indra*, king of gods
Mixture of yogurt, milk, and ghee (*naivedya*)—grants the ultimate worldly pleasures
Lamp—grants a body that shines like the sun
Incense—bestows the happiness found in the three worlds
Fruit—bestows one's desired results (*Bhāv*, vv. 470–77)

The worshiper should offer these substances and then stand in the *kāyotsarga* meditative pose and imagine a *jina* in his preaching assembly, omniscient and showing the eight *prātihārya*, or the miraculous phenomena that appear when a *jina* achieves enlightenment (*aśoka* tree, lion throne, fly whisks, triple umbrella, drums, rain of flowers, halo, and divine speech)

(*Bhāv*, v. 479). The worship is complete when the deities invited into the diagram have been dismissed (*Bhāv*, v. 481).

The *siddhacakra*, then, not only represents the liberated soul but also contains the mantras *oṃ* and *hrīṃ* that represent the Five Supreme Beings and the *tīrthaṅkaras*, respectively. It also can be used to imagine the Jina's Preaching Assembly. Because the physical worship of *yantras* in this way honors the ideals of Jainism, Devasena claims that the worshiper who writes out the Wheel of the Liberated Soul (*siddhacakra*) with sacred scented substances and worships it daily destroys bad karma and attracts good karma, engendering a variety of worldly profits. Propitiation of these diagrams expels evil spirits such as *guhas*, *piśācas*, *ḍākinīs*, and ghosts; it cures illnesses such as a fever; it generates love; and it brings about subjugation of others (*vaśīkaraṇa*), the attraction of a romantic partner (*ākṛṣṭi*), prevention of others' actions (*stambhana*), and the pacification of the bad influence of planets. Worship of the diagrams guarantees that enemies will not attack the worshipers and will instead become like friends. The practitioner will become the beloved of kings (*Bhāv*, vv. 455–60).

But the worship of the *siddhacakra* is certainly not simply about the here and now: these mundane things are a mere trifle when compared to the happiness of liberation the *siddhacakra* can confer (*Bhāv*, v. 461). If done properly, this type of worship of diagrams and icons ensures that the worshiper will begin on the path to liberation found in the *Ādipurāṇa*. The devotee will be reborn in heaven as a god and then eventually reincarnate on Earth as a universal emperor, who will renounce his kingly wealth to initiate as a Digambara monk (*Bhāv*, vv. 483–84). It is only at this stage, in the seventh *guṇasthāna*, that this soul will be able to undertake virtuous meditation without support, which is defined as meditation that is not focused on any syllable, or form, or any object of worship (*Bhāv*, v. 629). Then, in the twelfth *guṇasthāna*, when the monk has removed all the passions of pride, anger, deceit, and greed, he commences the ultimate form of meditation—pure meditation—whereby he achieves omniscience and eventual liberation. In the twelfth *guṇasthāna*, a monk undertakes the first two kinds of pure meditation, wherein he examines the origination, cessation, and continuity of a substance (*dravya*) such as one's soul (*Bhāv*, vv. 656, 663). In the thirteenth *guṇasthāna*, he undertakes the third category of pure meditation, in which all gross bodily activity has ceased (*Bhāv*, v. 667). Finally, in the moments just before death and liberation, in the fourteenth *guṇasthāna*, just as Mahāvīra is said to have done before enlightenment, the mendicant undertakes the fourth type of pure meditation, complete cessation of activity, the only type of meditation for which there is no influx of karma (*āśrava*) (*Bhāv*, vv. 681, 686).

Thus, while Devasena recognizes the worship of *yantra*s as a type of meditation that will not immediately bestow liberation, he maintains that ritual diagrams are a required component of the path to liberation. He explicitly chastises householders who claim that they will not perform meditation with support because they think the merit accrued in these acts will cause their souls to reincarnate. Nine hundred thousand souls are killed from sexual intercourse alone, Devasena reminds these misguided householders. When one thinks about all the violence that occurs in the day-to-day life of a householder, it is clear that a layperson cannot afford to skip ritual acts such as the worship of *yantra*s that destroy bad karma and create good karma (*Bhāv*, vv. 389–93).

RĀMASENA'S DEVELOPMENT OF TANTRIC MEDITATION IN THE TENTH CENTURY

Another impressive medieval work on the subject of Jain meditation, a lengthy text in Sanskrit verse, the *Tattvānuśāsana*, provides another way of integrating the ritual use of *yantra*s into the path to liberation. Compared to the *Bhāvasaṅgraha*, the *Tattvānuśāsana* can be considered more mystical than pragmatic.[48] While the *Bhāvasaṅgraha* is in many ways a practical text, outlining the practices such as temple worship, fasting, and charity (*dāna*) one must undertake to rid oneself of karma and progress toward liberation, the *Tattvānuśāsana* makes little mention of the fourteen levels of spiritual development (*guṇasthāna*) and is more indebted to the mystical strands of Digambara Jainism, most famously promoted in the writings of the renowned philosopher-monk Kundakunda (middle of the first millennium CE?), which posit that one can bypass ritual acts and achieve ultimate liberation through direct knowledge of the nature of one's soul.[49] Little is known about the author of this text, the Digambara monk Rāmasena, but he was influenced by the ninth-century Jinasena and is quoted by the thirteenth-century Āśādhara. Based on this knowledge and the development of ideas and expressions in Digambara texts, Jugalkiśor Mukhtār has placed him in the first half of the tenth century CE.[50]

Rāmasena's explanation for how *yantra*s and mantras should be considered objects of virtuous meditation is slightly more complicated than

Devasena's, though they both agree that *yantras* represent spiritually advanced souls, especially the Five Supreme Beings. He explains that because pure meditation is not possible in this time period, he will focus on virtuous meditation and analyze the nature of the meditator (*dhyātṛ*), meditation (*dhyāna*), the object of meditation (*dhyeya*), the fruits of meditation (*phala*), and where, when, and how to undertake meditation (*TA*, vv. 35–37). When discussing the object of meditation, he notes that among the six types of substances (*dravya*)—the soul (*puruṣa*), material objects (*pudgala*), time (*kāla*), motion (*dharma*), rest (*adharma*), and space (*ākāśa*)—the supreme object of meditation is the soul, including one's own and those of advanced practitioners such as the Five Supreme Beings (*TA*, vv. 117–19). But while the soul is the ultimate object of meditation, contemplating its nature can be difficult. Therefore, the meditator should focus on physical objects he can more easily comprehend that represent advanced souls.[51] To show the different ways meditators can focus on these souls, Rāmasena uses the analytical tool *nikṣepa* we discussed in chapter 1, in which a term is analyzed from the perspective of various categories. The soul can be thought of in different ways. It can be thought of in terms of these categories: (1) name (*nāman*), meaning that which is pronounced, (2) establishment (*sthāpanā*), referring to icons, (3) substances (*dravya*), which have qualities and modifications, and (4) modes (*bhāva*) of those substances, which can be either their qualities (*guṇa*) or the modifications of these qualities (*paryāya*) (*TA*, vv. 99–100).

The Ring of Disciples and other mantras and ritual diagrams are defined as objects of worship that belong to the first category, the "name" category, since they are words that represent advanced souls (*TA*, v. 101). In his discussion of these ritual diagrams, Rāmasena outlines with two verses a *siddhacakra* diagram that includes the Ring of Disciples:

> An eight-petaled lotus resides in the heart [of the meditator], situated in the middle of a four-sided earth *maṇḍala*.[52] On each petal the letters of the eight classes of the alphabet are inscribed. The pericarp has the name of the omniscient ones (*arhats*). It contains the Ring of Disciples (*gaṇabhṛdvalaya*) and is encircled three times by the seed syllable *hrīṃ*. It should be worshiped and meditated upon. (*TA*, vv. 105–6)

In contrast to Devasena, Rāmasena internalizes the worship of the diagrams, not mentioning external physical supports and instead placing the *siddhacakra* in the heart of the meditator.

But like Devasena, Rāmasena requires preliminary purification and integration (*sakalīkaraṇa*) rites. Before beginning meditation, he confirms, one should "successively focus upon the elements of wind, fire and water in order to create an appropriate body and effect purification."[53]

> Having filled and sustained the syllable "a" with wind, having burnt karma with his own body by means of the fire of the syllable "r," and having expelled the ash,
> The mantric syllable "ha," pouring ambrosia on the self, must be meditated upon in the sky after one has constructed a new body, itself nectar and refulgent.[54]

Sakalīkaraṇa rites follow these purifications. As in Devasena's *Bhāvasaṅgraha*, the worshiper should place the *pañcanamaskāra* on five different parts of his body (presumably the feet, naval, heart, mouth, and head mentioned in the *Bhāvasaṅgraha*). The outcome of this integration rite differs, however, from Devasena's understanding. Devasena's *sakalīkaraṇa* transforms the meditator into an *indra*, a king of the gods and the ideal worshiper of a *jina*, and his text describes a typical *pūjā* ceremony. In contrast, Rāmasena's *sakalīkaraṇa* rites and subsequent prescription of "meditation upon the self as the *arhat*" transform the worshiper into an enlightened soul.[55] Rāmasena removes the distinction between meditator and object of meditation, worshiper and object of worship, insisting that meditators "come into contact with the *arhat* within [one's] very self." Verse 190 articulates this vision of nonduality beautifully:

> The *yogin* becomes identical with that inner state into which his soul is transformed. And thus, immersed entirely in meditation on the enlightened one (*arhat*), he becomes himself the meditated enlightened one.[56]

For Rāmasena, purifying one's body through the visualization of the elements, transforming one's body through the placement of mantras, visualizing oneself as the *arhat*, and focusing on a diagram with the Ring of Disciples as situated inside of oneself can allow a worshiper to achieve identification with the enlightened one.

The ritual structure of this meditation is quite similar to descriptions of daily worship in texts of the Śaiva Siddhānta. In Aghoraśiva's twelfth-century *Kriyākramadyotikā*, for example, the practitioner first purifies himself by imagining "a fire arising from his right big toe that burns all the impurities of the elements located in the body." He then creates a pure body:

> Imagining it completely emptied of all that has the form of a fetter, the worshiper should bathe his entire body, inside and out, with streams of nectar flowing from the upside-down lotus at the top of his crown.[57]

With his body thus a pure vessel, the Śaiva worshiper imposes mantras on five parts of his body to recreate his body as "a Śiva-like instrument that will enable one to act as a Śiva within the domain of ritual."[58] While the Jain worshiper places the five lines of the *pañcanamaskāra* on his body—*arhat* on the head, *siddha* on the mouth, *ācārya* on the heart, *upādhyāya* on the navel, and *sādhu* on the feet—[59] in these Śaiva rites, the five *brahmamantra*s representing five aspects of Śiva are placed on five parts of the worshiper's body: Īśāna should be placed "on the top of the head, Tatpuruṣa on the mouth, Aghora on the heart, Vāma on the genitals, and Sadyojāta on the feet." Because "Śiva's body, beginning with the head, is composed of the five [brahma]mantras that are appropriate for the five activities," the placement of mantras allows the body of the worshiper to physically become Śiva, just as a temple icon (*liṅga*) is physically transformed into Śiva through these mantras.[60]

In Rāmasena's account, however, he does not argue that the *pañcanamaskāra* physically transforms a worshiper's body into a deity. Rather, the mantras are used to remind the worshiper that he is ultimately identical to the *arhat*. While his soul substance (*dravya*) has undergone modifications (*paryāya*) due to interactions with karma and thus is not enlightened, it still has the same inherent qualities (*guṇa*) as the *arhat*. Rāmasena reminds the worshiper, "The self's modifications, future and past, which constitute the *arhat*'s nature, always exist substantially in all entities."[61] Therefore, these meditations use mantras to advance a worshiper on a gradual path to liberation that is the same as the one described in the *Ādipurāṇa* and the *Bhāvasaṅgraha*, wherein the soul of the meditator will achieve worldly success, then be reborn in heaven, and then reincarnate in the body of "an emperor or some such person" who will initiate as a Digambara monk, perform pure meditation, and achieve liberation.[62]

Rāmasena agrees with Devasena that meditation on diagrams not only puts ghosts and witches at bay, pacifies the planets, grants knowledge, longevity, beauty, and wealth, and engenders many of the other profits the *Bhāvasaṅgraha* describes such as attraction (*ākārṣaṇa*), subjugation (*vaśīkāra*), immobilization (*stambhana*), delusion (*mohana*), quick movement (*druti*), the removal of poison (*nirviṣīkaraṇa*), and so on.[63] He also insists that it can also confer liberation:

> For the *yogin* occupying his final body, his delusion disappearing because of the excellence of his meditative practice, deliverance comes about at that very moment, while for the one who is not occupying his final body it will come gradually.[64]

Since pure meditation is not possible on Earth at this present moment, this rebirth as a Digambara monk has to occur in another time period and/or place in the universe, after the soul has spent eons (*TA*, v. 227: *sucira*) soaking up the pleasures of heaven. Presumably the *yogins* in their final bodies to whom Rāmasena refers in the verse above also reside in another time and place where pure meditation is possible.

Rāmasena's *Tattvānuśāsana* and Devasena's *Bhāvasaṅgraha* thus present two different ways of integrating the use of mantra-filled diagrams into the Jain path to liberation by arguing that *yantras* are icons of the Five Supreme Beings. However, redefining "meditation with support" and using the hermeneutical tool *nikṣepa* are not the only ways these two authors define the use of these diagrams as a type of Jain meditation. Both authors also use terms—what we can call the *stha* categories of meditation—that are foreign to early Jain texts.

JAIN MEDITATION WITH ŚAIVA TERMS: *PIṆḌASTHA, PADASTHA, RŪPASTHA,* AND *RŪPĀTĪTA*

By the tenth century, Digambaras had begun to split *dhyāna* into four divisions of meditation that are not found in early Jain sources but are popular in medieval Śaiva sources. These divisions translate literally as: "situated in a body" (*piṇḍastha*), "situated in a word" (*padastha*), "situated in a form" (*rūpastha*), and "beyond form" (*rūpātīta*). Several scholars have offered hypotheses as to how these terms entered Jainism. Johannes Bronkhorst has argued that Jains must have appropriated these *stha* terms from Śaiva sources because of the unpopularity of meditation practices among Jains and the subsequent necessity for the few Jains who wished to practice meditation "to start from scratch, so to speak . . . [and] look for a teacher, among the Jains but perhaps more often elsewhere."[65] He posits that "those later authors who had a practical interest in meditation felt free to work rather independently from the canonical description, often borrowing elements from non-Jaina schools of meditation."[66]

Olle Qvarnström has suggested that Jains adopted these *stha* terms in order to please royal patrons. Qvarnström has translated into English the most-discussed Jain text on meditation in English scholarship: the twelfth-century *Yogaśāstra* composed in Sanskrit verse by the influential Śvetāmbara monk Hemacandrasūri (1088–1173). In Qvarnström's account of this text, he suggests that Hemacandrasūri could have borrowed the *stha* terminology from the "Kashmirian Śaiva tradition"—specifically, the monistic Trika system of the Kulamārga, whose most famous theorist, Abhinavagupta, flourished in Kashmir in the eleventh century.[67] In other texts, Hemacandrasūri displays knowledge of Abhinavagupta's teachings;[68] so here too he could have drawn upon Kashmirian Śaiva doctrine to couch his Jain teachings in a terminology and perhaps ideology that would be familiar to his patron, the Śaiva-turned-Jain Cālukya king Kumārapāla.[69]

Both Bronkhorst and Qvarnström note the clear correspondences between Śaivas and Jains through the use of these *stha* terms, but Bronkhorst's claims are at best impossible to substantiate, and Qvarnström's analysis does not take into consideration the earlier Digambara texts we have analyzed in this chapter. Putting Hemacandrasūri's text in conversation with earlier Digambara texts on meditation suggests that Jain monks did not "start from scratch" with Śaiva meditative practices in the medieval period. It also shows that Hemacandrasūri did not take his interpretations of *stha* meditation from Abhinavagupta. Digambara sources on meditation from the tenth to twelfth centuries show the sophisticated ways in which Jain mendicants integrated *mantraśāstra* into earlier Jain ideas about meditation, making Jain tantric practices a key component of the path to liberation. Hemacandrasūri's works suggest great familiarity with a variety of Digambara texts on mantra-based meditation, and the four *stha*s had been commonplace in Digambara literature for around two centuries before the composition of the *Yogaśāstra*. The *stha* terms used in Jain texts on meditation thus seem to have entered Digambara Jainism in the first half of the tenth century not from Kashmir, but from west-central India.

Indeed, Alexis Sanderson has demonstrated that the contents of the key texts of the Western Transmission (*paśimāmnaya*) of the Śaiva Kūlamārga, the *Kubjikāmata* and the *Manthānabhairava*, are "product[s] of the Deccan," in west central and south India, so it is likely that "the whole tradition [of the

Western Transmission] emerged and developed in that region."[70] Because the Trika influenced the *Kubjikāmata*, "there is no need, then, to seek a connection with Kashmir to explain the fact that the Jaina Somadevasūri has referred to the Trika in his *Yaśastilaka*, completed in AD 959 at Gaṅgādhārā, near Vemulawada in the Karimnagar District of Andhra Pradesh."[71] Similarly, there is no need to look at the Gujarati Hemacandrasūri's interactions with the Kashmiri theorist Abhinavagupta in order to understand Jains' development of the *stha* categories of meditation. Instead, tenth-century Digambara texts of central India provide more proof that the Śaiva Kulamārga was well established in that region in the tenth century. In adopting these *stha* terms for different types of meditation, these Digambara authors did not import any ideology from Śaiva traditions, but instead used the literal meanings of the words to show that true virtuous meditation focuses on different aspects of a pure soul and the ascetics who are on the path to becoming that pure soul: the Five Supreme Beings.

Devasena's and Rāmasena's Tenth-Century Texts on Meditation

Devasena's *Bhāvasaṅgraha* and Rāmasena's *Tattvānuśāsana* contain some of the earliest Jain discussions of the *stha* categories of meditation.[72] In the *Bhāvasaṅgraha*, after outlining the worship of the *siddhacakra*, Devasena describes the nature of meditation. Echoing Patañjali's *Yogasūtra*, he defines meditation as the stopping of thought (*cittanirodha*)[73] and claims that there are four types of meditation: *piṇḍastha*, *padastha*, *rūpastha* and *rūpavarjita* (*Bhāv*, v. 619). *Piṇḍa* means body, he explains, and at the center of the body is one's own pure soul. Meditation on that pure soul is *piṇḍasthadhyāna* (*Bhāv*, vv. 620–22).

Rāmasena, in his *Tattvānuśāsana*, agrees with Devasena's definition of *piṇḍastha*. He explains that because the ideal object of meditation, the soul, is located (*stha*) in the body (*piṇḍa*) of the meditator, some people call the object of meditation *piṇḍastha* (*TA*, v. 134). Rāmasena does not, however, make any mention of the other three *stha* categories.

Devasena describes the other *stha* categories of meditation in a few verses. *Rūpasthadhyāna* is meditation on a pure soul that is outside one's body (*Bhāv*, v. 625). *Padasthadhyāna* destroys karma and is the recitation of the syllables associated with the Five Supreme Beings (*Bhāv*, v. 627). *Rūpavarjita* is the type of meditation in which the senses, attachment, and aversion are not engaged. It is meditation without support, or object (*nirālambana*), meaning the nondual realization of one's soul by means of the knowledge of the soul (*Bhāv*, vv. 629–30). In this meditation, which can be performed only in the seventh *guṇasthāna* when one is a monk, the soul directly knows the soul.

Padmasiṃha's Eleventh-Century Text on Meditation

Another short Prakrit poem on meditation, the *Jñānasāra* (*JñS*) (Pkt. *ṇāṇasāra*) by a Digambara monk named Padmasiṃha, provides another description of the *stha*s, but little is known about Padmasiṃha. He confirms at the conclusion of the *Jñānasāra* that he composed this text, which comprises just sixty-three verses, in 1029–30 CE, in a town called Ambaka that is today unidentifiable.[74] Because other locatable tenth- and eleventh-century Digambara texts to discuss the four *stha*s were composed in west-central India, it is tempting to put Padmasiṃha there as well, but for now his text will have to be examined not in terms of the specific motivations of the author, but in terms of earlier and later Digambara discussions of meditation.

After listing the four types of meditation found in early Jain texts—mournful, cruel, virtuous, and pure—*Jñānasāra* adds three more: *piṇḍastha*, *padastha*, and *rūpastha* (*JñS*, vv. 11–12). Padmasiṃha, like Devasena and Rāmasena before him, translates these terms literally, using the terms to focus on different forms of the *arhat*. He explains that to undertake *piṇḍasthadhyāna*, the meditator should imagine the enlightened one as placed on his own body: he should visualize the form of the enlightened one established in his naval glowing with the light of the sun, or the form of the *jina* glowing in his hand, forehead, throat, or heart (*JñS*, vv. 19–20). *Rūpasthadhyāna*, then, entails meditating on the form of the enlightened one itself, separate from one's body. The meditator should visualize a white *arhat* seated at the center of the Jina's Preaching Assembly, complete with the thirty-four characteristics of an enlightened being (*atiśaya*) such as fragrant breath and the accompaniment of pleasant weather, and eight miraculous accessories (*prātihārya*) such as a halo and throne (*JñS*, v. 21).

The third type of meditation, then, *padasthadhyāna*, places the *arhat* and the other supreme beings in different parts of the alphabet. Padmasiṃha summarizes the mantras of *padasthadhyāna* in the verse below:

> Meditate in turn on the white syllables that are one, five, seven, and thirty-five in number. This is the *padastha* meditation taught by those who are engaged in *yoga*. (*JñS*, v. 22)

He then provides some specific examples of the visual representations of these mantras. He describes a *siddhacakra* diagram with the Ring of Disciples in two Prakrit verses:

> Surround the seed syllable *arhaṃ*, situated at the center of an eight-petaled lotus, with the supreme seed syllables [*oṃ*]. Then [place] the syllables of the alphabet inside the petals, and at the edges of the petals, [inscribe] the mantra of seven syllables [*ṇamo arihaṃtāṇaṃ*]. Surround [the lotus] with the seed-syllable *hrīṃ* and the Ring of Disciples. In a half-second, whatever action one desires will be successful (*JñS*, vv. 26–27).[75]

In later Digambara and Śvetāmbara texts on meditation, *padasthadhyāna* became defined in this way as constituting mantras of different lengths that represent the Five Supreme Beings. An important Digambara account found in Vasunandin's Prakrit text on proper lay ritual practice, the *Śrāvakācāra* (ca. 1100), defines *padasthadhyāna* as focusing on mantras of one syllable and so on that represent the Five Supreme Beings (v. 464).[76] Often, the mantras Padmasiṃha mentions of one, five, seven, and thirty-five are understood as:

> One syllable: *oṃ*
> Five syllables: *a si ā u sā* (*a[rhat] si[ddha] ā[cārya] u[pādhyāya] sā[dhu]*)
> Seven syllables: *ṇamo arihaṃtāṇaṃ or ṇamo arahaṃtāṇaṃ*
> Thirty-five syllables: the *pañcanamaskāra*[77]

However, texts provide a variety of interpretations of these mantras of different lengths. For example, an undated manual that should be placed in the early modern period, Bhaṭṭāraka Jinadeva's *Bhavyamārgopadeśa Upāsakādhyayana*, provides the following list of different types of mantras whose uses should be classified as *padasthadhyāna*:

> One syllable: *oṃ*
> Two syllables: *arhaṃ*
> Four syllables: *arihaṃta* or *arahaṃta*
> Five syllables: *a si ā u sā* or *siddhebhyaḥ namaḥ*
> Six syllables: *oṃ namaḥ siddhebhyaḥ namaḥ* or *arahaṃta siddha*
> Seven syllables: *a si ā u sā namaḥ*
> Sixteen syllables: *arhatsiddhācāryādhyāyasarvasādhubhyo namaḥ*[78]

However, while texts may not agree on what constitutes these mantras of various lengths, they do agree that for an object of meditation to cause the destruction of karma, it must represent a liberated soul and the means of becoming one: the Five Supreme Beings.

Amitagati's Eleventh-Century Text on Meditation

The Digambara monk Amitagati's Sanskrit text on lay conduct, the *Śrāvakācāra*, provides another important interpretation of the four *sthas*' relationship to the Five Supreme Beings. Amitagati, a disciple of Mādhavasena, an *ācārya* of the Māthura Saṅgha, composed several important works on Jain philosophy and ritual in the late tenth and early eleventh centuries in Mālava, in west-central India.[79] In these texts, he claims to have been patronized by the Paramāra kings Vākpati Muñja (r. ca. 974–95), Sindhurāja (r. ca. 995–1010), and Bhoja (r. ca. 1011–55).[80] Thanks to the Paramāras' patronage, in his *Śrāvakācāra*, which was likely composed in the first quarter of the eleventh century, Amitagati could build on ideas about meditation formulated by Digambara monks like Devasena who had lived in Mālava in the century before him.

The fifteenth chapter of Amitagati's *Śrāvakācāra* places the topic of meditation in the framework of the fourteenth *guṇasthānas* and provides lay Jains even more access to virtuous meditation. While the earliest texts on meditation deny laypeople access to virtuous meditation and Devasena claims that laypeople in the fifth stage of purification who have taken the lay vows can undertake virtuous meditation, Amitagati expands the number of practitioners who can undertake *dharmadhyāna* further. He maintains that even people in the fourth *guṇasthāna* who have not taken lay vows but have obtained right vision (*samyaktva*) can undertake virtuous meditation. According to Amitagati, practitioners in the fourth, fifth, sixth, and seventh *guṇasthānas* are eligible to perform the practices of virtuous meditation (*Śrā* 15.17).

To explain what, exactly, constitutes virtuous meditation, Amitagati, like Rāmasena, establishes that practitioners should understand the nature of the meditator (*sādhaka*), of meditation (*sādhana*), of the object of meditation (*sādhya*), and of the fruit of meditation (*phala*) (*Śrā* 15.17). Here, his discussion of the object of meditation is the most important for understanding the history of the integration of the *stha* categories into Jain systems of meditation. In Digambara texts before Amitagati, there were two competing categorizations of meditation: the early fourfold scheme of mournful, cruel, virtuous, and pure, and the new *stha* categorizations of situated in the body, form, word, and beyond form. Amitagati ingeniously integrates these two schemes by keeping mournful, cruel, virtuous, and pure as the four types of meditation and identifying the four *stha*s as the different objects (*dhyeya*) of virtuous meditation (*Śrā* 15.30). These supports of meditation are *padastha*, mantras such as the *pañcanamaskāra* and so on; *piṇḍastha*, the miraculous body of the enlightened one; *rūpastha*, the form of a *jina* in a temple icon; and *rūpātīta*, the disembodied soul (*Śrā* 15.49–56).[81]

In Amitagati's quite lengthy discussion of *padasthadhyāna*, he outlines some representations of these mantras, including the Ring of Disciples diagram with the *apraticakrā*-mantra (*Śra* 15.31, 15.36–37).[82] He explains that at the center of the diagram, inside a hexagram, two mantras, *apraticakre phaṭ*, and *vicakrāya svāhā*, should be inscribed. The worshiper should concentrate on the seed syllable *arhaṃ* established at the very center of the diagram. Surrounding this central image, in a ring, the *ṛddhi-maṅgala* expanded to forty-eight lines should be established (*Śrā* 15.46–48).

Therefore, this text confirms that by at least the beginning of the eleventh century, Digambaras had developed the Ring of Disciples diagram with the *apraticakrā*-mantra for use in initiation *and* daily worship practices. Just as the *ṛddhi-maṅgala*'s association with the disciples of the *tīrthaṅkara*s made it an ideal mantra to use to call the disciples into a representation of the Jina's Preaching Assembly constructed for a mendicant's initiation or promotion, so too did the *maṅgala*'s reverence of superhuman powers make it a valuable component of diagrams used in "tantric" meditation. Since the obtainment of special powers was a dominant concern of tantric practices, non-Jain tantric traditions would include extraordinary powers in their *yantras*.[83] As a representation of what Jains can achieve through sustained ascetic practices and as a potent set of karma-destroying praises in and of itself, the *ṛddhi-maṅgala* became an ideal component of diagrammatic depictions of the Jain path to liberation.

Digambara Influence on Hemacandrasūri's Twelfth-Century Śvetāmbara Text on Yoga

By the eleventh century, discussions of the *stha* types of meditation had entered Śvetāmbara Jainism in a way quite distinct from Digambara accounts. An important discussion of these categories is found in the Śvetāmbara *ācārya* Śāntisūri's Prakrit text on temple image worship, the *Caityavandana*-

mahābhāṣya (Pkt. *Ceiyavaṃdaṇamahābhāsa*). Śāntisūri likely lived at the end of the eleventh century, as he is mentioned in a mid-twelfth-century play as the teacher of the teacher of Devasūri, the Śvetāmbara *ācārya* who faced the Digambara monk Kumudacandra in a debate over the legitimacy of the competing sects in 1125 in the Aṇahillapaṭṭana court in Gujarat.[84] Śāntisūri outlines in his text how a worshiper of a Śvetāmbara temple image should undertake *bhāvanā*s, or reflective meditations, on a *jina* in three states: *piṇḍastha*, before enlightenment (*chadmastha*); *padastha*, as an enlightened being; and *rūparahita*, as a liberated being.[85] Śāntisūri provides a different understanding of *pada* than the more commonly found explanation that *pada* means "word." He explains that *padastha* refers to the attainment of the station (*pada*) of the *tīrthaṅkara*.[86]

While more research needs to be done on this interpretation of the *sthas*, it does not seem to have become the most common interpretation in Śvetāmbara sources on meditation, because shortly after the composition of Śāntisūri's text, Hemcandrasūri wrote his massively influential Sanskrit text on the path to liberation, the *Yogaśāstra*, which followed Digambara sources in using the *stha* categories to integrate meditation on *yantra*s into the path to liberation. As noted, Hemacandrasūri composed the *Yogaśāstra* at the request of the Cālukya ruler Kumārapāla, a recent convert to Jainism from Śaivism, according to Jain tradition.

Scholars have long established the *Yogaśāstra*'s indebtedness to a Digambara text, Śubhacandra's *Jñānārṇava* (*JñA*). While virtually nothing is known about Śubhacandra, scholars have placed him in the century preceding Hemacandrasūri because many of the verses in chapters 7 through 10 of the *Yogaśāstra* are identical to ones from chapters 34 through 37 of the *Jñānārṇava*.[87] Śubhacandra aligns with tenth-century Digambara texts on *stha* meditation in some ways, develops a new interpretation of *piṇḍastha*, and seems to have influenced the twelfth-century Hemacandrasūri, so it is not unconceivable that he lived in the eleventh century. Because Śubhacandra's and Hemacandrasūri's texts were so influential that they have, in many ways, defined Śvetāmbara and Digambara meditation schemes to the present day, comparing how these two monks incorporated *yantra*s into Jain meditation schemes will complete our discussion of this formative period in the history of the tantricization of lay Jains' daily worship practices.

Both Śubhacandra's *Jñānārṇava* and Hemacandrasūri's *Yogaśāstra* chart the path to liberation in Sanskrit verses. The *Jñānārṇava* is massive, containing forty-two chapters, while the *Yogaśāstra* is more modest, comprising twelve. In their chapters on meditation, both Śubhacandra and Hemacandrasūri focus the majority of their discussions on virtuous meditation, presumably wanting to concentrate on the only form of meditation practitioners can undertake in the present time period to progress toward liberation.[88]

Like all the previous Digambara authors discussed except Amitagati, Śubhacandra lists the *stha*s as different types of meditation (*JñA*, v. 1877). However, in his description of *piṇḍasthadhyāna*, he proves to be quite innovative. He defines *piṇḍastha* meditation as the preliminary purification rites—the performance of different visualizations (*dhāraṇā*) related to five different substances: earth, fire, wind, water, and an omniscient soul (*ātman*) (*JñA*, vv. 1878–79).[89] Earlier Digambara texts also include purification rites using visualizations of the elements that make up the body, but Śubhacandra seems to have been the first to systematize them under the category of *piṇḍastha*. He also may have been the first to explicitly call these purification visualizations *dhāraṇā*, a technical term in non-Jain texts on tantric ritual that refers to both the practice of fixing the mind and the object of that fixation: the "elements (*bhūta*s) in their role as the cosmic supports that subdivide the cosmos as well as the disciple's body."[90] Buddhist, Śaiva, and Vaiṣṇava tantric manuals have various lists of elements to be used in these rites, with the five-element visualization of the Śaiva Siddhānta focusing on earth, water, fire, air, and space.[91] Here, Śubhacandra makes this five-element visualization "Jain" by defining the fifth *dhāraṇā* not as space, but as a pure soul.[92] In this Jain view of meditation, the soul is the most crucial component of the body that one should purify through meditation.

In Hemacandrasūri's discussion of virtuous meditation, he follows Amitagati in classifying the four *stha*s as the objects of virtuous meditation (*dhyeya*), agreeing that *piṇdastha*, *padastha*, *rūpastha*, and *rūpavarjita*[93] serve as the supports of meditation (*YŚ* 7.8). He follows Śubhacandra, however, in defining *piṇḍasthadhyāna* as the performance of different visualization practices related to the five different substances in the cosmos.[94] As in non-Jain tantric texts' descriptions of *bhūtaśuddhi*, Śubhacandra and Hemacandrasūri describe how the visualization of a *maṇḍala* associated with each of the elements is used to purify the body.[95] Hemacandrasūri's description of meditation on the element of fire, for example, recalls Devasena's description of the visualization of a fire *maṇḍala* to destroy karma:

> The fierce fire, which emanates from the meditation on the *mahāmantra* [*arhaṃ*], exclusively burns the eight petals [of the heart lotus] which have [their] face downward [and] which represents the eight kinds of karma.[96]

Since these rites purify the body, it makes sense that Śubhacandra and Hemacandrasūri would term them to be "situated in the body," *piṇḍastha*. In these two texts, *piṇḍastha* might be best translated as "visualizations to purify the body."

Hemacandrasūri's and Śubhacandra's descriptions of the other three *stha*s are similar to those of earlier Digambara authors. Hemacandrasūri explains that *padastha* means sacred syllables, *rūpastha* means the omniscient *jina* in his preaching assembly, and *rūpavarjita* is the pure consciousness and bliss of a disembodied soul (*YŚ* 8.1; 9.1–7; 10.1). His discussion of *padasthadhyeya* is quite lengthy, as he devotes a significant amount of chapter 8 to the discussion of the various mantras and *yantra*s, often drawing upon Digambara sources. For example, his verses on the eight-petaled *siddhacakra* in which the letters of the alphabet are inscribed are taken almost verbatim from Śubhacandra's *Jñānārṇava*,[97] and his verses that outline a diagram with the Ring of the Disciples align with Amitagati's *Śrāvakācāra*:

> One may [also] inscribe [from right] to left around a six-cornered figure each of the six syllables *a pra ti ca kre phaṭ*. Outside [the six-cornered figure], one should inscribe [from left] to right [each one of the six syllables] *vi ca krā ya svā hā*. Having inscribed [the syllable] *ha* together with an *anusvāra* in the middle of the [six-cornered figure], one should meditate [on it]. [The praises] that begin *namo jiṇāṇaṃ*, each preceded by *oṃ*, should be inscribed in circles outside [the six-cornered figure].[98]

The auto commentary on this diagram lists the praises to be inscribed on this diagram as the first seventeen lines of the *ṛddhi-maṅgala* (up to "praise to those who can travel in the sky," *ṇamo āgāsagāmīṇaṃ*), each prefaced with the seed syllable *oṃ*. These seventeen lines are followed by the syllables *oṃ jhauṃ śrī hrī dhṛti kīrti buddhi lakṣmī svāhā*,[99] invocations of the goddesses at the center of the Ring of Disciples diagram outlined in Digambara sources such as Nemicandra's *Pratiṣṭhātilaka* (see chapter 3). In the previous chapter, we saw that Śvetāmbara texts on the *sūrimantra* from the thirteenth century onward identified this diagram as the Cloth Diagram of the Mantra of the Mendicant Leader. Hemacandra says nothing about the *sūrimantra*, however, and sees it as a lay diagram. This is the earliest known description of the Ring of Disciples diagram with the *apraticakrā*-mantra in a Śvetāmbara text.[100]

After describing all the miraculous results of worshiping these and many other *yantra*s, Hemacandrasūri claims that he spends so much time discussing these practices as a way to motivate even spiritually unsophisticated people to eventually achieve liberation. Echoing earlier Digambara writers, he confirms that the *yogin* who undertakes virtuous meditation will reincarnate as a god, who, after enjoying the pleasures of heaven for eons, will be born into a prominent family in a "divine lineage" and will eventually initiate as a monk who can undertake pure meditation and achieve liberation (*YŚ* 10.18–24). Therefore, he explains,

> the result of these [different kinds of reverential repetitions of the *pañcanamaskāra*] has been told for the sole purpose of making [even foolish people] engage in these [practices], but in reality the result has been declared to be heaven and liberation (*YŚ* 8.39–40).

By using objects of meditation that represent the Five Supreme Beings in rites that are said to guarantee worldly successes, Hemacandrasūri encourages laypeople to undertake practices that ultimately lead to their liberation.

The *Yogaśāstra* marks the culmination of this formative period for Jain meditation, when monks were deciding how to insert *yantra*s into Jain orthodoxy. Beginning with Devasena's and Rāmasena's different experiments about how to place these diagrams into meditation schemes, Digambaras (and following them, Śvetāmbaras) eventually settled on using the term "*padastha*" to name the use of mantras and *yantra*s in virtuous meditation. In Śvetāmbara texts after the *Yogaśāstra*, Hemacandrasūri's interpretation of the *stha* categories became common.[101] Digambara *bhaṭṭāraka*s in the early modern period who expanded many of the diagrams outlined in these earliest texts into elaborate *vidhāna*s also consistently called *yantra*s objects of virtuous meditation, specifically naming them as *padasthadhyeya*,[102] and today Jain mendicants and laypeople continue to emphasize how the ritual use of these diagrams is a form of virtuous meditation that sheds karma.[103]

It is not clear why, exactly, *padastha* became the standard nomenclature for Jain meditation using mantras, since Jains were not influenced by non-Jain thinkers to completely disregard earlier Jain discussions of *dhyāna*, and could have simply identified *yantra*s as supports of meditation. With so little knowledge of the specific histories of the texts examined in this chapter, at this point we can say only that in the tenth and eleventh centuries in west-central India, aspects of the language of meditation in Śaiva and Śākta circles became popular enough that minority traditions saw it as a natural part of their own identifications of types of meditation. It does not seem to be the case that the influence of a single king, or a single Śaiva tradition, transformed Jains' language of meditation in this way. Different Śaiva-Śākta texts had various understandings of these terms. The *Yoginīhṛdayatantra*, for example, links *piṇḍa*, *pada*, *rūpa* and *rūpātīta* to different *cakras*, or centers of power in the subtle body, and to different *pīṭhās*, or pilgrimage places for the Goddess.[104] The *Mālinīvijayottaratantra*, on the other hand, relates these *stha* terms to earlier Upaniṣadic ideas about the four states of consciousness.[105] Jain authors, then, were not alone in using these terms to promote their vision of the path to liberation when they applied them to earlier Jain understandings of meditation on the Five Supreme Beings.

THE YANTRAS OF MODERN LAY JAINISM

The *yantras* described in the tenth- to twelfth-century Prakrit and Sanskrit texts on proper lay conduct outlined in this chapter fill modern Śvetāmbara and Digambara places of worship.[106] In Digambara temples, metal *yantras* sit alongside icons of *jinas*, and temple priests and laypeople will bathe them with water every morning. In Śvetāmbara temples, it is common to find these diagrams as reliefs carved into temple walls or as paintings hung in lecture halls. Indeed, an expanded form of the eight-petaled *siddhacakra* outlined by Hemacandrasūri, which includes a ring of the *ṛddhi-maṅgala* expanded to forty-eight lines, has become one of the most common Śvetāmbara *yantras* found in temples today.[107] Booklets with mantras and *yantras* also fill the shelves of Jain temples and homes. In image-worshiping Śvetāmbara homes, it is common to find Gujarati manuals called "No Fixed Sequence," *anānupūrvī*, which contain images of *yantras* and icons and tables that instruct the worshiper to silently recite different lines of the *pañcanamaskāra* in different sequences. And not only do Śvetāmbaras and Digambaras construct permanent representations of these diagrams out of cloth, paper, metal, and plaster, they also use colored powder and grains to fashion impermanent representations of the diagrams to be honored with foodstuffs for a variety of occasions, from a new marriage to a death to the completion of a fast. For Digambaras, a different ritual diagram is constructed for every major festival.[108]

Would it be correct, then, to call the ritual use of these objects of everyday Jain ritual culture "tantric meditation"? In literature on tantric traditions, *maṇḍala* worship is restricted to initiates only. "Tantric" practices are understood to be "designed for, or appropriate to, an inner circle of advanced or privilege disciples, communicated to, or intelligible by, the initiated exclusively."[109] But medieval Jains opened up these practices to Jain laypeople, and today these rites are anything but secret, with videos of the large Digambara *vidhānas* being uploaded to YouTube and broadcast on television channels like Paras TV, the Hindi-language twenty-four-hour station on Digambara Jainism founded in 2010 in Delhi. Anyone who has visited a temple of an image-worshiping sect of Jainism will confirm that the entrances to the temples are always plastered with posters advertising upcoming *vidhānas* or *mahāpūjanas*, and Jain pilgrimage sites are filled with venders' booths selling Jain merchandise, including DVDs of *vidhānas*.

In addition, many of these Jain rites do not on their surface resemble anything like meditation. John Cort has brought up this point, rightly criticizing academic literature for presenting Jain *yantras* and *maṇḍalas* as meditation tools.[110] Following a similar argument made by Robert Sharf,[111] Cort has noted that "fieldwork . . . does not confirm their use as a calming meditative aid, at least in the Jain context."[112] *Vidhānas* and *mahāpūjanas* involve hours of loud recitations of mantras, musicians blaring devotional songs, and pounds of offerings of coconuts and other foodstuffs. Jain *yantras* are not always objects of silent reflection.

There are benefits, however, in designating some Jain uses of *yantras* as "tantric meditation." Naming certain parts of the hours-long worship ceremonies of *yantras* (*vidhāna*, *mahāpūjana*) as tantric helps chart ritual change.[113] It highlights how elements of these modern Jain ceremonies arose in the medieval period when Jains developed their rites of temple worship in conversation with non-Jain tantric traditions. To this day, Digambara *vidhānas*, while certainly containing non-tantric elements, have the structure of the daily worship practices of tantric traditions (1) purification and protection rites of the ritual space and body (including visualization exercises related to the elements), (2) transformation into a different type of being via the placement (*nyāsa*) of mantras on one's body (*sakalīkaraṇa*), and (3) the use of mantras and *mudrās* to call and dismiss deities into a ritual diagram onto which physical offerings are made.

In addition, Jains for at least a thousand years have classified the ritual use of *yantras* as "meditation." They have seen these practices as a natural development of the meditation schemes found in early Jain texts. At least by the tenth century, mantra-filled diagrams that represent the Five Supreme Beings became the tools of meditation, or "the concentration of thought on a single object" (*TS* 9.26). Devasena, Rāmasena, Padmasiṃha, Amitagati, Śubhacandra, and Hemacandrasūri all categorize Jains' ritual uses of *yan-*

tras, whether physical or imagined, as a type of virtuous meditation that sheds karma and progresses the meditator toward liberation. It is for this reason that the modern Śvetāmbara monk Indrasenasūri, in his introduction to an *anānupūrvī* booklet, can claim that by reciting the lines of the *pañcanamaskāra* in the order described in the booklet, male and female worshipers can destroy as much bad karma as they would in a six-month fast.[114] For these Jain monks, the use of mantras and the physical worship of *yantras* is not simply a worldly pursuit, it is a type of *tapas*.[115] The use of mantras to identify as an *arhat*—an enlightened soul endowed with infinite knowledge, bliss, and power—became a natural progression of the meditation Mahāvīra is said to have adopted in the days leading up to his enlightenment: a focus on one's inherently omniscient soul.

5

THE TANTRIC RITUALS OF MODERN MONKS

IN THE FALL OF SEPTEMBER 2013, I was waiting at a bus stop in Ahmedabad, Gujarat, when a male college student approached me to chat. After hearing that I was in the city to study Jainism, his eyes lit up. He himself was Jain, he told me excitedly, and he was a devotee of a particular image-worshiping Śvetāmbara *ācārya* who was residing for the four-month-long rainy-season retreat in a temple complex just outside Ahmedabad. I must visit this *ācārya*, the student compelled me, not because of the monk's knowledge of scripture or his advanced practices of austerities, but instead because I could be sprinkled with his scented sandalwood powder, called "a throw of scent," or *vāsakṣepa*. The student insisted that if I were to be sprinkled with this *ācārya*'s *vāsakṣepa*, my wealth would multiply exponentially.

Any non-Jain who has spent time with Jains will immediately recognize this scene: lay Jains always want you to meet their favorite monk or nun. Mendicants are the earthly embodiments of the ideals of the liberated founders of the tradition, so they are seen as the perfect introduction to the tradition. For practicing Jain laypeople today, two of the six internal acts of asceticism in the *Tattvārthasūra*—respecting mendicants (*vinaya*) and serving mendicants (*vaiyāvṛttya*)—constitute a large part of their spiritual lives. Laypeople honor monks and nuns by welcoming them to stay in worship halls attached to their temple complexes, bowing before them, massaging their feet, singing devotional songs, offering them food, establishing institutions and temples in their names, and other acts of reverence. "This is the fundamental matter: Jains worship ascetics, and this is the most important single fact of Jain ritual culture," Lawrence Babb explains.[1] And this has been the case since the earliest known stages of Jainism—Jain mendicants have

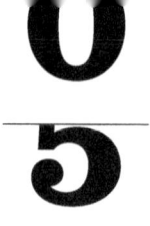

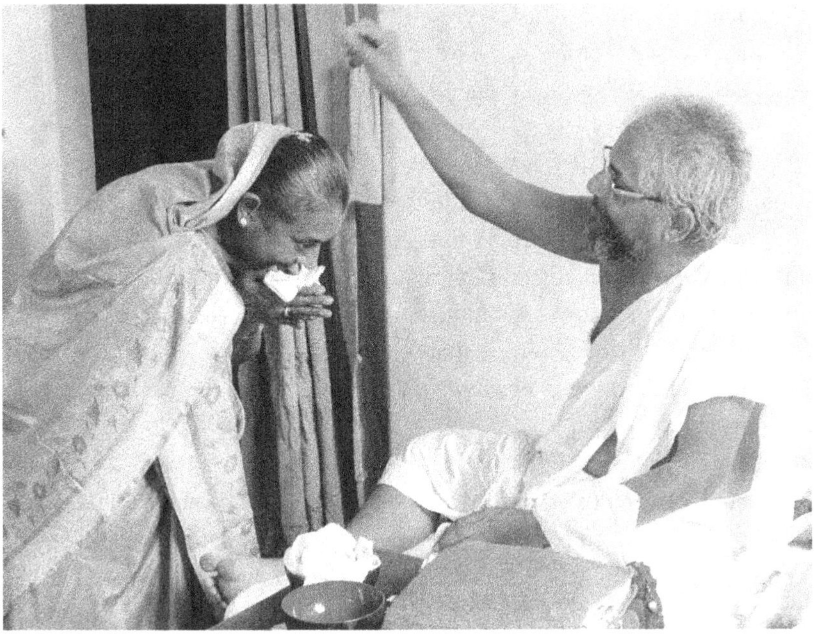

FIGURE 5.1. Ācārya Kalāprabhasāgarasūri of the Añcala Gaccha sprinkles *vāsakṣepa* onto the head of a lay devotee. Mumbai, August 2013.

consistently recognized that in order to have places to stay and food to eat, they needed to create incentives for lay support.[2]

For modern image-worshiping Śvetāmbaras, one way mendicants attract lay worshipers is by claiming that they can impart strength, wealth, and health to their followers by sprinkling them with *vāsakṣepa*. Indeed, my interaction with the college student in Ahmedabad was not the first time I had heard about this sandalwood powder scented with various substances, including camphor and saffron.[3] I have already recalled in the introduction to this book how one monk I met in Mumbai claimed that he cured a layman's seriously injured shoulder by sprinkling it with *vāsakṣepa*. Another time, when I was sitting in a lecture hall talking with an image-worshiping Śvetāmbara monk, a teenaged girl approached the *ācārya* to be sprinkled with his *vāsakṣepa* so that she could have the strength to complete an eight-day fast. From John Cort's experience in Gujarat with image-worshiping Śvetāmbara Jains, he confirms:

> [Some] *bhakt*s [lay devotees] keep a small supply of *vāskep* that has been blessed and given to them by their guru. One couple sprinkled a small

> amount on their own heads every day before leaving the house. Another man received a packet of *vāskep* from his guru in the mail every year. Many Jains believe that if one keeps *vāskep* in one's safe, one's money will increase.[4]

Along with increasing one's wealth, this powder also provides a blessing on one's path to liberation. While what is recited when the powder is sprinkled differs depending on the context, when some contemporary Śvetāmbara image-worshiping monks sprinkle the powder on a devotee's head, they recite, in Prakrit, the same phrase that they recite upon initiating a monk with a sprinkle of this powder: *nitthāragapāragāhoha*, "May you pass beyond the cycle of rebirth."

Because of the many uses of *vāsakṣepa*, Śvetāmbara monks and their followers will advertise their powder as particularly powerful. One *ācārya*, Nandighoṣasūri, even staged a public event where he showed he could scientifically prove the presence of "cosmic energy" in his *vāsakṣepa* using a metal device called the Lecher antenna that is said to measure electromagnetic wavelengths and frequencies just as a tuning fork can measure the wavelengths of sound. When placed above unconsecrated sandalwood powder, the Lecher antenna moved toward the experimenter, while when it was placed above a small amount of consecrated powder, the device moved forcefully in the other direction, showing that the energy levels in consecrated and unconsecrated powder were drastically different.

The question becomes, then: How does this powder become so powerful? While few lay Jains could answer this question, we will see in this chapter that the powder becomes sanctified through a secret ritual of daily worship that has the same structure as the daily worship practices of tantric traditions. This chapter draws upon ethnographic research and the analysis of the modern manuals used in these rites to show that Svetāmbara mendicants of higher ranks infuse *vāsakṣepa* with this "cosmic energy" through the daily worship of painted cloth diagrams that are imparted to them upon their promotions to higher ranks of mendicancy. In one of these diagrams, the Cloth Diagram of the Spell of Mahāvīra (*vardhamānavidyāpaṭa*), Mahāvīra sits at the center, surrounded by four goddesses and some of the praises of the *ṛddhi-maṅgala*; and in the other, the Cloth Diagram of the Mantra of the Mendicant Leader (*sūrimantrapaṭa*), Mahāvīra's disciple Gautama sits at the center of the diagram, surrounded by the four other deities and sections of the *sūrimantra*, the first of which is a variant of the *ṛddhi-maṅgala*.

Every day—often seated alone in a room in front of a shrine of icons—

these ascetics purify themselves and the ritual space with mantras and visualizations, display different *mudrās* and pronounce mantras to invite deities into the cloth diagrams, and sprinkle the scented sandalwood powder on the painted cloth while reciting the invocation they are imparted upon their promotions. The powder receives power by physically coming into contact with the divinities invited into these diagrams and by being associated with the mendicant whose soul has become more powerful and pure through the use of these karma-destroying mantras. Behind one of the more common Śvetāmbara lay-mendicant interactions, then, lies a ritual that many scholars would term "tantric."

I spent the rainy seasons of 2013, 2016, and 2019 in Ahmedabad, Palitana, and Mumbai, visiting dozens of image-worshiping Śvetāmbara monks from the Kharatara Gaccha, Tapā Gaccha, and Añcala Gaccha with the hope of discussing their worship of the Cloth Diagram of the Spell of Mahāvīra or the Cloth Diagram of the Mantra of the Mendicant Leader. I would visit monks whom laypeople recommended, and I would also wander around Jain parts of town, looking for banners hung outside Śvetāmbara temples advertising a monk within. In Ahmedabad, Ānandjī Kalyāṇjī, the trust that has been in charge of many Śvetāmbara temples and pilgrimage sites since 1730, publishes a yearly list of monks' places of stay for the rainy season, and by the end of the rainy season, the lay community publishes *Samagra Jain Cāturmās Sūcī*, a record of all the locations of Jain mendicants of all sects. Most monks I visited following these publications, however, refused to discuss in any detail the *sūrimantra* or *vardhamānavidyā*. They confirmed that these invocations are so powerful that only advanced ascetics should know about their ritual use. In the introduction to one publication of Siṃhatilakasūri's thirteenth-century text on the *sūrimantra*, the *Mantrarājarahasya*, the editor explains:

> Before books were printed, Mantras were meticulously concealed and given to deserving disciples in secrecy. But after the publication of books, all literature, including the one of Mantra-Sastra is made public. But it must be remembered that any practice of the Mantra merely on reading of books is not only not rewarding but is considered positively harmful.[5]

Because of the secrecy surrounding the use of the *vardhamānavidyā* and *sūrimantra*, only a handful of mendicants allowed me to see their diagrams. The Cloth Diagram of the Spell of Mahāvīra examined in the following pages was gifted to the Kharatara Gaccha monk Upādhyāya Vinayasāgara (d. 2013) upon his promotion to the rank of *upādhyāya* in 1951. Vinayasāgara would eventually leave the mendicancy in 1962, start a family, and become one of the most prominent Jain scholars of the twentieth century, publishing widely through the Prakrit Bharati Academy in Jaipur.[6] The Cloth Diagram of the Mantra of the Mendicant Leader examined in this chapter belongs to Ācārya Nandighoṣasūri, whose guru, Sūryodayasūri, promoted him to the rank of *ācārya* of the Tapā Gaccha sublineage (*samudāya*) of Ācārya Nemisūri in 2008. Nandighoṣasūri is also a published scholar who focuses primarily on science and Jainism, having published an examination of the topic of this book: superhuman powers in Jainism.[7]

I tried my best to communicate to the monks I met that I, as a non-initiate, have no desire to perform the practices documented in this chapter or to know the specifics of the rites. Each mendicant lineage, for example, has a slightly different version of the mantra they use in daily rites, and non-initiates have no right to know the details of these differences. At the same time, the Jain mendicant is the heart of Jainism, so overlooking key components of their daily routines would ignore a crucial part of the Jain tradition. A general understanding of the daily rites of image-worshiping Śvetāmbara monks provides important insights into how Jainism has developed and how many Jain monks attract the support of laypeople and define the path to liberation. It also provides insights into the development of tantric promotions and worship practices in India more broadly. In the case of the *mūrtipūjaka* Śvetāmbara rituals that sanctify this scented powder, it is asceticism—the requirement that Jain monks remain peripatetic—that in part has led to the popularity of these rituals.

THE REVITALIZATION OF TANTRIC PRACTICES IN THE TWENTIETH CENTURY

In the mid-nineteenth century, there were only a few dozen itinerant mendicants (*saṃvegī sādhu*) and few, if any, itinerant *ācāryas*.[8] Most Śvetāmbara *gaccha*s were instead led by what were called *śrīpūjya*s, sedentary ascetics who, like the Digambara *bhaṭṭāraka*s, could handle money, wear nonmendicant clothing such as ornamented shawls, and take permanent residence in the temple complexes they controlled.[9] In the late nineteenth century, however, a few members of the mendicant lineage Tapā Gaccha rejected these temple-dwelling *yati*s and reestablished groups of possessionless, peripatetic monks led by *ācārya*s who, outside of the four-month-long rainy season, spent only a few days at a time in one location. Without the immediate followers attached to the *yatis*' temple compounds, the increasing number of itinerant *ācārya*s who emerged in this period had to devise means of attracting lay devotees. It was at this time, after the reestablishment of orders of peripatetic Śvetāmbara monks at the end of the nineteenth century, that Śvetāmbara *mūrtipūjaka* mendicants reinvigorated the tradition of worshiping diagrams of the *sūrimantra* and the *vardhamānavidyā*. Monks in the Tapā Gaccha sublineage of the great reformer of the early twentieth century, Ācārya Nemisūri (1872–1948), claim that in 1907, Nemisūri was the first *ācārya* for at least 250 years to perform the "Five Sections," the *pañcaprasthāna*, an elaborate multiday worship ceremony of each of the five different sections of the *sūrimantra* that we will examine in depth in this chapter.[10]

It is not entirely clear how common the ritual use of the *sūrimantra* was between the sixteenth and nineteenth centuries, since few known texts on the mantra can be definitively dated to this period; but the transmission and daily ritual use of the *sūrimantra* likely continued during this time. Tapā Gaccha and Kharatara Gaccha hagiographies from the late sixteenth and early seventeenth centuries give great importance to the transmission of the *sūrimantra*,[11] and several *sūrimantrapaṭa*s dated between the sixteenth and nineteenth centuries have been published.[12] The temple-dwelling Ācārya Kuśalacandrasūri, who was initiated in Varanasi in 1778, is said to have always been reciting the "king of mantras," the *sūrimantra*;[13] and the great proponent of Śvetāmbara image worship, Vijayānandasūri (Ātmārāmajī; 1837–1896), who was promoted to the rank of *ācārya* in 1887, published a text on the *sūrimantra*.[14]

Even so, material and textual evidence suggests that the ritual use of cloth diagrams of the *sūrimantra* and *vardhamānavidyā* has never been as prevalent as it is today. After the reforms of the late nineteenth and early twentieth centuries, the number of peripatetic image-worshiping Śvetāmbara *ācārya*s grew exponentially: from perhaps none in the nineteenth century, there were 148 in 1996[15] and 300 in 2019.[16] From 1987 to 2013, the number of *ācārya*s in Nemisūri's *samudāya* alone increased from 19 to 29.[17] An increased number of *ācārya*s can mean more small groups of mendicants who travel separately, exerting a potentially wider influence. It also means, however, a greater need for support from the lay community. Each lineage must find some way of attracting these resources, so some monks such as the *ācārya*s of the lineages of Nemisūri have advertised themselves as innovators and experts in the worship ceremonies of the five sections of the *sūrimantra*.

Therefore, the splintering of the Śvetāmbara mendicant community into an increasing number of mendicant lineages has been one reason for the popularity of the *sūrimantra* in two different time periods. Just as monks composed a large number of texts on the *sūrimantra* between the thirteenth and fifteenth centuries, after the Tantric Age had ended, so too have monks in the twentieth and twenty-first centuries promoted these rites. This suggests that while it is helpful to see general trends in religious practices on the subcontinent, framing our understanding of the development of religious practices in terms of distinct, linear periods of time can also be limiting. Scholars often rely on historical periodization based on the religious affiliations of rulers—they use ideas about the Tantric Age or the periods of Muslim or colonial rule—to shape the arguments they make about their data. But this framing can overlook the more community-specific causes for the promotion of certain rituals or worldviews. In the case of Śvetāmbara image-worshiping Jainism, we might understand the emergence of religious ideas and practices both in terms of linear developments based on the influence of the state and in terms of cyclical developments based on the relationships between mendicant communities and laypeople. Developments in the nineteenth century such as European translations of the earliest Jain scriptures and the influence of the printing press played a role in both the Jain reforms of the late nineteenth century that sought to return Jainism to its "original" state and the promulgation of once-difficult-to-access texts on *mantraśāstra*.[18] The important scholar-monk Jambūvijaya's publication of a collection of manuscripts on the *sūrimantra*—the *Sūrimantrakalpasamuccayaḥ* (*SMKS*)—in 1969 and 1977 has played a huge role in the ritual use of the *sūrimantra* today. However, the proliferation of competing mendicant lineages that emerged from these nineteenth-century reforms is another reason modern monks have embraced the use of the *sūrimantra* and the *vardhamānavidyā*. My knowledge of the secret ritual use of the diagrams of Jain mendicants is necessarily partial, but from my discussions with a handful of Jain monks and an analysis of a few *paṭas*, I can provide a general understanding of the modern ritual practices of some image-worshiping Śvetāmbara monks, beginning with a discussion of how monks receive these diagrams in the first place.

RECEIVING THE CLOTH DIAGRAM OF THE SPELL OF MAHĀVĪRA

Today, modern image-worshiping Śvetāmbara monks rise through the ranks of mendicancy in a manner quite similar to the path outlined in Jinaprabhasūri's fourteenth-century *Vidhimārgaprapā* (*VMP*; see chapter 3). Indeed, members of the Kharatara Gaccha still follow the *Vidhimārgaprapā*'s instructions when initiating and promoting their mendicants. Members of the four other extant mendicant lineages—the Tapā Gaccha and others—follow the instructions in handbooks of various names, including "right conduct," *sāmācārī*, and "ritual manuals on monastic practices (*yoga*)," *yogavidhi*, which largely rely on the prescriptions of medieval texts on mendicant conduct like the *Vidhimārgaprapā*, another medieval text of the Kharatara Gaccha, Vardhamānasūri's *Ācāradinakara* (composed in Sanskrit in the early fifteenth century) and a Prakrit text, the *Subodhāsāmācārī* by the twelfth-century founding *ācārya* of the Candra Gaccha, Candrasūri.[19] Modern handbooks agree with their medieval sources that monks must combine the regular ritual use of a secret mantra with acts more commonly associated with Jain monasticism—austerities and scriptural study—to advance in the mendicant hierarchy. The two-hundred-page mid-twentieth-century Gujarati *bṛhadyogavidhi* from the lineage of the monks I saw promoted to the rank of *ācārya* in Surat in 2013, Pūrṇacandrasāgarasūri's *Bṛhad Yog Vidhi* (*BYV*), provides one of the most detailed instructions for mendicant initiation and promotion. This manual names five ranks of monk: (1) ordinary monk (*muni*), (2) leader of a smaller mendicant group (*gaṇin*) (3) mendicant scholar (*pannyāsa* or *paṇḍita*) (4) mendicant teacher (*upādhyāya* or *vācaka*), and (5) mendicant leader (*ācārya* or *sūri*).[20]

A monk receives a Cloth Diagram of the Spell of Mahāvīra only upon his promotion to the rank of *gaṇin*. This should occur after several years of mendicancy and the completion of the *yogavidhi*, or the study of key texts of the *mūrtipūjaka* Śvetāmbara "canon" in a systematic order that incorporates fasting and ritual exchanges between guru and disciple. It is worth examining this structured reading of scriptures briefly, because it relates to important scholarly debates over the use of the term "canon" as a translation for the group of scriptures image-worshiping Śvetāmbara mendicants must study in order to receive the *vardhamānavidyā*.

Building on foundational textbooks from the early twentieth century,[21] many introductory texts on Jainism claim that the "Jain canon" comprises forty-five scriptures (*āgama*): eleven "limbs" (*aṅga*) said to be the words of Mahāvīra recorded by his disciples, twelve subsidiary limbs (*upāṅga*), seven books of mendicant discipline (*chedasūtra*), four root scriptures (*mūlasūtra*), ten miscellaneous scriptures that tackle a variety of topics (*prakīrṇaka*), and two appendices (*cūlikā*). Some scholars have suggested that these forty-five texts were "committed to writing in [their] entirety" at the Council of

Valabhi in Gujarat in the fifth century CE.[22] More recent scholarship, however, has critiqued this use of the term "canon" for these texts, claiming that it was foisted upon the tradition by nineteenth-century Protestant Orientalists who modeled Jainism after their own tradition that requires a single, authoritative, ancient canon. They have noted that scholarship repeatedly cites the list of forty-five scriptures as the "Jain canon" not because all Jains since the fifth century have agreed that these texts are important, but because the German Orientalist Georg Bühler received the list from a *yati* of the Kharatara Gaccha, Śrīpūjya Jinamuktisūri, in 1871 and related it to Albrecht Weber, who then replicated it in his hugely influential work, "Über die heiligen Schriften der Jaina" (1883, 1885).[23] Many other lists of *āgama*s and classifications of scripture are found in Jain literature, this list of forty-five texts was not put into its final form until around the thirteenth century,[24] anti-iconic Śvetāmbaras only accept thirty-two of the forty-five scriptures, and Digambaras largely do not read any of these texts.[25] Indeed, the majority of lay Jains today could not name most of these texts.

Scholars such as Kendall Folkert and John Cort have thus encouraged their colleagues to avoid using the term "canon" solely for these forty-five texts and to also highlight different groupings of scriptures that are significant to Jains for various reasons.[26] In an important article, "The Intellectual Formation of a Jain Monk," John Cort undertakes this project by outlining the texts Tapā Gaccha monks should study according to a 1988 mendicant conference in Ahmedabad. In outlining the curriculum, which should be studied over a period of seven years and includes upward of seventy texts on various topics—from the hymn the *Bhaktāmarastotra*, to Pāṇini's Sanskrit grammar the *Āṣṭādhyāyī*, to a sixteenth-century text on different life forms—Cort shows that scholars have put too much emphasis on the forty-five *āgama*s, since only two of the texts in the curriculum belong to the "canon" (the *Daśavaikālika* and the *Oghaniryukti*).[27]

According to my conversations with modern Tapā Gaccha monks, however, few—if any—mendicants follow the curriculum outlined in 1988. In contrast, mendicants must follow the *yogavidhi* to be promoted through the ranks of mendicancy, so to this day they are quite familiar with different mendicant lineages' lists of *āgama*s, all of which are almost identical to the commonly found list of forty-five, mainly differing in their enumeration of the miscellaneous texts, the *prakīrṇaka*s.[28] In my conversations with lower-level monks, they would confirm to me that they are working through the curriculum in order to be promoted. Mendicants work at their own pace and take time to study other texts and topics that interest them, especially languages; but they all recognize that in order to become a *gaṇin*, they need to study the *āgamas*. This has likely been the case since the early stages of Jainism, since one of the *chedasūtras*, the *Vyavahārasūtra* that is dated the first few centuries BCE, defines many of the ranks of mendicancy in terms of the specific *āgamas* they have studied,[29] and in chapter 3, we saw that the chapters in Jinaprabhasūri's *Vidhimārgaprapā* on *yogavidhi* require the study of a collection of scriptures quite similar to the list of forty-five in order to rise through the ranks of mendicancy and receive the *vardhamānavidyā* and *sūrimantra*. Therefore, while the list of forty-five *āgamas* should not be understood as naming the most well-known, important texts for understanding the beliefs and practices of all Jains, if a "canon" delineates a collection of texts that religious leaders have codified to "provide an eternal norm for church doctrine," then image-worshiping Śvetāmbaras, in composing various lists of *āgamas* that must be read by monks to advance through the mendicant hierarchy, have an understanding of a canon.[30] While mendicants will continue to disagree over which texts, exactly, should claim canonical status, in practice today, according to Nandighoṣasūri, mendicants read only sixteen of these *āgamas* to advance to higher ranks of mendicancy (table 5.1).

The mendicant's study today, as in the *Vidhimārgaprapā*, begins after the initial renunciation with two "root scriptures"—the *Āvaśyakasūtra* and the *Daśavaikālikasūtra*—that outline foundational practices of Jain monasticism. The novice mendicant, after studying these two texts for a period of up to six months, may undertake the formal initiation and adopt the five vows of mendicancy (Guj. *vaḍī dīkṣā*). He then may work his way through the study of a third root text, the *Uttarādhyayanasūtra*; the first four limbs of the canon; two texts on mendicant discipline, the *Kalpasūtra* and the *Mahāniśīthasūtra*; the two appendices of the *āgamas*, the first four sub-limbs; and, finally, the fifth limb, the *Bhagavatīsūtra*. The study of each scripture should begin with the ceremony of *nandīkriyā*, in which the disciple circumambulates a model of the Jina's Preaching Assembly or the three sticks that makeup the tripod for the *sthāpanācārya* (Guj. *ṭhvaṇī*) and formally requests from his guru permission to study the scriptures in a formalized series of questions and answers in Prakrit. The guru grants his permission with a sprinkling of *vāsakṣepa*, and the disciple ends the ceremony by taking a vow to perform the fast required for the section of the scripture to be studied (Guj. *pacckkhāṇ*, Skt. *pratyākhyāna*).[31] Texts that should be studied at a specific time require the performance of *kālagrahaṇa* by the guru and disciple to determine the auspicious time for study (see chapter 3). In this study of the scriptures, the longest *āgama* by far, the *Bhagavatīsūtra*, or the *Vyākhyāprajñapti*, "Proclamation

TABLE 5.1. The canonical texts to be read by a modern *mūrtipūjaka* Tapā Gaccha Śvetāmbara monk in order to become a *gaṇin*

Text	Type of text	Promotion required for study	Number of days for study
Āvaśyakasūtra	*mūlasūtra* (root text)	*dīkṣā*	10
Daśavaikālikasūtra	*mūlasūtra*	*dīkṣā*	18
Uttarādhyayanasūtra	*mūlasūtra*	*vaḍī dīkṣā*	28
Ācārāṅgasūtra	*aṅga* (limb, or main, text)	*vaḍī dīkṣā*	55
Kalpasūtra (eighth chapter of the *Daśāśrutaskandha*)	*chedasūtra* (rules for mendicants)	*vaḍī dīkṣā*	40
Mahāniśīthasūtra	*chedasūtra*	*vaḍī dīkṣā*	45
Nandīsūtra and *Anuyogadvārasūtra*	*cūlikā* (appendix)	*vaḍī dīkṣā*	7
Sūtrakṛtāṅgasūtra	*aṅga*	*vaḍī dīkṣā*	35
Sthānāṅgasūtra	*aṅga*	*vaḍī dīkṣā*	21
Samavāyāṅgasūtra	*aṅga*	*vaḍī dīkṣā*	4
Aupapātikasūtra *Rājapraśnīyasūtra* *Jīvājīvābhigamasūtra* *Prajñāpanāsūtra*	*upāṅga* (sub-limb, or subsidiary, text)	*vaḍī dīkṣā*	14
Bhagavatīsūtra	*aṅga*	*vaḍī dīkṣā*	226

Source: Acārya Nandighoṣasūri, interviews with the author, July 2019

of Explanations [of Mahāvīra]," remains the most important text to understand. "*Savvānuyogabhagavaī*," Nandighoṣasūri recited to me in Prakrit, meaning: "The *Bhagavatī* [venerable scripture] contains all the scriptures." It is for this reason that a monk is eligible to lead a group of monks only after he has spent 226 days completing the study of this scripture.

One hundred and fifty days after his completion of the *Bhagavatīsūtra*, if his guru deems him to be honorable and knowledgeable enough, the monk will be ready for promotion to the rank of *gaṇin*. The guru will impart the *vardhamānavidyā* to the disciple by sprinkling consecrated *vāsakṣepa* onto his head and whispering the *vardhamānavidyā* three times into the disciple's ear. At this time, the disciple will also receive the cloth painting on which the *vardhamānavidyā* is inscribed, the Cloth Diagram of the Spell of Mahāvīra. The monk is now allowed to lead a group of monks, and he can continue to study the rest of the *āgama*s, though after being promoted to the rank of *gaṇin*, he is not required to study any more scriptures in a formalized way.[32] Usually after years of upholding supreme conduct, the *gaṇin*'s guru will determine if he has the intellect, knowledge, proper conduct, and leadership skills required to become a *pannyāsa*, a scholar monk, or an *upādhyāya*, a mendicant teacher (in India today there are few *upādhyāya*s). To promote a monk to these ranks, the guru will impart to him new versions of the *vardhamānavidyā*; each guru and lineage will develop different versions of the invocation, at times simply changing a single syllable to modify the effects of the spell.

Pūrṇacandrasāgarasūri's *Bṛhad Yog Vidhi* does not outline the required scriptural study for female mendicants, nor does it define their ranks. There are, however, three different ranks of female mendicant recognized today: ordinary nun (*sādhvī*); the female equivalent of an *upādhyāya*, a *pravartinī*; and the female equivalent of an *ācārya*, the *mahattarā*.[33] Nandighoṣasūri confirmed that in his Tapā Gaccha sublineage of Nemisūri, to be promoted to the rank of *pravartinī*, nuns read only the first four texts of the *yogavidhi* series, up to the *Ācārāṅgasūtra*, and they never receive the *vardhamānavidyā*.[34] Not all lineages agree about how to promote female mendicants, however. Ācārya *Yugabhūṣaṇasūri*, "Paṇḍit Mahārāj," who in February 2020 was declared the leader (*gacchādhipati*) of a new Tapā Gaccha sublineage of Ācārya Rāmacandrasūri, did impart the *vardhamānavidyā* and gift the Cloth Diagram of the Spell of Mahāvīra to the head nun in his lineage upon her promotion to *pravartinī*.[35] According to this nun, Pravartinī Sādhvī Kalānidhi, nuns in her lineage must study the *Āvaśyakasūtra*, *Daśavaikālika*, *Ācārāṅga*, *Uttarādhyāyana*, and two books on mendicant discipline, the *Piṇḍaniryukti* and *Oghaniryukti*, before this promotion. To become a *mahattarā*, then, the nun will receive a different version of the *vardhamānavidyā*.[36]

Once mendicants have received their version of the *vardhamānavidyā*, they are required to activate it daily through recitation. Indeed, in terms of daily conduct, the only required ritual difference between the three higher ranks of male mendicant—*gaṇin*, *pannyāsa*, and *upādhyāya*—is the recitation of a different version of the *vardhamānavidyā*. Each day, along with scriptural study, upholding the five vows of a mendicant, and the performance of the six essential duties, mendicants who have received the *vardhamānavidyā* must recite it 108 times while sprinkling *vāsakṣepa* on their cloth diagram of the spell.

THE CLOTH DIAGRAM OF THE SPELL OF MAHĀVĪRA

The lay community commissions the painting of a monk's cloth diagram upon the request of an *ācārya* wishing to promote his disciple. These mendicant leaders give the details of the mantras to be inscribed on the diagrams to male (often brahmin) artists.[37] In December 2013, I visited one of these brahmin artists in Jaipur named Mangal Kumar Sharma, who paints *sūri-mantrapaṭas* commissioned by various Śvetāmbara *ācāryas*. Sharma, like other artists who paint for Jain communities, maintains a long-standing relationship with Jain mendicant lineages, since his father also painted these diagrams. He confirmed that he uses oil-based paints and gold to make two different versions of the Cloth Diagram of the Mantra of the Mendicant Leader: the condensed (*saṃkṣipta*) and expanded (*bṛhat*) versions, priced at 21,000 rupees and 1.5 lakh rupees, respectively.[38] The Cloth Diagram of the Spell of Mahāvīra does not have an expanded version.

Throughout their years as *gaṇins*, *pannyāsas*, *upādhyāyas*, and *ācāryas*, laypeople will commission various versions of these diagrams from artists like Sharma. Laypeople will commission, for example, temple installations and portable renderings made on metal, sandalwood, and paper, among other materials. The key diagram used in daily ritual, however, is painted on cloth.

Examining the contents of a Cloth Diagram of the Spell of Mahāvīra that was painted in Jaipur and gifted to the Kharatara Gaccha Upādhyāya Vinayasāgara upon his promotion to the rank of *upādhyāya* in 1951 shows that these diagrams depict Mahāvīra's Preaching Assembly and use the *ṛddhi-maṅgala* as an auspicious border that signals the rank of the monk (fig. 5.2). Moving from the exterior to interior, three brick walls—one silver, one gold, and one green—surround three sections of the assembly where different classes of living beings have gathered to hear the teachings of the four-faced Mahāvīra at the center of the gathering. Monks, nuns, laymen, and laywomen, hands folded in reverence, sit in the innermost section, closest to Mahāvīra. Animals are gathered in harmony in the second section, with predators and prey—a cat and mouse, lion and goat, monkey and crocodile, peacock and snake—facing each other without animus. The third section, furthest from Mahāvīra, contains the vehicles of the gods, which take the shape of two-headed crocodiles, peacocks, and other forms. Outside the assembly, banners are established in each of the corners to mark the ritual space as auspicious, gods shower garlands from above the assembly,

FIGURE 5.2. A twentieth-century Cloth Diagram of the Spell of Mahāvīra from Rajasthan gifted to Upādhyāya Vinayasāgara of the Kharatara Gaccha. Jaipur, Rajasthan, March 2011.

musicians sound their instruments, and guards next to auspicious stepwells protect each of the four entrances to the assembly. Images of monks and footprints of the guru flank the bottom of the assembly, and Mahāvīra's tutelary deities—Mātaṅga with his elephant vehicle and Siddhāyikā on her lion—join Sarasvatī on her swan and Lakṣmī on her lotus at the bottom of the painting.

The focus of the diagram remains, however, Mahāvīra, who sits at the center of the diagram, and the *vardhamānavidyā*, which is inscribed in gold in the corners of the central triangle and represented by the four "victory goddess." Iconographical markers suggest that Mahāvīra is simultaneously established in his preaching assembly, seated in a temple shrine, and at the center of a tantric diagram. The dome with a flag above Mahāvīra signifies that he is enshrined: he is depicted as he might be in an image-worshiping Śvetāmbara temple, crowned and ornamented as a king—the true ruler of a devotee's actions—seated on a throne above his vehicle, the lion, and flanked by fly-whisk bearers. At the same time, Mahāvīra is the primary deity of a *yantra* with a six-pointed figure emerging from a lotus. He sits inside of two seed syllables traced in gold: *oṃ* and *hrīṃ*. The root spell of the diagram, the *vardhamānavidyā*, which names various epithets of Mahāvira, is inscribed in intersecting red triangles: *oṃ vīre vīre mahāvīre jayavīre seṇavīre vaddhamāṇavīre jae vijae jayante aparājie savvaṭṭhasiddhe nibue mahāṇase mahābale svāhā*. The terms for "victory" in the middle of the spell—in Sanskrit, *jaya*, *vijaya*, *jayanta*, and *aparājita*—are personified as four different goddesses seated in the ordinal directions. The blue Aparājitā sits in the upper left corner of the central square, the white Jayā in the upper right, the red Vijayā in the lower right, and Jayantā in the lower left.

Three concentric rings—one green and two red—surround the petals of the central lotus. Repetitions of seed syllables fill the six sections of the innermost ring, while a praise to Mahāvīra—*oṃ hrīṃ kṣuṃ hrīṃ vīrāya svāhā*—fills the six sections of the middle ring. The outermost ring contains a Sanskrit mantra asking for the production of continuous peace (*śānti*), satisfaction (*tuṣṭi*), prosperity (*puṣṭi*), wealth (*ṛddhi*), advancement (*vṛddhi*), intelligence (*buddhi*), happiness (*sukha*), well-being (*saubhāgya*), and great fortune (*mahodaya*) for the recipient of this *paṭa*, Vinayasāraga, whose guru is listed as Upādhyāya Maṇisāgara, disciple of Sumatisāgara.[39] In each of the four cardinal directions on the outside of the central circle, four red circles are filled with the seed syllables *oṃ* and *hrīṃ* surrounded by the Sanskrit mantra *arhaṃ hrūṃ hraḥ hrauṃ namo vardhamānasvāmine svāhā*.

The text inscribed in gold in the three red squares inside each of the walls of the three sections of the preaching assembly provides ritual prescriptions and expansions of the root spell. The inner red square contains instructions for different portions of the *vidyā* to be recited for different effects. The goddess Jayā can grant scriptural knowledge, Vijayā well-being, Jayantā victory over death, and Aparājitā attraction. To receive the effects related to these goddesses' powers, one should recite 108 times the portion of the spell associated with them: for scriptural knowledge, recite 108 times *oṃ hrīṃ jae hrāṃ svāhā*; for well-being, *oṃ hrīṃ vijae hrīṃ svāhā*; for victory over death, *oṃ hrīṃ jayante hrūṃ svāhā*; and for attracting people, *oṃ hrīṃ aparājie hrūṃ svāhā*.

The middle red square contains, in gold, the Prakrit mantra that Digambaras today are imparted upon their mendicant initiations. This Digambara mantra is also called the *vardhamānamantra*, providing more evidence of dialogues between the two sects when developing their mantras of initiation and promotion (see chapter 3). The outer red square contains Prakrit invocations related to the *sūrimantra*. It contains a spell (*vidyā*) to a goddess associated with a section of the *sūrimantra*, Tribhuvanasvāminī, and a version of the *ṛddhi-maṅgala*, which it calls the "second *vardhamānavidyā*":

> *oṃ hrīṃ namo jiṇāṇaṃ oṃ hrīṃ namo ohijiṇāṇaṃ oṃ hrīṃ namo paramohijiṇāṇaṃ oṃ hrīṃ namo savvohijiṇāṇaṃ oṃ hrīṃ namo aṇaṃtohijiṇāṇaṃ oṃ hrīṃ namo kuṭṭhabuddhīṇaṃ oṃ hrīṃ namo payāṇusārīṇaṃ, oṃ hrīṃ namo saṃbhinnasoāṇaṃ, oṃ hrīṃ namo caüddasapuvvīṇaṃ, oṃ hrīṃ namo aṭṭhagamahānimittakusalāṇaṃ, oṃ hrīṃ namo viuvvaṇaiḍḍhipattāṇaṃ, oṃ hrīṃ namo vijjāharāṇaṃ, oṃ hrīṃ namo paṇhasamaṇāṇaṃ, oṃ hrīṃ namo āgāsagāmīṇaṃ, oṃ hrīṃ krauṃ krauṃ prauṃ prauṃ svāhā oṃ hrīṃ klīṃ dhṛtiratimatibuddhikīrttilakṣmī svāhā*

The lines from the *ṛddhi-maṅgala*, without the seed syllables, read:

> Praise to the *jina*s; praise to the *jina*s who have clairvoyant knowledge, who have supreme clairvoyant knowledge, who have complete clairvoyant knowledge, who have infinite clairvoyant knowledge, praise to those whose intellects are like granaries that store the seeds of teachings; praise to those who can complete a text after knowing just one word; praise to those who can hear sounds beyond the range of normal hearing; praise to those who know the fourteen *pūrva*s; praise to those who have eight different types of prognostic abilities; praise to those who have the power of shape transformation; praise to the *vidyādhara*s; praise to those mendicants (*śramaṇa*) who have ascetic wisdom (*prajñā*); praise to those who can travel in the sky.

Therefore, in this diagram, as in other examples of the Cloth Diagrams of Mahāvīra, the *ṛddhi-maṅgala* forms a border, invoking the superhuman knowledge, healing powers, and austerities that monks cultivate in the propitiation of ritual diagrams and delineating a sacred space into which deities are invited. It appears that in some traditions, as mendicants are promoted from leader of a small group of mendicants to a mendicant scholar to a mendicant teacher, their *vardhamānavidyā*s include more parts of the *ṛddhi-maṅgala* that should be inscribed in the squares framing the preaching assembly.[40] The *ṛddhi-maṅgala* is appended in this way to *vardhamānavidyā*s of monks of higher ranks likely because the first section of the *sūrimantra* contains a version of the *ṛddhi-maṅgala*. Therefore, as monks move toward becoming a mendicant leader, they are imparted more components of the Mantra of the Mendicant Leader.[41]

WORSHIPING THE CLOTH DIAGRAM OF THE SPELL OF MAHĀVĪRA

In order to move toward promotion to the rank of *ācārya*, a *gaṇin*, *pannyāsa*, and *upādhyāya* must first spend years undertaking the daily propitiation of a cloth diagram of the *vardhamānavidyā*. In 2005, Nayacandrasāgara—the Tapā Gaccha monk whose promotion to the rank of *ācārya* was described in chapter 3—published a collection of premodern and modern Sanskrit, Prakrit, and Gujarati texts on this ritual propitiation called the *Vardhamāna Vidyā Kalpaḥ*. This collection includes selections from Jinaprabhasūri's *Vidhimārgaprapā* and Siṃhatilakasūri's *Mantrarājarahasya*; a Sanskrit hymn to the *vardhamānavidyā* by Jinaprabhasūri; the Sanskrit *Sūrimukhyamantrakalpa* by the fourteenth-century monk from the Añcala Gaccha, Merutuṅgasūri; anonymous Sanskrit texts on different versions and uses of the *vardhamānavidyā* by monks of the Pūrṇimā Gaccha and Añcala Gaccha; and Gujarati texts on the construction, consecration, and worship of the Cloth Diagram of the Spell of Mahāvīra by anonymous authors.

In interviews, Nayacandrasāgarasūri was tight lipped about which text, exactly, he follows in his daily worship of the Cloth Diagram of Mahāvīra, and he stressed that modern gurus draw from many medieval texts when deciding which version of the *vardhamānavidyā* to impart to their disciples. He did, however, confirm that the Gujarati description of the daily worship of the cloth diagram in his book, the *Śrī Vardhmānvidyā Nitya Ārādhnā Vidhi*, provides a general understanding of how a monk might worship a diagram, so I will summarize this text to provide an overview of these worship ceremonies.

Monks are required to make offerings of *vāsakṣepa* to their *paṭa* every day, and they usually do so in the morning, though there is no required time for worship. Especially during the rainy-season retreat, when they remain in one place for four months, some monks establish shrines for their cloth diagrams that are filled with images of Jain deities, *tīrthaṅkara*s, gurus, and other auspicious objects like conches and *yantra*s such as the *śrīcakra* (fig 5.3). The daily worship of the *paṭa* need not entail the establishment of a shrine, however, and I have seen the relatively open worship of the *paṭa*. One afternoon in Ahmedabad, when I was visiting with a lower-level monk in a large worship hall where he was residing with dozens of other mendicants for the rainy season, I looked across the hall to see another monk of a higher

FIGURE 5.3. Upādhyāya Maṇiprabhasāgara's shrine for the Cloth Diagram of the Spell of Mahāvīra. At bottom right, a bowl of *vāsakṣepa* and a rosary of 108 beads sit to the right of the cloth diagram. Palitana, Gujarat, October 2013.

rank seated alone, on a low table, legs crossed, with his *paṭa* placed in front of him, ready for worship. This is not a common sight, however, since the worship of the *paṭa* usually occurs in the early morning when laypeople are not visiting.

The Gujarati instructions in Nayacandrasāgara's texts describe the worship of the *paṭa* as follows:

(1) The ceremony begins with the recitation of a Prakrit confessional formula (*pratikramaṇa*) that is first found in the *Āvaśyakaniryukti* and should always be recited at the outset of one's performance of *caityavandana*, the praise of Jain temple images. This "Sūtra of the Path of One's Movement," the *īryāpathikīsūtra*, reads:

> I want to make amends (*pratikramaṇa*) for injury on the path of my movement, in coming and in going, in treading on living things, in treading on seeds, in treading on green plants, in treading on

dew, on beetles, on mold, on moist earth, and on cobwebs; whatever living organisms with one or two or three or four or five senses have been injured by me or knocked over or crushed or squashed or touched or mangled or hurt or affrighted or removed from one place to another or deprived of life—may all that evil bear no karmic consequence (*micchāmi dukkaḍaṃ*).[42]

(2) For the protection of his entire body (*ātmarakṣā*), the monk then recites a Sanskrit hymn of praise, the *Vajrapañjarastotra*, while performing arm gestures to place the nine lines of the *pañcanamaskāra* on his body to create mantra armor (*kavaca*) to protect him from evil influences while performing this ceremony.[43] There are ten Sanskrit lines that form this *stotra*:

a. With hands folded in a gesture of prayer in front of his chest, the monk should recite the first line: "*oṃ* I bring to mind the Praise to the Five Supreme Beings, the essence, which is made up of the Nine Parts (*navapada*) [and] protects me like an indestructible cage."

b. Placing both his hands over his head as if he is putting a helmet on his head, he should recite: "*oṃ namo arihaṃtāṇaṃ*, a helmet is placed on [my] head."

c. Placing his two hands over his mouth, he should recite: "*oṃ namo savvasiddhāṇaṃ*, on [my] mouth there is an excellent mouth shield."

d. Placing his hands on his chest and imagining he is wearing a coat of armor, he should recite: "*oṃ namo āyariyāṇam*, there is excellent protection of [my] limbs."

e. Imagining that he is holding swords or other weapons in his hands and that he is driving away evil forces, he should recite: "*oṃ namo uvajjhāyāṇaṃ*, there are weapons in [my] hands."

f. Placing his hands on his feet and imagining that he is wearing iron footwear, he should say: "*oṃ namo loe savvasāhūṇaṃ*, there is good footwear on [my] feet."

g. Touching the ground in front of him with both hands and imagining he is sitting on a rock made of *vajra*s (the hourglass-shaped weapon and ritual implement), he should recite: "*eso pañcanamukkāro*, [I am] on a surface that is a rock made of *vajra*s."

h. Hands in front of him, bent at the wrist, palms facing downward, he should imagine a wall of *vajra*s around himself, from the ground to his head, and should recite: "*savvapāvappaṇāsaṇo*, a *vajra*-rampart surrounds [me]."

i. Pointing in front of himself and imagining a moat surrounding himself, with flames burning in all four directions, he should recite: "*maṅgalāṇaṃ ca savvesiṃ*, there is a moat that has [burning] charcoal of acacia wood."

j. Lacing his hands together above his head and imagining he is closing the fort around himself with a cover made of *vajra*s, he should recite: "This line—*paḍamaṃ havai maṅgalaṃ*, ending with *svāhā*—should be known as a covering made of *vajra*s over the rampart for the protection of [my] body."[44]

(3) For the purification of his body, the monk should imagine that he is pure and rotate his hands over five key body parts (*pañcāṅga*): two legs, two arms, and his head.

(4) For purification of the space, or the *bhūmiśuddhi*, the monk takes *vāsakṣepa* in his right hand and sprinkles it in the eight directions, reciting three times a Sanskrit mantra that asks that the ground be purified.

(5) The monk then undertakes a "mantra bath" (*mantrasnāna*), for which he cups his hands together in front of himself in a gesture called *añjalimudrā*. Reciting a Sanskrit mantra asking for all the waters of pilgrimage places to purify him, he imagines these waters in his cupped hands and then gestures as if splashing the water on his head.

(6) He then performs *vastraśuddhi* for the purification of his clothes, reciting a Sanskrit mantra while gesturing as if dusting off his robes.

(7) Following the *vastraśuddhi*, he performs *aṅgulīnyāsa*, in which he places seed syllables on his fingers. He touches his index finger to his thumb and then one by one touches his thumb to rest of his fingers and recites the following seed syllables:

thumb—*hrāṃ*
index finger—*hrīṃ*
middle finger—*hrūṃ*
ring finger—*hrauṃ*
pinkie—*hraḥ*

(8) The monk then performs *kalmaṣadahana*, or the burning away of impurities, by reciting a Sanskrit mantra three times and essentially hugging himself while imagining all his impurities burning away.

(9) To purify his heart (*hṛdayaśuddhi*), the monk should then place his left hand on his heart and recite a Sanskrit mantra for purity of thought (*oṃ vimalāya vimalacittāya jvīṃ kṣīṃ svāhā*)

(10) The monk then places the Five Supreme Beings on his fingers, performing what is called *parameṣṭhinyāsa*. He touches his index finger to his thumb and then one by one touches his thumb to rest of his fingers and recites the following lines of the *pañcanamaskāra*:

thumb—*ṇamo arihaṃtāṇaṃ*
index finger—*ṇamo siddhāṇaṃ*
middle finger—*ṇamo āyariyāṇaṃ*
ring finger—*ṇamo uvajjhāyāṇam*
pinkie—*ṇamo loe savvasāhūṇaṃ*

(11) The monk then uses his left hand to place seed syllables on different parts of his upper body (*aṅganyāsa*):

heart—*hrāṃ*
throat—*hrīṃ*
top of the head—*hrūṃ*
eyebrows—*hrauṃ*
forehead—*hraḥ*

(12) To protect himself from bad dreams, bad results, misfortune, fear, enemies, lightning, and so on, he recites the Sanskrit mantra of protection (*rakṣāmantra*), *oṃ kuru kulle svāhā*, forward and backward, while touching the left and right sides of his body with his right hand:

forehead—*oṃ*
left shoulder—*ku*
left side—*ru*
left leg—*ku*
right leg—*lle*
right side—*svā*
right shoulder—*hā*
right shoulder—*hā*
right side—*svā*
right leg—*lle*
left leg—*ku*
left side—*ru*
left shoulder—*ku*
forehead—*oṃ*

(13) The monk then performs the *sakalīkaraṇa* rite, in which he places five different seed syllables on different parts of his body, each of which represents a color and one of the five elements: earth, water, fire, air, or sky. He should recite the seed syllables, forward and backward, three times:

kṣi	*pa*	*oṃ*	*svā*	*hā*
knee	navel	heart	mouth	top of head
yellow	white	red	blue	black
earth	water	fire	air (*vāyu*)	atmosphere (*ākāśa*)

(14) After these preliminary rites, he recites *oṃ oṃ namaḥ*, sprinkles *vāsakṣepa* on his cloth diagram, and opens the *paṭa* and places it in front of himself. He should sprinkle *vāsakṣepa* on Gautama in the middle of the *paṭa*. If he does not have a *paṭa*, the instructions confirm, he can imagine one.

(15) The monk then invites the deities of the diagram into the cloth through mantras and hand gestures:

i. Showing the invocation gesture, the *āhvānīmudrā*, he recites a Sanskrit mantra to Vardhamāna Svāmin and pulls his fingers toward his body, asking Mahāvīra to enter the *paṭa*.

ii. Showing the *sthāpanāmudrā*, he establishes Mahāvīra in the lotus's pericarp at the center of the *paṭa* through the recitation of another Sanskrit mantra, *tiṣṭha tiṣṭha ṭhaḥ ṭhaḥ*.

iii. Showing the *sannidhānamudrā* he recites another Sanskrit mantra asking for Vardhamāna Svāmin to remain near him.

iv. Showing the *sannirodhamudrā*, he recites a Sanskrit mantra requesting that Gautama remain in the *paṭa* until the *pūjā* is finished.

v. Showing *avaguṇṭhanamudrā*, he recites a Sanskrit mantra so that his ritual actions are hidden from other people. He then sprinkles *vāsakṣepa* on Mahāvīra and recites a Sanskrit mantra that asks Mahāvīra to accept perfumed substances, and so on.

(16) The monk then enlivens Mahāvīra in the *paṭa*. Showing the *surabhi* (also known as *amṛta* or *dhenu*) hand gesture, he performs the *prāṇapratiṣṭhā* of Gautama, to literally establish the breath of this saint in the painted cloth through the recitation of a Sanskrit mantra. The Gujarati text instructs the monk to imagine that Mahāvīra is alive and seated in his preaching assembly.

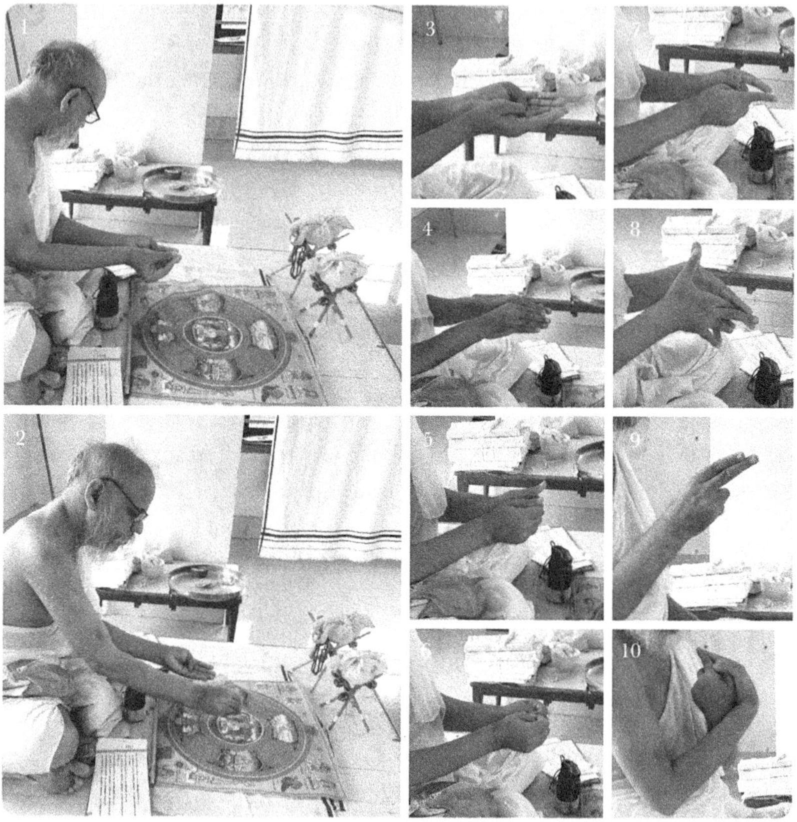

FIGURE 5.4. Nandighoṣasūri demonstrates the *mudrās* and motions of the daily worship of the Cloth Diagram of the Spell of Mahāvīra or the Cloth Diagram of the Mantra of the Mendicant Leader: (1) the welcoming gesture (*añjalimudrā*) used in the mantra bath, (2) the initial sprinkling of *vāsakṣepa* on the central deity, (3) the invitation gesture (*āhvāhanamudrā*), (4) establishing gesture (*sthāpanāmudrā*), (5) proximity gesture (*sannidhānamudrā*), (6) restraining gesture (*sannirodhamudrā*), (7) the hiding gesture (*avaguṇṭhanamudrā*), (8) the celestial cow gesture (*surabhimudrā*) used for *prāṇapratiṣṭhā*, (9) the weapon gesture (*astramudrā*), and (10) the dismissing gesture (*visarjanamudrā*). Mumbai, July 2016.

(17) After enlivening Mahāvīra at the center of his preaching assembly that is the Cloth Diagram of the Spell of Mahāvīra, the monk should undertake one of three ways to destroy obstacles, depending on his guru's tradition. He can say *hrūṃ* ten times as he sprinkles *vāsakṣepa* in the ten directions. He can recite a vowel of the alphabet (*svara*) for each sprinkle of *vāsakṣepa* in each of the ten directions, beginning with *a* in the east. Or he can recite mantras to each of the ten guardians of the directions (*dikpāla*) while sprinkling *vāsakṣepa*.

(18) The monk then recites the *vardhamānavidyā* 108 times, displaying five *mudrās*:

- **i.** gesture of well-being (*saubhāgyamudrā*)
- **ii.** gesture of the Five Supreme Beings (*parameṣṭhimudrā*)
- **iii.** celestial cow gesture (*dhenu/surabhimudrā*)
- **iv.** teaching gesture (*pravacanamudrā*)
- **v.** salutation gesture (*añjalimudrā*)

(19) After the completion of this recitation, the monk shows the *astramudrā*.

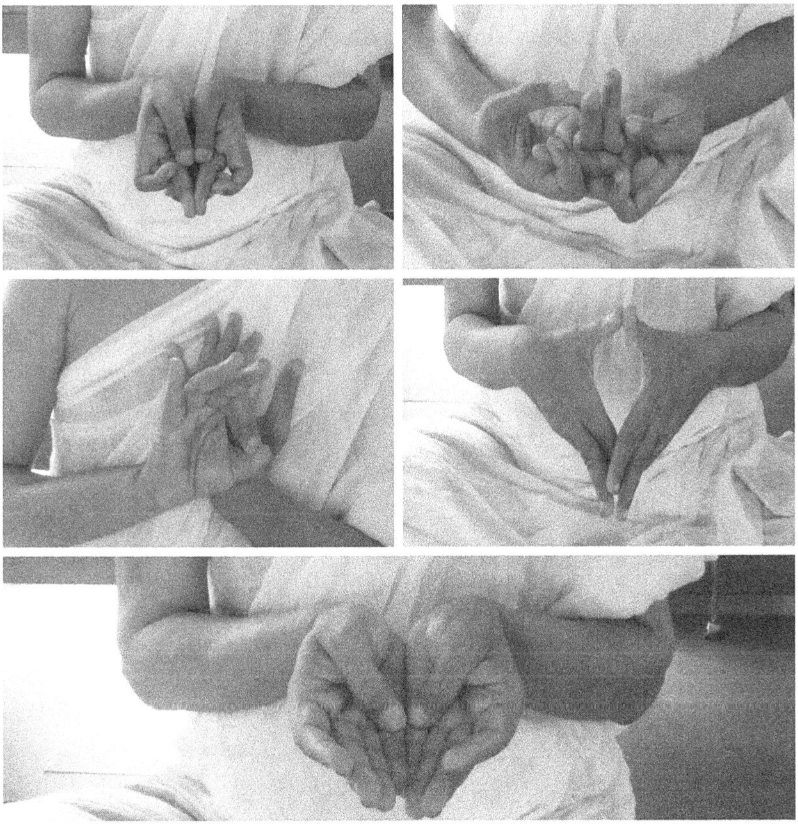

FIGURE 5.5. Nandighoṣasūri demonstrates, from the top to bottom: (1) the Gesture of Well-Being (*saubhāgyamudrā*), (2) the Gesture of the Five Supreme Beings (*parameṣṭhimudrā*), (3) the Teaching Gesture (*pravacanamudrā*), (4) the Celestial Cow Gesture (*surabhimudrā*), and (5) the Salutation Gesture (*añjalimudrā*). Ahmedabad, Gujarat, June 2013.

(20) The monk, with hands together on his forehead in a gesture of prayer, recites a Sanskrit verse asking for forgiveness from the Lord for any mistakes in mantras or actions that have been made during the worship ceremony.

(21) Finally, displaying the hand gesture of dismissal (*visarjanamudrā*), he recites a Sanskrit request for Mahāvīra to leave the *paṭa* and return to his own place (*punarāgamanāya svasthānaṃ gaccha gaccha yaḥ yaḥ yaḥ*).

While the specifics differ from text to text and from tradition to tradition, the general structure of this ritual corresponds in many ways to the daily worship practices of initiates of tantric Śaiva, Vaiṣṇava, and Buddhist traditions.[45] It also recalls the process of worshiping *yantra*s in medieval Digambara texts like the *Bhāvasaṅgraha* (chapter 4). All these ceremonies of worship begin with purification and divinization rites. Here, by first placing the Five Supreme Beings on his fingers, the monk, in touching five parts of his body and reciting the five syllables of the elements, performs *bhūtaśuddhi*, purifying the elements that constitute his body, and undergoes *sakalīkaraṇa*, transforming his body into a supreme instrument of worship by effectively becoming a supreme being through the imposition of mantras.[46]

Many of the hand gestures shown in these rites are also employed similarly in non-Jain tantric traditions. The *mudrā*s of inviting (*āhvāna/āvāhana*), establishing (*sthāpanā*), keeping near (*sannidhāna*), and retaining (*nirodhana/rodha/niṣṭura*) the deities in the diagram are also found in tantric scriptures.[47] The section on daily rites in the *Mṛgendrāgama* of the Śaiva Siddhānta, for example, prescribes that after "identifying five sections of the body with large segments of the universe, five parts of Śiva's fivefold mantra and five Śaiva ancillary mantras,"

> one should invoke the mantra-body [of Śiva] . . . with the gesture of Invocation. Then one should establish Him in a support made of His powers with the gesture of Establishing, and after receiving Him with the gesture of Homage, one should make him stay there with the Blocking gesture.[48]

In non-Jain texts, the *dhenumudrā* is used in purification rites, the *avaguṇṭhanamudrā* is used to hide rites,[49] and the *astramudrā* is used to purify or protect,[50] so it makes sense that the *dhenumudrā* and *avaguṇṭhanamudrā* are shown toward the beginning of the ceremony when monk purifies himself and his space and then hides the rite, and the *astramudrā* is shown near the end when the monk asks for forgiveness for potential mistakes. In addition, the *mudrā* used to represent the Five Supreme Beings is identical to the *pañcavaktramudrā* of the Śaiva *āgamas* that is used to evoke the five faces of Śiva.[51] While the exact paths of exchange cannot be determined at this point, it is clear that Jains have developed many of the same ritual techniques as found in tantric traditions.

With practice, a Śvetāmbara monk can undertake this whole process in under ten minutes. After the deities are dismissed from the cloth, the monk will transfer the *vāsakṣepa* consecrated in this worship ceremony to a pouch for later use. Jain mendicants are forbidden from worship with physical substances, but *vāsakṣepa* is understood as an exception: Śvetāmbara *mūrtipūjaka* monks employ it in every major ritual. It is sprinkled on mendicants during their initiations and promotions, sprinkled on laypeople to provide health, wealth, and blessings on the path to liberation, and sprinkled on temple icons in order to make them worthy of worship. Since most nuns[52] and *muni*s cannot perform the ritual worship of the cloth diagram to consecrate this powder, monks of higher ranks will also give these monks and nuns some of their *vāsakṣepa* to sprinkle on followers.[53]

While the secrecy surrounding the ceremony precludes me from knowing how common the above-outlined practice is, image-worshiping monks from a variety of mendicant branches in the Tapā Gaccha, Kharatara Gaccha, and Añcala Gaccha have confirmed to me that it is expected that a Śvetāmbara monk, after becoming a *gaṇin*, perform this worship ceremony every day. As leaders of a group of monks, *gaṇin*s should have the worldly power to protect their followers—the "cosmic energy" of the *vāsakṣepa*—and they should also develop the knowledge found in the texts they are required to study. After years of mendicancy and the daily worship of the Cloth Diagram of the Spell of Mahāvīra, a monk's guru will determine whether the monk is ready to receive the *sūrimantra* and be promoted to the highest rank of mendicancy, the rank of *ācārya*, or *sūri*, the leader of a large group of mendicants. After this promotion, he will begin his daily propitiation of the Cloth Diagram of the Mantra of the Mendicant Leader.

THE CLOTH DIAGRAM OF THE MANTRA OF THE MENDICANT LEADER

A close examination of the contents of the Cloth Diagram of the Mantra of the Mendicant Leader that was gifted to Nandighoṣasūri in 2008 upon his promotion to the rank of *ācārya* shows that the iconography of the diagram

FIGURE 5.6. Nandighoṣasūri's Cloth Diagram of the Mantra of the Mendicant Leader. Mumbai, July 2016.

argues for the superiority of the Jain path to liberation and places the worshiper of the diagram in the lineage of Mahāvīra. At first glance, the format of this modern diagram differs considerably from the earliest extant examples of the *sūrimantrapaṭa* from the fifteenth and sixteenth centuries.[54] Premodern examples of the Cloth Diagram of the Spell of the Mendicant Leader are devoid of images; they contain a mantra to Gautama, the disciple of Mahāvīra, at the center of a circle, and the sections of the *sūrimantra* are inscribed in concentric rings surrounding this central image. Modern *sūrimantrapaṭas*, however, situate the words of the *sūrimantra* and depictions of deities in an eight-petaled lotus, with Gautama placed in the lotus's pericarp.

Both older and modern versions of the Cloth Diagram of the Mendicant Leader do, however, contain a common feature of Śvetāmbara ritual diagrams—a pair of eyes that pop out at the top of the painting.[55] The eyes personify the entire cloth, suggesting the divinity of diagram. They also reference the ritual practice of viewing the divinities and the words of the *sūrimantra* to achieve the ultimate goal of the propitiation of the cloth: identification with the enlightened soul at the center of the painting, Gautama.

FIGURE 5.7. Diagram of fig. 5.6. showing the placement of (1) Sarasvatī, (2) Tribhuvan-asvāminī, (3) Lakṣmī, (4) Gaṇipiṭaka, (5) Gautama, seated below Mahāvīra, (6) Jayantā Devī, (7) Aparājitā Devī, (8) Jayā Devī, (9) Vijayā Devī, (10) Dikpāla Deva representing in the eight guardians of the directions, (11) Sūrya representing the nine planets, (12) Indrāṇī Devī representing the sixty-four *indrāṇīs*, (13) Indra representing the sixty-four *indras*, (14) Gomukha representing the twenty-four *yakṣas*, (15) Cakreśvarī representing the twenty-four *yakṣīs*, (16) Rohiṇī Devī representing the sixteen spell goddesses, (17) the guru's foot-prints, and (18) the nine treasures. Illustration by Lee-June Park.

When a monk looks at this cloth painting, he should be reminded that the nature of his soul is identical to Gautama's.

Lower-level protector deities and images of auspiciousness populate the space outside of the central circular image containing Gautama. The four "victory" goddesses of the Cloth Diagram of the Spell of Mahāvīra sit in the four corners of the diagram, with the blue Aparājitā in the upper-left corner, the white Jayā in the upper-right corner, the gold Jayantā in the lower left, and the red Vijayā in the lower right. Different sets of gods and goddesses—sixty-four kings of gods and sixty-four queens, twenty-four male and twenty-four female tutelary deities of each *jina*, sixteen spell goddesses, the eight guardians of the directions, and the nine planets—are represented by the first deity of the set. The footprints of the guru and golden vessels representing the nine treasures (*navanidhi*) of a universal emperor (*cakravartin*)[56]—houses, grains, ornaments, gems, clothing, the talent for divination, mines of precious metals, weapons, and the arts—are placed in the lower-right corner of the cloth.

The eight-petaled lotus at the focus of the cloth, then, contains the five sections of the *sūrimantra*[57] and the deities linked to each of these sections. Goddesses who in a non-Jain context would be associated with the "trinity" of Brahmā, Viṣṇu, and Śiva are the presiding deities (*adhiṣṭhāyaka*) of the first three sections of the *sūrimantra*, which are called *vidyā* because they are associated with goddesses. In the top petal of the cloth diagram sits the goddess Sarasvatī—the wife of Brahmā in a non-Jain contexts—riding a swan and holding her vina, a scripture, a lotus, and a rosary. Sarasvatī, associated with knowledge and the arts, presides over the first section of the mantra, termed the "Section of Knowledge," *vidyāpīṭha*, which is inscribed in the red ring around the lotus and is made up of a modified, shortened form of the *ṛddhi-maṅgala*:

> *oṃ namo jiṇāṇaṃ, oṃ namo ohijiṇāṇaṃ, oṃ namo paramohijiṇāṇaṃ, oṃ namo savvohijiṇāṇaṃ, oṃ namo aṇantohijiṇāṇaṃ, oṃ namo kevalīṇaṃ, oṃ namo bhavatthakevalīṇaṃ, oṃ namo abhavatthakevalīṇaṃ, oṃ namo cauddassapuvvīṇaṃ, oṃ namo dasapuvvīṇaṃ, oṃ namo ikkārasaṃgadhārīṇaṃ, oṃ namo kuṭṭhabudddhīṇaṃ, oṃ namo bījabuddhīṇaṃ, oṃ namo uggatavacaraṇakaraṇādhārīṇaṃ, oṃ namo gauyamassa laddhicintā, oṃ namo suhammasāmiṇo gaṇacintā, savvesiṃ eesiṃ namukkāraṃ kiccā jamiyaṃ vijjaṃ pauṃjāmi sāmevijjā pasijjau svāhā* || *vidyāpīṭham* || 12,000 *jāpaḥ* ||

> *oṃ* praise to praise the *jinas*, to the clairvoyant *jinas*, to the *jinas* who have supreme clairvoyance, who have complete clairvoyance, who have infinite clairvoyance, to the omniscient *jinas*, to the omniscient *jinas* who are still living, who are not living, to those who know the fourteen *pūrvas*, who know the ten *pūrvas*, who know eleven *aṅgas*, to those whose intel-

lects are like granaries and seeds from which ideas emerge, to those who can endure difficult fasts, to Gautama, to Sudharman Svāmin. Having undertaken all these praises, let whatever spell I employ be successful for me, *svāhā*. This is the *vidyāpītha*. Twelve thousand recitations.

This first section of the *sūrimantra* references many of the ideas about the *ṛddhi-maṅgala* found in texts from the early centuries CE to the present day. Śvetāmbaras have associated these superhuman powers with a deity of learning (Śrutadevatā, who is associated with Sarasvatī) since at least the time of the *Mahāniśīthasūtra*, perhaps because many of these powers are types of extraordinary knowledge (see chapter 1). This section of the mantra also references the *ṛddhis*' association with the disciples of the *tīrthaṅkaras*, linking the monk who recites these praises not only to scriptural knowledge, but also to early Jain ascetics. It praises two disciples of Mahāvīra: Gautama, who is famous for cultivating these superhuman powers,[58] and Sudharman, whom Śvetāmbaras recognize as the founder of their lineages.

The petal on the right contains the goddess of the three worlds, the four-armed Tribhuvanasvāminī, who sits on a cushioned stool in her abode, the Mānuṣontara Mountain, with her vehicle, a winged creature with the head of an elephant and the body of a tiger.[59] Tribhuvanasvāminī is reminiscent of the Śaiva goddess Tripurasundarī and presides over the second section of the mantra, the "Section of the Great Spell," the *mahāvidyāpīṭha*, written in the petal above her. This section contains the Prakrit "Spell of Bāhubali," the *bāhubalividyā*, that praises the strength and ascetic virtues of the son of Ṛṣabha.

The last three sections of the mantra contain different modifications of the syllable clusters that Jain monks interpret to represent various Jain teachings: *iri*, *kiri*, *giri*, *piri*, *siri*, *hiri*, and *āiri*. Śrī Lakṣmī Devī, the goddess associated with wealth who in a non-Jain context is understood as the wife of Viṣṇu, reigns over the third section of the mantra, the "Section of Lakṣmī," the *lakṣmīpītha*, also known as the "Section of the Secondary Spell," the *upavidyāpīṭha*. Śrī Devī is seen in the lowermost petal in her Gaja-Lakṣmī form, seated on a lotus and being bathed by two elephants. Her section of the mantra, inscribed in the petal on her right, makes the syllable combinations into feminine nouns—motion (*iriyā*), action (*kiriyā*), love (*piriyā*), praise (*giriyā*), wealth (*siriyā*), modesty (*hiriyā*), and conduct (*āyariyā*)—places them in the singular instrumental case, and adds invocations of Kālī to the end of the spell: *oṃ iriyāe kiriyāe giriyāe piriyāe siriyāe hiriyāe āyariyāe kāli kāli mahākāli.*

The elephant-headed, sixteen-armed personification of the scriptures, the *yakṣa* Gaṇipiṭaka, rides an elephant in the left petal and is reminiscent of the potbellied marker of auspiciousness, Gaṇeśa. Gaṇipiṭaka presides over the fourth section of the mantra, the *mantrapīṭha*, inscribed in gold on a red petal below him. This section contains the syllable clusters repeated and more invocations of Kālī: *oṃ iri iri kāli giri giri kāli kiri kiri kāli piri piri kāli siri siri kāli hiri hiri kāli āyariya āyariya kāli.*

Finally, at the center of the diagram, the primary divinity of the *sūrimantra*, Mahāvīra's disciple Gautama, sits cross-legged on a lotus, flanked by fly-whisk bearers, his left hand holding his robe and his right hand showing a gesture of teaching. A golden Mahāvīra floats above Gautama, and a mantra to Mahāvīra is inscribed in red: *oṃ srī mahāvīrasvāmipāragatāya namaḥ*, "Praise to Mahāvīra Svāmin, the one who has passed beyond rebirth." A mantra to Gautama is inscribed in gold at the bottom of the central circle: *oṃ śrī gautamasvāmisarvajñāya namaḥ*, "Praise to the one who has achieved omniscience, Gautama Svāmin." A red ring around Gautama contains the same Sanskrit mantra as found in the Cloth Diagram of the Spell of Mahāvīra that asks for the production of peace, satisfaction, prosperity, wealth, advancement, happiness, well-being, and great fortune for the recipient of this *paṭa*, Nandighoṣavijaya, whose lineage of gurus is listed as his initiatory guru, Ācārya Sūryodayasūri, whose guru was *Śubhaṅkarasūri*, whose guru was Yaśobhadrasūri, whose guru was Kastūrasūri, whose guru was Vijñānasūri, whose guru was Ācārya Nemisūri. Gautama presides over the fifth and final section of the mantra, painted in gold in the petal over his right shoulder. This section, the "Section of the King of Mantras," the *mantrādhirājapīṭha*, suffixes the word "*meru*" to each of the Prakrit syllable clusters: *irimeru, kirimeru, girmeru, pirmeru, sirimeru, hirimeru, āyarimeru.*

The iconography of this diagram, then, makes claims about lineage and the hierarchy of deities in the universe. By residing in the petals of the lotus, Sarasvatī, Tribhuvanasvāminī, and Lakṣmī become subservient not to their consorts, Brahmā, Śiva, or Viṣṇu, but to the true object of devotion at the center of the lotus, the monk Gautama. In addition, medieval and modern texts on the *sūrimantra* confirm that Gautama was the first disciple to receive the *sūrimantra* from Mahāvīra, so he represents an original transmission of this powerful invocation and a link between the present-day worshiper, who sits in front of him, and his guru and the last *tīrthaṅkara*, Mahāvīra, who sits above him.

WORSHIPING THE CLOTH DIAGRAM OF THE MANTRA OF THE MENDICANT LEADER

The daily and occasional worship ceremonies of the Cloth Diagram of the Mantra of the Mendicant Leader provide "Jain" interpretations of the common components of tantric ritual ceremonies. To understand the different ways *ācārya*s worship this diagram, Nandighoṣasūri directed me to a set of four Gujarati manuals on the *sūrimantra* compiled in 2013 by another member of Nemisūri's sublineage, Ācārya Somacandrasūri, to commemorate the completion of one of the few temples dedicated to a *sūrimantrapaṭa*, the Sūri Mahāmantra Mandir in the great pilgrimage center of Śvetāmbara Jainism in southern Gujarat, Palitana.[60] The temple houses a marble *sūrimantrapaṭa* under glass and icons to the five deities of the diagram along with icons of Ācārya Nemisūri and Ācārya Aśokacandrasūri, Nemisūri's disciple who completed the full multiday worship of all five sections of the *sūrimantra* (*pañcaprasthāna*) twenty-eight times and in whose memory the temple was established (*NĀV*, introduction).[61]

Somacandrasūri's set of manuals relies on Muni Jambūvijaya's collection of texts on the *sūrimantra* published in 1969 and 1977, the *Sūrimantrakalpasamuccayaḥ*. Somacandrasūri regularly cites Jambūvijaya's text, and he confirms that his ritual prescriptions mostly follow the manual of the fourteenth-century *ācārya* Rājaśekharasūri, with supplementations from texts on the *sūrimantra* by Siṃhatilakasūri, Jinaprabhasūri, and the Añcala Gaccha monk Merutuṅgasūri (fourteenth century).[62] In this way, Somacandrasūri, a Tapā Gaccha monk, draws upon the teachings of his own gurus and the published texts of monks from various lineages to create a version of the mantra and its worship unique to his lineage.[63] Somacandrasūri's modern manual shows that while monks of higher ranks will receive their lineage's versions of the *vardhamānavidyā* and *sūrimantra* in the handwriting of their initiatory guru upon their promotions, to know how to perform lengthy rites associated with these mantras, they will often rely on published sources.[64]

The first of Somacandrasūri's four manuals, the "Ritual for Daily Worship," the *Nitya Ārādhanā Vidhi* (*NAV*), outlines a ritual of daily propitiation of the Cloth Diagram of the Mantra of the Mendicant Leader that is very similar to the rite outlined above for the Cloth Diagram of the Spell of Mahāvīra. Somacandrasūri outlines in Gujarati sixty-one steps that constitute the daily worship of the cloth diagram. In this ceremony, the *ācārya* first purifies and protects himself and the space in the same way as he would for the worship of the Cloth Diagram of the Spell of Mahāvīra as previously outlined. He then sprinkles *vāsakṣepa* on the bound cloth diagram and his *sthāpanācārya*. He recites *oṃ hrīṃ namaḥ* and opens the cloth and places it in front of himself (*NĀV*, 1–5).

Following the preliminary purifications, the monk first makes offerings of *vāsakṣepa* to the deities that surround the main lotus of the diagram—the guardians of the directions, the nine planets, and the footprints of the guru. The *ācārya* sprinkles *vāsakṣepa* on the guardians of the directions and recites Sanskrit mantras of offering. He then sprinkles *vāsakṣepa* on the nine planets and requests that they and the guardians of the area (*kṣetrapāla*) grace the worship (*pūjāṃ pratīcchantu*). He requests that previous *ācārya*s, laypeople, and the four types of gods grace the worship. He sprinkles *vāsakṣepa* on the painted footprints and recites, in Sanskrit, the names of the gurus of his lineage. For Nandighoṣasūri, he begins by venerating Devasūri (1911–2002) and ends with his guru, Sūryodayasūri (d. 2012). He then opens the cloth bundle of his *sthāpanācārya*, sprinkles *vāsakṣepa* on the five shells inside the cloth that represent the Five Supreme Beings while reciting Sanskrit praises, and sprinkles *vāsakṣepa* in the eight directions inside the cloth while reciting the Prakrit *pañcanamaskāra* (*NĀV*, 5–8). In this way, he honors all Jain mendicants, in his lineage and beyond.

After honoring all the subsidiary divinities in the *paṭa*, the *ācārya* invites the five main deities of the *sūrimantra*, one by one, into the diagram by reciting mantras, displaying the gestures of invitation (*āhvānamudrā*), and so forth (see fig. 5.4) and sprinkling *vāsakṣepa* on them (*NĀV*, 1–10). The mantras the monk recites to invite the deities into the cloth demonstrate that these diagrams are also understood as embodiments of the Jina's Preaching Assembly. For example, the monk, showing the *āhvānamudrā* and then the *sthāpanāmudrā*, should recite in Sanskrit:

> Oh, Gautama Svāmin, who has all the superhuman powers! Come here, in the lotus of a thousand petals that is the Jina's Preaching Assembly! Please stay in this preaching assembly! (*NĀV*, 11)

After all the deities have been invited into the diagram and enlivened, the monk recites the entirety of the *sūrimantra* a number of times. Somacandrasūri recommends that the monk recite the mantra 108 times in order to destroy karma (*NĀV*, 24), but *ācārya*s confirmed to me that because of the length of the mantra, they do not often do so, preferring to recite it one, three, five, or twenty-seven times. Somacandrasūri outlines a specific way to recite the mantra five times in which the *ācārya* begins each recitation of the mantra with a different seed syllable and shows a different *mudrā* with each recitation:

> The seed-syllable *hrīṃ* and the *saubhāgyamudrā*
> The seed syllable *oṃ* and the *parameṣṭhimudrā*
> The seed syllable *śrī* and the *pravacanamudrā*
> The seed syllable *oṃ* and the *surabhimudrā*
> The seed syllable *oṃ* and the *añjalimudrā* (*NĀV*, 23).[65]

At the end of the propitiation of the cloth diagram, the monk should ask for forgiveness for mistakes and dismiss the deities from the diagram in the same way as he would for his worship of the Cloth Diagram of the Spell of Mahāvīra (*NĀV*, 24–25).

According to my interviews with a variety of *ācāryas*, performing a version of this daily ritual is an absolute requirement for *ācāryas*. It is meant to destroy karma and to ensure that the mendicant leader has the power to protect and lead his community of mendicants and lay followers. While this outline only approximates what *ācāryas* regularly perform, it provides an understanding of the daily rites of Śvetāmbara monks of higher ranks.

Worship Ceremony of the Five Sections of the Mantra of the Mendicant Leader

Along with their daily recitations of the mantra, some *ācāryas* also undertake the "Worship Ceremony of the Five Sections" (*pañcaprasthānavidhi*) that Nemisūri is said to have revived in the beginning of the twentieth century. These months-long ceremonies incorporate fasting, visualizations, recitation of the *sūrimantra*, the propitiation of a shrine of deities, and fire-offering ceremonies. *Ācāryas* who complete these ceremonies are celebrated: banners hung outside the temples where they spend their rainy-season retreats will advertise them as a "Sūrimantra Ārādhaka," or a "Worshiper of the *Sūrimantra*," partly because lay devotees will flock to these mendicant leaders to receive some of the sandalwood powder that has been consecrated in these complex rites.

In his Gujarati manual the *Śrīsūrimantrapañcaprasthānaprārambhavidhi* (*Śrī*), Somacandrasūri explains that it takes either eighty-three or eighty-four days in total to undertake this difficult worship ceremony, depending on one's guru's tradition. For the worship of each section, Somacandrasūri requires the establishment of a shrine, the recitation of the section of the mantra a certain number of times, the visualization of a certain color, and the display of particular hand gestures.[66] Each section also involves the performance of the six essential duties. The *ācārya* must perform the *kāyotsarga* meditative posture for the time it takes to recite either the Prakrit formula of praise to the twenty-four *tīrthaṅkaras* (*caturuviṃśati*) forty times or the *sūrimantra* 108 times. He also must undertake specific fasts, with the first and last day of the ceremony always requiring a complete fast (*upvāsa*) (*Śrī*, 16–28; table 5.2). "The results of the worship are great when one undertakes *tapas*, and little when one does not," Somacandrasūri declares in Sanskrit (*Śrī*, 17).

The worship of each of the five sections ideally begins or ends at auspicious times linked to the mythical origins of the mantra. Citing the *Mantrājarahasya*, Somacandrasūri describes how the first *tīrthaṅkara*, Ṛṣabha, imparted to his disciple Puṇḍarīka the original *sūrimantra* in three hundred verses; it remained this length until the eighth *tīrthaṅkara*, Candraprabha. However, after Candraprabha, as the mantra was passed from disciple to disciple, parts of it were gradually forgotten, until Mahāvīra eventually conveyed the remaining 2,100 syllables of the mantra to his disciple Gautama. It is for this reason that the worship of each section of the *sūrimantra* should begin or end on one of the five auspicious days (*kalyāṇaka*) of these *tīrthaṅkaras*, meaning the days of the conception, birth, renunciation, omniscience, or death of Ṛṣabha, Candraprabha, or Mahāvīra (*NĀV*, 8–9, citing *MRR*, vv. 87–91).

Nandighoṣasūri has performed the Worship Ceremony of the Five Sections every year since he became an *ācārya* in 2008. When I first met him in Ahmedabad in June 2013, he was in the middle of the eight-day-long worship of the fourth section of the *sūrimantra* dedicated to the elephant-headed Gaṇipiṭaka Yakṣa. In a small room attached to the temple's worship hall where he was residing with his two monk disciples before he began his rainy-season retreat, laypeople had established a shrine for this ceremony that included all the main deities of the *sūrimantra*. In figure 5.8, we can see Gaṇipiṭaka, the presiding deity of the fourth section, established at the front-and-center of the shrine, surrounded by icons of the other four deities connected to the other sections of the mantra. The three *tīrthaṅkaras* associated with the transmission of the *sūrimantra*—Ṛṣabha on the left, Mahāvīra in the middle, and Candraprabha on the right—are seated at the

TABLE 5.2. The required rites for the Worship Ceremony of the Five Sections according to the modern Tapā Gaccha monk Somacandrasūri*

Section of *sūrimantra* (*pīṭha, prasthāna*)	Presiding deity (*adhiṣṭhāyaka*)	Associated deities	Days of worship	Number of repetitions (*japa*)	Hand gestures (*mudrā*)	Required fasts (*tapovidhi*)
vidyāpīṭha	Goddess Brāhmī/ Sarasvatī		21	12,000	*parameṣṭhin* or *garuḍa*	• 2 days of eating no food (Guj. *upvās*) • 16 days of avoiding 10 types of modified foods (Guj. *nīvi*) • 3 days of eating unseasoned cereals (Guj. *āyambil*)
mahāvidyāpīṭha • *bāhubalividyā* • *mahāvidyā* • *vidyā*	Goddess Tribhuvanasvāminī		13 or 14	• *bāhubalividyā*: 12,000 • *mahāvidyā*: 16,000 • *vidyā*: 12,000	• *bāhubalividyā*: *yoni* • *mahāvidyā*: *saubhāyamudrā* • *vidyā*: *garuḍa*	• 2 *upvās* • 7 *nīvi* • 4 or 5 *āyambil*
upavidyāpīṭha	Goddess Śrī/ Lakṣmī	*jayādevīs*	25	12,000	*saubhāgya* or *parvata*	2 *upvās* 17 *nīvi* 6 *āyambil*
mantrapīṭha	God Gaṇipiṭaka Yakṣa		8	12,000	*parameṣṭhin*	2 *upvās* 5 *nīvi* 1 *āyambil*
mantrarājapīṭha	Mahāvīra's disciple Gautama	64 *indras* 16 *vidyādevīs* 24 *yakṣas* 24 *yakṣīs*	16	100,000	*parameṣṭhin* or *pravacana*	16 *āyambil* or 2 *upvās* 14 *āyambil*

Source: *Śrī*, 16–27

* Somacandrasūri's *sūrimantra* differs slightly from the one on Nandighoṣasūri's diagram in that it contains three different *vidyās* for the second section.

FIGURE 5.8. The shrine established for Nandighoṣasūri's worship of the fourth section of the *sūrimantra* dedicated to Gaṇipiṭaka Yakṣa. Ahmedabad, Gujarat, June 2013.

top of the shrine. Gautama, to whom his guru, Mahāvīra, passed the *sūrimantra*, sits below Mahāvīra. Gaṇipiṭaka sits at the feet of Gautama, which is fitting, since Gaṇipiṭaka embodies the scriptures that were passed from Mahāvīra to Gautama. In this shrine, the line from Mahāvīra to Gautama to Gaṇipiṭaka to the guru seated in front of the shrine can represent this scriptural transmission. Sarasvatī and Tribhuvanasvāminī, then, sit to the right of Gaṇipiṭaka, and Lakṣmī to his left. In the foreground of photo, we can see the progress the Nandighoṣasūri made in his worship: *vāsakṣepa* has been sprinkled on the different deities of the diagram and a clicker sits to the lower right of the *paṭa*, counting the number of times he recited the fourth section of the mantra.

For the completion of the worship of this fourth section, Nandighoṣasūri began each day's worship with the preliminary rites of purification and protection, and he then invited the five presiding deities of the *sūrimantra* into the cloth diagram with *mudrā*s and mantras, placing *vāsakṣepa* atop their images. He then spent a few hours each day reciting the fourth section of the mantra. In this way, for eight days, Nandighoṣasūri recited in soft voice (*upaṃśu*) the fourth section of the *sūrimantra*— *iri iri kāli kiri kiri kāli giri giri kāli*, and so on—twelve thousand times while sprinkling *vāsakṣepa* on the diagram.

The medieval texts on which Somacandrasūri bases his modern manual describe the meaning and purpose of the worship of this section. In these texts, Gaṇipiṭaka is the lord of the deities who are responsible for honoring and promulgating Jain teachings, and the syllables of this section of the mantra represent these deities. Quoting Jinaprabhasūri's *Sūrimantrabṛhatkalpavivaraṇa*, Rājaśekharasūri's *Sūrimantrakalpa*, and *Merutuṅgasūri Sūrimukhyamantrakalpa*, Somacandrasūri explains that *iri-iri* and *kirikiri* represent the ten *kalpendras*, the *vaimānika* gods who are chiefs of the heavens;[67] *girigiri* represents the *bhavanavāsin* deities; *piripiri* represents the *vyantara* deities; *sirisiri* represents the *jyotiṣka* deities; *hirihiri* represents Gaṇipiṭaka, the lord of the *indras*; and āyari represents the *laukāntika* deities, who are close to liberation and live near the top of the heavens (*SMKS*, 97, 119, 252, cited in *Śrī*, 24).[68] A Sanskrit hymn of praise to the *sūrimantra* by the fifteenth-century monk Munisundarasūri confirms the benefits Gaṇipiṭaka can confer as a commander of these powerful deities. Worship of him removes misfortunes for the whole mendicant community (*sakalasaṅgha*), Munisundarasūri proclaims.[69] It makes sense, then, that mendicant leaders should devote eight days a year to the propitiation of this boon-giving deity.

The Establishment of the Shrine and Concluding Fire Offerings for Goddess Lakṣmī

Ācāryas do not undertake these ceremonies entirely on their own, however. In the establishment of the shrine for worship of each of the sections of the *sūrimantra* and the fire offerings for the conclusion of the worship of the sections of the mantra dedicated to goddesses, lay and mendicant worshipers of all ranks together undertake rituals that are common to tantric worship ceremonies. When I returned to visit Nandighoṣasūri in July 2016 during his rainy-season retreat in Mumbai, I participated in the sanctification of his shrine for his twenty-five-day worship ceremony of Lakṣmī, who presides over the third section of the *sūrimantra*. To consecrate the shrine, about a dozen laymen and -women, having bathed and put on their *pūjā* clothes,[70] gathered at 6 a.m. at the temple's worship hall (*upāśraya*) where laypeople had established a shrine dedicated to the icons of the deities of the *sūrimantra* and other sacred images. In a two-hour-long ceremony, these laypeople joined Nandighoṣasūri and his two disciple monks in establishing next to the shrine two auspicious pots (*kumbha*), a lamp (*dīpaka*), the guardians of the area (*kṣetrapāla*), and the guru's footprints (*pādukā*).

The mantras and symbols used in the establishment of these objects linked them to common Jain symbols and teachings. For the establishment of the auspicious pots, Nandighoṣasūri, aided by two laymen, showed the "Lotus Gesture" (*padmamudrā*), recited softly to himself the third section of the *sūrimantra* dedicated to Lakṣmī, and filled with *vāsakṣepa* two silver pots decorated with the eight auspicious symbols of Śvetāmbara Jainism (*Śrī*, 2–3).[71] Laymen then covered the pots with green cloth, toped them with silver foil (Guj. *varakh*) and flowers, and placed them to the left of the shrine. To establish the lamp, Nandighoṣasūri recited three times a Sanskrit mantra asking that it shine in the darkness with the light of the five types of knowledge of an *arhat* (*Śrī*, 4).

Married laywomen who have a living son (*saubhāgyavatī*) then prepared a stand for the *kṣetrapāla*s, who were represented by foodstuffs. They used unbroken rice to form on a low wooden pedestal a symbol of the path to liberation commonly made for Śvetāmbara daily *pūjā*s. At the bottom of the platform, they formed an extended *svastika*, a *nandyāvarta*, that represents the four birth placements—plants and animals, deities, hell beings, and humans.[72] Above the *svastika*, they formed three circles of rice that represent the path to liberation, or right vision, knowledge, and conduct. Above these three piles of rice they formed a crescent moon symbolizing the result of the path, the abode of the liberated souls that is beyond karmic retribution and the suffering of the material world. On top of this diagram, they placed fruits, coconuts, and sweets representing the *kṣetrapāla*s. Nandighoṣasūri, showing the invitation gesture, recited Sanskrit mantras to invite these deities into the space, and laypeople then covered the foodstuffs with a white cloth and placed it next to the shrine.

Then, to pay homage to the gurus of his lineage, Nandighoṣasūri recited a Sanskrit mantra honoring all Jain gurus and laypeople and established coconuts decorated in silver (Guj. *varakh*) to represent the footprints of the guru on a low red platform ornamented with two piles of unbroken rice into which laywomen had traced *svastika*s (*Śrī*, 7–9). After the shrine was sanctified with objects of auspiciousness, protection, and one's lineage, Nandighoṣasūri invited the deities of the *sūrimantra* into their icons established in the shrine via mantras and the sprinkling of *vāsakṣepa* on the icons' heads. Laypeople placed flowers on these consecrated icons of Mahāvīra and the deities of the *sūrimantra*. The shrine was now ready for worship (fig. 5.9).

FIGURE 5.9. The shrine established for Nandighoṣasūri's worship of the third section of the *sūrimantra* dedicated to the goddess Lakṣmī, who sits at the center of the front row of the shrine, flanked by icons of three other deities of the *sūrimantra*. Each of the deities of the *sūrimantra* have their sections of the *sūrimantra* inscribed on copper plates placed in front of them. The flowers on the deities, the lamp, coconuts, and fruits bundled under a white cloth signal that the shrine has been sanctified. Mumbai, July 2016.

For each of the twenty-five days of the worship ceremony, Nandighoṣasūri remained seated in front of this shrine, his *paṭa* placed before him, for hours at a time. Day after day, after performing purification rites and the required daily recitation of the entire *sūrimantra*, he would repeat in a low voice the third section of the mantra associated with Lakṣmī—*iriyāe kīriyāe gīriyāe pīriyāe*, and so on—while sprinkling *vāsakṣepa* onto the center of the diagram. In his description of this section of the mantra, Somacandrasūri draws upon medieval texts to provide multiple meanings of these syllables. One interpretation claims that the syllable clusters up to āiri/āyari represent different goddesses, while the rest of the syllables represent the Jain ontological idea that matter is made up of substances (like souls) that have qualities (like infinite knowledge) that undergo modifications, or modes, when interacting with karma. Here, *kiri* represents substances (*dravya*), *giri* represents the qualities of those substances (*guṇa*), *piri* represents modifications of these substances (*paryāya*), *siri* represents the emergence of a new mode (*utpatti*), *hiri* represents the constancy of each quality (*dhrauvya*), and *āyari* represents the vanishing of a modification (*vigama*) (*Śrī*, 22).[73] In Nandighoṣasūri's recitation of this section, his rites lasted for twenty-five days, until he had recited these syllables twelve thousand times.

Once these twenty-five days had passed, to conclude the ceremony, laymen returned to the worship hall to use fire—the god Agni—to transport offerings to the goddesses associated with the *sūrimantra*. This fire offering (*āhuti*) is performed only to conclude the worship ceremonies of the sections of the *sūrimantra* associated with goddesses—namely, the first three sections presided over by Lakṣmī, Tribhuvanasvāminī, and Sarasvatī—and I was not able to observe them, because women are not allowed to participate. I can approximate what this offering entailed, however, with a summary of the rites described in a manual by the Tapā Gaccha monk Somasundaravijaya.

Triangular firepits are used for the worship of the goddesses of the *sūrimantra*.[74] At the outset of the rite, to ensure that the fire offerings will not harm living beings—a key reason why early Jain texts reject the Vedic sacrifice—the *ācārya* sprinkles *vāsakṣepa* and recites a mantra asking that the ceremony be free from the bad karma of violence and not harm single-sense living beings (*ekendriyajīva*) like fire.[75] The three goddesses of the *sūrimantra* are then invited into this firepit by means of Sanskrit mantras and *mudrā*s of invitation. The *ācārya* recites 108 times the root mantra of the fire offering—a Sanskrit mantra that offers scents (*gandha*), flowers (*puṣpa*), and fire offerings (*āhūti*) to Sarasvatī, Tribhuvanasvāminī, and Lakṣṃī and ends with the invocation *svāhā*. With each exclamation of *svāhā*, laymen offer to the fire ghee, powdered sap from the Gugal tree used as incense (Guj. gugaḷ), and sacrificial sticks (Guj. *samidh*), while other men present *vāsakṣepa* and flowers to the icons of these goddesses. The ceremony ends with a dismissal of the deities from the fire.[76]

The worship of the goddesses of the *sūrimantra* thus involve ritual components that, having been adapted from earlier Vedic models, became essential to tantric *maṇḍala* practice: the establishment of the ritual space with auspicious pots and a concluding rite of offerings into a fire. Charles

Orzech has identified an "emerging ritual synthesis" for esoteric Buddhists in Bodhiruci's *Scripture of the Mantra of Amoghapāśa's Miraculous Transformations*, composed in 707 CE. This text outlines how deities should be invited into a *maṇḍala* by the showing of *mudrās*, how the body and area of worship should be protected and sanctified through the recitation of mantras and the offering of "vases of *argya* water, incense, and flowers," and how the ceremony should conclude with a fire offering (*homa*).[77]

While Buddhist, Hindu, and Jain sources list a range of purposes for the propitiation of deities with *maṇḍalas* and fire offerings, from demonic expulsion, to expiation rites, to the identification of the worshiper with a supreme deity and ultimate liberation, the worship of the three goddesses of the *sūrimantra* primarily aids in goals related to prosperity.[78] Nandighoṣasūri confirmed that his twenty-five-day worship ceremony of Lakṣmī was for the laypeople involved in the establishment of the shrine and fire offering to gain the favor of this goddess of wealth and become more prosperous. The mantras of the fire offering to these goddesses reflect this goal. As the offerings progress, the *ācārya* recites a mantra that requests Agni to accept the offerings and grant the worldly goals of pacification, satisfaction, prosperity, wealth, advancement, and everything that one desires.[79] And in the root mantra to be recited in the fire offering, the goddesses who preside over sections of the mantra are designated as devotees (*bhakta*) of Gautama. Both in the iconography of the cloth diagram and in the mantras recited to them, these goddesses are designated as lower-level boon-givers. In this Jain vision of the cosmos, the deities of the *sūrimantra*—the male Gaṇipiṭaka and the three goddesses—can be compared to lay Jains, who use their wealth to support the people who are further along on the path to liberation: the monks, who identify with Gautama.

Becoming Gautama for Dīvālī

For *ācāryas* today, the most important section of the *sūrimantra*—the worship ceremony that is most intimately linked to the goal of liberation—is the fifth and final section dedicated to Mahāvīra's disciple Gautama, the central deity of the diagram and the transmitter of the *sūrimantra* for our age. The worship of this section lasts sixteen days, ending on Dīvālī so that it is completed on the day Mahāvīra was liberated and Gautama enlightened. In the *Kalpasūtra*, Mahāvīra's death and Gautama's omniscience are said to have taken place at the same moment in 527 BCE, on the new-moon day of the lunar month of Kārttika (October–November). On this date, Mahāvīra "died, went off, [quit] the world, cut asunder the ties of birth, old age, and death; [and] became a Siddha, a Buddha, a Mukta, a maker of the end (to all misery), finally liberated, freed from all pains."[80] Gautama, then, after his guru's death, was able to achieve the absolute detachment needed to destroy the karmas obscuring his soul's infinite knowledge. He "cut asunder the tie of friendship which he had for his master, and obtained the highest knowledge and intuition, called *kevala*, which is infinite, supreme, etc., complete, and full."[81] At that time, the eighteen kings that had gathered for Mahāvīra's passing proclaimed: "Since the light of intelligence is gone, let us make an illumination of material matter!"[82] Today, lay Śvetāmbara Jains cite this story as the reason why they light lamps for the celebration of "The Festival of Lights," Dīvālī, or Dīpāvalī, on the new-moon day of Kārttika each year.[83]

*Ācārya*s, however, have another way of observing this date. Dīvālī, as the day Mahāvīra died, commemorates the moment when Mahāvīra passed on the mendicant tradition to Gautama and his followers, so *ācārya*s use it to mark themselves as the true transmitters of the tradition. In 2013 in Ahmedabad and again in 2019 in Mumbai, I participated in the sanctification of Nandighoṣasūri's shrine for the ceremony of the fifth section of the *sūrimantra*. In the days leading up to the ceremony, laypeople organized the deities in the shrine in such a way to create a visual representation of the direct transmission of the *sūrimantra* from Mahāvīra, established at the top center of the shrine, to his disciple Gautama, seated at the bottom center, to the *ācārya* seated on the silver stool in front of the shrine. Smaller icons of Gautama filled much of the rest of the shrine (fig. 5.10). Sixteen days before Dīvālī, fewer than twenty laypeople gathered at the *upāśraya* early in the morning to sanctify and consecrate the ritual space in the way outlined above.

In both 2016 and 2019, from the day of the establishment of the shrine until Dīvālī, Nandighoṣasūri remained silent and undertook a fast called *āyambil* in Gujarati, eating only unseasoned rice or cereal once a day. When undertaking the other sections of the Worship of the Five Sections of the Sūrimantra, Nandighoṣasūri could receive lay visitors in the afternoon after his worship was complete, but for this final section, he had to remain as detached from the world as possible. In 2016, the shrine for the ceremony was established on a separate floor of the *upāśraya* from where the other monks slept, so Nandighoṣasūri remained alone, only being visited by his two disciple monks once a day to receive his meal that they had received from lay disciples.

Each day, Nandighoṣasūri undertook all the rites of purification, protection, and invocation before reciting the entirety of the *sūrimantra*, as he does

FIGURE 5.10. The shrine established for Nandighoṣasūri's worship of the fifth section of the *sūrimantra* is modeled after the Jina's Preaching Assembly, with three tiers. It establishes a line from Mahāvīra (center top and middle) to Gautama (center bottom) to the monk, who sits in front of the shrine. Mumbai, October 2019.

daily. He then remained in front of the shrine, repeating only the fifth section of the mantra, for hours at a time. In total, over this period of sixteen days, Nandighoṣasūri recited the final section of the *sūrimantra*—*oṃ irimeru kirimeru girimeru* and so forth—one hundred thousand times. Through this recitation, he moved himself closer to liberation. These syllables, Somacandrasūri confirms, represent the exact movement from worldly prosperity to renunciation and liberation that is outlined in the *sūrimantra* manuscript I found in the Digambara temple in Jaipur and in Jinaprabhasūri's *Sūrimantrabṛhatkalpavivaraṇa* (chapter 3). The path to liberation is present in these , from *irikiri*, which represents the wish-fulfilling tree, to *āyari*, which stands for the mendicant community and liberation (*Śrī*, 26–27). As Nandighoṣasūri recited these syllables, he would replicate Gautama's iconography, showing the "teaching gesture," the *pravacanamudrā*, and effectively establishing himself as a kind of Gautama in this world. Indeed, medieval and modern texts on the *sūrimantra* agree that by silently repeating the *sūrimantra*, the monk destroys karma and becomes equal (*tulya*) to Gautama himself (*NĀV*, 24; fig. 5.11).

At 4 a.m. on Dīvālī 2013 and 2019, Nandighoṣasūri completed this task and dismissed the deities from the ritual space; lay devotees returned to the temple to bow before the monk and receive a sprinkle of consecrated *vāsakṣepa* and one of the small icons of Gautama that had been sanctified in the rite. These icons of Gautama, established in the laypeople's shrines for daily worship, will be a reminder of Nandighoṣasūri's connection to the ascetic who gained superhuman powers and transmitted the teachings of Mahāvīra. From the organization of the shrine to the hand gestures of the monk to the words of the manual, the worship of the final section of the *sūrimantra* asserts that Nandighoṣasūri is not only connected to Gautama, he is identical to him.

In some ways, this recognition that the worshiper is identical to the object of worship parallels some of the mantra-based practices described in texts of tantric traditions, most famously the deity yoga (*devatāyoga*) of some traditions of Tibetan Buddhism.[84] In a well-known translation of two chapters of Tsong-kha-pa's fourteenth-century *Great Exposition of Secret Mantra*, Jeffrey Hopkins and the Dalai Lama present a performance of this deity yoga in the action and performance *tantra*s that parallels the worship of the Cloth Diagram of the Mantra of the Mendicant Leader. Just as Śvetāmbara monks can undertake rituals related to the *vardhamānavidyā* and *sūrimantra* only after receiving a cloth diagram in their promotions to higher ranks of mendicancy, the Dalai Lama confirms that in order to perform

FIGURE 5.11. Nandighoṣasūri shows the *pravacanamudrā* and the main icon of Gautama established for his worship of the fifth section of the *sūrimantra*, placed behind a sandalwood carving of all five deities of the *sūrimantra*. Ahmedabad, Gujarat, June and October 2013.

deity yoga, "at the least, one should have an initiation of Highest Yoga Tantra in a mandala of coloured powders or painted cloth."[85] Having undergone this initiation into a *maṇḍala*, one can undertake two forms of deity yoga: (1) meditation on a *buddha* in front of oneself who has been invited into a painting, sculpture, or imagined form by means of mantras, *mudrās*, and offerings of water, cloths, flowers, praises, and so on, or (2) meditation on oneself as a deity, or understanding the identical nature of oneself and the deity—emptiness—by imagining the sound of the deity's mantra, visualizing the letters of the mantra, visualizing the form of the deity, displaying the deity's *mudrās*, and seeing oneself as the deity.[86] Therefore, we can note two slightly different, though related, kinds of "divination" in texts of Śaiva, Vaiṣṇava, and Buddhist tantric traditions: the preliminary transformation into a deity through the imposition of mantras on one's body in order to perform the rites of worship, and the recognition of the identical nature of oneself and a deity without the necessary use of *nyāsa*, or the imposition of mantras on the body.[87]

Jains also undertake both kinds of divination. Since *ācāryas* bring about the latter form of divinization, becoming equal to Gautama, it is not entirely true that Jainism does not have "any cult parallel to that of the major Buddhist or Śaiva Tantric deities, with whom the practitioner identifies as a way of accessing the central liberating insight of the tradition."[88] In the centuries following the thirteenth century, because of Gautama's linkage to the *sūrimantra*, a significant Śvetāmbara cult did develop around this monk. According to some traditions, Gautama is said to have obtained twenty-eight superhuman powers, and the recitation of mantras that contain these powers—shortened versions of the *ṛddhi-maṅgala*—is said to engender eventual liberation.[89] Even so, the cult of Gautama does not seem to be as developed a component of the Jain path to liberation as the cults of some Śaiva and Buddhist tantric deities. In the lay and mendicant practices examined in the last two chapters, the divinity with whom Jains identify when performing mantra-based rituals is not a specific deity or personage, but an ideal: a purified soul.

TOWARD A HISTORY OF THE TANTRIC RITUALS OF JAIN MENDICANTS

At this point, there is no clear understanding of the history of the worship practices outlined in this chapter. Scholars do not know when, exactly, Jains began propitiating cloth diagrams inscribed with mantras. There is a gap of perhaps five hundred years between the earliest mention of the transmission of the *vardhamānavidyā* in the *Mahāniśīthasūtra* (see chapter 2) and the earliest known manual on the inscription of this spell on cloth diagrams, Siṃhatilakasūri's thirteenth-century *Vardhamānavidyākalpa*. Similarly, Haribhadrasūri may have mentioned the *sūrimantra* in the eighth century, but it is not until Siṃhatilakasūri's *Mantrarājarahasya* that a collection of prescriptions appears regarding the construction of the Cloth Diagram of the Mantra of the Mendicant Leader. Could it have been the case that Jains imparted the *vidyā* and mantra as early as the eighth century, but did not construct cloth diagrams until the thirteenth century? While we cannot answer this question definitively, we can show Jain knowledge of these types of diagrams in pre-thirteenth-century Jain texts on the cosmos and the Jina's Preaching Assembly. These texts suggest Jain knowledge of tantric ritual diagrams similar to the *sūrimantrapaṭa* and *vardhamānavidyāpaṭa* because of their description of four key goddesses common to Hindu, Jain, and Buddhist traditions: Jayā, Vijayā, Aparājitā, and Jayantī.

These four *jayādevīs* are often called the "Sisters of Tumburu," since they are described as the sisters of this manifestation of Śiva in mentions of what Alexis Sanderson terms "one of the earliest, perhaps the earliest, of the esoteric [aka tantric] Śaiva systems."[90] The earliest text of this system, the ca. seventh-century *Vīṇāśikhatantra*, describes the initiation into the cult of Tumburu and his sisters along with the daily rituals these initiates must undertake. In order to initiate into the cult, a devotee must first worship a square *maṇḍala* with a gate on each of its four sides. Tumburu, a four-faced manifestation of Śiva, sits at the center of the square, and at each gate sits one of his sisters: a white Jayā sits in the east, a red Vijayā is situated in the south, a yellow Jayantī is in the west, and a black Aparājitā sits in the north.[91] In the cloth diagrams of the *sūrimantra* and the *vardhamānavidyā*, the goddesses have the same coloring and positions. In addition, the four-headed Mahāvīra at the center of the *vardhamānavidyāpaṭa* recalls the descriptions of the Jina's Preaching Assembly, in which the *jina* faces all four directions, but it is also similar to a four-faced Tumburu seated between these four goddesses.

These goddesses are found not only in Śaiva and Jain sources, however. By the ninth century, their worship had spread to Southeast, East, and Central Asia.[92] In the Sanskrit Buddhist text the *Mañjuśriyamūlakalpa*, the *jayādevīs* became understood as the mothers of the bodhisattva of wisdom, Mañjuśrī, and were placed in the initiation *maṇḍala* of this cult, situated in the four directions surrounding the bodhisattva.[93] The founder of esoteric Buddhism in Japan, Kukai, also placed these goddesses facing the four directions in the Genzu, a version of the "Womb World Maṇḍala" that he brought from China to Japan in 806.[94] By the late medieval period, however, the goddesses had left India almost entirely: the cult of Tumburu seems to have died out, and the Buddhist traditions that had adopted their worship had left the subcontinent. While they are still worshiped in Japan, for example, as part of the Genzu *maṇḍala*,[95] existing scholarship suggests that they are no longer regularly worshiped as a group in India, and the Jain practices described in this chapter may be one of the few modern vestiges of this influential medieval cult.

But how old are these Jain practices? Since the cult of these goddesses seems to have flourished between the seventh and ninth centuries, did the Jain worship of these goddesses on cloth diagrams also develop during this time period? If so, why is there no known evidence of their worship? Buddhist and Hindu texts from the seventh to ninth centuries outline *maṇḍala*s with the *jayādevī*s surrounding the main object of reverence, so why is there no evidence of similar Jain diagrams until the thirteenth century?

Jain cosmological and mythological texts may provide evidence that pre-thirteenth-century Jains were at least aware of these types of diagrams. The earliest detailed description of the Jain cosmos, the Śvetāmbara *āgama Jīvājīvābhigamasūtra* that has been dated to the fourth century CE,[96] explains that the area of the universe where humans reside, the Middle World, is made up a series of concentric islands, each surrounded by an ocean. The island on which humans reside, Jambūdvīpa, has Mount Meru at its center, surrounded by four gates (*jagati*). When describing the doors to the gates surrounding this mountain at the center of the island, the *Jīvājīvābhigamasūtra* places the description in the mouth of Mahāvīra, who has just been asked a question by Gautama:

> *jaṃbuddīvassa ṇaṃ bhaṃte! dīvassa kati dārā paṇṇatta?*
> *goyamā! cattāri dārā paṇṇattā taṃ jahā—vijae vejayaṃte jayaṃte aparājie*
> [Gautama:] Oh Lord! How many doors are there on the island called Jambūdvīpa?
> [Mahāvīra]: Oh Gautama! There are four doors, which are: Vijaya, Vaijayanta, Jayanta and Aparājita. (*Jīvājīvābhigamasūtra, sūtra* 227)[97]

These names of the doors—masculine forms of the names of the *jayādevīs*—are standard in both Śvetāmbara and Digambara literature. The Śvetāmbara canonical text the *Jambūdvīpaprajñapti* 1.38 identifies *vijaya, vaijayanta, jayanta*, and *aparājita (terms for "victory")* as the names for the doors positioned in the four cardinal direction surrounding Mount Meru, as does the Digambara text on the Jain cosmos and universal history, the *Trilokaprajñapti* (*TP* 4.15).

The *jayādevī*s also found their way into descriptions of the Jina's Preaching Assembly. While they do not feature in the earliest description of the assembly in the *Āvaśyakaniryukti*, they do in the *Triṣaṣtiśalākāpuruṣacarita*, a version of the history of the universe by the twelfth-century Śvetāmbara Hemacandrasūri. In this text, in Ṛṣabha's Preaching Assembly,

> at the four gates of the second wall . . . beginning in the east, stood the goddesses Jayā, Vijayā, Ajitā and Aparājitā, each with one hand in the "fear-not" gesture (*abhayamudrā*) and the other three hands carrying the noose, the goad and the hammer. On the last rampart at each gate, stood a Tumburu as a door-keeper, carrying a skull-crowned club (*khaṭvāṅga*) having a garland of human skulls, and adorned with a coronet of matted hair.[98]

Here, Hemacandrasūri evinces his knowledge of the cult of Tumburu and his sisters and relegates Tumburu to the lowly position of doorkeeper of the gathering for the true object of worship, the *jina*.

Could the composer of the *Jīvājīvābhigamasūtra* also have been familiar with the cult of Tumburu and his sisters, or at least with ritual diagrams that contain the *jayādevīs*? Could ritual diagrams that place the *jayādevīs* as protectors of the directions have influenced Jain understandings of the makeup of the cosmos? If this is the case, then it suggests either that the cult of the *jayādevīs* as guardians of the directions was in existence as early as the fourth century or that this portion of the *Jīvājīvābhigamasūtra* dates much later than the fourth century. As previously noted, several scholars in the past few decades have rightly critiqued the accepted dating of the Śvetāmbara *āgamas*, which is often based on the idea that "the Canon of the white-robed has in essence remained unchanged" since the Council of Valabhi in Gujarat in the fifth century CE brought Jain monks together to codify their scriptures.[99] But little work has been done to develop a new understanding of the chronology of Jain texts. This passage in the *Jīvājīvabhigamasūtra* thus might be one piece of evidence to show the later dating of passages of the "canon."

Ritual diagrams did not necessarily influence Jain understandings of the cosmos, however. Male deities with similar names as the doors to the gates surrounding Mount Meru are already mentioned as early as the Sanskrit text on polity, the *Arthaśāstra*, whose final redaction has been placed between the second and third centuries CE. The section of the text that describes the ideal layout of a fort encourages the king to build in the middle of the city "shrines for Aparājita, Apratihata, Jayanta, and Vaijayanta, and abodes for Śiva, Vaiśravaṇa, Aśvins, Śrī, and Madirā."[100] The shrines to Aparājita, etc. are not necessarily positioned in the four directions, however, since the text explains that "the presiding deities of the gates are Brahmā, Indra, Yama, and Senāpati."[101] In short, it is not clear how, exactly, Jains developed the idea that Aparājita, etc. are the names of the doors facing the four directions on Jambūdvīpa.

This exercise does, however, highlight a potentially fruitful avenue of future research: using the material culture of Jainism to date—or at least to historicize and contextualize—parts of Jain scriptures that have been notoriously difficult to place in time and space.[102] John Cort has encouraged scholars to take up this methodology of letting material culture dictate how and what scholars of religion read, asking a simple question: "If we look first at the objects, and base our attempts at understanding [a religion] on them, will we emerge from our study with a different view of the tradition?"[103] Asking this question with regard to the objects of worship examined in this chapter provides a resounding yes for an answer. Beginning an examination of Jain mendicancy with the materials Śvetāmbara monks use—the *vāsakṣepa* with which many lay Śvetāmbara Jains have been sprinkled and the cloth diagrams and shrines that help sanctify this powder—not only provides new understandings of the formation of Jain ideas about the cosmos and the Jina's Preaching Assembly, but also challenges common accounts of Jain ascetics as austere renunciants who shun image worship and are "forbidden from even folding their hands and bowing to the gods in the temple."[104] The rituals outlined in this chapter confirm that many Jain monks lead lives filled with the worship of physical objects that in many ways parallel the daily ritual practices of initiates of tantric traditions.

This is not to say, however, that the sprinkling of *vāsakṣepa* on cloth diagrams should be seen as contradictory to renouncing the life of a householder. These practices have become popular in part *because* Jain monks have become homeless and need lay support. They include something not found in the equivalent Śaiva and Buddhist "divinization" rites: the consecration of *vāsakṣepa* to be used to give blessings to laypeople and to consecrate temples, signaling that these rites were developed in part to encourage lay-mendicant relationships and to establish Jain mendicants as leaders of certain communities. Many of the icons used for the establishment of the shrines used in the Worship of the Five Sections of the Mantra of the Mendicant Leader are also auctioned off to laypeople after the completion of the ceremonies, which brings funds to mendicant communities and the temples that house them. Therefore, while Jain monks may well have been propitiating their cloth diagrams using mantras, *mudrā*s, and visualization techniques continuously from at least the time of the earliest known mention of the *sūrimantra* in the eighth century to the present day, the two time periods when the production of texts on these rituals explodes mark periods of significant fracture in the mendicant community, when an increasing number of mendicant lineages needed to justify themselves as transmitters of the tradition of Mahāvīra: from the thirteenth to fifteenth centuries, and from the twentieth to twenty-first centuries. As mendicant lineages continue to grow and split, upcoming decades will surely usher in the increased production of texts, images, and temples dedicated to the Cloth Diagram of the Spell of Mahāvīra and the Cloth Diagram of the Mantra of the Mendicant Leader.

CONCLUSION

The Past Lives of Modern Mantras

THE *ṚDDHI-MAṆGALA*—FORTY-FOUR LINES of praise first found as an auspicious invocation in a text from the first half of the first millennium—is used not only in the rituals of initiation and daily worship outlined in the chapters of this book. Digambara laypeople recite a version of these Prakrit praises to ascetics with superhuman powers every morning, since the praises constitute a section of the daily ritual formula recited when Digambaras go to the temple to offer eight substances to the icon of a *jina*.[1] Digambara *ācārya*s recite the praises every two weeks, since they constitute part of one of their repentance formulas, the *pākṣikapratikramaṇa*.[2] The litany also constitutes a large section of the Digambara *bṛhadśāntimantra*, the invocation some devotees recite daily and that mendicants will sing during the performance of *abhiṣeka* ceremonies to pacify negative influences in people's lives (*śāntidhārā*).[3] In addition, while this book focuses on a few important *yantra*s that contain these praises—specifically, the Ring of Disciples (*gaṇadharavalaya*), the Wheel of the Liberated Soul (*siddhacakra*), the Cloth Diagram of the Spell of Mahāvīra (*vardhamānavidyāpaṭa*), and the Cloth Diagram of the Mantra of the Mendicant Leader (*sūrimantrapuṭa*)—versions of litany fill many more *yantra*s than were outlined in previous pages.[4] Since these modern uses of the *ṛddhi-maṅgala* have in many ways emerged from the premodern initiation and daily worship practices outlined in this book, looking at the impact and histories of some of these practices is a good way to review the developments of the preceding chapters.

Today, lay and mendicant Jains often focus on the practical uses of the versions of the *ṛddhi-maṅgala*. When I would spend afternoons sitting with

Digambara and Śvetāmbara mendicants, I was quite surprised at how often laypeople would approach the mendicants to ask for mantras to help them with a variety of problems, from bankruptcy to infertility. In September 2013, during one of my visits to the Jain pilgrimage site Palitana in Gujarat, I had gone to visit a prominent Śvetāmbara *ācārya* to ask him about his use of the *sūrimantra*. Seated at the feet of this monk in a worship hall, I was working through a series of questions about the monk's daily worship of the *sūrimantrapaṭa* when a layman with a pained expression approached the monk, halting our conversation. After leaning over in reverence and pronouncing the traditional greeting of a Śvetāmbara monk—*matthaeṇa vaṃdāmi*—"I honor you with my [bowed] head," the man confided that he had been having trouble sleeping for months. He needed a remedy. The monk, sitting cross-legged and straight-backed on his wooden platform, recited the thirty-fourth line of the *ṛddhi-maṅgala* of the *Ṣaṭkhaṇḍāgama: ṇamo savvosahipattāṇaṃ*, "praise to those who can heal through all parts of their bodies." He instructed the man to recite the mantra 108 times when trying to fall asleep. "*ṇamo*. . . ?" Not knowing Prakrit, the devotee initially had difficulty in pronouncing the mantra, so the monk carefully wrote the words on a slip of paper, sprinkled the man with *vāsakṣepa*, and turned back to our conversation.

In other visits to temples and shops, I found the *ṛddhi-maṅgala* in *yantra*s representing the verses of one of the most popular Jain hymns of praise, the *Bhaktāmarastotra* (ca. sixth to thirteenth centuries CE?). Indeed, the *ṛddhi-maṅgala*'s most common use today in conjunction with this Sanskrit poem that honors the first *tīrthaṅkara*, Ṛṣabha. Many practicing Jains today—both Digambara and Śvetāmbara—can recite at least a few of the Sanskrit verses of this praise poem, with Digambaras accepting forty-eight verses and Śvetāmbaras accepting forty-four. Followers of all sects of Jainism, however, accept a set of forty-eight *yantra*s that represent the poem. In each of these *yantra*s, one line of the *Bhaktāmarastotra*, one mantra, and one line of the *ṛddhi-maṅgala*, expanded to forty-eight lines, are inscribed. Visitors to Jain temples will find dozens of ritual manuals that outline the different effects of reciting the contents of these *yantra*s, which are found installed in Jain homes and temple shrines throughout India. In the past twenty years, monks have commissioned several temples dedicated to the *Bhaktāmarastora* and its attendant forty-eight *yantras*. Śvetāmbara temples in Gujarat include one commissioned by (then) Upādhyāya Maṇiprabhasāgara in Palitana, one commissioned by Ācārya Rājayaśasūri in Bharuch, one commissioned by disciples of Ācārya Surendrasūri in Shankheshwar, and one commissioned by disciples of Ācārya Rāmacandrasūri at Sammet Shikhar.

Digambara temples include one commissioned by Ācārya Jñānasāgara in Vehalna, near Muzaffarnagar, and one commissioned by Ācārya Vimalasāgara at Sammet Shikhar.

But the opportunities to encounter the forty-eight *yantras* are not limited to the physical space of the temple. Jains and non-Jains are also increasingly encountering these *yantras* through the online presence of the businesswoman whom we met at the outset of this book, Manju Jain, who has found great success in promoting her book *Jaina Method of Curing* on her website and other social media platforms. Manju Jain, like many Jains, grew up reciting the *Bhaktāmarastotra*, and as an adult she became a devoted follower of the Terāpanthī Digambara monk Ācārya Vidyāsāgara. In more recent years, she has supported the publication of her guru's teachings, writing her first book, *Saadhak: A Journey of Divine Image (2009)*, on some of his discourses, and then becoming inspired to research the healing effects of the *Bhaktāmarastotra* and its *yantras*. The result of this research, *Jaina Method of Curing* (2011), draws upon Hindi-language popular literature to document the problems that can be solved by reciting each verse of the poem and by pouring water over the poem's metal *yantras*. In her book, she replicates the *yantras* and the miraculous stories associated with each verse that are given in the Digambara monk Kāmakumāranandī's publication *Kāvya kā Kariśmā*. She also draws upon Piyush Pandit's ritual manual *Bhaktāmar Vidhān* to outline how practitioners should offer nuts to a circular diagram of powder as they recite each verse, mantra, and *ṛddhi*.[5]

On July 10, 2016, I attended an English-language workshop in Mumbai on the use of the *Bhaktāmarastotra* given by one of Manju Jain's pupils. The eight-hour workshop was designed, according to promotional materials, for participants to "connect with universal frequencies" in order to "become champions of life." When I arrived at the conference hall, I and a couple dozen other participants—doctors, businesspeople, retirees, students, and owners of homeopathic clinics—paid the fee of four thousand rupees and filed into the conference room as speakers blared a tape of a man repeating "*oṃ*." Women and men were evenly represented, and the participants' ages ranged from a four-year-old child joining his parents to an elderly man, perhaps in his early eighties. Many of the participants were Jains who had grown up reciting the *Bhaktāmarastotra*—both Śvetāmbaras and Digambaras were represented—but about half the participants were non-Jain. A lot of the participants had found the workshop through word of mouth on social media and had signed up for a variety of reasons, many of them regarding health or monetary concerns.

The leader of the workshop, Jigar Mehtalia, a Śvetāmbara in his thirties, had first come to the recitation of the *Bhaktāmarastotra* through the recommendation of a Jain monk, the Śvetāmbara *muni* Jinacandra (Bandhu Tripuṭī), who had recommended that he chant the sixth verse associated with developing one's IQ and memory. At this Jain monk's urging, every day for sixth months, Mehtalia recited the verse twenty-one times and chanted its associated *ṛddhi* 108 times: *oṃ arhaṃ ṇamo kuṭṭhabuddhīṇāṃ*, "praise to those whose intellects are like granaries that store the seeds of teachings."[6] In the workshop, however, Mehtalia did not stress the "Jain" nature of the *Bhaktāmarastotra*. Instead, he systematically worked through *Jaina Method of Curing*, which he had come to about six months before the workshop after a friend sent him a link to one of Manju Jain's videos. Working through this book, he led us in the recitation of each verse, mantra, and *ṛddhi*, and he supplemented our practice with inspirational videos on the power of sound vibrations. Throughout the day, the majority of the attendees' questions related to which verse, *ṛddhi*, and mantra one should recite for specific problems that might not be mentioned in the book.

A question related to Jain traditions did, however, come from an older Śvetāmbara Jain couple in the audience. Noting that *Jaina Method of Curing* follows the Digambara tradition, which insists that the *Bhaktāmarastotra* contains forty-eight verses, the couple inquired about the Śvetāmbara tradition they had grown up with, which recognizes a *Bhaktāmarastotra* of forty-four lines. Having spent hours in the conference hall being told about the power of a single syllable to change the outcomes of events, Śvetāmbara attendees were rightly concerned that the forty-eight-versed *Bhaktāmara*, or at least the four extra verses, might be inauthentic and ineffective. Mehtalia was not interested in the history of the sectarian development of these two versions of the poem, however. He assured his participants that both Digambaras and Śvetāmbaras associate forty-eight *yantra*s with the *Bhaktāmarastotra*, so they should follow the tradition of forty-eight verses when using the *Bhaktāmarastotra* for healing and other worldly purposes.

For Manju Jain, the layman who could not sleep, and the attendees of the conference on the *Bhaktāmarastotra*, their confidence in the power of the recitations came from the testimony of their peers and community leaders. The layman who could not sleep likely left his meeting with the Śvetāmbara *ācārya* relieved because a prominent monk—an *ācārya*—was confident in the mantra's powers. Similarly, Manju Jain and Jigar Mehtalia came to the *ṛddhi-maṅgala* through the advice of monks. Evidently, confidence in the effectiveness of reciting the forty-eight *ṛddhi*s does not require an understanding of their meaning or history, no more than one needs a pharmacological survey of antibiotics when taking routine medication for an ear infection. Those willing to look further into the development of the *ṛddhi*s, however, will find themselves rewarded with an understanding not only of the "what" of the *ṛddhi-maṅgala*, but also the "how" and the "why" of its powers, vis-à-vis the Jain path to liberation.

THE LIFE OF THE *ṚDDHI-MAṄGALA*

I have argued that the *ṛddhi-maṅgala* rose to prominence in the medieval period through the tantricization of the ascetic Jain path to liberation. What this means is the development and integration of the components of a tantric ritual syntax from, and into, an ascetic one. In the orthodox account of the Jain path to liberation, the fourth- to fifth-century *Tattvārthasūtra*, a soul achieves omniscience, bliss, and freedom from the cycle of rebirth through the systematic destruction of karma through asceticism (*tapas*). Twelve acts constitute *tapas*: six external (fasting, limiting one's food, restricting what one eats, abstaining from delicious food, sleeping alone, and avoiding temptation), and six internal (expiation of faults, respecting mendicants, serving mendicants, study, meditation, and ignoring the needs of the body). These acts might be called the components of a Jain ritual syntax of asceticism. Ascetic initiation through the adoption of the five vows of a mendicant and the subsequent performance of the six essential duties of a mendicant are part of this syntax and are outlined in texts from the early centuries BCE and CE.

We can compare this ascetic path to liberation with the ritual syntax of early tantric traditions that Dominic Goodall and Harunaga Isaacson have outlined. Drawing upon Śaiva and Buddhist texts from the sixth-eighth centuries, they have argued that the components of this syntax include varied uses of mantras for the attainment of the "shared goals" of tantric systems: *bhukti*, worldly success and the attainment of superhuman powers (*siddhi*) like becoming a possessor of spells (*vidyādhara*); and *mukti*, or omniscience and liberation. These mantras are often "repeated nonsense words (some of which resemble imperatives)," and they often include inflections (*jāti*) such as *phaṭ* and *huṃ*. In tantric traditions, mantras are linked to the elements, colors, shapes, and body parts. They are used in the "shared ritual technology" of fire rites and magical rites, in the showing of *mudrā*s, and in "the pervasive use of the *maṇḍala*," especially in a liberating initiation. They are also placed on the body for *sakalīkaraṇa*—so that the initiate can become identical to God—and they are repeated at length (*japa*). Early tantric traditions also developed a "social religion" that included a hierarchy of initiates and a sequence of promotions, with the *ācārya* responsible for initiations.[7] When all these aforementioned components are grouped together into a soteriological system, scholars call it a "tantric tradition."

Jains, from perhaps the eighth century onward, were able to seamlessly integrate the above-noted components of a tantric ritual syntax into their existing ascetic path to liberation because many of these components already existed, in different forms, in their tradition. The pre-sixth-century Jain ascetic path to liberation included the development of superhuman powers (such as becoming a *vidyādhara*), invocations that destroyed karma, *maṇḍala*-like circular diagrams that represented the ideals of the tradition, a non-Vedic soteriological initiation into a hierarchy of initiates led by an *ācārya*, and meditative rites that acknowledged the identical nature of one's soul and the "godhead" of Jainism, the enlightened soul. Examining instances of this natural integration of the tantric path into the ascetic path of liberation in Jain sources can encourage scholars to examine more specific ways in which some Śaiva, Vaiṣṇava, and Buddhist tantric practices also emerged from earlier ascetic ones.

The *ṛddhi-maṅgala*, a Prakrit litany of forty-four lines first found in the *Ṣaṭkhaṇḍāgama*, became a perfect tool to use to tantricize Jain mendicant initiations and daily ritual practices because of its connection to the superhuman powers of the disciples of the twenty-four enlightened founders of Jainism. Texts from the first half of the first millennium agree that the destruction of karma obscuring the soul's innate qualities of infinite energy, power, and knowledge leads to the manifestation of superhuman powers of intellect, healing, physical strength, bodily transformation, the ability to undertake extreme austerities, the abilities to transform speech or food from ordinary to sweet, and the powers to make food and dwellings inexhaustible. In his commentary on the *ṛddhi-maṅgala* in the early ninth-century *Dhavalā*, the Digambara monk Vīrasena draws upon earlier Jain literature to describe how the original disciples of the twenty-four *tīrthaṅkara*s possessed these powers. Praising advanced souls like these disciples, Vīrasena explains, destroys karma that inhibits the successful reading of a text. Because the *ṛddhi-maṅgala* was, in this way, associated with the disciples of the *tīrthaṅkara*s and their acquisition of superhuman powers through the destruction of karma, during the medieval period the litany began to be inscribed on diagrams used for mendicant initiations, promotions, and daily worship practices designed to grant Jains extraordinary powers and eventual liberation.

By at least the time of the Śvetāmbara Haribhadrasūri's eighth-century *Pañcāśakaprakaraṇa* and the Digambara Jinasena's ninth-century *Ādipurāṇa*, making offerings to a *maṇḍala*-like ritual diagram became a crucial component of one's initiation into a life of mendicancy. In both of these texts, the diagram to be constructed for the initiation ceremony is understood to be a model of an image found in early Jain texts: the Jina's Preaching Assembly, in which a newly enlightened *jina* gives his first teaching to all the living beings in the cosmos seated around him in three concentric circles. For Digambaras, many of the earliest known descriptions of the exact contents of these models of the assembly are found in texts on temple image consecration, since the consecration of a temple image is partially modeled on the initiation of a living monk.

Other early descriptions of ritual diagrams are found in tenth- to twelfth-century texts on meditation, since these texts define the ritual use of *yantras* as types of virtuous meditation (*dharmadhyāna*). In fact, the earliest known description of the diagram Digambaras honor on the eve of their initiations—the Ring of Disciples—is found in the eleventh-century Digambara monk Amitagati's section on meditation in his *Śrāvākācāra*. This text outlines the components of the forty-eight-petaled Ring of Disciples diagram that uses the *ṛddhi-maṅgala* to create a figure that is reminiscent of Ṛṣabha's Preaching Assembly. The center of the diagram is filled with a hexagram at the center of which a praise to an omniscient being, an *arhat*, is inscribed. In all likelihood the *arhat* represents Ṛsabha, because his tutelary goddess, Apraticakrā, is called into the six corners of the figure surrounding him via the *apratcakrā*-mantra that names the diagram as unsurpassable (*vicakra*): *apraticakre phaṭ vicakrāya svāhā*. Six more goddesses surround the six-cornered figure: Śrī, Hrī, Dhṛti, Kīrti, Buddhi, and Lakṣmī. With Ṛṣabha thus established at the center of this diagram, the *ṛddhi-maṅgala* plus four additional lines fill the forty-eight petals encircling this central image, invoking the disciples of the *jina*, who sit in concentric circles around the Ṛṣabha to hear him give his first teachings (*Śrā* 15.46–48). To this day, Digambaras, on the eve of their initiations into a life of mendicancy, make offerings of coconuts to a colored Ring of Disciples diagram, symbolically joining the assembly of disciples to hear the teachings of the *jina*.

By at least the thirteenth century, Śvetāmbaras began to inscribe this *ṛddhi-maṅgala*-filled diagram on cloth to create the *sūrimantrapaṭa* that is gifted to monks upon their promotions to the highest rank of mendicancy. Śvetāmbara image-worshiping *ācāryas* up to the present day use this painted cloth in their daily rituals, explicitly calling the diagram the Jina's Preaching Assembly. They use mantras and *mudrās* to purify and divinize themselves prior to making offerings of scented sandalwood powder (*vāsakṣepa*) to the *sūrimantrapaṭa*, concluding some rites with a fire offering. While modern diagrams do not contain the *apraticakrā*-mantra, some of the earliest known Sanskrit manuals on these diagrams—such as Siṃhatilakasūri's thirteenth-century *Mantrarājarahasya* and Jinaprabhasūri's fourteenth-century *Sūrimantrabṛhatkalpavivaraṇa*—do outline some forms of the cloth diagram that match the Digambara Ring of Disciples diagram, with the *apraticakrā*-mantra at its center.

THE *ṚDDHI-MAṄGALA* AND THE *BHAKTĀMARASTOTRA*

The use of the *ṛddhi-maṅgala* in Digambara and Śvetāmbara diagrams of initiation, promotion, and daily worship eventually led Jain mendicants to connect the litany with the *Bhaktāmarastotra*. The descriptions of Ṛṣabha's virtues, as contained in the *Bhaktāmarastotra*, naturally complemented the forty-eight praises of the *ṛddhi-maṅgala*, which called the disciples into a diagram that is reminiscent of Ṛṣabha's preaching assembly. To my knowledge, the *ṛddhi-maṅgala* was first connected to the *Bhaktāmarastotra* in the fourteenth century, when the poem began its ascent to the status of one of the most popular Jain hymns of praise. While the poem is often dated to the sixth-seventh centuries CE, and both Digambaras and Śvetāmbaras attribute it to the Jain monk Mānatuṅga, whose recitation of its verses allowed him to escape an unfair imprisonment, very little can be said about the history of the *Bhaktāmarastotra* before the thirteenth century, and there is no solid evidence that it was composed before then.[8] The earliest hagiography of Mānatuṅga, the *Prabhāvakacarita* by the Śvetāmbara monk Prabhācandrasūri, was composed in 1277 CE, and the earliest commentary on the hymn was not completed until the fourteenth century.[9] It is not until this time—the end of the fourteenth century—that the *Bhaktāmarastotra* became associated with mantras and various rituals that could effect miraculous results.

In 1369, a Śvetāmbara monk from the Rudrapallīya Gaccha named Guṇākarasūri composed in Sanskrit the most famous commentary (*vṛtti*) on the *Bhaktāmarastotra* known today, at least among Śvetāmbaras.[10] This commentary associates different verses of the poem with different mantras, or spells, and it includes twenty-eight tales of how devotees recited these verses and invocations to overcome obstacles such as being stuck in a well, being paralyzed, and being lost in the jungle.[11] Thirteen of these mantras contain parts of the *ṛddhi-maṅgala*, or the first section of the *sūrimantra*. Guṇākarasūri uses lines of what he explicitly calls the *sūrimantra* to create different powerful invocations. The first invocation is connected to the seventh verse of the hymn. In the story related to this verse, Guṇākarasūri recounts how a *yogin* became infuriated with two Jain merchants when they refused to worship him, and so he covered their homes in dust, plunging them into darkness. The merchants were freed from this dust by reciting the seventh verse of the *Bhaktāmarastotra*, along with the following mantra:

> *oṃ hrāṃ hrīṃ hrūṃ ṛṣabhaśāntidhṛtikīrtikāntibuddhilakṣmīhrīṃ apraticakre phaṭ vicakrāya svāhā (Bhaktāmara, 20).*[12]

A variant of this mantra is at the center of the Ring of Disciples diagram, providing another piece of evidence for the historical link between the Śvetāmbara *sūrimantra* and the Digambara Ring of Disciples. The mantra pays homage to the "unassailable wheel" (*vicakra*), which refers to the hexagram at the center of the diagram, and it invokes Ṛsabha, Apraticakrā, and goddesses at the center of the Ring of Disciples—Hrī, Dhṛti, Kīrti, Buddhi, and Lakṣmī—plus Śāntī and Kāntī.

Other parts of the *ṛddhi-maṅgala* are associated with verses 12 through 19 of the *Bhaktāmarastotra*:

> Verse 12, Spell of Sarasvatī (*sarasvatīvidyā*): *oṃ hrīṃ* praise to those who know the fourteen *pūrvas*, *oṃ hrīṃ* to those who can complete a text after knowing just one word, *oṃ hrīṃ* to those who know the eleven *aṅgas*, *oṃ hrīṃ* to those who can read minds, *oṃ hrīṃ* to those who can extensively read minds, *svaha*.

> Verse 13, Spell That Rids One of Illness (*rogāpahāriṇī*): *oṃ hrīṃ* praise to those whose touch is medicinal, *oṃ hrīṃ* to those whose urine, excrement, and semen is medicinal, *oṃ hrīṃ* to those whose phlegm, saliva, and so on is medicinal, *oṃ hrīṃ* to those whose sweat is medicinal, *oṃ hrīṃ* to those who can heal with all parts of their bodies, *svāhā*.

Verse 14: Spell That Gets Rid of Poison (*viṣāpahāriṇī*): *oṃ hrīṃ* praise to those who have poisonous speech, *oṃ hrīṃ* to those who have milk-like speech, *oṃ hrīṃ* to those who have honey-like speech, *oṃ hrīṃ* to those who have nectar-like speech, *svāhā*.

Or: Spell of Tribhuvanasvāminī, Giver of All Desires: *oṃ hrīṃ śrīṃ klīṃ a si ā u sā culu culu kulu kulu mulu mulu*, grant me my desires, *svāhā*.

Verse 15: Spell That Frees One from Bonds (*bandhamokṣiṇī*): *oṃ hrīṃ* praise to the *jinas*, *oṃ hrīṃ* to the *jinas* who have clairvoyant knowledge, *oṃ hrīṃ* to those who have supreme clairvoyant knowledge, *oṃ hrīṃ* to those who have infinite clairvoyant knowledge, *oṃ hrīṃ* to ordinary omniscient beings, *oṃ hrīṃ* to the omniscient beings who exist, *oṃ hrīṃ* to the omniscient beings who do not yet exist.

Verse 16: Spell That Bestows Wealth (*śrīsampādinī*): *oṃ hrīṃ* praise to those who can understand entire teachings from a single word, to those whose intellects are like granaries that store the seeds of teachings, to those who can hear sounds beyond the range of normal hearing, to those who can provide an inexhaustible supply of food, to those who have all superhuman powers, *svāhā*.

Verse 17: Spell That Neutralizes Other Spells (*paravidyocchedinī*): *oṃ hrīṃ* praise to those who can endure difficult fasts, *oṃ hrīṃ* to those who can glow from performing austerities, *oṃ hrīṃ* to those who reduce food to its elements, *oṃ hrīṃ* to those who have passed through all eleven spiritual stages that culminate in renunciation (*pratimā*), *svāhā*.[13]

Verse 18: Spell That Destroys Faults (*doṣanirnāśinī*): *oṃ hrīṃ* praise to those who can fly by using their legs, *oṃ hrīṃ* to those who can fly using spells, *oṃ hrīṃ* to those who have the power of shape transformation, *oṃ hrīṃ* to those who can travel in the sky, *svāhā*.

Verse 19: Spell That Pacifies Dangerous Things (*aśivopaśamanī*): *oṃ hrīṃ* praise to those who can read minds, to those who can manifest streams of cool air, to those who can manifest streams of fire, to those who have poisonous speech, to those who have a poisonous gaze, to those who have extraordinary powers of movement, to those who know the Śvetāmbara scriptures the *Mahāsvapnabhāvana* and the *Tejogninisarga* (*Bhaktāmara*, 32–53).[14]

Here, Guṇākarasūri likely connected the components of the Śvetāmbara *sūrimantra* to the *Bhaktāmarastotra* because of their shared association with the goddess Apraticakrā. While the object of praise of the *Bhaktāmarastora*, Ṛṣabha, as a liberated soul cannot help practitioners in need, Ṛṣabha's tutelary goddess grants devotees favors when they praise her and her main object of reverence. In the fourteenth century, when Śvetāmbara monks from various competing mendicant lineages were composing a large number of texts on the worldly and soteriological powers of the *sūrimantra*, Guṇākarasūri would have been well aware of the connection between the *ṛddhi*s of the *sūrimantra* and Apraticakrā due to her invocation at the center of some of the diagrams on which the *sūrimantra* was inscribed. Therefore, in his stories associated with verses 12 through 19 of the *Bhaktāmarastotra*, Guṇākarasūri has practitioners in trouble recite these different sections of the *ṛddhi-maṅgala*, and sure enough, Apraticakrā always swoops in to save the day.

Perhaps around the fifteenth century, Digambaras also began to associate the *ṛddhi-maṅgala* with the *Bhaktāmarastotra*. The earliest known Digambara commentary on the poem comes from the monk Nāgacandra, in 1475.[15] It was at this time—in the early modern period—that leaders of Digambara communities, *bhaṭṭāraka*s, attracted laypeople and funds to their temple compounds through the performance of days-long worship ceremonies to colored diagrams that were said to grant worldly well-being and eventual liberation. These *bhaṭṭāraka*s expanded on earlier discussions of *yantra*s and mantras to compose dozens of ritual manuals for these ceremonies, including a number of *pūjā*s to diagrams that visually represent the *Bhaktāmarastotra*. One of these rites to have been published, a *pūjā* to a *maṇḍala* in the shape of a forty-eight-petaled lotus, has been attributed to a *bhaṭṭāraka* Somasena, who may have lived at the end of the fifteenth century.[16] In this ceremony, as worshipers make offerings to the diagram, they are to recite a line of the *Bhaktāmarastotra*—a Sanskrit mantra of seed syllables and praises to Jain divinities/entreaties for worldly well-being—and a line of the *ṛddhi-maṅgala* expanded to forty-eight lines (the *gaṇadharavalayamantra*).[17] In the centuries following the fifteenth century, more Digambara texts associated the *Bhaktāmara* were composed, with Rāyamalla Brahmacārin, disciple of Sakalacandra, writing in 1610, in northwest India, a Sanskrit collection of stories about the miraculous effects of reciting the *Bhaktāmarastotra* in 1610, and codifying in forty-eight yantras the connection between the *ṛddhi*s and verses of the *Bhaktāmara*.[18] These *yantra*s are commonly found in temples, booklets, and home shrines to this day.

For a specific example of how Digambaras split up the expanded *ṛddhi-maṅgala* of the Ring of Disciples and inscribed it on forty-eight different *yantra*s, let us examine the *yantra* associated with the first verse of the *Bhaktāmarastotra* (fig. 6.1). The square frame of the *yantra* contains the first verse of the *Bhaktāmara*. Inside the next smaller square, the seed syllables *oṃ* and *klīṃ* are repeated. At the center of the *yantra* sits the seed syllable *oṃ*, surrounded by a swirl that culminates in another *oṃ*. The ring around the central circle contains sixteen repetitions of the seed syllable *hrīṃ*. The ring surrounding these *hrīṃ*s reads: "*oṃ hrīṃ arhaṃ ṇamo arhihaṃtāṇaṃ, ṇamo jiṇāṇaṃ, hrāṃ hrīṃ hrauṃ hraḥ a si ā u sā apraticakre phaṭ vicakrāya jhrauṃ jhrauṃ svāhā, oṃ hrāṃ hrīṃ hrūṃ śrīṃ klīṃ klūṃ krauṃ oṃ hrīṃ namaḥ*." This ring contains what texts on the *Bhaktāmara* call the *ṛddhi* and the mantra associated with the verse. The *ṛddhi* is the first line of the *ṛddhi-maṅgala* (*ṇamo jiṇāṇam*) plus the *apraticakrā*-mantra from the center of Ring of Disciples diagram (ending in *svāhā*), and the mantra is a series of seed syllables, beginning with *oṃ*. In this way, each *yantra* of the *Bhaktāmarastotra* contains on it a line from the expanded *ṛddhi-maṅgala* of forty-eight lines in the Ring of Disciples diagram.

Digambaras, like Śvetāmbaras, linked the *ṛddhi-maṅgala* to the *Bhaktāmara* because they both understood these praises to ascetics with superhuman powers to be an extension of the invocation of the Apraticakrā at the center of their initiation diagrams. They both saw the power in praising Ṛṣabha alongside his tutelary goddess. But while Śvetāmbara *sūrimantra-paṭas* contain varying numbers of praises to practitioners with superhuman powers inscribed in rings around the central image, Digambara Ring of Disciples diagrams always contain forty-eight praises to maintain a common structure of initiation diagrams: one in which rings of petals, in multiples of eight, surround a central figure.

Could the differences between these Digambara and Śvetāmbara diagrams of mendicant initiation and promotion be the reason why Digambaras and Śvetāmbaras disagree on the length of the *Bhaktāmarastotra*? The question of why the sects maintain different lengths of the *stotra* has perplexed scholars for decades, since there does not seem to be a clear reason why the lengths should differ. The discrepancy between the sects' versions of the hymn comes in the middle of the poem, when the poet describes the

FIGURE 6.1. The first *yantra* of the *Bhaktāmarastotra*. This *yantra* is established in a shrine in the Śvetāmbara Bhaktāmar Mandir that was commissioned by monks of Ācārya Rāmacandrasūri's lineage. Sammet Shikhar, Jharkhand, December 2019.

prātihārya, or the miraculous phenomena that appear when a *jina* achieves enlightenment and sits in his preaching assembly. Svetambaras name the *aśoka* tree, the lion throne, fly whisks, and the triple umbrella, and Digambaras add drums, a rain of flowers, a halo, and divine speech to the list. This discrepancy is perplexing, because both Śvetāmbara and Digambara texts accept eight *prātihārya*.

To date, Madhusudan Dhaky and Jitendra Shah have provided the most reasonable explanation for the different lengths, compiling Śvetāmbara and Digambara lists of the *prātihārya*s from various texts to show that while Śvetāmbara sources do not always agree on the number of *prātihārya* and some early texts list only four, Digambaras almost always name a set of eight, so to keep this consistency, a Digambara poet must have added four lines to the initial forty-four lines of the poem.[19] Building on this suggestion that Digambaras lengthened the poem, we can hypothesize that the association of the forty-eight-lined *ṛddhi-maṅgala* of the Ring of Disciples with the *Bhaktāmarastotra* may have influenced Digambaras to lengthen their version of the *Bhaktāmarastotra* by four lines. If each verse of the *Bhaktāmarastotra* was to be connected to one petal of the Ring of Disciples diagram, it had to be lengthened to forty-eight verses.

While this hypothesis may or may not be correct—the associations of *yantra*s with the poem may or may not be the reason for the different lengths of the *stotra*—Jains of all sects today accept the forty-eight *yantra*s Digambaras developed. Despite accepting only forty-four verses, the Śvetāmbara temples dedicated to the *Bhaktāmarastotra* in Bharuch, Shankheshwar, Palitana, and Sammet Shikhar display forty-eight *yantras*.[20] These specific *yantra*s have likely prevailed because of their connection to an ancient invocation both Śvetāmbaras and Digambaras recognize from its use in key soteriological rites: the *ṛddhi-maṅgala*. Indeed, another Śvetāmbara set of forty-four *yantra*s of the *Bhaktāmarastotra* attributed to an unknown monk named Haribhadrasūri has also been published, but these *yantra*s are not commonly found in Jain homes and places of worship, likely because of their contents.[21] Haribhadrasūri's *yantra* associated with the first verse of the *stotra*, for example, contains a ten-cornered figure made of intersecting triangles with the syllable *oṃ* at its center. Seed syllables are inscribed around the figure and at its corners; these include *jhrīṃ* and *hrīṃ* as well as repetitions of the four semi-vowels paired with the first four vowels of the Devanagari alphabet: *ya yā yi yī*, *la lā li lī*, *ra rā ri rī*, and *va vā vi vī*. There is no explicit link between these seemingly random seed syllables and Jain teachings or ritual culture. The *ṛddhi-maṅgala* that fills the other *yantra*s, however, represents the first Jain monks, the power of Jain austerities, and is used in the initiations, promotions, and daily worship practices of Jain laypeople and mendicants. It is no surprise, then, that the forty-eight *yantras* have reigned supreme. While Manju Jain and her students may claim her healing practices as nonsectarian, examining the history of the contents the forty-eight *yantras* she promotes actually sheds quite a bit of light on the formation of the Jain path to liberation.

THE *ṚDDHI-MAṄGALA* AND MODERN SCHOLARSHIP ON JAINISM

From 1879 until his death in 1900, the German Sanskritist Friedrich Max Müller (1823–1900) oversaw the publication of one of the great scholarly endeavors of modern period: *The Sacred Books of the East* (*SBE*), a fifty-volume series of translated sacred scriptures that "effectively defined the parameters of the 'major religions of the world.'"[22] In the introduction to the series from 1879, Müller stressed that "in order to have a solid foundation for a comparative study of the religions of the East, we must have before all things complete and thoroughly faithful translations of their sacred books."[23] In other words, to establish the field of comparative religion, distinct religious traditions first had to be established based on the Protestant idea that a religion must have a foundational scripture. Müller initially was not going to include Jain scriptures in the series, noting in its introduction that apart from Christianity and Judaism, "the only great and original religions which profess to be founded on Sacred Books" are Hinduism, Buddhism, Zoroastrianism, Islam, Confucianism, and Taoism.[24] But after Hermann Jacobi (1850–1937) established for academics that Jainism is an independent religion in 1879, he was tasked to translate two volumes of Jain scriptures for the series.[25] The scriptures he was to translate had to conform to Müller's definition of "Sacred Books" as texts that "had received a kind of canonical sanction,"[26] so Jacobi selected four texts that German scholars had recently classified as belonging to the "Jain Canon," the list of forty-five Śvetāmbara *mūrtipūjaka āgamas* that Georg Bühler had received from the monk Śrīpūjya Jinamuktisūri in 1871.[27]

In 1884 and 1885, Jacobi contributed to the *Sacred Books of the East* translations of the *Ācārāṅgasūtra* and *Kalpasūtra* (*SBE*, vol. 22) and the *Uttarādhyayanasūtra* and *Sūtrakṛtāṅgasūtra* (*SBE*, vol. 45). Four texts of a Śvetāmbara image-worshiping tradition that date to before the sixth century CE and outline the strict rules of the self-denying mendicant and reject the use of invocations (*Sūtrakṛtāṅgasūtra* 2.2.27; *Uttarādhyayanasūtra* 36.264)[28] were to define Jainism for this project of the comparative study of religion. And the influence of Jacobi's translations cannot be overstated. Equivalent Digambara texts thought to contain Mahāvīra's sermons and teachings on mendicant conduct such as the *Ṣaṭkhaṇḍāgama* and the *Mūlācāra* have yet to be translated in their entirety into English, and almost all the medieval and early modern texts on ritual and material culture discussed in this book have not been examined in any depth outside of India. Jacobi's translations of the four Śvetāmbara scriptures, however, are consistently referenced in scholarship on Jainism. While scholars of other religions have long since moved beyond the translations of the *Sacred Books of the East*, with Spalding Professor of Eastern Religions and Ethics at Oxford R. C. Zaehner claiming in 1958 that "many of the translations are now quite out of date,"[29] in the study of Jainism, Jacobi's versions of these texts remain the best and most-cited translations of these scriptures. Though the last few decades have seen scholars use anthropology, art history, philology, and other disciplines to address an impressively diverse range of topics from all sects of Jainism, Jain studies still lacks the critical mass of scholars to move the field forward at the pace of other fields.

Jacobi had the option, however, of enshrining another Jain text as the scripture that would help define the field. In 1876, three years before he would classify Jainism as a distinct tradition, he published a German translation of the *Bhaktāmarastotra* and another Sanskrit hymn to Pārśva likely modeled on the *Bhaktāmara*, the *Kalyāṇamandirastotra*. This was his first translation of Jain scriptures and, indeed, was "one of the first publications in [his] career as a Sanskritist." Jacobi chose the *Bhaktāmara* to translate in part because he had encountered its manuscripts so many times and had recognized its popularity among Jains, who recited the "prayer for help in the dangers and trials under which men suffer."[30] From 1873 to 1874 he had traveled in Rajasthan with Georg Bühler, collecting manuscripts with the help of the monk Jinamuktisūri, who admitted the two scholars to the Śvetāmbara collection of manuscripts in Jaisalmer.[31] By the nineteenth century, partially because Jains wished to record representations of the *yantra*s that could be copied onto metal, cloth, or other objects of worship, the *Bhaktāmarastotra* had become one of the most commonly found texts in Jain manuscript collections. Therefore, while Jacobi in the introduction to his translation showed no interest in the *yantra*s associated with the poem and instead focused on the *Bhaktāmara*'s author, history, and literary qualities, the association of the *ṛddhi-maṅgala* with the *Bhaktāmara* was one reason he encountered the poem in the first place.

We could thus lament Jacobi's missed opportunity at properly presenting Jainism at this formative juncture for the study of world religions. In choosing to translate for the *Sacred Books of the East* four "canonical" Prakrit Śvetāmbara texts, Jacobi furthered a bias toward image-worshiping Śvetāmbara Jainism and the earliest texts of the tradition that promote its ascetic core. Had he defined Jainism in terms of the *Bhaktāmarastotra*, he could have begun the project of this book: a comparative historical study of the texts, images, and practices of modern Jainism. With the clarity of hindsight, we could wish that Jacobi had offered to Müller for the *Sacred Books of the East* a translation of the *Bhaktāmara*, accompanied by the commentary of the Śvetāmbara Guṇākarasūri and the *pūjā* of the Digambara Somasena, both replete with discussions of the power of the *ṛddhi-maṅgala*.

In entertaining such ideas, however, we must guard against the temptation to overcorrect for biases of the past, lest we suggest that the teachings of the *Ācārāṅgasūtra*, *Kalpasūtra*, *Uttarādhyayanasūtra*, and *Sūtrakṛtāṅgasūtra* somehow misrepresent Jainism and contradict the "lived reality" of Jains. This is simply not the case. Digambara and Śvetāmbara monks to this day adopt the five vows of mendicancy first outlined in the *Ācārāṅgasūtra*, and Śvetāmbara monks are required to study all four of these scriptures before they can be promoted to higher ranks of mendicancy, receiving the *vardhamānavidyā*. Śvetāmbara laypeople are also intimately familiar with the *Kalpasūtra*, since every year for the main festival Paryuṣaṇa, they reenact the biographies of the *tīrthaṅkara*s found in the text.

Thus, a fuller comprehension of Jainism requires a twofold understanding: one of the extensive use of tantric ritual components in both lay and mendicant practices, and another of the role of early scriptures in shaping and enabling the use of said components. The many powers of the *ṛddhi-maṅgala*, as listed in the commentaries on the *Bhaktāmarastotra*, derive from the earliest discourses on the acquisition of superhuman powers through asceticism and the use of invocations to destroy karma. Jacobi's translation of the *Uttarādhyayanasūtra*, for example, contains a dialogue between Mahāvīra's disciple Gautama and a follower of Pārśva, Keśi, who is said to have the power that is named in the first section of the *ṛddhi-maṅgala*, clairvoyance (*avadhi*) (*Uttarādhyayanasūtra* 23.3). Meanwhile, the *Kalpasūtra* provides a crucial Jain explanation of how praises to advanced ascetics destroy karma. Jacobi's translation of the *Kalpasūtra* opens with the nine lines of the image-worshiping Śvetāmbara version of the *pañcanamaskāra*, which declares that this praise to the Five Supreme Beings of Jainism destroys all bad karma (*pāpa*).

The difficulty in identifying the strictly "tantric" components of Jain rituals and material culture gives credence to their deep scriptural roots. The modern Jain monks who see fasting and the use of mantras as equally effective in progressing toward liberation remind us that religious traditions rarely reduce themselves to the neat boundaries of analytical categories. As reflected in the evolution of the *ṛddhi-maṅgala*, a tantric ritual syntax lives on in Jain religious culture not in spite of the ascetic teachings of Jainism, but precisely because of them.

ACKNOWLEDGMENTS

THIS BOOK DOCUMENTS THE POWER OF praising teachers of Jainism, so it seems fitting that I include in it an homage to the people and institutions that have made my study of Jainism possible. My year of research in India on which much of this book is based was funded by a Fulbright-Hays grant, and I conducted follow-up interviews while in India on a Fulbright-Nehru Senior Research Fellowship. Funding for participation in the International Summer School for Jain Studies, a grant from Yale's South Asian Studies Council, a Foreign Language and Area Studies (FLAS) fellowship, and funding for the yearlong Hindi program through the American Institute of Indian Studies also made possible language study and travel to India crucial for this project. I thank Nidhi Sharma (with Will, George, and Katie!) and the family of Archana Patel for providing homes away from home in Jaipur and Ahmedabad during my research.

In India, I have been overwhelmed by the generosity of the Jain community. It is impossible to thank all the Jains who have invited me into their homes for meals and overnight stays, driven me to far-flung sites of worship, gifted books and other resources, and sat patiently with me for hours as I worked through basic questions. In Delhi, Shugan Chand Jain provided guidance and resources. In Jaipur, I must especially recognize the support of Dr. Shivprasad, Vipin Baj, Vimalkumar Jain, Jyoti Kothari, Yashwant Golccha, the staff at Prakrit Bharati Academy, and the late Mahopādhyāya Vinayasāgarajī. At the Apabhraṃśa Institute in Jaipur, Kamal Chand Sogani and Shakuntala Jain not only read Prakrit with me and provided contacts and resources, but they and all the staff at the institute always made me feel at home. In Mumbai, the most thanks go to Manish Modi, for being a tireless promotor of all things Jain and just an all-around great guy. Thanks also go to Pandit Pradipkumar Jain and Pandit Vijaykumar Jain, Muni Suyaśavijayajī, Ācārya Hemacandrasūrijī, Muni Amoghakīrtijī, and Muni Amarakīrtijī.

The final chapter of this book would not exist without the patience, open-mindedness, and vast knowledge of Ācārya Nandighoṣasūrijī. He has read through a draft of the chapter and spent countless hours instructing me on scripture and practice. Despite his efforts, I know mistakes and oversights remain, so I apologize for these and pay my respects to him here: *matthaeṇa vaṃdāmi.*

During my research in India and at home, I have benefited from choosing a field of study populated with the loveliest scholars imaginable. Many of the ideas in this book developed in conversation with Peter Flügel, who advised my master's thesis on Jain *mantraśāstra* and continues to provide much-needed support, wisdom, and resources. I thank John Cort for answering and asking important questions, vastly improving various drafts, and providing resources and contacts. Tillo Detige has been a huge help in this project, and Finnian Gerety, Kristi Wiley, Whitney Kelting, Christoph Emmrich, Steven Vose, and Paul Dundas have also provided indispensable guidance along the way.

I have also been supported by incredible mentors, colleagues, and friends during my time as a PhD student at Yale and my years as an assistant professor at Emory. At Emory, support for this project has come in particular from Joyce Flueckiger, Sara McClintock, and the members of the writing groups Devin Stewart organized. At Yale, David Brick was the most careful reader of this project yet, and formative conversations with Lang Chen, Mark Holum, Aleksandra Restifo, Jay Ramesh, Kedar Deshpande, and Andrew More have surfaced in various parts of this book. Lynna Dhanani provided important contacts and organized the writing group with Yong Cho I needed to keep going. Alexandra Kaloyanides has improved much of what I have written in the last decade, saved me from one too many Ellen-related debacles, and helped form most of my scholarly ideas. And the brilliant, big-hearted Marko Geslani has influenced my thought so much that much of this book might be considered plagiary.

As for Phyllis Granoff and Koichi Shinohara, it is not possible to properly thank them, since they have played such a fundamental role in shaping me. Koichi taught me how to read carefully, and his questions always force me to widen my thinking. When I first came to Yale, I knew Phyllis was a brilliant scholar and a master of Sanskrit and Prakrit, but I could not have anticipated her unbounded generosity. Phyllis has the rare combination of great expertise and uncompromising care for her students, and I could not be more grateful for her support.

For providing much-needed editorial assistance, I should also thank Ellen Goldlust, the anonymous reviewers of the manuscript, and Kyle Wagner, Johanna Rosenbohm, and the other editors at Chicago, especially Kathryn Lofton, for her faith in the project. Parts of chapters 2 and 3 have previously been published in "Tantric Ritual Elements in the Initiation of a Digambara," in *Tantric Communities in Context*, ed. Nina Mirnig, Marion Rastelli, and Vincent Eltschinger (Vienna: Austrian Academy of Sciences, 2019), 233–73; and a part of chapter 3 draws upon my publication "The Tantricization of Jain Image Consecration," in *Consecration Rituals in South Asia*, ed. István Keul (Leiden: Brill, 2017), 265–308. Parts of chapter 4 have been previously published in "Wheel of the Liberated: Jain Siddhacakras, Past and Present," in *Objects of Worship in the South Asian Religions: Forms, Practices, and Meanings*, ed. Knut Jacobsen (New York: Routledge, 2015), 85–108.

To conclude, I must thank the ones closest to me. As an undeclared undergrad, I took my first class in religious studies at the recommendation of my brother. Sung Park was the patient, supportive presence I needed in India, and with support from Lucky and Coco, he edited significant parts of the manuscript, always asking the most incisive questions. Finally, my parents, both academics, have not only given me critical advice about research, teaching, and writing, they have also taught me the importance of integrity and kindness. I dedicate this book to them.

NOTES

PREFACE

1 *Pañcanamaskṛtistuti*, v. 31, in *Namaskāra Svādhyāya*, Saṃskṛta Vibhāga, comp. Dhurandharavijaya Gaṇi and Muni Jambūvijaya, ed. Muni Tattvānandavijaya (Bombay: Jain Sāhitya Vikās Maṇḍal, 1962), 181; Steven M. Vose, "The Making of a Medieval Jain Monk: Language, Power and Authority in the Works of Jinaprabhasūri (c. 1261–1333)" (PhD diss., University of Pennsylvania, 2013), 300.

2 For a discussion of this verse, see Christopher Wallis, *Tantra Illuminated: The Philosophy, History, and Practice of a Timeless Tradition* (Petulama, CA: Mattamayūra Press, 2012), 26; and Sir John Woodroffe, *Shakti and Shâkta: Essays and Addresses on the Shâkta Tantrashâstra*, 3rd ed. (London: Luzac, 1929), 50–51. For a discussion of this verse and a similar one found in another Śaiva *āgama*, the *Ajitāgama, Kriyāpāda*, 1.115, see Jean Filliozat, "Introduction: Les Āgama Çivaïtes," in *Rauravāgama*, ed. N. R. Bhatt (Pondicherry: Institut Français d'Indologie, 1961), 1:vii.

3 *tanoti vipulān arthān tattvamantrasamanvitān* | *trāṇaṃ ca kurute yasmāt tantram ity abhidhīyate* || I summarize the Hindi explanation of this verse in Sagarmal Jain, "Tantra-Sādhnā aur Jain Jīvan Dṛṣṭi," in *Śvetāmbar Sthānakvāsī Jain Sabhā Hīrak Jayanti Granth*, ed. Sagarmal Jain and Ashok Kumar Singh (Varanasi: Pārśvanāth Śodhpīṭh, 1994), 481. This uncited verse by Jain differs slightly from *Kāmikāgama, Pūrvabhāga* 1.29, which uses *samāśritān*, a synonym of *samanvitān*.

INTRODUCTION

1 Manju Jain, *Jaina Method of Curing* (Nagpur: Metalfab High Tech, 2011), 18.

2 Government of Maharashtra, Social Justice and Special Assistance Department, *Translation in English of the Maharashtra Prevention and Eradication of Human Sacrifice and Other Inhuman, Evil and Aghori Practices and Black Magic Ordinance, 2013 (Mah. Ord. XIV of 2013)* (Mumbai, August 26, 2013), 6. This bill was pushed through the legislature after the murder of its most vocal proponent, Narendra Dabholkar, in August 2013.

3 Douglas Renfrew Brooks, *The Secret of the Three Cities: An Introduction to Hindu Śākta Tantrism* (Chicago: University of Chicago Press, 1990), 5. See also the summary of several other scholarly discussions of modern Indians' negative opinion of tantra in Patton E. Burchett, *A Genealogy of Devotion: Bhakti, Tantra, Yoga, and Sufism in North India* (New York: Columbia University Press, 2019), 385–86n1.

4 I will translate *labdhi*, *ṛddhi*, and *siddhi* interchangeably as "special powers," "extraordinary powers," and "superhuman powers." I avoid the translation "supernatural" to acknowledge the belief that these powers are within the realm of the laws of nature (*dharmatā*). For a useful comparison of European and Indian understandings of miracles, the "supernatural" and natural law, see David V. Fiordalis, "Miracles and Superhuman Powers in South Asian Buddhist Literature" (PhD diss., University of Michigan, 2008), 1–10.

5 I use the terms "geometric diagram," "diagram," and "ritual diagram" to refer to objects of worship variously named *cakra*, *valaya*, *maṇḍala*, *yantra*, *paṭa*, *mahāpūjana*, and *vidhāna*. In Hindu traditions, the term "*yantra*," which in Sanskrit means "instrument," "machine," or "mystical diagram," is often used for smaller, portable geometric designs, while the term "*maṇḍala*" refers to larger, impermanent diagrams made of colored powder into which divinities are called for a special occasion. Gudrun Bühnemann, "Maṇḍala, Yantra and Cakra: Some Observations," in *Maṇḍalas and Yantras in the Hindu Traditions*, ed. Bühnemann (Leiden: E. J. Brill, 2003), 15. No such distinction exists, however, in Jainism. The term "*yantra*" is used for a geometric diagram made of any material. Śvetāmbaras call impermanent structures made of colored powers and foodstuffs *mahāpūjana* (great worship ceremony), while Digambaras call them *vidhāna* (worship ceremony). The terms "*maṇḍala*" (circle), "*cakra*" (wheel), and "*valay*" (ring) refer to the shapes of different diagrams. The term "*paṭa*" often refers to a cloth diagram, but it can also refer to diagram in general—for instance, one carved on a wall of a temple. For an example of how these terms are used, the *Ṛṣimaṇḍalayantravidhāna* refers to the construction of a circular (*maṇḍala*) diagram (*yantra*) of divinities (*ṛsi*) that is made out of powder (*vidhāna*). For a discussion of these terms, see Ellen Gough, "Jain *Maṇḍala*s and *Yantra*s," in *Brill's Encyclopedia of Jainism*, ed. Knut A. Jacobsen, John E. Cort, Paul Dundas, and Kristi L. Wiley (Leiden: Brill, 2020), 585–93.

6 From the medieval period to the present day, texts affirm the hidden nature of Jain mantras and diagrams. The medieval Sanskrit hymn outlining one popular Jain diagram, the *Ṛṣimaṇḍalastotra*, confirms: "This great *stotra* is to be concealed. It is not to be given to anyone. Giving it to a wrong-believer is like killing a child in every step." *etād gopyaṃ mahāstotraṃ na deyaṃ yasya kasyacit | mithyātvavāsino deyaṃ bālahatyā pade pade ||* (v. 66). As of 2019, non-Jains cannot access one of the largest collections of Śvetāmbara *yantra*s housed in the Acharya Shri Kailasasagarsuri Gyanmandir, in Koba, Gujarat, because of the conservative stance of the mendicant advisors to the administration.

7 For some potential dates of the *Tattvārthasūtra*, see W. J. Johnson, *Harmless Souls: Karmic Bondage and Religious Change in Early Jainism with Special Reference to Umāsvāti and Kundakunda* (Delhi: Motilal Banarsidass, 1995), 46–47.

8 In his important study of contemporary Śvetāmbara ritual practices, John E. Cort has called these teachings the "*mokṣa-mārg* ideology," or the worldview that promotes

ascetic practices as the path (*mārga*) to liberation (*mokṣa*). Cort, *Jains in the World: Religious Values and Ideology in India* (New York: Oxford University Press, 2001). This list of twelve types of *tapas* is commonly found in Jain literature, from the Śvetāmbara canon (*āgamas*) to the present day. For other discussions of the twelve types of *tapas*, see Cort, *Jains in the World*, 120; and Johannes Bronkhorst, *The Two Traditions of Meditation in Ancient India* (Delhi: Motilal Banarsidass, 1993), 16.

9 Judith Bennett, *Sex Signs: Every Woman's Astrological and Psychological Guide to Love, Men, Sex, Anger, and Personal Power* (New York: St. Martin's Press, 1980), 477; Gavin Flood, *The Tantric Body: The Secret Tradition of Hindu Tradition* (London: I. B. Tauris, 2006), 9.

10 The first known use of the term "*tantra*" in English occurred in 1799. Herbert Guenther, *The Tantric View of Life* (Berkeley: Shambala Publications, 1972), 1, cited in Richard K. Payne, ed., *Tantric Buddhism in East Asia* (Boston: Wisdom, 2006), 5.

11 Robert L. Brown, introduction to *The Roots of Tantra*, ed. Katherine Anne Harper and Robert L. Brown (Albany: State University of New York, 2002), 1.

12 Brooks, *The Secret of the Three Cities*, xvii.

13 Donald S. Lopez Jr., *Elaborations on Emptiness: Uses of the Heart Sūtra* (Princeton, NJ: Princeton University Press, 1996), 102. For some historiographies of Tantra, see Hugh B. Urban, "The Extreme Orient: The Construction of 'Tantrism' as a Category in the Orientalist Imagination," *Religion* 29 (1999): 123–46; Hugh Urban, *Tantra: Sex, Secrecy, Politics and Power in the Study of Religions* (Berkeley: University of California Press, 2003); and Christian K. Wedemeyer, "Tropes, Typologies, and Turnarounds: A Brief Genealogy of the Historiography of Tantric Buddhism," *History of Religions* 40, no. 3 (February 2001): 223–59.

14 André Padoux, "Hindu Tantrism," in *The Encyclopedia of Religions*, ed. Mircea Eliade (New York: Macmillan, 1986), 14:273, cited in David Gordon White, *Kiss of the Yoginī: "Tantric Sex" in Its South Asian Contexts* (Chicago: University of Chicago Press, 2003) 15; and Gerald James Larson, "Differentiating the Concepts of 'yoga' and 'tantra' in Sanskrit Literary History," *Journal of the American Oriental Society* 129, no. 3 (2009): 492.

15 Dominic Goodall and Harunaga Isaacson, "On the Shared 'Ritual Syntax' of the Early Tantric Traditions," in *Tantric Studies: Fruits of a Franco-German Collaboration on Early Tantra*, ed. Goodall and Isaacson (Pondicherry: Institut Français de Pondichéry, 2016), 1–76.

16 Bühnemann, "Maṇḍala, Yantra and Cakra," 13.

17 Gavin Flood, "The Purification of the Body in Tantric Ritual Representation," *Indo-Iranian Journal* 45 (2002): 25–43.

18 The foundational article distinguishing between the Atimārga and Mantramārga is Alexis Sanderson, "Śaivism and the Tantric Traditions," in *The World's Religions*, ed. S. Sutherland et al. (London: Routledge, 1988), 660–704. For an overview of the five streams of Śaivism outlined in the *Niśvāsamukha*, see Nirajan Kafle, "The Niśvāsamukha, the Introductory Book of the Niśvāsatattvasaṃhitā: Critical Edition, with an Introduction and Annotated Translation Appended by Śivadharmasaṅgraha 5–9" (PhD diss., Leiden University, 2015), 23–29.

19 Alexis Sanderson summarizes the sources of the terms "*atimārga*" and "*mantramārga*," including the *Niśvāsamukha* 4.132 and later texts such as the *Kāmikāgama*, in "The Śaiva Literature," *Journal of Indological Studies*, 24 and 25 (2012–13): 4n14. It is important to note that not all Śaiva texts interpret the terms "*atimārga*" and "*mantramārga*" the same, so Sanderson privileges the *Niśvāsamukha*'s characterization of the terms in formulating his sectarian history of Śaivism. See Alexis Sanderson, "The Lākulas: New Evidence of a System Intermediate between Pāñcārthika Pāsupatism and Āgamic Śaivism," *Indian Philosophical Annual* 24 (2006): 158–63.

20 Sanderson, "Śaivism and the Tantric Traditions," 664.

21 Ronald M. Davidson, *Indian Esoteric Buddhism: A Social History of the Tantric Movement* (New York: Columbia University Press, 2002), 183. The term the Pāśupatas adopted for their final life stage—"*siddha*"—was used in Jain texts from the early centuries BCE to refer to a liberated soul that had been freed from karma. The *Pāśupatasūtra* 20, which has been dated to about the third century CE, agrees with the Jain idea of a *siddha*, claiming that a *siddhayogin is* not besmeared by karma or immoral action: "*siddhayogī na lipyate karmaṇā pātakena va.*" Cited in Davidson, *Indian Esoteric Buddhism*, 382n45, with a fuller discussion of the early history of the term *siddha* on 173–84.

22 On the date of the *Mūlasūtra*, see *Niśvāsatattvasaṃhitā*, ed. and trans. Dominic Goodall, in collaboration with Alexis Sanderson and Harunaga Isaacson, as *The Niśvāsatattvasaṃhitā: The Earliest Surviving Śaiva Tantra* (Pondicherry: Institut Français de Pondichéry, 2015), 19–73.

23 Dominic Goodall and Harunaga Isaacson, "Tantric Traditions," in *The Continuum Companion to Hindu Studies*, ed. Jessica Frazier (London: Continuum, 2011), 125.

24 Sanderson, "The Lākulas," 147. This distinction between the Atimārga and Mantramārga was formulated later, with a description found in Abhinavagupta's eleventh-century *Tantrāloka*: "For the doctrine that while the Atimārga teaches only the means of liberation the Mantramārga teaches both such means and the means of accomplishing supernatural effects (*siddhiḥ*) see *Tantrāloka* 37.14–16." Sanderson, "The Śaiva Literature," 5n14.

25 Lākula Śaivas, who belong to the Atimārga, did develop an initiation that was said to effect liberation, but they are still considered to be ascetics, not tantrics, because their tradition does not include the tantric initiation of nonbrahmin males and householders, the emphasis on the development of superhuman powers (*siddhi*), and the use of a *maṇḍala*. On the Lākula initiation also conferring liberation, see Sanderson, "The Lākulas," 188–93.

26 In the Pāñcarthika initiation ceremony described in Kauṇḍinya's commentary (*bhāṣya*) to the *Pāśupatasūtra* (dated between 400 and 550), the initiand sits facing the right face of an icon (*mūrti*) of Śiva and the guru then sprinkles ash consecrated with the five Vedic *brahmamantras* on the head of the initiand. While the commentary on another Pāñcārthika text, the *Gaṇakārikā*, confirms that the "icon" here is an area of land hidden from view by means of a structure such as a hut (*kūṭi*), suggesting a sort of proto-*maṇḍala*-like ritual space into which deities are invited, a clear description of a *maṇḍala* constructed at the time of the initiation is not found until the *Mūlasūtra* of the *Niśvāsatattvasaṃhitā*. Dominic Goodall does note, however, that in the *Mūlasūtra*, "the

fact that so many options [for the iconography of the *maṇḍala*] are mentioned plainly suggest that, although the *Mūlasūtra* may give the earliest tantric account known to us of the drawing of a *maṇḍala*, it certainly was not the first." *Niśvāsatattvasaṃhitā*, ed. and trans. Goodall as *The Niśvāsatattvasaṃhitā*, 267.

27 On the history of a key component of this meditative practice, the purification of the body through the identification with the elements (*bhūtaśuddhi*), see Flood, *The Tantric Body*, 107–8. Goodall and Isaacson claim that the earliest Śaiva mentions of *bhūtaśuddhi* are the "non-eclectic Kālottara recensions," one of which likely predates the eighth-century *Guhyasiddhi*, which mentions it. Goodall and Isaacson, "Shared 'Ritual Syntax,'" 7n16.

28 Flood, *The Tantric Body*, 106.

29 These practices belong to the so-called non-Saiddhāntika Mantramārga—cults that focus their worship not only on Śiva, as in Śaiva Siddhānta, but on Śiva and Śakti, a form of the Goddess. These non-Saiddhāntika cults, Vaiṣṇava Pāñcarātra, and the Śaiva Siddhānta "are essentially variants of a single ritual system." Sanderson, "The Śaiva Literature," 32.

30 *Vinaya* i.82–4, cited in Rupert Gethin, *The Foundations of Buddhism* (Oxford: Oxford University Press, 1998), 87.

31 Gethin, *Foundations of Buddhism*, 89–90.

32 Charles D. Orzech, "The 'Great Teachings of Yoga,' the Chinese Appropriation of the Tantras, and the Question of Esoteric Buddhism," *Journal of Chinese Religions* 34 (2006): 46–47.

33 For a summary of the *abhiṣeka* rites in the *Mahāvairocana* and the *Sarvatathāgatatattvasaṃgraha*, see Ryūichi Abé, *The Weaving of Mantra: Kukai and the Construction of Esoteric Buddhist Discourse* (New York: Columbia University Press, 2000), 133–49.

34 See, for example, the prescription to construct the seats of different deities out of different-colored lotuses in *Mahāvairocanatantra* 13.25–27, trans. Stephen Hodge as *The Mahā-Vairocana-Abhisambodhi Tantra with Buddhaguhya's Commentary* (New York: Routledge Curzon, 2003), 269–70.

35 Ronald M. Davidson, "Abhiṣeka," in *Esoteric Buddhism and the Tantras in East Asia*, ed. Charles D. Orzech, Henrik H. Sørensen, and Richard K. Payne (Leiden: Brill, 2011), 75.

36 From the seventh century onward, Buddhist tantric texts understand that mantra-based rituals could destroy karma and confer a similar state of omniscience as described in texts of the Śaiva Mantramārga. See, for example, *Mahāvairocanatantra* 5.11: "The Buddhas, most excellent of men, describe this as its result. He who abides thus in the Mantra Method will certainly become a Buddha." *Mahā-Vairocana*, trans. Hodge as *Mahā-Vairocana-Abhisambodhi Tantra*, 165. See also the section on "Abhiṣeka as a General Theory of Enlightenment" in Abé, *Weaving a Mantra*, 141–49.

37 On the history of deity yoga in Buddhist texts, see Charles Orzech, "Tantric Subjects: Liturgy and Vision in Chinese Esoteric Ritual Manuals," in *Chinese and Tibetan Esoteric Buddhism*, ed. Yael Bentor and Meir Shahar (Leiden: Brill, 2017), 36.

38 See, for example, *Mahāvairocanatantra* 13.7.

39 For the process of achieving superhuman powers and becoming a *buddha* through the recitation of mantras, the construction of a *maṇḍala*, and visualization practices,

see *Mahāvairocanatantra*, chapter 5, "The Accomplishment of Mundane *Siddhi*," in *Mahāvairocanatantra*, trans. Hodge as *Mahā-Vairocana-Abhisambodhi Tantra*, 164–65. For another discussion of becoming a deity, see *Mahāvairocanatantra* 6.47.

40 See *Mañjuśriyamūlakalpa* 4.20 and 39.12, cited in Goodall and Isaacson, "Shared 'Ritual Syntax,'" 4n6.

41 Robert H. Sharf, *Coming to Terms with Chinese Buddhism* (Honolulu: University of Hawai'i Press, 2002), 263–78. For an overview of the use of the terms "tantric" and "esoteric" in studies of East Asian religions, see Charles D. Orzech, Richard K. Payne, and Henrik H. Sørensen, "Introduction: Esoteric Buddhism and the Tantras in East Asia: Some Methodological Considerations," in *Esoteric Buddhism and the Tantras in East Asia*, ed. Charles D. Orzech, Richard K. Payne, and Henrik H. Sørensen (Leiden: Brill, 2011), 3–18; and Richard D. McBride II, "Is There Really 'Esoteric' Buddhism?" *Journal of the International Association of Buddhist Studies* 27, 2 (2004): 329–56.

42 Jacob Dalton, "A Crisis of Doxography: How Tibetans Organized Tantra during the 8th–12th Centuries," *Journal of the International Association of Buddhist Studies* 28, no. 1 (2005): 115–81.

43 *Guhyasamājatantra*, chapter 5, trans. Christian Wedemeyer, "Antinomianism and Gradualism: The Contextualization of the Practices of Sensual Enjoyment (*Caryā*) in the Guhyasamāja Ārya Tradition," *International Journal of Buddhist Studies* 3 (2002): 185.

44 Christian Wedemeyer, *Making Sense of Tantric Buddhism: History, Semiology, and Transgression in the Indian Traditions* (New York: Columbia University Press, 2013), 9.

45 For a recent discussion, see Patton E. Burchett's distinction between ascetic (*tapasvī*) and tantric yoga, typified by the "ascetic" Rāmānandīs and the "tantric" Nāthas. Burchett, *A Genealogy of Devotion*, 173–77.

46 See, for example, the claim by James Mallinson and Mark Singleton that "ascetic traditions are not inclined toward magical mantra practice." Mallinson and Singleton, *Roots of Yoga* (London: Penguin Classics, 2017), 263.

47 Peter Flügel, "The Invention of Jainism: A Short History of Jaina Studies," *International Journal of Jaina Studies (Online)* 1, no. 1 (2005): 1–14. See also Hermann Jacobi, "Kalpasūtra of Bhadrabāhu," *Abhandlungen für die Kunde des Morgenlandes* 7, no. 1 (1879). Mitch Numark has shown that Bombay-based Protestant Scottish missionaries in the first half of the nineteenth century recognized Jainism as an independent religion, but their writings have not had a significant impact on the academic study of Jainism. Numark, "The Scottish 'Discovery' of Jainism in Nineteenth-Century Bombay," *Journal of Scottish Historical Studies* 33, no. 1 (2013): 20–51. As Peter Flügel explains, "Jaina Studies as an academic field was established around the 1880s by [German] scholars belonging to the wider circle of Albrecht Weber." Flügel, "Life and Work of Johannes Klatt," in *Jaina-Onomasticon*, ed. Flügel and Kornelius Krümpelmann (Wiesbaden: Harrassowitz Verlag, 2016), 80. For another examination of eighteenth- and nineteenth-century Orientalists' and missionaries' accounts of Jainism as a sect of Hinduism or Buddhism, see Leslie C. Orr, "Orientalists, Missionaries, and Jains: The South Indian Story," in *The Madras School of Orientalism: Producing Knowledge in Co-*

lonial South India, ed. Thomas R. Trautman (New York: Oxford University Press, 2009), 263–87.

48 For a fuller account of this formation of Jaina Studies as an academic field, see Flügel, "Life and Work of Johannes Klatt," 9–164.

49 Padmanabh Jaini, *The Jaina Path of Purification* (Berkeley: University of California Press, 1979), 254, 254n20.

50 Jeffery D. Long, *Jainism: An Introduction* (London: I. B. Tauris, 2009), 69.

51 "Salvation . . . depends solely on the asceticism of the individual," Max Weber claimed of Jainism in 1915, and scholars maintain this stance today. Weber, *The Religion of India: The Sociology of Hinduism and Buddhism*, trans. Hans H. Gerth and Don Martindale (Glencoe, IL: Free Press, 1958), 194.

52 Alexis Sanderson notes that "unlike Śaivism, Pāñcarātra, and Tantric Buddhism in its mature form, Jaina Tantrism did not claim to offer Jainas a new path to liberation. It remained entirely focused on mundane benefits." Sanderson, "The Śaiva Age—the Rise and Dominance of Śaivism during the Early Medieval Period," in *Genesis and Development of Tantrism*, ed. Shingo Einoo (Tokyo: Institute of Oriental Culture, University of Tokyo, 2009), 244. John E. Cort agrees that "most Jain Tantric rituals are aimed at accomplishing a variety of goals in this world, such as health, wealth, and power." Cort, "Worship of Bell-Ears the Great Hero," in *Tantra in Practice*, ed. David Gordon White (Princeton, NJ: Princeton University Press, 2000), 417. Olle Qvarnström explains: "Despite the fact that Hindu Tantrism and Jainism were conceptually incompatible, the Jains were . . . able to adopt certain Tantric elements by regarding Hindu Tantrism as basically a system of different means (*sādhana*), not for the attainment of liberation (*mokṣa*), but for merely mundane objectives (*bhukti*)." Qvarnström, "Stability and Adaptability: A Jain Strategy for Survival and Growth," *Indo-Iranian Journal* 41 (1998): 37.

53 Monier-Williams helped construct this multivalent, contradictory "Hinduism" to emphasize its weaknesses compared to Christianity: "The ancient fortress of Hindūism, with its four sides, Monotheism, Pantheism, Dualism, and Polytheism, is everywhere tottering and ready to fall." Monier-Williams, *Hinduism* (London: Society for Promoting Christian Knowledge, 1877), 185.

54 John E. Cort has argued that because scholars have viewed Jain *bhakti* "as an 'accretion' that is marginal to the ascetic core that constitutes the 'guiding project' of 'true' and 'original' Jainism," they believe these practices "can safely be ignored by scholarship." Cort, "Bhakti in the Early Jain Tradition: Understanding Devotional Religion in South Asia," *History of Religions*, 42, no. 1 (2002): 59.

55 See Padmanabh Jaini, "Is There a Popular Jainism?" in *The Assembly of Listeners: Jains in Society*, ed. Michael Carrithers and Caroline Humphrey (Cambridge: Cambridge University Press, 1991), 187–200. The most influential article to posit Śaiva influence on the development of tantric practices is Sanderson, "The Śaiva Age," which asserts that Jainism "developed a Tantric ritual culture along Śaiva lines" (243).

56 André Padoux, *The Hindu Tantric World* (Chicago: Chicago University Press, 2017), 31.

57 Monier-Williams, *Hinduism*, 131. For three popular surveys used today, see chapter 7,

"Śaiva and Tantric Religion," in Gavin Flood, *An Introduction to Hinduism* (Cambridge: Cambridge University Press, 1996), 148–73; chap. 13, "Tantra," in Hillary P. Rodrigues, *Introducing Hinduism* (New York: Routledge, 2006), 257–69; and "Tantrism," and "Tantrism and Bhakti" in Nirad C. Chaudhuri et al., *The Hinduism Omnibus* (New Delhi: Oxford University Press, 2003), 148–58.

58 Eugène Burnouf, *Introduction to the History of Indian Buddhism*, trans. Katia Buffetrille and Donald S. Lopez Jr. (Chicago: University of Chicago Press, 2010), 479–504. For modern surveys, see chap. 5.5, "Tantric Buddhism, or the Vajrayāna," in John S. Strong, *The Experience of Buddhism: Sources and Interpretations*, 2nd ed. (Belmont, CA: Wadsworth Thompson Learning, 2002), 193–208; and "Mahāyāna Holy Beings, and Tantric Buddhism," in Peter Harvey, *Introduction to Buddhism: Teachings, History and Practices*, 2nd ed. (Cambridge: Cambridge University Press, 2013), 149–93.

59 See John E. Cort, "Śvetāmbar Mūrtipūjak Jain Scripture in a Performative Context," in *Texts in Context: Traditional Hermeneutics in South Asia*, ed. J. Timm (Albany: State University of New York Press, 1991), 171–94.

60 For other surveys of nineteenth-century scholarship on Jainism, see the essay "Jain Studies" in Kendall W. Folkert, *Scripture and Community: Collected Essays on the Jains*, ed. John E. Cort (Atlanta: Scholars Press, 1993), 23–33; Padmanabh S. Jaini, "The Jainas and the Western Scholar," *Sambodhi* 5, nos. 2–3 (1976): 121–31; Peter Flügel, "Jainism and the Western World: Jinmuktisūri and Georg Bühler and Other Early Encounters," *Jinamañjari* 18, no. 2 (1998): 36–47; and the bibliography to Kristi L. Wiley, *The A to Z of Jainism* (Lanham: Scarecrow Press, 2009), 285–86.

61 For some early English-language Jain introductions to the tradition, see Jagmanderlal Jaini, *Outlines of Jainism* (Cambridge: Cambridge University Press, 1916); A. B. Latthe, *An Introduction to Jainism* (1905; repr., Delhi: Jain Mittra Mandal, 1964); and U. D. Barodia, *History and Literature of Jainism* (Bombay: Jain Graduates' Association, 1909).

62 One early study stands out for its presentation of the most detailed overviews of Jain *mantraśāstra* of any introductory textbook to date. Helmuth von Glasenapp's *Der Jainismus: Eine indische Erlösungsreligion* (1925) integrates data from texts and fieldwork to outline Jain mantras and to explain the performance of "placing" mantras and deities on the body (*nyāsa*), displaying ritual hand gestures (*mudrā*), and the use of *yantra*s and secret mantras in the temple image installation ceremony. Glasenapp, *Jainism: An Indian Religion of Salvation*, trans. Shridhar B. Shroti (Delhi: Motilal Banarsidass, 1998). Unfortunately, no subsequent studies built on Glasenapp's observations, placing them in a larger context of tantric rites that were being identified in various overviews of Hinduism and Buddhism.

63 On the Jain manuscript archive and how scholars have ignored the "pragmatic" texts that fill these collections—especially shorter manuals that focus on practices such as alchemy, astrology, or the ritual use of mantras—see Ulrich Timm Kragh, "Localized Literary History: Sub-text and Cultural Heritage in the Āmer Śāstrabhaṇḍār, a Digambara Manuscript Repository in Jaipur," *International Journal of Jaina Studies (Online)* 9, no. 3 (2013): 1–53.

64 See Dhīrajlāl Ṭokarśī Śāh, *Tantronuṃ Tāraṇ* (Mumbai: Jain Sāhitya Prakāśan Mandir, 1961), 56–59. Śāh has published widely on Jain *mantraśāstra* (see bibliography).

65 Muni Jambūvijaya, ed., *Catalogue of the Manuscripts of the Pāṭaṇa Jain Bhaṇḍāras*, pt. 3, comp. Muni Puṇyavijaya (Ahmedabad: Sharadaben Chimanbhai Educational Research Centre, 1991), 442–45, 496. The abundance of manuscripts of the *Bhaktāmarastotra* has been noted by John E. Cort, "Devotional Culture in Jainism: Mānatuṅga and His Bhaktāmara Stotra," in *Incompatible Visions: South Asian Religions in History and Culture: Essays in Honor of David M. Knipe*, ed. James Blumenthal (Madison: University of Wisconsin Center for South Asia, 2005), 105.

66 Some readers might notice that this book barely references the texts that have come to represent "Jain Tantra" in many surveys of Tantra: two Digambara manuals on the ritual propitiation of goddesses from south India, the *Jvālāmālinīkalpa* composed by the monk Indranandin in Karnataka in 939, and the *Bhairavapadmāvatīkalpa* completed by Malliṣeṇa in 1057. This is because the invocation at the focus of this book does not appear in these texts. I chose to focus on the life of a mantra that is found in an early text and is popular today to highlight the history of tantric practices that have been central to the Jain path to liberation. While interesting texts that should one day be studied properly, the *Bhairavapadmāvatīkalpa* and *Jvālāmālinīkalpa* are not often discussed by monks or laypeople today and should not represent "Jain Tantra."

67 David Germano, "The Funerary Transformation of the Great Perfection (*Rdzogs chen*)," *Journal of the International Association of Tibetan Studies* 1 (2005): 2. See also David Germano, "The Shifting Terrain of the Tantric Bodies of Buddhas and Buddhists from an Atiyoga Perspective," in *The Pandita and the Siddha: Tibetan Studies in Honour of E. Gene Smith*, ed. Ramon N. Prats (Dharamshala: Amnye Machen Institute, 2007).

68 In using the idea of a "life" of a mantra, this book follows the historians, sociologists, and anthropologists who have promoted the study of the "social life of things," though in this case the object of study is an invocation, not a material object. Igor Kopytoff summarizes the usefulness of this biographical approach well: "In doing the biography of a thing, one would ask questions similar to those one asks about people: What, sociologically, are the biographical possibilities inherent in its 'status' and in the period and culture, and how are these possibilities realized? Where does the thing come from and who made it? . . . What are the recognized 'ages' or periods in the thing's 'life,' and what are the cultural markers for them? How does the thing's use change with its age, and what happens to it when it reaches the end of its usefulness?" Kopytoff, "The Cultural Biography of Things: Commoditization as Process," in *The Social Life of Things: Commodities in Cultural Perspective*, ed. Arjun Appadurai (Cambridge: Cambridge University Press, 1986), 66–67.

69 See Catherine Bell, *Ritual Theory, Ritual Practice* (Oxford: Oxford University Press, 1992).

70 See, for example, Mohanlal Bhagwandas Jhavery, *Comparative and Critical Study of Mantrashastra (with Special Treatment of Jain Mantravada)* (Ahmedabad: Sarabhai Manilal Nawab, 1944); Umakant P. Shah, "Supernatural Beings in the Jain Tantras," in *Acharya Dhruva Smaraka Grantha* (Ahmedabad: Gujarat Vidya Sabha, 1946); Rājeś Dīkṣit, *Jain Tantra-Śāstra* (Agra: Dīp Publication, 1984); Sagarmal Jain, *Jaindharm aur Tāntrik Sādhnā* (Varanasi: Pārśvanāth Vidyāpīṭh, 1997); and Muni Prārthanāsāgara, *Mantra Yantra aur Tantra*, 4th ed. (n.p.: Muni Śrī Prārthnā Sāgar Foundation, 2011).

71 I follow scholars of South Asia who label the sixth through fifteenth centuries as the medieval period and ca. 1500–1750 as the early modern period. I do this simply to organize developments in ritual change in time, not because the developments charted in this book necessarily align with European ideas about the medieval or modern. For a table of different scholars' understandings of when the medieval period begins and ends, see Wedemeyer, *Making Sense of Tantric Buddhism*, 60. For the use of the term "early modern" to define India between 1500 and 1750, see John F. Richards, "Early Modern India and World History," *Journal of World History* 8, no. 2 (1997): 197–209.

72 As should be clear in this introduction, scholars have long recognized that the Śaiva Mantramārga and certain tantric Buddhist practices emerged from the ascetic Śaiva Atimārga and early monastic Buddhism. Shaman Hatley, for example, recognizes how tantric sexual rituals evolved from an earlier ascetic discipline, the *asidhārāvrata*, in which a man must remain celibate while sleeping next to a woman. Hatley, "Erotic Asceticism: The Knife's Edge Observance (*asidhārāvrata*) and the Early History of Tantric Coital Ritual," *Bulletin of the School of Oriental and African Studies* 79, 2 (2016): 329–45. Gavin Flood recognizes that Kaula ritualized sex, because it is "transgressive of dharmic values," performs the same function as asceticism, which "is traditionally seen in terms of celibacy and fasting." Flood, *The Ascetic Self: Subjectivity, Memory and Tradition* (Cambridge: Cambridge University Press, 2003), 96. Christian Wedemeyer also notes that Buddhist tantra was the logical conclusion of the ca. fifth-century BCE "ascetical zeitgeist" in which "observances were practiced and propagated across traditions" and "the antinomian traditions of the later Buddhist tantras grew out of and were initially practiced within Buddhist monastic or quasi-monastic enclaves." Wedemeyer, *Making Sense of Tantric Buddhism*, 155, 163, 177. For two recent discussions of the emergence of tantric practices out of asceticism, see Judit Törzsök, "How Śāktism Began" (lecture handout, 17th World Sanskrit Conference, Vancouver, July 13, 2018); and Alexis Sanderson, "Keynote Lecture: The Śākta Transformation of Śaivism" (lecture handout, World Sanskrit Conference, Vancouver, July 10, 2018). In Jain Studies, the foundation of later Jain tantric practices in early texts is outlined in Umakant P. Shah, "A Peep into the Early History of Tantra in Jain Literature," in *Bhārata-Kaumudī: Studies in Indology in Honor of Dr. Radha Kumud Mookerji*, part 2, ed. N. K. Sidhanta et al. (Allahabad: Indian Press, 1946), 839–54.

73 Many scholars have noted the continuities between non-ascetic Vedic practices and later "tantric" ones. Shingo Einoo has shown that the creation of *maṇḍala*s may have developed from formation of *sthandila*s in the Vedic *Gṛhyapariśiṣṭa*s and that discussions of *kāma*s in earlier Vedic literature set the basis for ideas about the development of "tantric" superhuman powers (*siddhi*). Einoo, "The Formation of Hindu Ritual," in *From Material to Deity: Indian Rituals of Consecration*, ed. Einoo and Jun Takashima (New Delhi: Manohar, 2005), 24–33; and Einoo, "From *kāma*s to *siddhi*s—Tendencies in the Development of Ritual towards Tantrism," in *Genesis and Development of Tantrism*, ed. Einoo (Tokyo: Institute of Oriental Culture, University of Tokyo, 2009), 17–40. Koichi Shinohara has drawn upon the work of Marko Geslani to show that pacification (*śānti*) rites outlined in the appendices of the *Atharvaveda* from the first half of the first millennium provide much of the ritual structure of the initiation (*abhiṣeka*)

rites of early esoteric Buddhism. Shinohara, *Spells, Images, and Maṇḍalas: Tracing the Evolution of Esoteric Buddhist Rituals* (New York: Columbia University Press, 2014), 64–90. See also Marko Geslani, *Rites of the God-King: Śānti and Ritual Change in Early Hinduism* (New York: Oxford University Press, 2018). Ronald Davidson has hypothesized about how fire-offering rites moved from Brahmanical to esoteric Buddhist sources in Davidson, "Some Observations on the Uṣṇīṣa Abhiṣeka Rites in Atikūṭa's *Dhāraṇīsaṃgraha*," in *Transformations and Transfer of Tantra: Tantrism in Asia and Beyond*, ed. István Keul, (Berlin: Walter de Gruyter, 2012), 91–93. Vrajavallabha Dviveda notes that a key idea of tantric texts, becoming a god to worship one, is found in the *Bṛhadāraṇyakopaniṣad*. Dviveda, "Having Become a God, He Should Sacrifice to the Gods," in *Ritual and Speculation in Early Tantrism: Studies in Honor of André Padoux*, ed. Teun Goudriaan (Albany: State University of New York Press, 1992), 121–38.

74 Sharf, "Thinking through Shingon Ritual."

75 *Bhāgavatapurāṇa*. 11.27.7, trans. J. L. Shastri and G. V. Tagare as *The Bhāgavata Purāṇa*, pt. V (1955; repr. Delhi: Motilal Banarsidass, 2003), 2087, cited in Sanjukta Gupta, Dirk Jan Hoens, and Teun Goudriaan, *Hindu Tantrism* (Leiden: E. J. Brill, 1979), 124.

76 Sādhvī Candanākumārī, in her 1964 Hindi code of conduct for the Loṅkā Gaccha—the mendicant followers of the fifteenth-century anti-iconic lay Jain reformer Loṅkā Śāh—explicitly forbids the practices at the focus of this book: "Monks should not practice the spells of *mantra-tantra* and *yantra*, etc." (*sādhuoṃ ko mantra-tantra tathā yantra ādi vidyāoṃ kā prayog nahīṃ karnā cāhie*). Transcribed in Peter Flügel, "The Unknown Loṅkā: Tradition and the Cultural Unconscious," in *Jaina Studies*, ed. Colette Caillat and Nalini Balbir (Delhi: Motilal Banarsidass, 2008), 276.

CHAPTER 1

1 See, for example, *Chāndogya Upaniṣad* 4.5 and *Kaṭha Upaniṣad* 2.16, trans. Patrick Olivelle, *The Early Upaniṣads: Annotated Text and Translation* (New York: Oxford University Press, 1998), 175, 276. For an early history of the syllable *oṃ*, see Finnian Gerety, "This Whole World Is OM: Song, Soteriology, and the Emergence of the Sacred Syllable" (PhD diss., Harvard University, 2015).

2 For a good discussion of the attitudes of Buddhists, Jains, Mīmāṃsakas, and other Indian philosophers to ritual language, see Phyllis Granoff, "Buddhaghoṣa's Penance and Siddhasena's Crime: Remarks on Some Buddhist and Jain Attitudes towards the Language of Religious Texts," in *From Benares to Beijing: Essays on Buddhism and Chinese Religion*, ed. Koichi Shinohara and Gregory Schopen (Oakville: Mosaic Press, 1991), 17–33.

3 Alexis Sanderson, "The Doctrine of the Mālinīvijayottaratantra," in *Ritual and Speculation in Early Tantrism: Studies in Honour of André Padoux*, ed. Teun Goudriaan (Albany: State University of New York Press, 1992), 286.

4 On Jains' use of both Sanskrit and Prakrit mantras, see Paul Dundas, "Becoming Gautama: Mantra and History in Śvetāmbara Jainism," in *Open Boundaries: Jain Commu-

nities and Cultures in Indian History, ed. John E. Cort (Albany: State University of New York Press, 1998), 34; and Paul Dundas, "Jain Attitudes towards the Sanskrit Language," in Ideology and Status of Sanskrit, ed. J. E. M. Houben (Leiden: E. J. Brill, 1996), 154–55.

5 Different lists of *vargaṇā*s exist in Jain literature. Digambara texts such as the *Ṣaṭkhaṇḍāgama* list twenty-three different combinations of matter. For this list and references to other texts, see Jinendra Varṇī, ed., *Jainendra Siddhānt Koś*, 6th ed., 6 pts. (Delhi: Bhāratīya Jñānpīṭh, 2002), s.v. *vargaṇā*. Śvetāmbara texts such as the *Bhagavatīsūtra* list eight. See Devendra Muni Shastri, *Source Book in Jaina Philosophy* (Udaipur: Sri Tarak Guru Jain Granthalaya, 1983), 171–72. The aggregates of matter that cause karma (*kārmaṇavargaṇā*) and speech (*bhāṣāvargaṇā*) are found in both lists. See also Małgorzata Glincka, "Materiality of Language in Jain Philosophy: Introductory Matters," *Internetowy Magazyn Filozoficzny Hybris* 35 (2016): 156–76.

6 Not all Jain texts agree on the qualities of the soul, but by the end of the first half of the Common Era, Jains had agreed that each soul contains infinite knowledge (*jñāna*) and perception (*darśana*). See S. C. Jain, *Structure and Functions of Soul in Jainism* (Delhi: Bharatiya Jnanpith, 1978), 98–142. For a brief discussion of consciousness (*caitanya*), bliss (*sukha*), and energy (*vīrya*) as the qualities (*guṇa*) of the soul, see P. S. Jaini, *Jaina Path*, 104–6.

7 Dundas, "Jain Attitudes towards the Sanskrit Language," 139.

8 The *Paümacariya* of Vimalasūri (ca. first to fifth centuries CE) has one of the earliest lists of *vidyā*s. See U. P. Shah, "A Peep into the Early History," 851. Jhavery, *Critical Study of Jain Mantraśāstra*, 271–87, provides an impressive overview of discussions of *vidyā*s and mantras in Śvetāmbara *āgama*s and their commentaries. For other references to *vidyā*s in Jain texts, see Kalipada Mitra, "Magic and Miracle in Jaina Literature," *Indian Historical Quarterly* XV, no. 2 (1939): 175–82.

9 André Padoux, "Mantras—What Are They?" In *Understanding Mantras*, ed. Harvey P. Alper (Albany, NY: State University of New York Press, 1989), 295. While this claim is contested by Dundas, "Becoming Gautama," 32, few scholars have done much work to undermine it.

10 Vincent Eltschinger, "Dharmakīrti on Mantras and Their Efficiency," in *Esoteric Buddhist Studies: Identity in Diversity. Proceedings of the International Conference on Esoteric Buddhist Studies, Koyasan University, 5 Sept.–8 Sept. 2006*, ed. ICEBS Editorial Board (Koyasan: Koyasan University, 2008), 273–89.

11 Phyllis Granoff, "Unspoken Rules of Debate in Medieval India and the Boundaries of Knowledge" (lecture, Scholasticisms' Practice, and Practices' Scholasticism, second workshop, CNRS, Paris, April 2015).

12 Granoff, "Unspoken Rules of Debate."

13 *Sūtrakṛtāṅga* 2.2.27, trans. Jacobi, *SBE*, 22:366–67. For other examples of early Jain texts' criticisms of occult practices, see John E. Cort, "Medieval Jaina Goddess Traditions," *Numen* 34, no. 2 (1987): 238; U. P. Shah, "A Peep into the Early History," 114–15; and Nalini Balbir, "The Jain Tradition on Protection and Its Means," in *Katā me rakkhā, kata me parittā: Protecting the Protective Texts and Manuscripts*, ed. Claudio Cicuzza (Bankok / Lumbini: Fragile Palm Leaver Foundation / Lumbini International Research Institute, 2018), 251–55.

14 For a manuscript of the original *Praśnavyākaraṇa* recently found in Nepal, see Diwakar Acharya, "The Original *Paṇhavāyaraṇa / Praśnavyākaraṇa* Discovered," *International Journal of Jaina Studies (Online)* 3, 6 (2007): 1–10.

15 Christopher Minkowski, "Why Should We Read the Maṅgala Verses?" in *Śāstrārambha: Inquiries into the Preamble in Sanskrit*, ed. Walter Slaje (Wiesbaden: Harrassowitz Verlag, 2008), 17.

16 On these superhuman powers, see Kristi L. Wiley, "Supernatural Powers and Their Attainment in Jainism," in *Yoga Powers: Extraordinary Capacities Attained through Meditation and Concentration*, ed. Knut A. Jacobsen (Leiden: E. J. Brill, 2012), 145–94; and Peter Flügel, "Sacred Matter: Reflections on the Relationship of Karmic and Natural Causality in Jaina Philosophy," *Journal of Indian Philosophy* 40, no. 2 (2012): 125–33.

17 The best English introductions to this mantra are Gustav Roth, "Notes on Pamca-Namokkāra Parama-Maṅgala," in *Indian Studies: Selected Papers by Gustav Roth*, ed. Heinz Bechert and Petra Kieffer-Pülz (Delhi: Sri Satguru Publications, 1986), 129–46; Paul Dundas, *The Jains*, 2nd ed. (London: Routledge, 2002), 81–83; and Umakant P. Shah, *Jaina-Rūpa-Maṇḍana (Jaina Iconography)* (New Delhi: Abhinav, 1987), 41–46.

18 Knut A. Jacobsen, ed., *Yoga Powers: Extraordinary Capacities Attained through Meditation and Concentration* (Leiden: E. J. Brill, 2012). The eight classical *siddhi*s most commonly found in Brahmanical texts are famously found in the *Yogasūtrabhāṣya* I.44–45 (ca. 325–425 CE). The powers can be translated as: (1) smallness (*aṇimā*), (2) lightness (*laghimā*), (3) greatness (*mahimā*), (4) obtaining (*prāpti*), (5) willfulness (*prākāmya*), (6) pervasion (*vaśitva*), (7) lordship (*īśitṛtva*), and (8) the suppression of desire (*kāmāvasāyitva*) (Sarbacker, "Power and Meaning in the Yogasūtra of Patañjali," in Jacobsen, *Yoga Powers*, 204). A comprehensive discussion of South Asian Buddhists' understandings of superhuman powers is found in Fiordalis, "Miracles and Superhuman Powers."

19 For approximate dates for early Jain literature, I rely on the canonical stages established by Suzuko Ohira, *A Study of the Bhagavatīsūtra: A Chronological Analysis* (Ahmedabad: Prakrit Text Society, 1994), 1–39. Ohira assigns discussions of superhuman powers to the early fifth canonical stage, or the second half of the fourth century CE.

20 Sonya Rhie Quintanilla, *History of Early Stone Sculpture at Mathura, ca. 150 BCE–100 CE* (Leiden: Brill, 2007), 101, citing figs. 112, 168, and 170 in the same book.

21 For a discussion of energy or the power to act (*vīrya*) as a quality of the soul, see Flügel, "Sacred Matter," 7–9.

22 For a summary of the scholarship on the dating of the *Trilokaprajñapti*, see Jyoti Prasad Jain, *The Jaina Sources of the History of Ancient India (100 B.C.–A.D. 900)* (Delhi: Munshi Ram Manohar Lal, 1964), 137–39.

23 *Aup, sūtra* 24, p. 58, lists superhuman powers from each of the eight Digambara categories except the power to perform austerities (*tapas*). See Surendra Bothara's discussion in *Aup*, 55–64. Other Śvetāmbara sources from the first half of the first millennium on *labdhi*s include the *Sthānāṅgasūtra* 4.2.168, *Bh* 8.2.71–78, and what Śvetāmbaras believe to be Umāsvāti's autocommentary (*Svopajñabhāṣya*) on *TS* 10.7, which outlines thirty-six different *labdhi*s.

24 *Bh* 15.1.543, cited in Ācārya Hastīmala, *Jain Dharm kā Maulik Itihās*, pt. 1, 4th ed. (Jaipur: Samyagjñān Pracārak Maṇḍal, 1999), 567.

25 For a *paṭṭāvali* that places the composition of the *Ṣaṭkhaṇḍāgama* by Bhūtabali and Puṣpadanta 683 years after the death of Mahāvīra in 527 BCE, see Rudolf A. F. Hoernle, "Three Further Pattavalis of the Digambaras," *Indian Antiquary* XXI (1892): 58.

26 Scholars have hypothesized a variety of dates for the *Ṣaṭkhaṇḍāgama*, from the first century BCE to the sixth century CE. For a good overview of the scholarly debate over the dating of the *Ṣaṭkhaṇḍāgama*, see Kristi L. Wiley, "Early Śvetāmbara and Digambara Karma Literature: A Comparison," in *Jaina Studies: Papers of the 12th World Sanskrit Conference*, ed. Colette Caillat and Nalini Balbir (Delhi: Motilal Banarsidass, 2008), 57n36.

27 According to Jain philosophy, there are five types of knowledge: (1) sensory (*mati*), (2) scriptural (*śruta*), (3) clairvoyance (*avadhi*), mind reading (*manaḥparyaya/manaḥparyāya*), and (5) omniscience (*kevala*). See Wiley, *A to Z of Jainism*, 112. For a discussion of different types of clairvoyance, see Kristi L. Wiley, "Extrasensory Perception and Knowledge in Jainism," in *Essays in Jaina Philosophy and Religion*, ed. Piotr Balcerowicz (Delhi: Motilal Banarsidass, 2003), 89–109.

28 See *TP* 4.978–79 for a description of *koṣṭhabuddhiṛddhi*. *Dh* 4.1.6 (*SKhĀ*, *khaṇḍa* 4, *bhāga* 1, line 6) explains that a mendicant who has this power "has the ability to retain what he has learned for a minimum of countable years to a maximum of uncountable years." Wiley, "Supernatural Powers," 168.

29 Literally, "praise to those who have seed-intellect"—i.e., those who can understand a teaching from a single word in the form of a seed. See *TP* 4.975–77.

30 *TP* 4.980–83 outlines three different types of this power: (1) knowing the text after a keyword (*anusārin*), (2) knowing the text before the keyword (*pratisārin*), and (3) knowing the text before and after the keyword (*ubhayasārin*). Peter Flügel, "The Power of Death" (unpublished manuscript, 2008).

31 *TP* 4.984–86 and *Dh* 4.1.9 agree that those who possess this power can decipher and respond to multiple animals and humans speaking to them in their own languages from a great distance outside the range of normal hearing. Śvetāmbaras have slightly different understandings of this power. For these interpretations, see Wiley, "Supernatural Powers," 160, and *Yogaśāstra* of Hemacandrasūri, trans.Olle Qvarnström as *The Yogaśāstra of Hemacandra: A Twelfth Century Handbook on Śvetāmbara Jainism* (Cambridge, MA: Harvard University Press, 2002), 21n21.

32 *Ṛjumati* and *vipulamati* are the two divisions of the fourth type of knowledge in Jainism, mind reading. See *TS* 1.24.

33 The fourteen *pūrva*s are understood as the earliest Jain scriptures composed during the lifetime of the twenty-third *tīrthaṅkara* Pārśva. Those sages who know all fourteen *pūrva*s are called "Śrutakevalin" or "Sarvākṣarasannipātin." According to Digambaras, Bhadrabāhu I, the last to know all fourteen *pūrva*s, passed ten of them to Sthūlabhadra, the eighth patriarch of the Jain community after Mahāvīra. The next seven patriarchs, Sthūlabhadra to Vajra, knew the contents of these ten *pūrva*s, and after Vajra, the entirety of the fourteen *pūrva*s were forgotten. See Rudolf A. F. Hoernle, "Two Pattavalis

of the Sarasvati Gachchha of the Digambara Jains," *Indian Antiquary* 20 (1891): 341–61. In Jain texts of both sects, Daśapūrvins and Śrutakevalins are known for their superhuman abilities. *Bh* 5.4.36 declares that Śrutakevalins are capable of producing a thousand identical versions of a single object such as a pitcher or an umbrella, while *TP* 4.998–1000 describes how those who have studied ten *pūrva*s can approach the gods to receive 1,200 different magical spells.

34 *TP* 4.1002–16 outlines eight *naimittika*s, or types of divination. Wiley, "Supernatural Powers," 169–70, translates them as prognostication: "(1) by signs in the heavens (*nabba*) . . . (2) by signs of the earth (*bhauma*) . . . (3) by limbs (*aṅga*) [of the body, e.g., bodily secretions] . . . (4) by sound/voice (*svara*) . . . (5) by marks (*vyañjana*) . . . (6) by bodily marks [(e.g., lotuses on hands or feet (*lakṣaṇa*)] . . . (7) by indicatory marks (*cihna*) . . . such as clothing that is torn . . . [and] (8) by dreams (*svapna*)."

35 *Dh* 4.1.15 and *TP* 4.1024–32 list eight and eleven different types of *vikriyārddhi*, respectively. Both texts agree that the first eight types correspond to the eight classical *siddhi*s of yoga philosophy (*aṇimā*, etc.). The *Trilokaprajñapti* adds three other types to this list: nonresistance (*apratighāta*), invisibility (*adṛṣyatā*), and changing form at will (*kāmarūpitva*). Flügel, "The Power of Death," n.p.

36 Wiley, "Supernatural Powers," 176–80, discusses different types of Digambara and Śvetāmbara *cāraṇa*s at length. For another English translation of some Śvetāmbara accounts of different *cāraṇas*, such as flying by using one's legs (*jaṅghācāraṇa*) and flying by using spells (*vidyācaraṇa*), see *Triṣaṣtiśalākāpuruṣacarita* of Hemacandra, trans. Helen Johnson as *The Lives of Sixty-Three Illustrious Persons*, vol. 1 (Baroda: Oriental Institute, 1931), 79n114.

37 *TP* 4.1017–21 and *Dh* 4.1.18 list four types of ascetic wisdom (*prajñāśramaṇa*): (1) related to actions in a previous existence (*autpattika*) (2) resulting from one's birth placement (*pāriṇāmika*), (3) related to good behavior (e.g., knowledge of the twelve key canonical scriptures, the *aṅgas*) (*vainayika*), and (4) resulting from austerities alone (*karmajā*). See Wiley, "Supernatural Powers," 171.

38 *TP* 4.1078 and *Dh* 4.1.20 explain this power as having the ability to directly effect action through one's words (e.g., saying "die" will cause someone to die). See Wiley, "Supernatural Powers," 171–72.

39 *TP* 4.1079 confirms that by the power of this *ṛddhi*, a great sage filled with anger can merely look at someone and they will die just as someone dies when bitten by a snake.

40 *TP* 4.1051 and *Dh* 4.1.22 explain that *ugratapas* involves fasting for one day after mendicant initiation, breaking the fast, beginning another fast, and continuing this pattern by successively adding one day to the length of the fasts for either six months (*avasthita-ugratapas*) or until the mendicant eventually fasts to death (*ugra-ugratapas*). The mendicant thus fasts for one day, eats for one day, fasts for two days, eats for one day, fasts for three days, and so on. See Wiley, "Supernatural Powers," 172.

41 See *TP* 4.1052 and *Dh* 4.1.23 for an explanation of *dīptatapa*s, which does not refer to a specific fast, since various fasts can result in humans glowing as bright as the sun.

42 *TP* 4.1053 lists only urine and excrement. *Dh* 4.1.24 adds semen to the list and claims that four types of food can be transformed in this way. Johnson, in *Triṣaṣtiśalākāpu-*

ruṣacarita, trans. Johnson as *Lives of Sixty-Three Illustrious Persons*, 5:299n294, claims these four types are "solid food (*aśana*), drink (*pāna*), fruit (*khādya*), and betel, ginger, etc. (*svādhya*) usually taken after a meal."

43 Here I follow the explanation given in *TP* 4.1054, which explains that by the power of this *ṛddhi*, mendicants, with the strength of the first four types of right knowledge (*mati*, *śruta*, *avadhi*, *manaḥparyāya*), can undertake all types of fasts (*upavāsa*). *Dh* 4.1.25, on the other hand, claims that these advanced practitioners have obtained a variety of extraordinary powers, including the eight classical *siddhi*s of yoga philosophy (*aṇimā*, etc.); the eight different types of extraordinary powers of movement (*cāraṇa*); the ability to heal with all parts of the body (*sarvauṣadhi*); the powers of poisonous sight and touch; and clairvoyance.

44 See *TP* 4.1055; and *Dh* 4.1.26.

45 *TP* 4.1056–7 and *Dh* 4.1.27 agree on the definition of *ghoraparākramaṛddhi*, naming objects such as fire, mountains, and lightning that these mendicants can cause to rain from the sky.

46 This *ṛddhi* is the only one in the *maṅgala* not found in *TP*. *Dh* 4.1.28 explains that *ghora* means "fierce" (*raudra*) and this power can arise in order to perform a fierce act.

47 *Dh* 4.1.29 describes how fear, disease, famine, enmity, and the like will not arise by the power of the austerities of those mendicants who have adopted the five *samiti*s (care in walking, speaking, accepting alms, picking up and putting down objects, and relieving oneself), and three *gupti*s (restraining body, speech, and mind). *TP* describes several interpretations of the superhuman power *aghorabrahmacāritva*: *TP* 4.1058 claims that thieves, strife, or wars will not happen in the vicinity of a mendicant with this power, *TP* 4.1059 claims that this power rids oneself of bad dreams, and *TP* 4.1060 claims that by the arising of this power, great people undertake celibacy (here termed *aghora*).

48 See *TP* 4.1068.

49 *TP* 4.1069 describes how with this power, saliva, phlegm, and mucus from one's eyes and nose can cure diseases.

50 See *TP* 4.1070.

51 Here I follow the description in *TP* 4.1072. *Dh* 4.1.33 includes semen in the list of medicinal bodily substances.

52 *TP* 4.1073 explains how water or wind that comes into contact with the nails, hair, etc. of mendicants who have undertaken severe austerities and obtained this power becomes curative. *Dh* 4.1.34 describes how "all the impurities of the body, . . . including the seven secretions (*dhātu*) chyle, blood, flesh, fat, bone, marrow, and semen, become medicinal." Wiley, "Supernatural Powers," 175. The commentary in *Aup*, 60–64, discusses these curative powers in a Śvetāmbara context.

53 *TP* 4.1062 explains that with this power, one can understand the entirety of the scriptural teachings of the *tīrthaṅkaras* (*śruta*) in under a *muhūrta* (forty-eight minutes). *Dh* 4.1.35 explains that with this power, even after thinking about all the realities of the three worlds described in the twelve *aṅgas*, one does not become fatigued.

54 *TP* 4.1063–64 describes how *vacanabalaṛddhi* is the ability to pronounce and understand all the teachings of the *tīrthaṅkaras* in under a *muhūrta* without tiring. *Dh* 4.1.36

describes this power as the ability to recite the twelve *aṅga*s many times without tiring. In the Śvetāmbara context, Bothara, in *Aup*, 57, translates *vacanabalin* as one who has the "strength of speech which include[s] resolutely sticking to [a] promise."

55 *TP* 1065–66 and *Dh* 4.1.37 both define *kāyabalaṛddhi* as the ability to lift the three worlds with a single finger. In the Śvetāmbara context, Bothara, in *Aup*, 57, translates *kāyabalin* as one who has the "strength of body which include[s] the untiring capacity to endure hunger, thirst, heat, cold, and other torments."

56 Flügel, "Power of Death," explains that lines 38–41 refer to either hearing (*śrava*) speech that is like these substances, or the influx (*āsrava*) of these substances. Thus, while *TP* 4.1080, 1082, 1084, and 1086 explain these powers as the ability to transform food into milk, ghee, honey, and nectar, respectively, by a mere touch, *TP* 4.1081, 1083, 1085, and 1087 confirm that these powers allow one to pacify the sadness of people and animals with one's speech. *Dh* 4.1.38–41 agrees that both understandings are possible.

57 *TP* 4.1089–90 explains that if a mendicant with this power eats from a certain place, the food he leaves behind will remain permanently, no matter how many people are fed from it. Even if that same day an army of a universal emperor (*cakravartin*) comes to eat, not a single particle of food will be depleted. For a more detailed discussion of all the powers mentioned in this *maṅgala*, see Wiley, "Superhuman Powers," 168–75.

58 For English introductions to this text, see the introduction by Moti Chandra to *Aṅgavidyā*, ed. Muni Shri Punyavijyaya as *Aṅgavijjā: Science of Divination through Physical Signs & Symbols* (Banaras: Prakrit Text Society, 1957), 35–55; and Paul Dundas, "A Non-imperial Religion? Jainism in Its 'Dark Age,'" in *Between the Empires: Society in India 300 BCE to 400 CE*, ed. Patrick Olivelle (New York: Oxford University Press, 2006), 403–5.

59 The *Mahāniśīthasūtra* has been notoriously difficult to date. Walther Schubring, *Studien zum Mahānisīha, Kapitel 6–8* (Hamburg: Cram, de Gruyter, 1951), 66, discusses a prophecy in *Mahāniśīthasūtra* VII, para. 44, that predicts a historical event from the beginning of the eighth century. Jozef Deleu notes that a text likely composed in 900 CE has borrowed extensively from *Mahāniśīthasūtra*. See Deleu, "A Preliminary Note on the Mahānisīha," in Deleu and Walther Schubring, *Studien zum Mahānisīha, Kapitel 1–5* (Hamburg: Cram, de Gruyter, 1963), 1n2.

60 On this *ācāmāmla* fast, which is called *āyambil* in Gujarati and Hindi and requires practitioners to eat only certain types of unseasoned rice or cereal once a day, see Cort, *Jains in the World*, 135–36.

61 See the summary of scholarship on Śrutadevatā in Acharya, "The Original *Paṇhavāyaraṇa*," 6n11.

62 For a helpful list of names of Jain spells listed alphabetically, see Jagdish Chandra Jain, *Life in Ancient India as Depicted in the Jain Canons* (Bombay: New Book Company, 1947), 226–35.

63 Minkowski, "Why Should We Read the Maṅgala Verses?" 18. On the development of astrology in India and the introduction of Greek astrology around the second century CE, see the second chapter of David Pingree, *Jyotiḥśāstra: Astral and Mathematical Literature* (Wiesbaden: Otto Harrassowitz, 1981).

64 Minkowski, "Why Should We Read the Maṅgala Verses?" 7.

65 Minkowski, 9.

66 Richard Salomon, *Indian Epigraphy: A Guide to the Study of Inscriptions in Sanskrit, Prakrit, and the Other Indo-Aryan Languages* (New York: Oxford University Press, 1998), 67–68.

67 For the original inscription and translation, see Alexander Cunningham, *Inscriptions of Asoka* (Calcutta: Office of the Superintendent of Government Printing, 1877), 132 and plate XVII. For some context for the inscription, see P. S. Jaini, *Jaina Path*, 278.

68 Based on *paṭṭāvali*s, the earliest date for the completion of this Śvetāmbara text is put at 80 CE by Leumann, *Outline*, 78. The final compilation of the *Āvaśyakaniryukti*, after a long period of development, is placed in the fourth to fifth centuries CE by Ohira, *Bhagavatī Sūtra*, 11, 163. On the similarities between the *Mūlācāra* and the *Āvaśyakaniryukti*, see Ernst Leumann, *An Outline of the Āvaśyaka Literature*, trans. George Baumann (Ahmedabad: L. D. Institute of Indology, 2010), 44–58. See also Nalini Balbir, *Āvaśyaka-Studien 1: Introduction générale et traductions* (Stuttgart: Franz Steiner, 1993), 39.

69 I follow Vasunandin's twelfth-century commentary on verse 513, which glosses *karaṇa* as "body, speech, and mind." See Mūl, 360. A slightly different version of *Mūl*, v. 514 (*eso paṃcaṇamoyāro savvapāvapaṇāsaṇo | maṃgalesu ya savvesu paḍamaṃ havadi maṃgalaṃ ||*), is now the final portion of the *pañcanamaskāra* of image-worshiping Śvetāmbaras. The version is found in the *Mahāniśīthasūtra* and is termed *paṃcamcaṃgala: namo arahantāṇaṃ, namo siddhāṇaṃ, namo āyariyāṇaṃ, namo uvajjhāyāṇaṃ, namo loe savvasāhūṇaṃ*. Its final lines (*anuṣṭubh*) correspond to the description of the *maṅgala* in the *Mulācāra* (Mūl, v. 514): *eso paṃcanamokkāro, savvapāvapaṇāsaṇo, maṅgalāṇaṃ ca savvvesiṃ, paḍhamaṃ havaï maṅgalaṃ*, "this fivefold praise destroys all bad karma and is the foremost *maṅgala* of all the *maṅgalas*." Present-day Digambaras do often recite these final four lines in certain rituals, but they are not as commonly found in Digambara versions of the mantra, since Digambaras believe they are not an essential part of the mantra but instead simply explain its power. Members of the two Śvetāmbara anti-iconic sects, Sthānakavāsīs and Terāpanthīs, also reject these four lines, since they do not accept the *Mahāniśīthasūtra* as authoritative.

70 Vīrasena mentions in the *Dhavalā* that he composed the text during the rule of the Rāṣṭrakūṭa king Jagatuṅga, father of Amoghavarṣa. See *Hīrālāl* Jain's introduction to the *Dhavalā* in *ṢKhĀ*, *khaṇḍa* 1, *bhāga* 1, *pustaka* 1, pp. 35–36.

71 In his introduction to the *Mahābandha*, for example, Devendrakumār Śāstrī insists that the *pañcanamaskāra* must be uncomposed. One piece of evidence he provides is the claim that the first *tīrthaṅkara* Ṛṣabha is said to have performed the repentance rite *pratikramaṇa*, which includes the recitation of the *pañcanamaskāra*. Because Puṣpadanta lived thousands of years after Ṛṣabha, he could not have composed these praises, Śāstrī claims. These types of arguments, however, have little basis in history. Devendrakumār Śāstrī, "Prastāvanā," in *Mahābaṃdho*, book 1, 3rd ed., ed. and trans. Sumeru Divākar (Delhi: Bhāratīya Jñānpīṭh), 48–56.

72 *Dh* 4.1.44, in *ṢKhĀ*, *khaṇḍa* 4, *bhāga* 1, *pustaka* 9, p. 103, cited in Wiley, "Supernatural Powers," 157.

73 Bhadrabāhu I (ca. third century BCE) is supposedly the last monk to have remembered the entirety of the contents of the *pūrvas*. See Wiley, *A to Z of Jainism*, 176.

74 See *TP* 1.9–11, cited in *ṢKhĀ*, *khaṇḍa* 4, *bhāga* 1, *pustaka* 9, p. 33n5–6.

75 See also *TP* 1.14–15, cited in *ṢKhĀ*, *khaṇḍa* 4, *bhāga* 1, *pustaka* 9, p. 34n4–5.

76 For an introduction these concepts, see Jayandra Soni, "Dravya, Guṇa and Paryāya in Jaina Thought," *Journal of Indian Philosophy* 19 (1991): 75–88.

77 On *bhavya* and *abhavya jīvas*, see Padmanabh S. Jaini, "Bhavyatva and Abhavyatva: A Jaina Doctrine of 'Predestination,'" in *Mahāvīra and His Teachings*, ed. A. N. Upadhye et al. (Bombay: Mahāvīra Nirvāṇa Mahotsava Samiti, 1977), 95–111.

78 For a discussion of *nikṣepa*, see Bansidhar Bhatt, *The Canonical Nikṣepa. Studies in Jaina Dialectics* (Leiden: E. J. Brill, 1978).

79 A brief summary of Vīrasena's application of *nikṣepa* to the term "*maṅgala*" is as follows: *Nāmamaṅgala* refers to words (*nāman*) that are auspicious in and of themselves, without reference to the objects they denote (*nimitta*) (*Dh* 1.1.1, p. 18). *Sthāpanāmaṅgala* designates a depiction written, carved, and so on of something auspicious, either representationally (*sadbhāva*), such as an icon that physical resembles a *jina*, or nonrepresentationally, as in something like a shell that is imagined to be a Jain ideal (*asadbhāva*) (*Dh* 1.1.1, p. 21). *Dravyamaṅgala* refers to a physical substance (*dravya*), living or nonliving, that is inclined toward an auspicious modification, such as an unmarried girl (*kanyā*) or a pot (*Dh* 1.1.1, pp. 21–29). Places where ascetics have practiced austerities, such as Ūrjayanta (aka Girnar), Champapur, and Pavapuri, are known as *kṣetramaṅgala* (*Dh* 1.1.1, p. 30), and auspicious times when ascetics obtain omniscience (*kevalajñāna*) due to the destruction of karmas, such as the thrice-yearly occasion of the festival on Nandīśvaradvīpa, are called *kālamaṅgala* (*Dh* 1.1.1, p. 30). Finally, *bhāvamaṅgala* is present when the current mode (*bhāva*) of a substance is auspicious (*Dh* 1.1.1, pp. 30–31).

80 Chapter 4 of this book discusses pure meditation in depth.

81 Even though he mentions that the disciples are associated with these powers, Vīrasena insists that all forty-four praises of the *ṛddhi-maṅgala* refer to *jinas* with superhuman powers, presumably to emphasize that only praises to the most advanced practitioners of Jainism are powerful enough to create change in the universe (*Dh* 4.1.3, pp. 55–56). His commentary on the praises to those who know the ten *pūrvas*, for example, insists that while there were many people who knew these ten texts, this praise is not to the *daśapūrvins* who were not *jinas* (*Dh* 4.1.12, pp. 69–70).

82 This verse is atypical. The seven different types of superhuman powers listed here do not correspond with the seven types of powers that are described in the *ṛddhi-maṅgala*. It is not clear why clairvoyance and mind-reading are listed separately from the powers of intellect (*buddhiṛddhi*), since they are usually included in this category. See *TP* 4.969.

83 For an English translation and the original text of this story in the *Āvaśyakacūrṇi* and Haribhadrasūri's *Āvaśyakaṭīkā* (eighth century), see Rolf Heinrich Koch, "Āvaśyaka-Tales from the Namaskāra-Vyākhyā," *Indologica Taurinensia* XVII–XVIII (1991–92): 242–45.

84 Granoff, "Buddhaghoṣa's Penance," makes this same point.

85 Another of the most popular recitations among Digambaras and Śvetāmbaras, the Prakrit "Fourfold Maṅgala," the *cattārimaṅgala*, honors the four auspicious entities of

the soul (*arhat*), the liberated soul (*siddha*), the mendicant (*sādhu*), and the *dharma* taught by the omniscient one (*kevalin*): *arahantā maṅgalaṃ, siddhā maṅgalaṃ, sāhū maṅgalaṃ, kevalipannatto dhammo maṅgalaṃ*. For a story in a ninth-century commentary on the *Uttarādhyāyana* on how this invocation protected a queen lost in a forest, see Balbir, "The Jain Tradition on Protection," 268.

CHAPTER 2

1 Suketu Mehta, *Maximum City: Bombay Lost and Found* (New York: Vintage Books, 2004), 532, 511, 512.

2 S. Mehta, *Maximum City*, 520.

3 For two documentaries on Jainism that include presentations of initiation ceremonies, see *Frontiers of Peace: Jainism in India* (1986; Madison: University of Wisconsin Center for South Asia), DVD; and Michael Tobias, dir., *Ahimsa: Non-violence* (1987; Direct Cinema Limited), DVD. For a fictionalized account of Jain initiation in the first person, see the second chapter of Gita Mehta, *A River Sutra* (New York: Vintage Books, 1993). For some studies of Śvetāmbara renunciation today, see B. C. Agrawal, "Diksha Ceremony in Jainism: an Analysis of Its Socio-political Ramifications," *Eastern Anthropologist* 25 (1972): 13–20; John E. Cort, "The Śvetāmbar Mūrtipūjak Jain Mendicant," *Man (N.S.)* 26 (1991): 651–71; and S. Holmstrom, "Towards a Politics of Renunciation: Jain Women and Asceticism in Rajasthan" (PhD diss., University of Edinburgh, 1988). The most detailed portraits of *dīkṣā* found in English-language literature is N. Shāntā, *The Unknown Pilgrims: The Voice of the Sādhvīs: The History, Spirituality and Life of the Jaina Women Ascetics*, trans. M. Rogers (Delhi: Sri Satguru Publications, 1997), 444–72, 653–60.

4 Michael Carrithers, "Jainism and Buddhism as Enduring Historical Streams," *Journal of the Anthropological Society of Oxford* 21, no. 2 (1990): 153–54.

5 Carrithers, "Jainism and Buddhism as Streams," 154.

6 For a detailed analysis of the renunciation of Mahāvīra in the *Ācārāṅgasūtra* and *Kalpasūtra* in the context of an examination of some early Śvetāmbara texts on renunciation, see Peter Flügel, "The *Nikkhamaṇa* of Mahāvīra according to the Old Biographies," in *Cāruśrī: Essays in Honour of Svastiśrī Cārukīrti Bhaṭṭāraka Paṭṭācārya*, ed. Jayandra Soni and Hampa Nagarajaiah (Bengaluru: Sapna Book House, 2019), 67–80.

7 *ĀS* 766.7–9; 24–26, 769.1–4, in *SBE*, trans. Jacobi, 22:199–200, translation emended. P. S. Jaini, *Jaina Path*, 15–20, drawing upon earlier sources (mentioned in Dundas, *The Jains*, 31), has explained that in early Jain texts, a single vow of equanimity, rather than the five vows that were later codified, was taken at the time of initiation.

8 See, for example, *Sūtrakṛtāṅga* 1.1.2.12: *savvappagaṃ viukkassaṃ savvaṃ ṇūmaṃ vihūṇiyā | appattiyaṃ akammaṃse eyam aṭṭhaṃ mige cue* || "Shaking off greed, pride, deceit and wrath, one becomes free from karman. This is a subject (which an ignorant man, like) a brute animal, does not attend to." Trans. Jacobi, *SBE*, 22:241.

9 The details of the Digambara initiation I witnessed are published in Ellen Gough,

"Tantric Ritual Elements in the Initiation of a Digambara," in *Tantric Communities in Context*, ed. Nina Mirnig, Marion Rastelli, and Vincent Eltschinger (Vienna: Austrian Academy of Sciences, 2019), 233–73.

10 Of the two main branches of Digambara Jainism—the Bīsapantha and the Terāpantha—Vairāgyanandī identifies as a Bīsapanthī. He was initiated in 1994 by Ācārya Kunthusāgara, a disciple of Ādisāgara Aṅkalīkara's successor Mahāvīrakīrti (1910–1972), and he became an *ācārya* in 2005. Ācārya Vairāgyanandī confirmed that the rites of initiation he follows are found in the manual *Vimal Bhakti Saṅgrah*, which was compiled by the nun Āryikā Syādvādamatī, who belongs to a lineage called the Vimala Saṅgha, which traces its origins to another of Ādisāgara Aṅkalīkara's disciples, Vimalasāgara (1915–1961).

11 Modern Digambaras have not standardized which scripture is imparted at the time of initiation. When I participated in an initiation in Pushpagiri, Madhya Pradesh, the initiating guru, Ācārya Puṣpadantasāgara, gifted the initiates, both male and female, a modern Hindi book on mendicant discipline titled *Vimal Bhakti Puṇya*.

12 Not all Digambara *vidhāna*s end with a fire offering (*homa*), but many do. Whether there is a fire offering depends on the amount of time devoted to the ceremony; shortened ceremonies do not include one.

13 Nayacandrasāgara and Pūrṇacandrasāgara became the twenty-sixth and twenty-seventh *ācārya*s of Ānandasāgarasūri's *samudāya* in the Sāgara Śākhā of the Tapā Gaccha (on this *śākhā*, see Peter Flügel, "Demographic Trends in Jaina Monasticism," in *Studies in Jain History and Culture*, ed. Flügel, [London: Routledge, 2006], 373n66). The rites of promotion they followed are outlined in detail in the *Bṛhad Yog Vidhi*, a lengthy mid-twentieth-century Gujarati manual on initiation, promotion, and the daily rites of mendicants by the monk Pūrṇacandrasāgarasūri, who also belongs to Ānandasāgarasūri's *samudāya*. I discuss this text in more detail in chapter 5.

14 On the *sthāpanācārya*, see Cort, *Jains in the World*, 101–3. See also figure 5.4 for two *stāpanācārya*s placed in front of the *sūrimantrapaṭa* Nandighoṣasūri worships.

15 For some datings of Kundakunda to between the first and third centuries CE, see A. N. Upadhye's introduction to *Pravacanasāra* of Kundakunda, ed. and trans. A. N. Upadhye as *Pravacanasāra (Pavayaṇasāra): A Pro-canonical Text of the Jainas* (Bombay: Parama-Śruta-Prabhāvaka-Maṇḍala, 1964), 10–16. For a placement of him in the eighth century, see M. A. Dhaky, "The Date of Kundakundācārya," in *Pt. Dalsukhbhai Malvania Felicitation*, Vol. 1, ed. M. A. Dhaky and Sagarmal Jain (Varanasi: P. V. Research Institute, 1991), 187–206.

16 The twelfth-century commentator Jayasena understands the first "mark" (*liṅgam*) of this verse to be the "mark of one's physical appearance" (*dravyaliṅgam*), and the second the "mark of one's internal disposition" (*bhāvaliṅgam*) (Sanskrit text in *Pravacanasāra*, trans. Upadhye as *Pravacanasāra* (*Pavayaṇasāra*), 279).

17 *Pravacanasāra* 3.1–5. The translation is adapted from *Pravacanasāra*, trans. Upadhye as *Pravacanasāra* (*Pavayaṇasāra*), 405–6.

18 On the *samiti*, see Robert Williams, *Jaina Yoga: A Survey of the Mediaeval Śrāvakācāras* (1963; repr. Delhi: Motilal Banarsidass, 1991), 32.

19 On the *āvaśyaka*, see Williams, *Jaina Yoga*, 184, 187–215.

20 For a more detailed summary of Megha's renunciation, see Shantaram Bhalchandra Deo, *History of Jaina Monachism from Inscriptions and Literature* (Poona: Deccan College Postgraduate and Research Institute, 1956), 142. This story seems to have been drawn from a template for royal initiations, as King Śailaka's initiation in *Jñā* 5.53–57 is described in essentially the same way as Prince Megha's. *Bh* 9.33.21–82 also contains a similar description of the renunciation of Prince Jamāli.

21 For this same statement of intent to renounce (*ālitte ṇaṃ bhante loe, palitte ṇaṃ bhante loe*, "The world is ablaze, oh Lord! The world is on fire, oh Lord"), see also Skandaka's initiation in *Bh* 2.1.34, Kālodāyī's renunciation in *Bh* 7.10.12, Ṛṣabhadatta's initiation in *Bh* 9.33.16, and Devānandā's renunciation in *Bh* 9.33.17 (the latter two initiations are modeled on Skandaka's). The *upāṅga* the *Puṣpikāḥ* 3.4.4 also has Subhadrā recite this formula upon her renunciation, citing Devānandā's initiation in the *Bhagavatīsūtra* (see *Puṣpikāḥ*, in *Nirayāvaliyā-Suyakkhandha Uvaṅgas 8–12 of the Jain Canon*, trans. J. W. de Jong and Royce Wiles[Tokyo: Chuo Research Foundation, 1996], 94). In contrast, the account of the initiation of the nineteenth *tīrthaṅkara*, Mallī, in *Jñā* 8.162, has her recite a much more concise formula upon renunciation, saying "praise to the liberated ones" and taking the vow of equanimity. This account parallels the description of Mahāvīra's renunciation in the *Ācārāṅgasūtra* and could be an attempt to distinguish the earlier renunciation ceremonies of the *jina*s (who are thought to have taken a single vow of equanimity) from the later model of renunciation that was, according to the tradition, developed during Mahāvīra's time.

22 See Flügel, "The *Nikkhamaṇa* of Mahāvīra," 77.

23 Many scholars have discussed these models. For a recent discussion of the *samavasaraṇa* in both Digambara and Śvetāmbara art, see Julie A. B. Hegewald, "Visual and Conceptual Links between Jaina Cosmological, Mythological and Ritual Instruments," *Journal of Jaina Studies (Online)* 6, no. 1 (2010): 1–20. John E. Cort, *Framing the Jina: Narratives of Icons and Idols in Jain History* (New York: Oxford University Press, 2010), 115–21, 303n5, cites several important scholarly discussions of this model.

24 Ohira, *Study of the Bhagavatīsūtra*, 11, 163. Another early account of the *samavasaraṇa* occurs in the *bhāṣya*, or Prakrit commentary in verse form, on the Śvetāmbara *āgama* the *Kalpasūtra*, the *Bṛhatkalpabhāṣya* attributed to the sixth-century Saṅghadāsa (*Bṛhatkalpabhāṣya*, vv. 1176–217).

25 On the deities in the Jain cosmos, see Glasenapp, *Jainism: An Indian Religion of Salvation*, 262–65.

26 For the Prakrit description of the Jina's Preaching Assembly, see *Āvaśyakaniryukti*, vv. 543–74, in Nalini Balbir, "An Investigation of Textual Sources on the *samavasaraṇa* ("The Holy Assembly of the Jina")," in *Festschrift Klaus Bruhn*, ed. Nalini Balbir and J. K. Bautze (Reinbek: Verlag für Orientalische Fachpublikationen, 1994), 77–80. See also U. P. Shah, *Studies in Jaina Art* (1955; Varanasi: Parsvanatha Vidyapitha, 1998), 86–89.

27 Balbir, "Investigation of Textual Sources on the *samavasaraṇa*," 91. For a discussion of the divine sound of *jina*s in their preaching assemblies, see Johannes Bronkhorst, "Divine Sound or Monotone? Divyadhvani between Jaina, Buddhist and Brahmani-

cal Epistemology," in *Sanmati: Essays Felicitating Professor Hampa Nagarajaiah on the Occasion of His 80th Birthday*, ed. Luitgard Soni and Jayandra Soni (Bengaluru: Sapna Book House, 2015), 83–96.

28 Balbir, "Investigation of Textual Sources on the *samavasaraṇa*," 89.

29 Balbir, 87.

30 Quintanilla, *History of Early Stone Sculpture*, 98–100, 114–15, fig. 140. Because the three-pronged symbol is often called *triratna*, or "three jewels," scholars of art history have interpreted it to mean right vision, knowledge, and conduct and have argued that the *triratna*s placed in the four directions surrounding the *jina* in some *āyagapaṭa*s must symbolize the *jina* preaching in all the directions in the *samavasaraṇa*. See Quintanilla, *History of Early Stone Sculpture*, 93; and Shah, *Studies in Jaina Art*, 81. These claims are speculative, however, and we cannot be sure what exactly the *triratna* symbol represented at the turn of the first millennium.

31 See Phyllis Granoff, "Jain Lives of Haribhadrasūri: An Inquiry into the Sources and Logic of the Legends," *Journal of Indian Philosophy* 17 (1989): 105–28; Phyllis Granoff, "My Rituals and My Gods: Ritual Exclusiveness in Medieval India," *Journal of Indian Philosophy* 29, nos. 1–2 (2001): 109–34; and Christopher Key Chapple, *Reconciling Yogas: Haribhadrasūri's Collection of View on Yoga* (Albany: State University of New York Press, 2003), 75–85.

32 Robert Williams has attributed this text to the Haribhadrasūri who lived in the sixth century. Williams, "Haribhadra," *Bulletin of the School of Oriental and African Studies, University of London*, 28, no. 1 (1965): 104. However, many scholars have questioned this dating; see Paul Dundas, "Haribhadra on Giving," *Journal of Indian Philosophy* 30 (2002): 23. The flower-throwing rite in the initiation ceremony in the *Pañcāśakaprakaraṇa* also suggests a later dating for the text. For now, then, I will attribute the *Pañcāśakaprakaraṇa* to the Haribhadrasūri who is said to have died in 750 CE.

33 *dikkhāvihāṇam eyaṃ bhāvijjataṃ tu taṃtaṇītīe | saïapuṇabaṃdhagāṇaṃ kuggahavirahaṃ lahuṃ kuṇaï ||* (*PP* 2.44). Haribhadrasūri uses the term "*tantra*" in other texts as well. The *Yogadṛṣṭisamuccaya* also refers positively to the *tantra* and *tantra*s as teachings on yoga (*Yogaviṃśikā* of Haribhadrasūri, vv. 74, 206, ed. and trans. K. K. Dixit as *Yogadṛṣṭisamuccaya and Yogaviṃśikā of Ācārya Haribhadrasūri* [Ahmedabad: Lalbhai Dalpatbhai Bharatiya Sanskriti Vidyamandira, 1970], 50, 91). The *Lalitavistarā* also refers to *tantra* as a tradition (*sampradāya*) within Jainism. See Sagarmal Jain, "Tantra-Sādhnā," 481.

34 See Dominic Goodall and Marion Rastelli, eds., *Tāntrikābhidhānakośa III: Dictionnaire des termes techniques de la littérature hindoue tantrique / A Dictionary of Technical Terms from Hindu Tantric Literature / Wörterbuch zur Terminologie hinduistischer Tantren* (Vienna: Verlag de Österreichischen Akademie der Wissenschaften, 2013), s.v. *dīkṣānāman* and *puṣpakṣepa*.

35 *Niśvāsatattvasaṃhitā* 4.1–3b, trans. Goodall as *The Niśvāsatattvasaṃhitā*, 259.

36 *Niśvāsatattvasaṃhitā* 4.1, trans. Goodall as *The Niśvāsatattvasaṃhitā*, 259.

37 *Svāyambhuvasūtrasaṅgraha* 13.8c–9, trans. Goodall and Isaacson, "Shared 'Ritual Syntax,'" 51.

38 *Sātvatasaṃhitā* 199.39c–41b, trans. Marion Rastelli, "Maṇḍalas and Yantras in the Pāñcarātra Tradition," in *Maṇḍalas and Yantras in the Hindu Tradition*, ed. Gudrun Bühnemann (Leiden: E. J. Brill, 2003), 133–34.

39 Shinohara, *Spells, Images, and Maṇḍalas*, 50–63.

40 For a full summary of the worship of the All-Gathering Maṇḍala in the *Collected Dhāraṇī Sūtras*, see the appendix of Shinohara, *Spells, Images, and Maṇḍalas*, 205–25.

41 Shinohara, *Spells, Images, and Maṇḍalas*, 66.

42 Shinohara, xiii.

43 For an example of how the iconography of the initiation *maṇḍala* described in Abhinavagupta's eleventh-century *Tantrāloka* encodes the hierarchy of deities in the Trika tradition, see Alexis Sanderson, "Maṇḍala and Āgamic Identity in the Trika of Kashmir," in *Mantras et Diagrammes Rituelles dans l'Hindouisme*, ed. André Padoux (Paris: Centre National de la Recherche Scientifique, 1986), 183.

44 David Gordon White, "Introduction: Tantra in Practice: Mapping a Tradition," in *Tantra in Practice*, edited by White (Princeton, NJ: Princeton University Press, 2000), 25.

45 This idea that the flower-throwing determines the efficacy of the ritual is not unique to Jainism. The eighth-century Buddhist *Guhyatantra*, like the *Pañcāśakaprakaraṇa*, prescribes the rejection of the blindfolded candidate if, on the final day of the seven-day initiation ritual, he cannot land a flower, after three tries, in the proper place on the *mahāmaṇḍala* of Buddhist divinities. In the initiation rite in the *Mahāvairocana* as well, "where the flower falls reveals how far the candidate has come through spiritual practice in the course of his past births" (Shinohara, *Spells, Images, and Maṇḍalas*, 153, 162). In a text of the Vaiṣṇava Pāñcarātra, the *Īśvarasaṃhitā*, the initiand's worthiness should be tested by seeing if he shows the signs of devotion such as the bristling of hair, tears, etc., after throwing the flower onto the *maṇḍala* (Rastelli, "Maṇḍalas and Yantras in the Pāñcarātra," 134).

46 Aditya Chaturvedi has examined the use of the most famous "Vedic" mantra—the *gāyatrīmantra* that initiates a brahmin male into the Vedic fire sacrifice—in a likely early modern tantric Śākta text from Bengal, the *Gāyatrītantra*, to show that mantras should not be deemed to be inherently tantric or Vedic. Instead, their ritual use and interpretation determine what they should be called. Chaturvedi, "Of Revelation and Sādhanā: The Gāyatrī Mantra in the Gāyatrī Tantra" (unpublished manuscript, 2018). On the *gāyatrīmantra* in tantric texts, see also Gupta, Hoens, and Goudriaan, *Hindu Tantrism*, 111, 123.

47 This pronouncement relates to the idea that monks should daily recite the Prakrit ritual formula that praises Jain temples, the *caityavandana*. Different texts are in disagreement about how often a monk should recite this formula. On the ritual requirement for mendicants to perform the *caityavandana* seven times a day, see Williams, *Jaina Yoga*, 198.

48 *Mahāniśīthasūtra* 3.29.10–15, transcribed in Deleu and Schubring, *Studien zum Mahānisīha*, 64. This translation is based on Deleu, *Studien zum Mahānisīha*, 139.

49 Goodall and Isaacson, "Tantric Traditions," 125.

50 *Brahmasiddhāntasamuccaya*, v. 219, in Dundas, "Becoming Gautama," 36.

51 *uttamaṃ cātra samavasaraṇaṃ maṇḍalaṃ matam | tatra puṣpādipātena jñeyaṃ sthānādi cāsya tu || Brahmasiddhāntasamuccaya*, v. 221.

52 P. S. Jaini, *Jaini Path*, 292–304; Dundas, "Becoming Gautama," 35.

53 Anant Sadashiv Altekar, *The Rāshṭrakūṭas and Their Times* (Poona: Oriental Book Agency, 1934), 19–23; Hampa Nagarajaiah, *A History of the Rāṣṭrakūṭas of Maḷkhēḍ and Jainism* (Bangalore: Ankita Pustaka, 2000), 19–23.

54 *tae ṇaṃ mallī arahā ṇamo'tthu ṇaṃ siddhāṇaṃ ti kaṭṭu sāmāiyacarittaṃ paḍivajjai* | (Mallī's renunciation described in *Jñā* 8.163).

55 Orzech, "Tantric Subjects," 19–20.

56 Orzech, 20.

57 See Padmanabh S. Jaini, *Gender and Salvation: Jaina Debates on the Spiritual Liberation of Women* (Berkeley: University of California Press, 1991), 98n2.

58 Patrick Olivelle, "Celibacy in Classical Hinduism," in *Celibacy and Religious Traditions*, ed. Carl Olson (Oxford: Oxford University Press, 2008), 152.

CHAPTER 3

1 *Gaṇdharvalay Vidhān*, ed. Āryikā Jñānamatī (Hastinapur: Digambar Jain Trilok Śodh Saṃsthān, 2008), 6.

2 Brahmacārī Indū Jain, "Prastāvanā" of *Gaṇdharvalay Vidhān*, 5.

3 For an example of a Śvetāmbara Cloth Diagram of the Mantra of the Mendicant Leader from Gujarat, dated 1650–1700, that calls itself the *gaṇadharavalayayantra*, see Pratapaditya Pal, *The Peaceful Liberators: Jaina Art from India* (Los Angeles: Los Angeles County Museum of Art / Thames and Hudson, 1994), 228–29. This diagram has been discussed in Richard J. Cohen, "The Art of Jain Meditation," in *Glimpses of Jainism*, ed. Surender K. Jain (Delhi: Motilal Banarsidass, 1997), 127–38.

4 See Ellen Gough, "The Digambara *Sūrimantra*."

5 In a chapter on the modern worship of Jain *maṇḍala*s, John Cort also identifies the similarities between these Digambara and Śvetāmbara diagrams, noting that "the Śvetāmbara *sūrimantra* is also known as the Gaṇadhara Valaya," which "is evidence of the interaction between Śvetāmbara and Digambara ritual cultures. The rituals are not the same, however, as the Śvetāmbara Sūri Mantra ritual is performed only by an initiated *ācārya* whereas the Digambara Gaṇadhara Valaya ritual is performed at one's initial initiation as a monk." Cort, "Contemporary Jain Maṇḍala Rituals," in *Victorious Ones: Jain Images of Perfection*, ed. Phyllis Granoff (New York: Rubin Museum of Art, 2009), 156n25.

6 I have outlined the prescriptions for initiations and promotions in Cāmuṇḍarāya's *Cāritrasāra* (ca. 1000) and Āśādhara's *Anagāradharmāmṛta* (composed in 1240), in Gough, "Tantric Ritual Elements in the Initiation of a Digambara." The five verses that constitute the *dīkṣāvidhi* in the *Vidyānuśāsana*, pp. 263–64, are too cryptic and corrupt to examine at this point.

7 Sagarmal Jain, ed., *Samaṇ Suttaṃ*, 2nd ed., comp. Jinendra Varni (New Delhi: Bhagwan Mahavir Memorial Samiti, 1999).

8 Deo, *History of Jaina Monachism*, 143–45.

9 Deo, 224.

10 Shantaram Bhalchandra Deo, *Jaina Monastic Jurisprudence* (Banaras: Jaina Cultural Research Society, 1960), 23.

11 Deo, *History of Jaina Monachism*, 218–19; Deo, *Jaina Monastic Jurisprudence*, 25. The *Vyavahārasūtra* is attributed to Bhadrabāhu I, who is said to have died 170 years after Mahāvīra's death. Deo, *History of Jaina Monachism*, 24. While this tradition cannot be verified historically, the content and language of the text suggests that it must belong to an earlier layer of Jain scriptures. On the dating of this text to the "second canonical period," see Ohira, *Study of the Bhagavatīsūtra*, 1.

12 *Sthānāṅgasūtra* 4.3.422, for example, defines four different types of *ācārya*s in terms of whether or not they can oversee *pravrajyā*, *upasthāpanā*, both, or neither. Deo, *History of Jaina Monachism*, 223, provides a list of eight different types of *ācārya*s found in the *Vyavahārasūtra*.

13 Deo, 222.

14 Deo, 225.

15 Deo, *Jaina Monastic Jurisprudence*, 28.

16 *Mūl*, vv. 155–56, discussed in Dundas, *The Jains*, 181.

17 *Mūl*, v. 158. In my summary, I rely on Vasunandin's twelfth-century Sanskrit commentary on this verse.

18 In Brahmanical texts such as the *Manusmṛti*, the term "*ācārya*" also designates a teacher and one who initiates a student. See Paul Dundas, *History, Scripture and Controversy in a Medieval Jain Sect* (New York: Routledge, 2007), 25.

19 Goodall and Isaacson, "Tantric Traditions," 127.

20 For a good overview of the different types of initiation found in the Śaiva *āgama*s, the three initiations (*samaya*, *viśeṣa*, and *nirvāṇa*) codified in later ritual manuals (*paddhati*), and the levels of initiate (*sādhaka*, *ācārya*), see N. R. Bhatt, introduction to *Mataṅgapārameśvarāgama (Vidyāpāda) avec le commentaire de Bhaṭṭa Rāmakaṇṭha*, ed. Bhatt (Pondicherry: Institut Français d'Indologie, 1977), xviii–xxiii. See also Flood, *The Tantric Body*, 133–38. For a description of the role of the *sādhaka* in the Śaiva Mantramārga and the Pāñcarātra, respectively, see Hélène Brunner, "Le sādhaka: Personage oublié du Śivaisme du sud," *Journal Asiatique* 263 (1975): 411–43; and Marion Rastelli, "The Religious Practice of the 'Sādhaka' according to the Jayākhyasaṃhitā," *Indo-Iranian Journal* 43, no. 4 (2000): 319–95. On the evolution of Śaiva initiation from one to three initiations and a summary of the three types of initiation and the consecration of a *sādhaka* and *ācārya* presented in the eleventh-century *Somaśambhupaddhati*, see Hélène Brunner, introduction to *Somaśambhupaddhati, Troisième Partie* (Pondicherry: Institut Français d'Indologie, 1977), xxx–xlvii.

21 For an overview of Pāñcarātra initiation rites, see Sanjukta Gupta, "The Changing Pattern of Pāñcarātra Initiation: A Case Study in the Reinterpretation of Ritual," in *Selected Studies on Ritual in the Indian Religions: Essays to D. J. Hoens*, ed. Ria Kloppenborg (Leiden: E. J. Brill, 1983), 69–91.

22 Abé, *Weaving of Mantra*, 124.

23 I have discussed the tantric development of the requirement that the *ācārya* lead the image-consecration ceremony in Gough, "The Digambara *Sūrimantra*." In earlier Saiddhāntika texts, "*pratiṣṭhā* was in fact a concern of the *sādhaka*." Jun Takashima, "Pratiṣṭhā in the Śaiva Āgamas," in *From Material to Deity: Indian Rituals of Consecration*, ed. Shingo Einoo and Takashima (New Delhi: Manohar, 2005), 137. This was the case for Vaiṣṇavas as well. While in the earlier Pāñcarātrika text the *Jayākhyasaṃhitā*, "the *sādhaka* leads the ceremony under the guidance of the preceptor," the later *Kapiñjalasaṃhitā* has the *ācārya* head the rite. Hiromichi Hikita, "Consecration of Divine Images in a Temple," in Einoo and Takashima, *From Material to Deity*, 187–88. This shift from *sādhaka* to *ācārya* as the main officiant could align with tantric cults' increasing emphasis on public consecration of large, state-supported temples over the personal shrines of the *sādhaka*.

24 Brunner cites *Somaśambhupaddhati*, pt. 3, pp. 486, 496, and *Mṛgendrāgama, Kriyāpāda*, chap. 8, 214–16. Brunner, "Ātmārthapūjā versus Parārthapūjā in the Śaiva tradition," in *The Sanskrit Tradition and Tantrism*, ed. Teun Goudriaan (Leiden: E. J. Brill, 1990), 23n27.

25 Goodall and Isaacson explain, "In the case of Buddhist tantrism, the old social division into *bhikṣus*, *bhikṣuṇīs*, *upāsakas* and *upāsikās* . . . remain largely in place, with the new identities of *ācārya* and *sādhaka/mantrin* not supplanting but supplementing these traditional ones." In the earliest "tantric" Śaiva text, the *Niśvāsatattvasaṃhitā*, while there is mention of an initiating *ācārya* and lower-level initiates, *sādhakas*, no hierarchy of initiates has been established. Goodall and Isaacson, "Shared 'Ritual Syntax,'" 63–64.

26 A list of some of these texts is provided under "*Sāmācārī Granth*" in *Vidhimārgaprapā* of Jinaprabhasūri, trans. Sādhvī Saumyaguṇā as *Vidhi Mārg Prapā* (Mumbai: Śrī Mahāvīr Svāmī Jain Derāsar Trust, 2005), 112; and in Sādhvī Saumyaguṇā, *Jain Vidhi-Vidhān Sambandhī Sāhitya kā Bṛhad Itihās*, pt. 1 (Shajapur: Prācya Vidyāpīṭh, 2006), 180–264. To date, the earliest known source for the contents of the Śvetāmbara *sūrimantra* is the eleventh- to twelfth-century Sanskrit ritual manual the *Nirvāṇakalikā*, parts of which have been copied from a Śaiva source. See Gough, "The Digambara *Sūrimantra*."

27 For a summary of scholarship that has accepted this period as the Tantric Age, see Burchett, *A Genealogy of Devotion*, 321n1. Sanderson, "The Śaiva Age," calls it the Śaiva Age.

28 One example of a text that claims that Jains gained favor with kings through the use of mantras is Merutuṅgasūri's fourteenth-century *Prabandhacintāmaṇi*, which claims that the "kingdom of the Gurjaras, even from the time of King Vanarāja, was founded with Jain mantras (*jainais tu sthāpitaṃ mantraih*); its foe indeed had no cause to rejoice" (cited in Balbir, "The Jain Tradition on Protection," 433).

29 Because Jains integrated a tantric initiation into a *maṇḍala* and a monastic initiation, they could not, like the Saiva Saiddhāntikas, develop a special liberation-granting tantric initiation for a king to attract his patronage. On this Saiddhāntika development of a special seedless (*nirbīja*) initiation for the king that guarantees liberation and worldly powers without the requirement of subsequent daily rites, see Sanderson, "The Śaiva Age," 254–62.

30 Dundas, "Becoming Gautama"; Paul Dundas, "The Jain Monk Jinapati Sūri Gets the

Better of a Nāth Yogī," in *Tantra in Practice*, ed. David Gordon White (Princeton, NJ: Princeton University Press, 2000), 231–38; and Dundas, *History, Scripture and Controversy*, 26–28.

31 Dundas, *The Jains*, 138–45. Peter Flügel has outlined the six extant Śvetāmbara image-worshiping *gacchas*, with their traditional dates of founding in parentheses: "(1) the Kharatara Gaccha (1023), (2) the A(ñ)cala Gaccha or Vidhi Pakṣa (1156), (3) the Āgamika or Tristuti Gaccha (1193) and (4) the Tapā Gaccha (1228), from which (5) the Vimala Gaccha (1495), and (6) the Pārśvacandra Gaccha (1515) separated." Flügel, "Demographic Trends," 317.

32 Phyllis Granoff has thus argued that "in the late medieval period Jains retreated from the pan-Indian rhetoric which linked proper worship with the security of the state as a whole and shifted their focus from that larger community to the smaller community of the Jain faithful." Granoff, "The Jina Bleeds: Threats to the Faith and the Rescue of the Faithful in Medieval Jain Stories," in *Images, Miracles, and Authority in Asian Religious Traditions*, ed. Richard H. Davis (Boulder, CO: Westview Press, 1998), 129. On the relationship between lay supporters and medieval Śvetāmbara monks from competing lineages, see Phyllis Granoff, "The Place of Ritual: Geographic Boundaries and Sectarian Identity in Medieval Indian Religions," in *Territory, Soil, and Society in South Asia*, ed. Daniela Berti and Gilles Tarabout (Delhi: Manohar, 2009), 143–76.

33 Dundas, "The Jain Monk Jinapati Sūri," 235.

34 On the various biographies of Jinaprabhasūri, see Phyllis Granoff, "Jinaprabhasūri and Jinadattasūri: Two Studies from the Śvetāmbara Jain Tradition," in *Speaking of Monks: Religious Biography in India and China*, ed. Granoff and Koichi Shinohara (Oakville, ON: Mosaic Press, 1992), 1–96; and Vose, "The Making of a Medieval Jain Monk."

35 Dundas, *The Jains*, 140–42. On the miracle-working Kharatara Gaccha monks, see Phyllis Granoff, "Religious Biography and Clan History among the Śvetāmbara Jains in North India," *East and West* 39, nos. 1–4 (1989): 195–215.

36 Dundas notes that the *Vṛddhācāryaprabandhāvali* recording this account should predate 1617. Dundas, "The Jain Monk Jinapati Sūri," 235.

37 Vose, "The Making of a Medieval Jain Monk," 157–60.

38 Introductions to Jainism often list four *mūlasūtras*: the *Āvaśyaka*, *Daśavaikālika*, and *Uttarādhyayana*, plus the *Oghaniryukti* and *Piṇḍaniryukti*, verses on begging for food and monastic equipment (see, e.g., Dundas, *The Jains*, 75). However, the *Vidhimārgaprapā* explicitly says that the *Oghaniryukti* is part of the *Āvaśyakasūtra*, so there is no separate ceremony (*upadhāna*) to study it (*VMP*, p. 49, line 6), and the *Piṇḍaniryukti* is listed as a chapter of the *Daśavaikālikasūtra* (*VMP*, p. 49, line 12). The formation of the image-worshiping Śvetāmbara "canon" will be discussed in more detail in chapter 5.

39 The twelfth limb is said to have been forgotten (*VMP*, p. 56, line 30).

40 The *prakīrṇakas* are listed as: *Devendrastava, Taṇḍulavaitālika, Maraṇasamādhi, Mahāpratyākhyāna, Āturapratyākhyāna, Saṃstāraka, Candravedhyaka, Bhaktaparijñā, Catuḥśaraṇa, Vīrastava, Gaṇividyā, Dvīpasāgaraprajñapti, Saṅgrahaṇī, Gacchācāra*, etc. (*VMP*, pp. 57–58, para. 62).

41 On the requirement of *nandīracanā* in all levels of initiation and promotion to this day, see Sādhvī Saumyaguṇā, *Jain Muni ke Vratāropaṇ kī Traikālik Upyogitā Navyayug ke*

Sandarbh meṃ (Ladnun: Jain Viśva Bhāratī Viśvavidyālay, 2014), 23–46. Saumyaguṇā, ibid., 23, quotes the *Nandīsūtra*'s explanation of the term "*nandi*" as something by which living beings become happy and that which brings prosperity. Peter Flügel has translated from Gujarati fifty-four rhetorical questions, *Whose Tradition Is That?* (*te keha nī paramparā chai?*), attributed to Loṅka, the fifteenth-century reformer who rejected image worship and argued for Śvetāmbaras to return to the "original" practices of Jainism. The questions critique a number of practices of image-worshiping Śvetāmbaras. No. 38, which questions the performance of *nāndi maṇḍāvai*" is likely a reference to the erection of a model of the Jina's Preaching Assembly for rites of initiation, promotion, and the *nandīkriyā*, or the rite required for a mendicant to begin scriptural study. Flügel, "The Unknown Loṅkā," 240, 274. These rituals will be discussed further in chapter 5.

42 *VMP*, p. 30, line 2, also mentions that the assembly is traced with superior, beautifully colored cow dung.

43 Chapter 37 of the *Vidhimārgaprapā* outlines twenty-nine different *mudrās*. The *muktāśukti*, the tenth *mudrā* outlined, is found in *VMP*, p. 116, line 14. See also the only English-language source on Jain *mudrās*, Priyabala Shah, ed., *Mudrāvicāraprakaraṇam and Mudrāvidhiḥ* (Baroda: Oriental Institute, 1956).

44 See, for example, the video of the April 22, 2017, *dīkṣā* of a Jain nun (*sādhvī*) into the mendicant community of Ācārya Guṇodayasāgarasūri, the head (*gacchādipati*) of the Śvetāmbara mendicant lineage the Añcala Gaccha, in Mumbai: "Diksha Samaroh Of Bhaviben from Ghatkopar," YouTube video, 4:14:58, posted by Shree K. D. O. G. V. C Jain Sangh, April 22, 2017, https://www.youtube.com/watch?v=yZ9D33rBdJE. Beginning at 2:37:00, the initiand begins to circumambulate the model of the Jina's Preaching Assembly and then is sprinkled with scented sandalwood powder and rice by her gurus.

45 Śvetāmbaras have the same six essential duties as Digambaras, but swap the position of *pratyākhyāna* and *kāyotsarga*. See Cort, *Jains in the World*, 122–27.

46 On the fasts and rituals required for study of these texts in the days after *pravrajyā*, see *VMP*, 48–49.

47 The *Nandīsūtra* lists seventy-two texts divided into two groups: twelve "within the limbs" (*aṅgapraviṣṭa*) and fifty "outside the limbs" (*aṅgabāhira, anaṅgapraviṣṭa)* (79). It lists twelve limbs, from the *Ācārāṅgasūtra* to the *Dṛṣṭivāda* (83–96), though the contents of the *Dṛṣṭivāda* are thought to have been forgotten shortly after Mahāvīra taught them, so they are not part of a mendicant's curriculum. It lists fifty texts that are outside of the limbs, twenty-nine of which can be studied at any time (*utkālika*; 81), and thirty that can only be studied at designated times (*kālika*; 82). See Dundas, *The Jains*, 77–78; and Hiralal Rasikdas Kapadia, *A History of the Canonical Literature of the Jainas* (1941; repr. Ahmedabad: Sharadaben Chimanbhai Educational Research Centre, 2000), 23–26.

48 On this fast, which is called *nīvi* in Hindi and Gujarati, see Cort, *Jains in the World*, 136.

49 Today this ceremony in Hindi is called *baḍī dīkṣā*. See Wiley, *A to Z of Jainism*, 79–80.

50 The *Vidhimārgaprapā* records the number of years a monk should have spent in mendicancy in order to be able to study certain scriptures. For example, he must have four years' standing to study the second *aṅga* the *Sūtrakṛtāṅgasūtra*, five for the *chedasūtras* the *Daśaśrutaskandha*, etc., eight for the *aṅga* the *Sthānāṅgasūtra*, and so on (*VMP*, p. 56, para. 60).

51 On the details of the study of all the scriptures, see the chapters on *yogavidhi* in *VMP*, 40–62.

52 On the Cloth Diagram of the Spell of Mahāvīra, see Umakant P. Shah, "Varddhamāna [*sic*] -Vidyā-Paṭa," *Journal of the Indian Society of Oriental Arts* IX (1941): 42–51. See also chapter 5.

53 The *Vidhimārgaprapā*, chapter 28, outlines the promotion of the *upādhyāya*. This ceremony is identical to the ceremony of promotion to the rank of *vācanācārya*, but the *upādhyāya* should receive a slightly different version of the Spell of Mahāvīra. For the spell of the *upādhyāya*, the *pañcanamaskāra* and the four lines of the *ṛddhi-maṅgala* that praise *jinas* with different types of clairvoyant knowledge should preface the *vardhamānavidyā*. This makes sense, since the *upādhyāya* is one step closer to becoming a mendicant leader, and the *ṛddhi-maṅgala* constitutes the first section of the *sūrimantra*. The promotion of the *pravartinī* is also the same as the *vācanācārya*, though the *pravartinī* will also receive a garment that *sādhvīs* wear called a *skandha-karaṇī* (*VMP*, p. 71, para. 72). The *mahattarā* should also receive the *upādhyāyaman-tra* in her right ear that has been decorated with sandalwood (*VMP*, p. 72, para. 73, lines 9–10).

54 The mantra is here termed the "mantra of the guru's tradition" (Skt. *guruparamparā*) (*VMP*, p. 67, para. 70, lines 8–9).

55 For a different interpretation—a comparison of the *sādhaka* and the Jain householder—see Collette Caillat, "Le Sādhaka Śaiva à lumière de la discipline Jaina," in *Studien zum Jainismus und Buddhismus: Gedenkschrift Für Ludwig Alsdorf*, ed. Klaus Bruhn and Albrecht Wezler (Viesbaden: Franz Steiner, 1981), 51–59.

56 For the *sādhyamantra* in the Śaiva Siddhānta, see *Mṛgendrāgama, Kriyāpāda*, chap. 4, in Hélène Brunner, *Mṛgendrāgama, section des rites et section du comportement, traduction, introduction et notes* (Pondicherry: Institut Français d'Indologie Pondichéry, 1985), 75–82.

57 Jean-Michel Creismeas, "Le yoga du Mataṅgapārameśvaratantra à la lumière du commentaire de Bhaṭṭa Rāmakaṇṭha" (PhD diss., Sorbonne Université, 2015), 55.

58 John E. Cort, "World Renouncing Monks and World Celebrating Temples and Icons: The Ritual Culture of Temples and Icons in Jainism," in *Archaeology and Text: The Temple in South Asia*, ed. Himanshu Prabha Ray (Oxford: Oxford University Press, 2010), 267–95.

59 Paul Dundas, "How Not to Install an Image of the Jina: An Early Anti-Paurṇamīyaka Diatribe," *International Journal of Jaina Studies (Online)* 5, no. 3 (2009): 1–23.

60 Flügel, "Demographic Trends," 343.

61 Flügel, "Demographic Trends," 380.

62 Tillo Detige, "Digambara Renouncers in Western and Central India," in *Brill's Encyclopedia of Jainism*, ed. Knut A. Jacobsen, John E. Cort, Paul Dundas, and Kristi L. Wiley (Leiden: Brill, 2020), 182–215.

63 For accounts of the origins of the *bhaṭṭāraka* rank, see Flügel, "Demographic Trends," 345–47.

64 Detige, "Digambara Renouncers," 188.

65 Tillo Detige, "'*Tataḥ Śrī-Gurus-Tasmai Sūrimantraṃ Dadyāt*,' 'Then the Venerable Guru Ought to Give Him the *Sūrimantra*': Early Modern Digambara Jaina *Bhaṭṭāraka* Consecrations," *Religions* 10, no. 369 (2019): 1–31.

66 Ratancandra Jain, *Jainparamparā aur Yāpnīyasaṅgh*, pt. 2 (Agra: Sarvoday Jain Vidyāpīṭh, 2009), 116.

67 R. Jain, *Jainparamparā aur Yāpnīyasaṅgh*, 121, does not specify whether the guru himself or a ritual specialist performs these rites. The text on the promotion of a *bhaṭṭāraka* has a ritual specialist (*paṇḍita*) perform the *abhiṣeka*, and the *gītas* Detige has examined mention both *yatis* and *paṇḍitas* performing the rites of promotion ("'*Tataḥ Śrī-Gurus-Tasmai Sūrimantraṃ Dadyāt*,'" 19).

68 R. Jain, *Jainparamparā aur Yāpnīyasaṅgh*, p. 121, lines 7–10. These same mantras are recited today to promote *upādhyāyas* and *ācāryas* and, indeed, were recited in the promotion of the three Digambara *ācāryas* I witnessed in Pushpagiri in 2019. See *Vimal Bhakti Saṅgrah*, 451–52.

69 R. Jain, *Jainparamparā aur Yāpnīyasaṅgh*, p. 121, lines 4–5, p. 116, lines 22–23. The five golden pots could represent the five types of proper conduct (*pañcācāra*) an *ācārya* is said to possess: *jñāna*, *darśana*, *cāritra*, *tapas*, and *vīrya*. Deo, *Jaina Monastic Jurisprudence*, 24. Indeed, in promotional materials for the promotion I witnessed in Pushpagiri in 2019, the rank of *ācārya* was termed the *pañcācār bhagavat pad*, or the "rank of the lord who has five types of right conduct."

70 Detige, "'*Tataḥ Śrī-Gurus-Tasmai Sūrimantraṃ Dadyāt*,'" 15.

71 Tillo Detige, "'*Guṇa kahuṃ śrī guru*': Bhaṭṭāraka Gītas and the Early Modern Digambara Jaina Saṅgha," in *Early Modern India: Literature and Images, Texts and Languages*, ed. Maya Burger and Nadia Cattoni (Heidelberg: CrossAsia-eBooks, 2019), 271–85.

72 Detige, "'*Tataḥ Śrī-Gurus-Tasmai Sūrimantraṃ Dadyāt*,'" 19–20.

73 Vasunandin's *Pratiṣṭhāpāṭha* has been published in *Pratiṣṭhā Vidhi Darpaṇ*, comp. Ācārya Kunthusāgara (Jaipur: Śrī Digambar Jain Kunthu Vijay Granthmālā Samiti, 1992). On dating Vasunandin to around 1100, see Williams, *Jaina Yoga*, 25.

74 R. Nagaswamy, "Jaina Temple Rituals: Pratishtha tilaka of Nemicandra—a Study," http://tamilartsacademy.com/journals/volume2/articles/jain-temple.html (accessed August 15, 2013).

75 On Āśādhara, see Williams, *Jaina Yoga*, 26–28.

76 Saumyaguṇā, *Jain Vidhi-Vidhān Sambandhī Sāhitya kā Bṛhad Itihās*, 427.

77 On these sects, see Flügel, "Demographic Trends," 339–44.

78 *Pratiṣṭhātilaka* of Nemicandra, 2nd ed., ed. Āryikā Jñānamatī (Hastinapur: Digambar Jain Trilok Śodh Saṃsthān, 2012).

79 *Pratiṣṭhā Ratnākar*, ed. Darbārī Lāl Koṭhiyā and Jaykumār "Niśānt" (Delhi: Prati Vihār Jain Samāj, n.d.), 48

80 Eight days after the completion of the purification rites and establishment of the ritual space on the first day of the ceremony (*aṅkurārpaṇādi*, the establishment of pots of grains, etc.) (*PrT* 10.1, p. 234).

81 For another mention of the *vardhamānamantra*, see *PrT* 10.8, p. 236.

82 The mantra takes different forms in different sources. One version reads: *oṃ ṇamo bha-*

yavado vaḍḍhamāṇassa risahassa cakkaṃ jalaṃtaṃ gacchaï āyāsaṃ pāyālaṃ loyāṇaṃ bhūyāṇaṃ jaye vā vivāde vā thaṃbhaṇe vā raṇaṃgaṇe vā rāyaṃgaṇe vā moheṇa vā savvajīvasattāṇaṃ aparājido bhavadu rakkha rakkha svāhā (*Vimal Bhakti Saṅgrah*, 444). See also *Laghuvidyānuvād*, ed. Gaṇadharācārya Kunthusāgara (Jaipur: Śrī Digambar Jain Kunthuvijay Granthmālā Samiti, 1986), *khaṇḍ* 2, p. 236. For a slightly different version, see the *vardhamānayantra* outlined in Varṇī, *Jainendra Siddhānt Koś*, pt. 3, p. 359. More research on the history of the Digambara *vardhamānamantra* needs to be done, however. Tillo Detige has confirmed that the seventeenth-to-eighteenth-century manuscripts on the initiation of a Digambara *muni* he has photographed contain no references to a *vardhamānamantra*. Detige, email to author, May 26, 2019.

83 On these *atiśaya*, see Cort, *Framing the Jina*, 21–22. Qvarnström, in *Yogaśāstra* of Hemacandrasūri, trans. as *The Yogaśāstra of Hemacandra: A Twelfth Century Handbook*, 165n1, outlines the thirty-four *atiśayas* given in Hemacandrasūri's *Abhidhānacintāmaṇi* 1.57–64.

84 *prāṇapratiṣṭhāpy adhivāsanā ca saṃskāranetrocchṛtisūrimantrāḥ* | *mūlaṃ jinatvāgamane kriyā 'nyā bhaktipradhānā sukṛtodbhavāya* || (*Pratiṣṭhāpātha* of Jayasena, ed. Hīrācand Nemcand Dośī (Solapur: Śeṭh Hīrācand Nemcand Dośī, 1925), 136). "The foundational rites in the [icon's] obtainment of the status of the Jina are the *sūrimantra*, the eye-opening, the imparting of the rites of passage (*saṃskāra*), the *adhivāsanā*, and the establishment of breath (*prāṇapratiṣṭhā*). The other rites, characterized by devotion, are for the production of merit."

85 The requirement in Jayasena's *Pratiṣṭhāpāṭha* that an *ācārya* must remove his clothes before imparting the *sūrimantra* to the icon suggests that this was originally the practice of naked monks. See Gough, "The Digambara *Sūrimantra*."

86 On the construction of the *siddhacakra* to consecrate a temple image of a liberated soul (*siddha*), see Ellen Gough, "Wheel of the Liberated: Jain *Siddhacakras*, Past and Present," in *Objects of Worship in the South Asian Religions: Forms, Practices, and Meanings*, ed. Knut Jacobsen (London: Routledge, 2015), 85–108.

87 For images of *yāgamaṇḍalas*, see Jyotindra Jain and Eberhard Fischer, *Jaina Iconography, Part Two: Objects of Meditation and the Pantheon* (Leiden: E. J. Brill, 1978), plate VI; and Gough, "Jain *Maṇḍalas* and *Yantras*," 590–91.

88 See also *Pratiṣṭhāsāroddhāra* of Āśādhara, ed. Paṇḍit Manoharlāl Śāstrī (Bombay: Jaingranth Uddhārak Kāryālay, 1917), 230a–31a.

89 *PrT*, 326, says that the *siddhacakra* for a *siddhapratimā* should be made of five colors.

90 Phyllis Granoff explains: "In the Jain tradition . . . the chief characteristic of a *pratyekabuddha* according to such texts as the commentaries on the *Nandīsūtra* is that *pratyekabuddhas* unlike *svayambuddhas* require some external sign in order to achieve enlightenment. *Pratyekabuddhas* are experienced in the scriptures, whereas scriptural study is not a prerequisite for a *svayambuddha*, and *prateykabuddhas* have no human teacher from whom they may get their monastic insignia." Granoff, "The Miracle of a Hagiography without Miracles: Some Comments on the Jain Lives of the Pratyekabuddha Karakaṇḍa," *Journal of Indian Philosophy* 14 (1986): 394.

91 Detige, "Digambara Renouncers," 190, has noted that the names for the branches

(*śākhā*) of the Balātkāra Gaṇa were devised by Vidyādhar P. Johrāpurkar in *Bhaṭṭārak Sampradāy* (Sholapur: Jain Saṃskṛti Saṃrakṣak Saṅgh, 1958).

92 On the four different well-known *bhaṭṭārakas* who went by the name of Prabhācandra, see Kastūrcand Kāslīvāl, *Rājasthān ke Jain Sant: Vyaktitva evaṃ Kṛtitva* (Jaipur: Śrī Digambar Jain Atiśay Kṣetra Śrī Mahāvīrjī, 1967), 183–86. For the manuals by Sakalakīrti, Śubhacandra, Padmanandin, and Prabhācandra, see *Śrīgaṇdharvalay Pūjan Saṅgrah*, comp. Muni Ajitasāgara (Udaipur: Śrī Paṇḍit Guljārī Lāl Caudhrī, 1967). For the dates of these *bhaṭṭārakas*, see Hoernle, "Three Further Pattavalis of the Digambaras."

93 They followed a Hindi adaptation of this Sanskrit text: *Bṛhad Gaṇdhar Valay Vidhān* of Āryikā Rājaśrī, ed. Ācārya Guptinandī (Jaipur: Śārdā Prakāśan, 2003).

94 See Kāslīvāl, *Rājasthān ke Jain Sant*, 93–105.

95 The final verse and colophon of the version of the *MRR* published by Jambūvijaya claims the text was completed on Dīpāvalī of Saṃvat 1327 (1271 CE) by Siṃhatilakasūri, disciple of Vibudhacandrasūri, disciple of Yaśodhadevasūri (*SMKS*, 74).

96 *Ṛṣimaṇḍalastavayantralekhanam* of Siṃhatilakasūri, ed. Tattvānandavijaya, trans. Gujarati Dhurandharavijaya (Mumbai: Śrī Navīncandra Aṃbālāl Śāh, 1961). Dundas, "Becoming Gautama," 38, places Siṃhatilakasūri in the Kharatara Gaccha. For more information on Siṃhatilakasūri, see Alessandra Petrocchi, *The Gaṇitatilaka and Its Commentary: Two Medieval Sanskrit Mathematical Texts* (New York: Routledge, 2019), 11–15.

97 There is significant evidence to suggest Śvetāmbaras developed the *sūrimantra* in conversation with Digambaras. First, it is slightly out of place for Śvetāmbaras to credit Gautama with the composition of the *sūrimantra* (*MRR*, vv. 87–90, summarized in Dundas, "Becoming Gautama," 39), since while Digambaras trace their mendicant lineages back to Gautama, Śvetāmbaras begin with Mahāvīra's disciple Sudharman. It is possible that medieval Śvetāmbaras developed the connection between Gautama and this mantra via traditions of the Digambaras, who also believe that Gautama composed the present form of the *gaṇadharavalayamantra* (Jñānamatī, *Gaṇdharvalay Vidhān*, 43). It is also unusual that part of the second section of the Śvetāmbara *sūrimantra* is dedicated to Ṛṣabha's son Bāhubali, since a hugely popular cult to this figure developed among medieval Digambaras but Śvetāmbaras rarely worship him (Dundas, "Becoming Gautama," 41). Śvetāmbara texts on the *sūrimantra* also have the same language as Digambara texts; compare, for example, *MRR*, vv. 448–49, and the ca. eleventh-century Digambara text the *Jñānārṇava*, vv. 1916–1917. See also Jinaprabhasūri's mention of the *Siddhabhakti*, a hymn found in Digambara but not Śvetāmbara ritual culture (*SMKS*, 88). Finally, in her study of superhuman powers in Jain texts, Kristi Wiley has noted that Śvetāmbara sources do not usually discuss the powers related to austerities (*tapas*). One of these powers of austerities of the *ṛddhi-maṅgala*, *ghoraguṇa*, the "fierce quality" that Jinasena in his *Dhavalā* explains will banish fear, disease, famine, enmity, etc., "is not found in any other list that [she is] aware of." Wiley, "Supernatural Powers," 174. This quality is, however, found in the Digambara *gaṇadharavalayamantra* formed from the praises of the *ṛddhi-maṅgala*, and this mantra seems to have found its way into Śvetāmbara sources. Jinaprabhasūri's *Sūrimantrakalpabṛhatvivaraṇa* (*SMKS*, 87),

the *Paṭālekhanavidhi* (*SMKS*, 251), and the *Labdhipadaphalaprakāśakakalpa* (*SMKS*, 214–15) all mention this power in their lists of the *labdhi*s of the first section of the *sūrimantra*.

98 For a slightly different version of the five *prasthāna*s as found in the fourteenth-century Rājaśekharasūri's text on the *sūrimantra*, see Dundas, "Becoming Gautama," 39–42.

99 Dundas, 41.

100 Dundas, 50n49, cites *MRR*, v. 223, which relates *kiri*, *giri*, etc., to the ontological Jain categories of *guṇa*, *dravya*, and *paryāya*. I discuss this further in chapter 5.

101 The manuals repeatedly link the *apraticakrā*-mantra with the *labdhipada*. A text by an anonymous author called the "Ritual Manual Explaining the Fruits of the *Labdhipada*," the *Labdhipadaphalaprakāśakakalpa*, opens with this mantra that it says removes cholera: *oṃ namo arahaṃtāṇam namo jiṇāṇaṃ hrāṃ hrīṃ hrūṃ hrauṃ hraḥ apraticakre phaṭ vicakrāya svāhā oṃ hrīṃ arhaṃ a si ā u sā hrauṃ hrauṃ svāhā*. It then outlines the curative effects of reciting forty-six different praises to *labdhi*s (*SMKS*, 213–15).

102 Jambūvijaya has replicated this diagram and the diagram with the *apraticakrā*-mantra mentioned by Siṃhatilakasūri in the *Sūrimantrakalpasamuccayaḥ* (*SMKS*, *yantra*s 1, 26), and he recognizes the importance of what he calls the *apraticakrā yantra* with forty-eight *labdhi*s in Śvetāmbara sources. He acknowledges that of all the texts on the *sūrimantra* compiled in the *Sūrimantrakalpasamuccayaḥ*, there are no *labdhipada*s with forty-eight lines, but he notes that Ācārya Lakṣmīsūri's *sūrimantrapaṭa* from 1518/19 contains forty-eight *labdhi*s. *SMKS*, 301–2.

103 The *labdhipada* Jinaprabhasūri outlines that should fill the *nāndipada*, or *samavasaraṇa*, corresponds exactly with the Digambara forty-eight praises that fill the Ring of Disciples diagram, the *gaṇadharavalayamantra* (*SMKS*, 86–87).

104 Jambūvijaya, in *SMKS*, 87n9, notes that this section does not appear in the primary manuscript on which he relied.

105 U. P. Shah, *Jaina-Rūpa-Maṇḍana*, 204–300; 224–46.

106 I thank David Brick for this hypothesis.

107 Pandit Chandrakant, WhatsApp message to author, November 28, 2019.

108 Śubhacandra and Padmanandin require that the forty-eight-petaled *gaṇadharavalayayantra* be made on copper (*Śrīgaṇdharvalay Pūjan Saṅgrah*, 1–4). Śubhacandra requires that each day's worship of the Ring of Disciples begin with the series of *abhiṣeka*s of the metal *yantra*, and with each *abhiṣeka*, the *ācārya* should recite the mantra at its center. When laypeople and ritual specialists perform the *abhiṣeka* with sugarcane juice, for example, the *ācārya* leading the initiation ceremony should recite: *oṃ hrīṃ jhvīṃ śrīṃ arhaṃ a si ā u sā apraticakre phaṭ vicakrāya jhrauṃ jhrauṃ pavitratarekṣurasena snapayāmi svāhā* (*Bṛhad Gaṇdhar Valay Vidhān*, 17). After the *abhiṣeka*s, Śubhacandra prescribes that the disciples with superhuman powers should be made present in the metal *yantra* through the recitation of three verses that outline a version of the Ring of Disciples very similar to the one Nemicandra describes in his image-consecration manual, with the seed-syllable *kṣmā* at the center of a six-sided figure and the expanded *ṛddhi-maṅgala* placed in petals surrounding that central image. The final verse describes how the mantras should be inscribed on copper or cloth and worshiped with scented substances (*Bṛhad Gaṇdhar Valay Vidhān*, 56).

109 For a collection of essays on Ācārya Ādisāgara Aṅkalīkara, see Brahmacārī Maināb̄āī Jain, comp., *Ācārya Śrī Ādisāgar (Aṅkalīkar) kī Jhalak* (Delhi: Ācārya Śri Sanmati Sāgarjī Saṅgh, 1996). Biographical information and photographs can also be found on the Facebook page "C. C. Muni-Kunjar Prathamacharya sh.AcharyaAdisagar g [ank-likar] ke bhakt," accessed February 19, 2015, https://www.facebook.com/pages/CCMuni-Kunjar-Prathamacharya-shAcharya-Adisagar-g-anklikar-ke-bhakt/473919165963964?sk=timeline.

110 For brief biographies of each of these *bhaṭṭārakas*, see *Jain Tīrthvandanā: Bhāratvarṣīya Digambar Jain Tīrthkṣetra Kameṭī kā Mukhpatra*, 2, no. 11 (May 2012): 26–47.

111 R. Jain, *Jainparamparā aur Yāpnīyasaṅgh*, 116.

112 For some modern Digambara *sūrimantras*, see Gough, "The Digambara *Sūrimantra*." More research needs to be done on the promotion of *bhaṭṭārakas* in south India today to determine whether or not their *sūrimantra* traditions predate the twentieth century.

113 Dundas, "Becoming Gautama," 36, 48n21, also notes that Jinaprabhasūri mentions a Digambara version of the *sūrimantra*.

114 Śrī Digambar Jain Candraprabhujī Mandir, Aṅkroṃ kā Rāstā, Kiśanpol Bāzār, Jaipur, MS no. 24.

115 *sarvakarmakṣayakārī mokṣarūpo mantrarājo* (*SMKS*, p. 98, line 3). Here Jinaprabhasūri describes the fifth section of the mantra, termed the "king of mantras," the *mantrarāja*. This fifth section is recited in the promotion of an *ācārya* as a shortened form of the mantra thought to represent the entire invocation.

CHAPTER 4

1 I have discussed the history and present-day celebration of this festival in Gough, "Wheel of the Liberated."

2 Amṛtacandra, in *Tattvārthasāra* 10.37–40 (ca. tenth century), lists these eight root qualities of a pure soul. This is the most common classification, though some texts differ on a few qualities. See S. C. Jain, *Structure and Functions of Soul*, 231–32.

3 For the preliminary rites of *aṅgaśuddhi*, *vastraśuddhi*, *sakalīkaraṇa*, and *digbandhana*, see *Śrī Siddhcakra Vidhān*, ed. Sanat Kumār Vinod Kumār (Delhi: Jain Sāhitya Sadan, Śrī Digambar Jain Lāl Mandirjī, n.d.), 7–12. See also the "Indratva Sthāpanā" and "Sakalīkaraṇa Vidhāna" in *Siddhacakra Maṇḍala Vidhāna (Saṃskṛta)*, ed. Rāmeścandra Jain and Aśok Kumār Jain, comp. Ācārya Vimalasāgara (Lalitpur: Pārśvajyoti Mañc, 1990), 10–14.

4 On the eightfold (*aṣṭaka*) of Digambaras, see Wiley, *A to Z of Jainism*, 44–45. The eight substances of a modern Bīsapanthī *pūjā* are: (1) water (for *abhiṣeka*), (2) sandalwood paste, (3) rice grains (*akṣata*), (4) flowers, (5) sweets (*naivaidya*), (6) a lamp (*dīpa*), (7) incense (*dhūpa*), and (8) fruit (*phala*).

5 For the entirety of this *bhajana*, see *Śrī Siddhcakra Vidhān*, 243.

6 On this story, see Gough, "Wheel of the Liberated."

7 Flood, *The Tantric Body*, 106.

8 P. S. Jaini, *Jaina Path*, 254n20.

9 "... *devaṃ dhyāyati yaḥ sa muktisubhago.*" See also *Pratiṣṭhāsāroddhāra* of Āśādhara 6.14.

10 For Williams's section on *dhyāna*, see *Jaina Yoga*, 239–41. For this argument that *Jaina Yoga* is weakened by Williams's understanding of Jainism as an austere tradition gradually subjugated by "non-Jain" practices, see Paul Dundas, "A Digambara Jain Saṃskāra in the Early Seventeenth Century: Lay Funerary Ritual according to Somasenabhaṭṭāraka's *Traivarṇikācāra*," *Indo-Iranian Journal* 54 (2011): 100–102.

11 Williams, *Jaina Yoga*, xxiii–xxiv.

12 Dundas, "Digambara Jain Saṃskāra," 100.

13 *samaṇe bhagavaṃ mahāvīre vosaṭṭha[kāe] cattadehe. . . . appāṇaṃ bhāvemāṇe viharaï.* *ĀS* 770.11–14, trans. Jacobi, *SBE*, 22:200.

14 *ĀS* 773.7–11, trans. Jacobi, *SBE*, 22:201.

15 For an overview of Śvetāmbara canonical discussions of *dhyāna*, see Bronkhorst, *Two Traditions of Meditation*, chapter 3. For a shorter account that includes Digambara texts, see Johannes Bronkhorst, "Remarks on the History of Jaina Meditation," in *Jain Studies in Honour of Jozef Deleu*, ed. Rudy Smet and Kenji Watanabe (Tokyo: Hon-no-Tomosha, 1993), 151–62. See also Nathmal Tatia, *Studies in Jaina Philosophy* (Banaras: Jain Cultural Research Society, 1951), 281–85.

16 This definition of *dhyāna*, standard in later texts, is first found in the *Tattvārthasūtra*. See Suzuko Ohira, "Treatment of Dhyāna in the *Tattvārthādhigamasūtra*," *Indian Philosophical Quarterly* 3, no. 1 (1975): 51.

17 *Sarvārthasiddhi* is Ācārya Pūjyapāda's ca. eighth-century commentary that records the Digambara version of the *Tattvārthasūtra*, which differs only slightly from its Śvetāmbara counterpart. Both versions of the text are recorded in the *Tattvārthasūtra*, trans. Nathmal Tatia as *That Which Is*.

18 Other Digambara and Śvetāmbara discussions of meditation being the cause of liberation are discussed in Samani Pratibha Pragya, "Prekṣā Meditation: History and Methods" (PhD diss., SOAS, University of London, 2017), 18–21. Pragya notes that the Śvetāmbara Jinabhadrasūri, for example, in his ca. sixth-century *Dhyānaśataka*, confirms that "meditation is the highest religious practice and also the foremost means to liberation" (v. 96: *jhāṇaṃ ca pahāṇagaṃ tavassa to mokkha heūṃ*).

19 On the Jain universe and the different time periods, see P. S. Jaini, *Jaina Path*, 29–32.

20 Williams, *Jaina Yoga*, 239–40. See also *TS* 9.37.

21 *Sthānāṅga* 4.1.61–72 and *Bh* 25.7.237–49. The *Aupapātikasūtra*'s discussion of meditation with support is trans. in Bronkhorst, "Remarks on the History of Jaina Meditation," 152.

22 The *Dhyānaśataka*, v. 42, also adds the six essential duties as supports (*ālambana*) of *dhyāna*.

23 In the *Ādipurāṇa*, "kingship itself became a path to renunciation," notes Sarah Pierce Taylor, "Aesthetics of Sovereignty: The Poetic and Material Worlds of Medieval Jainism" (PhD diss., University of Pennsylvania, 2016), 230.

24 On the *Bhāvasaṅgraha* and the *Darśanasāra*, see Jugal Kishore "Yugvir," Mukhtar,

ed. and comp., *Puratana-Jainvakya-Suchi*, pt. 1 (Saharanpur, U.P.: Vir-Sewa-Mandir, 1950), 59–61.

25 Perhaps the most famous Jain work to hail from tenth-century Mālava is the Śvetāmbara Dhanapāla's *Tilakamañjarī*, a romantic tale composed in Sanskrit prose at the end of the tenth century. See Ganga Prasad Yadava, *Dhanapāla and His Times: A Socio-cultural Study Based upon His Works* (New Delhi: Naurang Rai, 1982). On the Śaiva Saiddhāntika guru Purandara hailing from Malwa, see Sanderson, "Śaiva Age," 263–64. On the importance of Śaiva Mattamayūras in Central India in the tenth century, see Richard H. Davis, "Aghoraśiva's Background," *Journal of Oriental Research, Madras* 56–62 (1986–92): 374–75.

26 Sanderson, "The Śaiva Literature," 13n51.

27 *Sarvārthasiddhi* 9.1, summarized in *Tattvārthasūtra*, trans. Nathmal Tatia as *That Which Is*, 213–14. The *guṇasthāna*s are first outlined in the *Ṣaṭkhaṇḍāgama* and are much more popularly employed among Digambaras. Early Śvetāmbara references to the list of fourteen stages include the *Āvaśyakaniryukti* and the *Prajñāpanāsūtra*. See Ohira, "Dhyāna in the Tattvārthādhigamasūtra," 58; and Nalini Balbir, "Stories from the Āvaśyaka Commentaries," in *The Clever Adulteress and Other Stories*, ed. Phyllis Granoff (Oakville: Mosaic Press, 1990), 17–74. For charts of all the *guṇasthānas*, see P. S. Jaini, *Jaina Path*, 272–73; and Wiley, *A to Z of Jainism*, 243–44. On the different types of karma, see Helmuth von Glasenapp, *The Doctrine of Karman in Jain Philosophy*, trans. Barry Gifford (Bombay: Bai Vijibai Jivanlal Panalal Charity Fund, 1942).

28 Ohira, "Dhyāna in the *Tattvārthādhigamasūtra*," 51.

29 Dalsukh Malvani, Jayandra Soni, and Karl H. Potter, eds., *Encyclopedia of Indian Philosophies, Vol. X: Jain Philosophy*, pt. 1 (Delhi: Motilal Banarsidass, 2007), 219.

30 See Tatia, *Studies in Jaina Philosophy*, 284.

31 Vīrasena in his *Dh* 5.4.26 maintains that only monks can perform *dharmadhyāna*. See Ohira, "Dhyāna in the *Tattvārthādhigamasūtra*," 64n12. Cāmuṇḍarāya's *Cāritrasāra* (ca. 1000) and Āśādhara's *Anagāradharmāmṛta* (thirteenth century) also identify *dhyāna* as a mendicant ritual (Williams, *Jaina Yoga*, 240).

32 On the five minor vows (*anuvrata*), the three *guṇavrata*s, and the four *śikṣāvrata*s, see P. S. Jaini, *Jaina Path*, 187.

33 Because it is a complete version of the text, I cite from *Bhāvasaṅgraha* of Devasena, Hindi commentary by Lālārām Śāstrī (Solapur: Āryikā Sumatimatī Digambar Jain Granthmālā, 1987). A better edition of the section of the text on laypeople's duties, however, can be found in *Śrāvakācār Saṅgrah*, pt. 3, ed. and trans. Hīrālāl Śāstrī into Hindi (Solapur: Jain Saṃskṛti Saṃrakṣak Saṅgh, 1998), 440–64.

34 For a helpful overview of what scholars have seen as the components of a tantric *pūjā*, see Michele Stephen, "Sūrya-Sevana: A Balinese Tantric Practice," *Archipel* 89 (2015): 95–124. For a summary of the preliminary purification and protection rites of a tantric *nityāpūjā* that align closely with the *pūjā* of the *siddhacakra* outlined in the *Bhāvasaṅgraha*, see Gupta, Hoens, and Goudriaan, *Hindu Tantrism*, 134–38.

35 For the wording of the Digambara *īryāpathaśuddhi*, which is quite similar to the Śvetāmbara wording of the *īryāpathikīsūtra* (the formula that Śvetāmbaras to this day

recite at the outset of the worship of a temple icon, *caityavandana*; see chapter 5), see *PrT*, 13.

36 As in non-Jain texts, a fire *maṇḍala* in Jain texts (often called a *śikhi* or *agni-maṇḍala*) is often understood as a triangle in which the syllable *ra* is inscribed in each of the corners. For a description of a Digambara fire (here called *hutāśana*) *maṇḍala*, see *Vidyānuśāsana*, 3.34, p. 99; see p. 100 for a depiction of the diagram. For a detailed description of this rite involving the *agnimaṇḍala*, see Lālārām Śāstrī's Hindi commentary, which cites an unknown Sanskrit verse, in *Bhāv*, 193–96.

37 While it is not clear how this hand gesture was formed, both Digambaras and Śvetāmbaras to this day use a hand gesture in ritual called the *pañcaparameṣṭimudrā*. For some Sanskrit descriptions of these hand gestures in Śvetāmbara texts, see P. Shah, *Mudrāvicāraprakaraṇam and Mudrāvidhiḥ*, 23, 27, 35. For a depiction of the Digambara *parameṣṭhimudrā* as performed today, see *Laghuvidyānuvād, khaṇḍ* 1, p. 23, *citra* no. 20. See also figure 5.5 of this book.

38 For a history of *bhūtaśuddhi* and a description of a very similar purification ritual in which the body is burned to ashes and subsequently "divinized" into Viṣṇu in the text of the Vaiṣṇava Pāñcarātra, the *Jayākhyasaṃhitā*, see Flood, *The Tantric Body*, 106–15; and Flood, "The Purification of the Body." For a similar process in texts of the Śaiva Siddhānta, see Richard Davis, *Ritual in an Oscillating Universe: Worshiping Śiva in Medieval India* (Princeton, NJ: Princeton University Press, 1986), 47–60. See also Goodall and Isaacson, "Shared 'Ritual Syntax,'" 7–9.

39 On Śaiva *sakalīkaraṇa*, see Hélène Brunner, *Somaśambhupaddhati, Première Partie: Le rituel quotidien dans la tradition śivaïte de l'Inde du Sud selon Somaśambhu* (Pondicherry: Institut Français d'Indologie, 1963), 323–25. For an example of a Buddhist text, the *Mahāvairocana* XIV.1–2 also discusses burning up one's body to create a new mantra body at the outset of a worship ceremony (trans. Hodge, 301). See also Goodall and Isaacson, "Shared 'Ritual Syntax,'" 45–49.

40 In this rite, like most Digambara *vidhāna*s, worshipers transform themselves into *indra*s and *indrāṇī*s, but other *vidhāna*s require other transformations. The *Kalpadrumavidhāna*, for example, requires worshipers to transform themselves into universal emperors, *cakravartins*. See *Kalpdrum Vidhān*, 14th ed., ed. Āryikā Jñānamatī (Hastinapur: Digambar Jain Trilok Śodh Saṃsthān, 2008), 4.

41 For this story and for a description of Śvetāmbara lay worshipers understanding themselves as *indra*s and *indrāṇī*s to worship images of the *jina*s, see Lawrence A. Babb, *Absent Lord: Ascetics and Kings in a Jain Ritual Culture* (Berkeley: University of California Press, 1996), 79–82. Śvetāmbaras, to my knowledge, do not undertake these *sakalīkaraṇa* rites to perform communal *pūjā* ceremonies, but they do adopt the appearance of gods and goddesses, wearing crowns and orange garments.

42 For a description of an earth (here termed *pṛthvī*) *maṇḍala* in a Digambara text, see *Vidyānuśāsana* 3.34, p. 99; see p. 100 for a depiction of the diagram.

43 On the lotus as a common *maṇḍala* motif, see Bühnemann, "Maṇḍala, Yantra and Cakra," 21–24.

44 On *oṃ* representing the Five Supreme Beings in Jainism, see P. S. Jaini, *Jaina Path*, 163–64; and Ellen Gough, "When Sound Becomes an Image: Picturing Oṃ in Jainism,"

Material Religion, forthcoming. On the connection of the *tīrthaṅkaras* to *hrīṃ*, see Ellen Gough, "Shades of Enlightenment: A Jain Tantric Diagram and the Colours of the Tīrthaṅkaras," *International Journal of Jaina Studies (Online)* 8, no. 1 (2012): 1–47.

45 On these spell goddesses, see Umakant P. Shah, "Iconography of the Sixteen Jaina Mahāvidyās," *Journal of the Indian Society of Oriental Art* 15 (1947): 114–77.

46 For some examples of images of hourglass-shaped protective *vajras* drawn at the corners of Digambara *yantras* so evil spirits do not enter the ritual space, see *Jainendra Siddhānt Koś*, pt. 3, pp. 360, 362, 368.

47 On the nine treasures associated with a universal emperor in Jain texts, see Glasenapp, *Jainism: An Indian Religion of Salvation*, 283.

48 For an introduction to this text and a partial English translation, see Paul Dundas, "A Digambara Jain Description of the Yogic Path to Deliverance," in *Yoga in Practice*, ed. David Gordon White (Princeton, NJ: Princeton University Press, 2012), 143–61.

49 This is noted by Dundas, "Digambara Jain Description of the Yogic Path," 147, who cites verse 221 as an example of one of the few times the text references the *guṇasthānas*.

50 A. N. Upadhye, preface to *Tattvānuśāsana*, ed. and trans. Jugalkiśor "Yugvīr" Mukhtār, (Delhi: Vīrsevāmandir Trust Prakāśan, 1963), 14.

51 See *TA*, vv. 181–82, in Dundas, "Digambara Jain Description of the Yogic Path," 156.

52 The Hindi commentary on *Tattvānuśāsana* explains the contents of the *pṛthvīmaṇḍala* by citing a description of a *bhūmaṇḍala* in the ca. sixteenth-century Digambara text the *Vidyānuśāsana*. This *bhūmaṇḍala* is a four-sided yellow diagram divided at the center by *vajras* and containing the seed syllable *kṣiṃ* at its cardinal points and *laṃ* in its corners (*TA*, 105–6).

53 *TA*, vv. 123–26, in Dundas, "Digambara Jain Description of the Yogic Path," 158. What Dundas translates as "unification" (*sakalīkaraṇa*) here refers to the practice of *nyāsa* in which the Five Supreme Beings are placed on the meditator's body.

54 *TA*, vv. 183–85, in Dundas, "Digambara Jain Description of the Yogic Path," 156.

55 *TA*, vv. 186–87, in Dundas, 156.

56 *TA*, v. 190, in Dundas, 156–57, translation emended.

57 Aghoraśiva, *Kriyākramadyotikā*, 57, cited in Richard H. Davis, "Becoming Śiva, and Acting as One, in Śaiva Worship," in *Ritual and Speculation in Early Tantrism: Studies in Honor of André Padoux*, ed. Teun Goudriaan (Albany: State University of New York Press, 1992), 113.

58 Davis, "Becoming a Śiva," 113.

59 For another Digambara example of *sakalīkaraṇa* in which the five lines of the *pañcanamaskāra* are placed on the head, face, heart, navel, and feet, see the eleventh-century *Bhairavapadmāvatīkalpa* 2.3–4.

60 Davis, "Becoming a Śiva," 114. For the five *brahmamantras* that become associated with the five faces of Śiva (Īśāna, Tatpuruṣa, Aghora, Vāma and Sadyojāta) in the *Pāśupatasūtra* and later tantric Śaiva texts, see *Taittirīya Āraṇyaka* X.43–47. The five *brahmamantras* are also often used in ritual in conjunction with five of the six limb mantras (*aṅgamantra*) that correspond to other aspects of Śiva: his eye (*netra*), heart (*hṛd*), head (*śiras*), topknot (*śikhā*), armor (*kavaca*), and weapon (*astra*). Davis, *Ritual in an Oscillating Universe*, 48–50, 116. For a Jain linkage of the *aṅgamantras* (minus *netra*)

and the five lines of the *pañcanamaskāra*, see the fourteenth-century Śvetāmbara Jinaprabhasūri's description of *sakalīkaraṇa* in his chapter of the *Vidhimārgaprapā* on image consecration. In this *sakalīkaraṇa*, the *ācārya* should pronounce: "*oṃ namo arahaṃtāṇaṃ hṛdaye, oṃ namo siddhāṇaṃ śirasi, oṃ namo āyariyāṇaṃ śikhāyām, oṃ namo uvajjhāyāṇaṃ kavacam, oṃ namo savvasāhūṇaṃ astram.*" *VMP*, pp. 97–98, lines 38, 39, 1.

61 *TA*, v. 192, in Dundas, "Digambara Jain Description of the Yogic Path," 157.

62 For this gradual path to liberation, see *TA*, vv. 225–29, in Dundas, 159.

63 *TA*, vv. 198–99, 211–12, in Dundas, 158.

64 *TA*, v. 224, in Dundas, 159.

65 Bronkhorst, "Remarks on the History of Jaina Meditation," 158.

66 Bronkhorst, 157–58.

67 Sanderson, "Śaivism and the Tantric Traditions," 681.

68 Hemacandra's "*Kāvyānuśāsana* quotes Abhinavagupta extensively." Qvarnström, "Stability and Adaptability: A Jain Strategy," 41. See also Gary A. Tubb, "Hemacandra and Sanskrit Poetics," in *Open Boundaries: Jain Communities and Culture in Indian History*, ed. John E. Cort (Albany: State University of New York Press, 1998), 53–66.

69 Qvarnström, "Stability and Adaptability: A Jain Strategy," 41–43.

70 Sanderson, "The Śaiva Literature," 62.

71 Sanderson, 63.

72 An early mention of the fourfold *stha* classification is found in the Digambara Yogīndu's *Yogasāra (v. 98)*, a short work of Apabhraṃśa verses that is often placed in the sixth century, but should probably not be dated earlier than the tenth century. This text does not define what it means by the *stha*s, however, so it says little of the development of Jain ideas about meditative practices. On the *Yogasāra* containing the oldest mention of these *stha*s, see Sudhā Jain, *Jain evaṃ Baudh Yog: Ek Tulnātmak Adhyayan* (Varanasi: Pārśvanāth Vidyāpīṭh, 2001), 201.

73 *Yogasūtra* 1.2 defines *yoga* as the "cessation of the turning of thought" (*citta*), with *citta* in Sāṃkhya philosophy referring to the combination of mind (*manas*), ego (*ahaṃkāra*), and intellect (*buddhi*): *yogaścittavṛttinirodhaḥ. Yogasūtra* of Patañjali, trans.Barbara Stoler Miller as *Yoga: Discipline of Freedom: The Yoga Sutra Attributed to Patanjali* (New York: Bantam, 1998), 29–30.

74 See *JñS*, vv. 61–62 in *Jñānasāra* of Padmasiṃha, ed. and trans. Kailāścandra Siddhāntśāstrī (Varanasi: Vīr-Sevā-Mandir-Trust Prakāśan, 1984), 15.

75 *aṭṭhadalakamalamajjhe aruhaṃ veḍeha paramavīyehiṃ* | *pattesu taha ya vaṇṇā dalatare sattabaṇṇā ya* || *gaṇaharavalayeṇa puṇo māyāvīeṇa dharayalakkaṃte* | *jaṃ jaṃ icchaha kammaṃ sijjhaï ta ta khaṇaddheṇa* ||. The meaning of *dharayalakkaṃte* is not clear. For an analysis of these two verses and a discussion of the *gaṇadharavalaya*, see *TĀ*, 105–6.

76 For Vasunandin's outline of the four *stha*s, see *Śrā*, vv. 456–76. Vasunandin defines *piṇḍasthadhyāna* as meditation (on the *jina*) with the symbols of the eight *prātihārya* and white sunbeams (behind his head), describing the standard depiction of a temple icon of a *jina* (*Śrā*, v. 456), or imagining the *jina* in different places in one's body (*Śrā*, v. 476).

77 On some of these different interpretations, see Muni Sunīlasāgara's Hindi commentary in *Vasunandi-Śrāvakācāra*, ed. Bhāgcandra Jain "Bhāskar" and Vimalkumār Sauṃrayā (1999; repr., Mumbai: Hindī Granth Kāryālay, 2006), 489–90; and Mukhtār's commentary in *TA*, 103–4. For an example of how a Śvetāmbara interpreted these different "numbered" mantras, see *YŚ* 8.38–46, which draws upon *JñA*, vv. 1962–78.

78 *Bhavyamārgopadeśa Upāsakādhyayana*, vv. 286–87, in *Śrāvakācār Saṅgrah*, pt. 3, 393.

79 See the *praśasti* of the *Śrāvakācāra*, where Amitagati claims to be the disciple of Mādhavasena, who belonged to the Māthura Saṅgha (in *Śrāvakācār Saṅgrah*, pt. 1, 420–21).

80 Kailash Chandra Jain, *Malwa through the Ages* (Delhi: Motilal Banarsidass, 1972), 401, 471.

81 See also Williams, *Jaina Yoga*, 240.

82 Amitagati also includes a description of what is presumably a *siddhacakra*—an eight-petaled lotus with the enlightened one (*arhat*) at its center—but this diagram does not include the Ring of Disciples (*Śrā* 15.36–37).

83 The *śrīcakra*, for example, of the Śrīvidyā tradition will most often include a ring of ten superhuman powers (*siddhi*) at its periphery. These ten *siddhi*s include the eight classical yogic *siddhi*s (*aṇimā*, etc.) and the power to obtain pleasures (*bhukti*) and to "actualize all intentions" (*sarvakāmasiddi*). S. K. Ramachandra Rao, *Śrī-Chakra: Its Yantra, Mantra and Tantra* (Bangalore: Kalpatharu Research Academy, 1982), 18.

84 See Paul Dundas, "Shutting Kumudacandra's Mouth: Yaśaścandra's *Mudritakumudacandra* as a Source for the Intra-Jain Debate at Aṇahillapaṭṭana in 1125" (lecture, World Sanskrit Conference, Vancouver, Canada, July 10, 2018).

85 *Caityavandanamahābhāaṣya*, v. 217. I thank John Cort for pointing me to this text. For more information on different meditations on these states and their relationship to iconography—the three states of *piṇḍastha*, eight *prātihārya*s of *padastha*, and the two postures of *rūparahita*—see John E. Cort, "The Jina as King or the Jina as Renouncer: Seeing and Ornamenting Temple Images in Jainism" (Mohini Jain Presidential Chair in Jain Studies, inaugural lecture series, University of California, Davis, February 1, 2018). See also John E. Cort, "Dios como rey o asceta," in *La Escultura en los Templos Indios: El Arte de la Devoción*, ed. John Guy, trans. Carlos Mayor (Barcelona: Fundación "la Caixa," 2007), 171–79.

86 In the early twentieth century, the Śvetāmbara *yati* who lived in Varanasi, Bālacandrasūri (established as *ācārya* in 1883), in his Hindi commentary (*vṛtti*) on an early modern Hindi text on Jainism by the Brahmanical *sādhu* and scholar Kāṣṭhajihvā Svāmī, also discussed the four *stha*s and interpreted *padastha* in the same way (*tīrthaṃkar padvī par dhyān*). *Jain Bindu Vṛtti* in *Śrīkuśalacandrasūripattapraśastih*, 44.

87 Both Muni Jambūvijaya in his Sanskrit edition of the *Yogaśāstra* and Qvarnström in his English translation have noted the many verses Hemacandrasūri lifted directly from Śubhacandra with little modification.

88 Hemacandrasūri agrees with the *Tattvārthasūtra* that only those who know the fourteen *pūrva*s can undertake *śukladhyāna* (*YŚ* 11.2).

89 A preliminary discussion of the *dhāraṇā*s in the *Jñānārṇava* is found in Christopher Key Chapple, "Tantric Yoga in the *Mārkaṇḍeya Purāṇa* of Hinduism and the *Jñānārṇava* of Jainism," *Religions* 8, no. 11 (2017): 235–57.

90 Wayne Edward Surdam, "South Indian Śaiva Rites of Initiation: The Dīkṣāvidhi of Aghoraśivācārya's Kriyākramadyotikā" (PhD diss., University of California, Berkeley, 1984), 94n258. For these meditative practices involving the elements in non-Jain tantric texts, see Dominic Goodall and Marion Rastelli, eds. *Tāntrikābhidhānakośa III*, s.v. *dhāraṇā*; and Goodall and Isaacson, "Ritual Syntax," 7–9.

91 For a good overview of *dhāraṇā* in tantric texts, see Mallinson and Singleton, *Roots of Yoga*, 496-7n7–8.

92 Śubhacandra (*JñA*, v. 1879) terms this meditation *tattvarūpavatī dhāraṇā*, and Hemacandrasūri (*YŚ* 7.9) terms it *tattvabhū dhāraṇā* and describes how the pure-minded meditator should imagine themselves as an omniscient soul ("*sarvajñakalpam ātmānaṃ śuddhabuddhiḥ smaret*" *YŚ* 7.23).

93 For another example of an author using the term "*rūpavarjita*" in place of *rūpātīta*, see the Digambara Bhāskaranandi's *Dhyānastavaḥ*, v. 24 (early twelfth century).

94 Compare *YŚ* 7.9 and *JñA*, vv. 1878–79.

95 Davis, "Becoming Śiva," 112.

96 *YŚ*, 7.16, trans. Qvarnström as *The Yogaśāstra of Hemacandra: A Twelfth Century Handbook*, 147–48 (brackets in the original).

97 See *YŚ*, 8.74–75, and *JñĀ*, 2020–23.

98 *YŚ* 8.64–65, trans. Qvarnström as *The Yogaśāstra of Hemacandra: A Twelfth Century Handbook*, 160–61, translation emended (brackets in the original).

99 Jambūvijaya, *Yogaśāstra*, 3:1119. See also Qvarnström, *Yogaśāstra*, 161.

100 To my knowledge, the only other Śvetāmbara text on lay conduct to mention the *apraticakrā*-mantra diagram is mentioned by Muni Jambūvijaya in *SMKS*, 300. He notes that the diagram is also outlined in the *Mantradvātriṃśikākalpa*, a Sanskrit text of unknown provenance that has been attributed to Bhadraguptācārya, who may have lived in the fourteenth or fifteenth century. Paul Dundas, "Tantra without 'Tantrism': The Quotidian Jain Mantra according to Somasena Bhaṭṭāraka" (lecture handout, Jaina Studies Workshop on Jaina Tantra, School of Oriental and African Studies, University of London, 2015). See also *Mantradvātriṃśikākalpa*, vv. 12–13.

101 Some Śvetāmbara texts composed after Hemacandrasūri that describe the *stha*s include the *Dhyānavicāra* (unknown author, ca. fifteenth to sixteenth centuries), the *Dhyānadīpikā* of Sakalacandragaṇin (seventeenth century) and the *Dhyānadīpikā* of Devacandra in (1766 Vikram Samvat). Upādhyāya Vinayasāgara has interestingly noted that the latter two texts are also based on Śubhacandra's *Jñānārṇava*. Vinayasāgara, "Upādhyāy Sakalcandrakaṇi [*sic*] Racit Dhyānadīpikā (Saṃskṛt) Saṅgrah Granth hai," *Anusandhān* 47 (March 2009): 76–80. While modern Śvetāmbaras uphold these categories of meditation, they do not worship most of the *yantra*s Hemacandrasūri outlines in his *Yogaśāstra*. The *Yogaśāstra*'s chapters on meditation read more like a Digambara than Śvetāmbara text.

102 See, for example, from the early modern period: *Puruṣārthānuśāsanagata Śrāvakācāra* 5.36–66, in *Śrāvakācār Saṅgrah*, pt. 3, 518; and *Upāsakādhyayana*, vv. 286–87, in *Śrāvakācār Saṅgrah*, pt. 3, 393. See also the nineteenth-century Paṇḍit Daulatrām's *Kriyākoṣa*, vv. 48–65, in *Śrāvakācār Saṅgrah*, pt. 5, 353–54.

103 See, for example, Pratapkumar Toliya (whose august title I was tempted to use for

this chapter), *Meditation & Jainism: A Very Important, Deeply Studied & Condensed Research Paper* (Bangalore: Vardhaman Bharati International, 1986); and Sādhvī Priyadarśanā, *Jain Sādhnā Paddhati meṃ Dhyānyog* (Ahmednagar: Śrī Ratna Jain Pustakālay, 1986).

104 *Yoginīhṛdayatantra*, vv. 42–43. This text uses the term "*kaṇḍa*" in place of "*piṇḍa*." For a discussion, see André Padoux and Roger-Orphé Jeanty, trans., *The Heart of the Yogini: The Yoginīhṛdaya, a Sanskrit Tantric Treatise* (Oxford: Oxford University Press, 2013), 40.

105 Qvarnström, "Stability and Adaptability: A Jain Strategy," 40–41.

106 For an examination of the 162 *yantras* collected at the Digambara Neminātha temple in Amer, Rajasthan, see Kastūrcandra "Suman" Jain, *Āmer ke Digambar Jain Mandir Sāṃvalājī Nemināth ke Yantralekh* (Digambar Jain Atiśay Kṣetra Śrī Mahāvīrjī, Rajasthan: Jain Vidyā Saṃsthān, 2012).

107 I have shown the historical relationship between Śvetāmbara and Digambara versions of the *siddhacakra* in Gough, "Wheel of the Liberated." The contents of this Śvetāmbara *siddhacakra* are first outlined in a fourteenth-century Prakrit narrative tale by Ratnaśekharasūri, the *Sirivālacariya*. The *labdhipada* of the Śvetāmbara *siddhacakra* contains the exact same forty-eight praises of the *gaṇadharavalaya*, slightly rearranged.

108 For some images of these impermanent diagrams, see Cort, "Contemporary Jain Maṇḍala Rituals"; and Gough, "Jain *Maṇḍalas* and *Yantras*."

109 Wedemeyer, *Making Sense of Tantric Buddhism*, 9, quoting the *Oxford English Dictionary*'s definition of "esoteric."

110 For some examples of this literature, see J. Jain and Fischer, *Jaina Iconography*, pt. 2, 1–12. In their study of Jain ritual objects, these scholars place *yantras* in a category called "objects of meditation" (*dhyeya*). Richard Cohen, following Jain and Fischer, similarly focuses on these diagrams as objects of meditation, claiming that "the *raison d'être* of the *yantra* is to inspire the meditator, focus attention and provide mantras and other texts to be recited." Cohen, "The Art of Jain Meditation," 127.

111 Robert H. Sharf, "Visualization and Mandala in Shingon Buddhism," in *Living Images: Japanese Buddhist Icons in Context*, ed. Sharf and Elizabeth Horton Sharf (Stanford: Stanford University Press, 2001), 151–97.

112 Cort, "Contemporary Jain Maṇḍala Rituals," 141.

113 It is also important to note that some Jain monks themselves call these practices tantric. In an introduction to a *Siddhacakra Mahāpūjana* manual, the contemporary Śvetāmbara monk Ācārya Pradyumnasūri explains in Gujarati that worship of the *siddhacakra* is a *pūjā* that is filled with pure (*sattvika*) mantras and tantric spells (*taṃtravidyā*). *Śrī Siddhcakra Mahāpūjan Vidhi*, ed. Pradyumnasūri (Ahmedabad: Śrī Arunoday Foundation, 2000), 8.

114 Ācārya Indrasenasūri, ed., *Anānupūrvī* (n.p., 1997), 9.

115 Johannes Bronkhorst has called it "a plain absurdity" that all four types of *dhyāna*, including mournful and cruel, which "cannot possibly be considered forms of asceticism," have been classified as types of internal *tapas* in the *Bhagavatīsūtra* and *Aupapātikasūtra* (the *Tattvārthasūtra* agrees with these earlier texts) (Bronkhorst, *Two Traditions of Meditation*, 16). While these schemes can seem artificial, taking them seriously can provide new perspectives on what constitutes "asceticism" and "meditation."

CHAPTER 5

1 Babb, *Absent Lord*, 23.

2 Inscriptions from Mathura from the early centuries CE to the medieval period record laypeople's donations for the establishment of images in temples and monasteries at the urging of mendicants. See, for example, Quintanilla, *History of Early Stone Sculpture*, appendix II; John E. Cort, "Doing It for Others: Merit Transfer and Karma Mobility in Jainism," in *Jainism and Early Buddhism: Essays in Honor of Padmanabh S. Jaini*, ed. Olle Qvarnström (Freemont, CA: Asian Humanities Press, 2003), 133–34; and Cort, "Bhakti in the Early Jain Tradition," 69.

3 For a description of how *vāsakṣepa* is made, see James Burgess, "Papers on Shatrunjaya and the Jainas," *Indian Antiquary* 7, no. 13 (1884): 191.

4 Cort, *Jains in the World*, 115. Cort (114–15) explains that some image-worshiping Śvetāmbara monks have formalized this lay-mendicant exchange of *vāsakṣepa* in Gujarati handbooks, calling it *gurupūjā*, or worship of the guru. In this rite, the layperson will sprinkle *vāsakṣepa* on the right big toe of a monk, place some money for the monk on a metal plate, and then bow before the monk, hands in *pranāma*, or a gesture of prayer. The guru will then reciprocate the gesture by sprinkling his powder on the crown of the layperson's head. In my experiences witnessing *gurupūjā*, laypeople did not sprinkle *vāsakṣepa* on the toe of the monk, but they did offer money to a plate in exchange for a sprinkling of *vāsakṣepa. For another image and discussion of gurupūjā, see Babb, Absent Lord*, 61–62.

5 Jayantakrishna Harikrishna Dave, introduction to *Mantrarājarahasya* of Siṃhatilakasūri, ed. Ācārya Jinavijaya as *Mantrarāja Rahasyam of Śrī Siṃhatilakasūri*, (Bombay: Bharatiya Vidya Bhavan, 1980), 6. For some medieval demands that the *sūrimantra* be kept secret, see Dundas, "Becoming Gautama," 49n34.

6 Nāgendra, *Mahopādhyāy Vinaysāgar: Jīvan, Sāhitya aur Vicār* (Jaipur: Prākṛt Bhāratī Academy, 1999), 45.

7 Ācārya Nandighoṣasūri, *Labdhi: Ek Vaijñānik Viśleṣaṇ (Labdhi: A Scientific Analysis)* (Ahmedabad: Research Institute of Scientific Secrets from Indian Oriental Scriptures, 2017).

8 Flügel, "Demographic Trends," 373n67.

9 For an introduction to *yati*s and the nineteenth-century *saṃvegī sādhu* reformers, see Cort, *Jains in the World*, 44–46.

10 Muni Śīlacandravijaya, *Śāsan Samrāṭ* (Ahmedabad: Tapāgācchīya Śeṭhśrī Jindās Dharmdās Dhārmik Trust, Kadambgiri Vāṭī, 1973), 90.

11 Dundas, *History, Scripture, and Controversy*, 26–27; Dundas, "The Monk Jinapati Sūri."

12 For an excellent discussion of a *sūrimantrapaṭa* housed at the Royal Asiatic Society that dates to 1499, see Nalini Balbir, "Sūri-mantra-paṭa," *Jainpedia*, n.d., http://www.jainpedia.org/themes/principles/sacred-writings/highlights-of-jainpedia/suri-mantra-pata/index.html. Another *sūrimantrapaṭa* dated to the fifteenth century has been published in Philip S. Rawson, *Tantra: Hayward Gallery, London, 30 September–14 November 1971* (London: Arts Council of Great Britain, 1971), 106, fig. 494, but has been misidentified

as "Yantra 'Oṃ Klīṁ' in Circles." It can be found online at https://www.pinterest.com/pin/506795764309274293/?nic_v1=1awEnTeuAVh8SvcR8MExNs9uHuHUJdfpKvYxqAaXBYwqknSFabUL458qX8ueDzXCd%2F, accessed April 14, 2020. Several early modern *sūrimantrapaṭas* are published in Ambālāl Premcand Śāh, ed., *Śrīsūrimantrakalpasandoha* (Ahmedabad: Sarabhai Manilal Nawab, 1948). For a *sūrimantrapaṭa* dated to 1650–1700, see Pal, *The Peaceful Liberators*, 228–29. For one dated to the fifteenth century (but should probably be dated a century later) and one to the nineteenth century, see Shridhar Andhare and Pandit Laxmanbhai Bhojak, *Jain Vastrapatas: Jain Paintings on Cloth* (Ahmedabad: Lalbhai Dalpatbhai Institute of Indology, 2015), 58–59. Another *sūrimantrapaṭa* dated to the eighteenth century has been published on pp. 66–67 of *Jain Vastrapatas*, though it has been misidentified as a *siddhacakra*.

13 *Śrīkuśalacandrasūripaṭṭapraśastiḥ*, p. 6, v. 40.

14 *SMKS*, 267, cited in Dundas, "Becoming Gautama," 49n32; Dundas, afterword to *History, Scripture, and Controversy*.

15 Flügel, "Demographic Trends," table 12.1, 322–23.

16 Bābūlāl "Ujjval" Jain, comp., *Samagra Jain Cāturmās Sūcī* (Mumbai: Gajendra Sandeś Kāryālay, 2019), 158.

17 Muni Suyaśavijaya, pers. comm., Mumbai, September 2013.

18 Flügel, "The Invention of Jainism," 1–2.

19 *Śrīsubodhāsamācārī* [sic] (Bombay: Sheth Devchand Lalabhai Jain Pustakoddhar Fund, 1924). For a discussion of a thirteenth-century *sāmācārī* text by Tilakācārya, see Saumyaguṇā, *Jain Muni ke Vratāropaṇ*, 113–14.

20 On the formulas recited to advance to these different ranks, see *BYV*, 195–97. Some sources list the *vācaka* and *upādhyāya* as different ranks with different *vardhamānavidyās*. In conversations in 2016 and 2019, Nandighoṣasūri confirmed to me that, technically, *pannyāsa* is not a rank (*pada*) but instead should be understood as an advanced *gaṇin*. The *Bṛhad Yog Vidhi* does, however, name *pannyāsa* as a *pada*.

21 See esp. Walther Schubring, *Mahāvīra's Words*, trans. Willem Bollée and Jayandra Soni (Ahmedabad: L. D. Institute, 2004).

22 P. S. Jaini, *Jaina Path*, 52.

23 On the history of this list, see the essays "The 'Canons' of 'Scripture': Text, Ritual and Symbol" and "The Jain Scriptures and the History of Jainism: The Study of 'Scripture' as a Category in Comparative Religion" in Folkert, *Scripture and Community*, 53–81; 85–112; and Cort, "Śvetāmbar Mūrtipūjak Jain Scripture," 171–94.

24 For an excellent overview of scholarly accounts of the dating and events of the Jain councils, see Royce Wiles, "The Dating of the Jaina Councils: Do Scholarly Presentations Reflect the Traditional Sources?" in *Studies in Jaina History and Culture: Disputes and Dialogues*, ed. Peter Flügel (London: Routledge, 2006), 61–85.

25 For a good overview of some lists of Śvetāmbara *āgamas* and Digambara classifications of scripture, see Dundas, *The Jains*, 76–81.

26 Folkert suggests the use of "Canon I" for texts familiar to Jains through regular (usually ritual) contact, and "Canon II" for "normative texts that are more independently and distinctively present with a tradition" (Folkert, *Scripture and Community*, 69). Cort, influenced by Clifford Geertz's categories of "experience-near" and "experience far,"

renames Folkert's typologies "Canon-near" and "Canon-far" (Cort, "Śvetāmbar Mūrtipūjak Jain Scripture," 175). I do not think these categories work for Jainism, however, because texts become important only through ritual. The *āgamas*, for example, have been codified into lists not because of their intrinsic value, but because they are used in the *yogavidhi*, or at least are listed in texts on the *yogavidhi*.

27 John E. Cort, "The Intellectual Formation of a Jain Monk," *Journal of Indian Philosophy* 29 (2001): 329.

28 For an excellent examination of some of the various lists of *prakīrṇaka* texts, from the list in the *Nandīsūtra*, which lists 84,000, to texts from the twentieth century, see Kapadia, *History of the Canonical Literature of the Jainas*, 44–48. For different collections of *prakīrṇakas* in manuscripts, see Nalini Balbir, "Functions of Multiple-Text Manuscripts in India: The Jain Case," in *The Emergence of Multiple-Text Manuscripts*, ed. Alessandro Bausi, Michael Friedrich, and Marilena Maniaci (Berlin: De Gruyter, 2019), 15–17. See also chap. 3, n99, for the fourteen *prakīrṇakas* listed in Jinaprabhasūri's *Vidhimārgaprapā*. Kapadia notes that "at least since the time of Bhāvaprabha Sūri [of the Pūrṇimā Gaccha in the early eighteenth century,] the number of [*prakīrṇakas*] is fixed as ten . . . [but] there is no uniformity as to which works are to be looked up" (Kapadia, *History of the Canonical Literature*, 45). This does not seem to be entirely true, however, since manuscripts after the early nineteenth century continue to contain collections of more than ten *prakīrṇakas* (Balbir, "Functions of Multiple-Text Manuscripts," 17). According to the twentieth-century Pūrṇacandrasāgarasūri, there are nineteen *prakīrṇakas*: *Āturapratyākhyāna*, *Mahāpratyākhyāna*, *Devendrastava*, *Taṇḍulavaitālika*, *Saṃstāraka*, *Bhaktaparijñā*, *Ārādhanāpatākā*, *Gaṇividyā*, *Aṅgavidyā*, *Catuḥśaraṇa*, *Dvīpasāgaraprajñapti*, *Jyotiṣakaraṇḍaka*, *Maraṇasamādhi*, *Tīrthodgālī*, *Siddhaprābhṛta*, *Narakavibhakti*, *Candravedhyaka*, *Pañcakalpa*, and *Jītakalpa* (*BYV*, 192). The last two texts are placed in the *Chedasūtra* category in English-language lists of *āgamas*. For comparison, another twentieth-century Tapā Gaccha monk, Gaṇin Nityānanda of the Vijaya Śākhā in Premasūri's lineage, names the exact same ten *prakīrṇakas* that are listed in English-language scholarship. *Śrī Pravrajyā-Yogādi Vidhi Saṅgrah*, ed. Gaṇi Nityānanda (Dabhoi, Vadodara: Ārya Śrī Jambūsvāmī Jain Muktābhāī Āgam Mandir, 1975), 159.

29 See Deo, *Jaina Monastic Jurisprudence*, 25–26.

30 Brevard S. Childs, *The New Testament as Canon: An Introduction* (Philadelphia: Fortress Press, 1984), 6.

31 On this ritual (called *nandīkriyā*, *nandīvidhi*, or *nandī*) for the beginning of study (Guj. *yog praveś*), see *BYV*, 26–27. For the instructions on the construction of the model of the Jina's Preaching Assembly, see *BYV*, 1–2.

32 For a chart on the number of days, fasts, and performances of *kāyotsarga* required for the study of each *āgama*, see *BYV*, 168–92. While this text prescribes the formalized study of *āgamas* after the *Bhagavatīsūtra*, in practice these texts are not required reading. Monks do not undertake *nandīkriyā* to study these texts, and they read them according to their own desire.

33 The equivalencies with male mendicant ranks were provided by Pravartinī Kalānidhi, pers. comm., Mumbai, October 2019.

34 Ācārya Nandighoṣasūri, pers. comm., Mumbai, July 2019. Multiple mendicants of the

Tapā Gaccha confirmed to me that nuns used to read the *prakīrṇakas* as well (see *BYV*, 192), but this is no longer practiced.

35 This appears to be an innovation by Ācārya Yugabhūṣaṇasūri. Another disciple in Rāmacandrasūri's *samudāya* in the Tapā Gaccha (Vijaya Śākhā), Sādhvī Jinaprajñā, disciple of Ācārya Kīrtiyaśasūri, confirmed to me that female mendicants only read the first four texts of the *yogavidhi* and do not receive the *vardhamānavidyā*. Sādhvī Jinaprajñā, pers. comm., Mumbai, July 2019.

36 Kalānidhi, pers. comm.

37 Ācārya Yugabhūṣaṇasūri confirmed that his *sūrimantrapaṭa* was painted by an artist in Mumbai named Dharmindar who is not Jain but is a follower of Osho. Yugabhūṣaṇasūri, pers. comm., Mumbai, September 2019.

38 Two expanded versions of the *sūrimantra*, which depict all the subsidiary deities—the four *jayādevīs*, the nine treasures (*navanidhi*), the eight guardians of the directions (*dikpāla*), the sixteen spell goddesses (*vidyādevī*), the sixty-four *indras* and *indrāṇīs*, and the *yakṣa* and *yakṣī* of each of the twenty-four *tīrthaṅkaras*—are published in Andhare and Bhojak, *Jain Vastrapatas*, 62–63, 66–67 (the latter being misidentified as a *siddhacakra*).

39 Vinaysāgara's guru is also called Jinamaṇisāgara. Nāgendra, *Mahopādhyāy Vinaysāgar*, 45.

40 See chap. 3, n112. See also a manual from the Añcala Gaccha in which the *vardhamānavidyā* for the *vācanācārya* (*vācaka*) does not include part of the *ṛddhi-maṅgala*, and the version of the spell for the *upādhyāya* includes the beginning of the *ṛddhi-maṅgala*: four praises to *jinas* with clairvoyance (*namo ohijiṇāṇaṃ*, etc.) (*VVK*, pp. 72–73). Merutuṅgasūri's *Sūrimukhyamantrakalpa*, however, includes a different *vardhamānavidyā* for an *upādhyāya*, *pravartaka*, *sthavira*, *gaṇavacchedaka*, and *paṇḍita*, but only the *sthavira*'s *viydā* contains part of the *ṛddhi-maṅgala* (*Vardhamāna Vidyā Kalpaḥ*, 66–71). For representations of the different cloth diagrams that should be made for monks of different ranks according to Siṃhatilakasūri's thirteenth-century *Vardhamānavidyākalpa*, see *VVK*, 14–17.

41 In a modern Gujarati booklet from the Tapā Gaccha that includes different versions of the *vardhamānavidyā*, the *vidyā* for the *upādhyāya* begins with the *pañcanamaskāra* and part of the *ṛddhi-maṅgala*: the four praises to *jinas* with clairvoyance (*namo ohijiṇāṇaṃ*, etc.). The *vidyā* for the *sthavira* contains ten more lines of the *ṛddhi-maṅgala*. This text also includes an expanded spell, a *bṛhadvardhamānavidyā*, that includes even more lines of the *ṛddhi-maṅgala*. Muni Divyaratnavijaya, ed., *Māro Svādhyāy* (n.p: n.p, n.d), 39–42.

42 Williams, *Jaina Yoga*, 203–4, translation emended. On this formula, see Paul Dundas, "Textual Authority in Ritual Procedure: The Śvetāmbara Jain Controversy Concerning *Īryāpathikīpratikramaṇa*," *Journal of Indian Philosophy* 39 (2011): 327–50.

43 For a transcription, translation, and discussion of the *Vajrapañjarastotra*, see Balbir, "The Jain Tradition on Protection," 283–85.

44 For the *vajrapañjarastotra* with illustrations of the movements, see *Śrī Sūrimantra Mahāpūjan evaṃ Vardhamān Vidyā Mahāpūjan*, ed. Gaṇi Somasundaravijaya (n.p., 2007–8), 8–9.

45 Compare the steps of the daily worship of a higher-level Jain monk with the steps of the daily worship practices of an initiate in the Vaiṣṇava Pāñcarātra outlined in Rastelli, "The Religious Practice of the 'Sādhaka,'" 323–29, and those of an initiate in the Śaiva Kulamārga outlined in Gupta, Hoens, and Goudriaan, *Hindu Tantrism*, 139–57.

46 For the placement of mantras first on one's fingers and then on key parts of the body in the *Jayākhyasaṃhitā* to transform the practitioner into Viṣṇu, see Flood, *The Tantric Body*, 114–15; and Rastelli, "The Religious Practice of the 'Sādhaka,'" 323–324. For a Śaiva equivalent, see Davis, *Ritual in an Oscillating Universe*, 47–51.

47 On these four *mudrās*, see Brunner, *Somaśambhupaddhati, Première Partie*, 188–89 and plate I. For another image of these *mudrās*, see Sanjukta Gupta, "The Worship of Kālī according to the *Toḍala Tantra*," in *Tantra in Practice*, ed. David Gordon White (Princeton, NJ: Princeton University Press, 2000), 477.

48 *Mṛgendrāgama, Kriyāpāda* 3.12–14, trans. Judit Törzsök, "The Search in Śaiva Scriptures for Meaning in Tantric Ritual," in *Mélanges tantriques à la mémoire d'Hélène Brunner / Tantric Studies in Memory of Hélène Brunner*, ed. Dominic Goodall and André Padoux (Pondicherry: Ecole Française d'Extrême Orient, 2007), 462.

49 For the use of the *dhenumudrā* in symbolically transforming water into *amṛta*, see Gupta, Hoens, and Goudriaan, *Hindu Tantrism*, 131, 135. For the use of the *dhenu* and *avaguṇṭhanamudrās* in the *Toḍalatantra* and accompanying photos of these *mudrās*, see Gupta, "The Worship of Kālī," 477, 487.

50 Brunner, Oberhammer, and Padoux, eds., *Tāntrikābhidhānakośa I*, s.v. *astramudrā*.

51 For a photograph of this *mudrā*, see *Somasambhupaddhati*, vol. 1, appendix I, image 27.

52 Even though the *Vidhimārgaprapā* prescribes that *pravartinī*s receive the *vardhamānavidyā* (see chap. 3, n53), this is not common today, and Ācārya Yugabhūṣaṇasūri seems to have be innovative in imparting the spell to Pravartinī Kalānidhi.

53 Nuns and lower-level monks also sometimes consecrate their own *vāsakṣepa* through the use of the *pañcanamaskāra* or by sprinkling it on metal *yantra*s of boon-giving deities like Padmāvatī. Nandighoṣasūri, pers. comm., July 5, 2019.

54 For two examples, see Pal, *The Peaceful Liberators*, 228–29; and Balbir, "Sūri-mantra-paṭa," http://www.jainpedia.org/themes/principles/sacred-writings/highlights-of-jainpedia/suri-mantra-pata/contentpage/1.html.

55 The eyes that are often painted atop Śvetāmbara ritual diagrams and auspicious images such as pots are reminiscent of the eyes painted on the Buddhist *stūpa*s of Nepal. See Micah Issitt and Carlyn Main, *Hidden Religion: The Greatest Mysteries and Symbols of the World's Religious Beliefs* (Santa Barbara, CA: ABC-CLIO, 2014), 188–89.

56 On the *navanidhi*, see Helmuth von. Glasenapp, *Jainism*, 283–85.

57 Interviews with monks from the Tapā, Kharatara, and Añcala *gaccha*s confirmed that today, all modern Śvetāmbaras accept that the *sūrimantra* contains five different components. This does not seem to have always been the case, as the *Mantrarājarahasya* contains versions of the *sūrimantra* that contain a variety of sections, from one to six (see chapter 3).

58 The best study of the cult of Gautama is Mahopādhyāya Vinayasāgara, *Gautam Rās: Ek Pariśīlan* (Jaipur: Prākṛt Bhāratī Academy, 1987).

59 Texts consistently claim that Tribhuvanasvāminī has a thousand arms, though she is depicted with various numbers of arms. For descriptions of Tribhuvanasvāminī, see Dundas, "Becoming Gautama, 50n47, which references *Mantradvātriṃśikākalpa* 1.19 and 4.32; and *SMKS*, 204, where she is said to have been a laywoman in Bāhubali's time. For a story of Hemacandra's propitiation of Tribhuvanasvāminī, see Sanderson, "Śaiva Age," 248.

60 See Ācārya Somacandrasūri, *Śrīsūrimantrapañcaprasthāna Prārambhavidhi, Nitya Ārādhanāvidhi, 21 Divasīya Ārādhanāvidhi & Pañcaprasthānapūrṇāhutipūjāvidhi* (Surat: Śrī Rānder Road Jain Saṅgh, 2013).

61 This temple is established at the base of the Śatruñjaya hill, in front of the Samosaraṇ Mandir.

62 The order of deities Somacandrasūri follows, where Lakṣmī presides over the third section of the mantra and Gaṇipiṭaka presides over the fourth section, agrees with Siṃhatilakasūri's *Mantrarājarahasya*. In the manuals by Rājaśekharasūri, Jinabhadrasūri, and Merutuṅgasūri, Gaṇipiṭaka presides over the third section, and Lakṣmī the fourth. In addition, since Rājaśekharasūri does not outline the worship of the ten guardians of the directions and the nine planets, Somacandrasūri also supplements his text with the descriptions of the worship of these deities in the texts by Jinabhadrasūri and Merutuṅgasūri. *NĀV*, 15–16.

63 Somacandrasūri interestingly compares the sixty steps of modern worship of the *paṭa* to the steps required for the worship of the *sūrimantrapaṭa* in the premodern Sanskrit manuals collected in the *SMKS*, providing citations from the *SMKS* for nearly every step of the daily ritual and noting which steps are not found in premodern manuals (*NĀV*, 41–56).

64 For examples of handwritten *vidyā*s imparted to disciples, see the first few pages of *VVK*.

65 For the details of the showing of these *mudrā*s, see *NĀV*, 53–54, citing *SMKS*, 120, 127, 147.

66 These directions are taken from the medieval manuals of the *SMKS*. Nandighoṣasūri confirmed to me that he does not visualize colors or show *mudrā*s while performing the rites, though other *ācārya*s might.

67 On the *kalpendra* gods, see *TS* 4.17–20. For Śvetāmbaras, since there are only two chiefs for the last four heavens, there are twelve heavens and ten chiefs. *Tattvārthasūtra*, trans. Tatia, *That Which Is*, 106.

68 On the *laukāntika* gods, see *TS* 4.25.

69 Muni Kuśalakīrtivijaya, comp., *Jinśāsan Adhiṣṭhāyak Samput*, pt. 1 (Ahmedabad: Gītārth Gaṅgā, 2018), 20.

70 On the unstitched, clean clothes that laymen and -women wear only for *pūjā*—usually a *dhoti* and a cotton wrap for men and a sari for women—see Cort, *Jains in the World*, 89, 98, 221n22.

71 The eight auspicious symbols in Śvetāmbara Jainism are the *svastika*, *śrīvatsa*, *nandyāvarta*, powder box (*vardhamānaka*), throne (*bhadrāsana*), full water jug (*kalaśa*), pair of fish (*matsyayugma*), and mirror (*darpaṇa*).

72 For a photo of a *nandyāvarta*, see Cort, *Jains in the World*, 77.

73 See also *MRR*, v. 223. On substances and their modifications, see Soni, "Dravya, Guṇa and Paryāya."

74 Somasundaravijaya outlines the different types of *havanas* for *mūrtipūjaka* Śvetāmbaras and the required *kuṇḍas* for these ceremonies. For the three-day ceremony for prosperity (*pauṣṭikavidhāna*), an eight-cornered firepit of three levels should be constructed. For the worship of the *nandyāvarta* diagram, a six-cornered *kuṇḍa* should be constructed. For the male boon-giving deities Maṇibhadra, Ghaṇṭākarṇa, Nākoḍābhairava, and Bhomīyājī, a square *kuṇḍa* should be established. For goddesses like Padmāvatī, Cakreśvarī, Ambikā, Pañcagulī, and Jvālāmālinī, a triangle-shaped *kuṇḍa* should be constructed. *Śrī Sūrimantra Mahāpūjan*, 8.

75 For an objection to fire sacrifice, see *Sūtrakṛtāṅga*, 1.7.6–7, trans. Jacobi, *SBE*, 45:293: "He who lights a fire, kills living beings; he who extinguishes it, kills the fire. Therefore a wise man who well considers the Law should light no fire. Earth contains life, and water contains life; jumping (or flying) insects fall in (the fire); dirt-born vermin (and beings) living in the wood: all these beings are burned by lighting a fire."

76 *Śrī Sūrimantra Mahāpūjan*, 71–78.

77 Charles D. Orzech, "Ritual Subjects: Homa in Chinese Translations and Manuals from the Sixth through Eighth Centuries," in *Homa Variations: The Study of Ritual Change across the Longue Durée*, ed. Richard K. Payne and Michael Witzel (New York: Oxford University Press, 2016), 271.

78 Several recent essays on *homa* in tantric traditions are found in Payne and Witzel, *Homa Variations*.

79 *Śrī Sūrimantra Mahāpūjan*, 73.

80 *Kalpasūtra* 5.123, trans. Jacobi, *SBE*, 22:264–65.

81 *Kalpasūtra* 5.127, trans. Jacobi, *SBE*, 22:265–66.

82 *Kalpasūtra* 5.128, trans. Jacobi, *SBE*, 22:266.

83 For the Śvetāmbara lay celebration of Dīvālī, see James Laidlaw, *Riches and Renunciation: Religion, Economy, and Society among the Jains* (Oxford: Clarendon Press, 1995), part V; and Cort, *Jains in the World*, 164–75.

84 Jeffrey Hopkins, drawing upon the distinction between *sūtra* and *tantra* by the fourteenth-century founder of the Geluk school of Tibetan Buddhism Tsong-kha-pa, explains that "visualizing oneself as a deity and identification with that deity comprise the central distinguishing feature of tantric meditation." Hopkins contrasts tantric deity yoga with earlier non-tantric Buddhist forms of meditation by noting that early forms do not encourage visualization of one's physical body as a *buddha*, but instead encourage practitioners to identify an enlightened mind of a *buddha* within themselves. Hopkins, "The Ultimate Deity in Action Tantra and Jung's Warning against Identifying with the Deity," *Buddhist-Christian Studies* 5 (1985): 160.

85 Tsong-kha-pa, H.H. the Dalai Lama, and Jeffrey Hopkins, *Tantra in Tibet: The Great Exposition of Secret Mantra, Vol. 1* (Delhi: Motilal Banarsidass, 1987), 21.

86 Tsong-kha-pa, H.H. the Dalai Lama, and Jeffrey Hopkins, *Deity Yoga* (Ithaca, NY: Snow Lion Publications, 1987), 103–38.

87 For a distinction between *nyāsa*-based *sakalīkaraṇa* rites and identification with the deity through "a series of transformations," see Goodall and Isaacson, "Shared 'Ritual Syntax,'" 45–49. To see how these two types of divinization are intimately linked, one can look at the description of daily rites in chapter 2 of the Śaiva *Svacchandatantra*, which first outlines the *nyāsa*-based preliminary rites of purification and deification of the body required for worship, and then prescribes the divinized worshiper to undertake an elaborate visualization to "[meditate] upon Bhairava as one's own self." Simone McCarter, "The Body Divine: Tantric Śaivite Ritual Practices in the *Svacchandatantra* and Its Commentary," *Religions* 5 (2014): 739–42, 744–45.

88 Geoffrey Samuel, *The Origins of Yoga and Tantra: Indic Religions to the Thirteenth Century* (Cambridge: Cambridge University Press, 2008), 268.

89 One manual ensures that the practitioner who fasts and recites the *mahāmantra* of twenty-eight lines listing Gautama's powers will first become an *ācārya* and then eventually achieve liberation. The mantra contains a variant of the *ṛddhi-maṅgala*. *Labdhinidhān Śrī Gautam Svāmī*, ed. Muni Harṣabodhivijaya (Mumbai: Śrī Andherī Jain Saṅgh, n.d.), n.p.

90 Sanderson, "The Śaiva Age," 129n301.

91 *Vīṇāśikhatantra*, ed. and trans. Teun Goudriaan as *Vīṇāśikha Tantra: A Śaiva Tantra of the Left Current* (Delhi: Motilal Banarsidass, 1985), 48.

92 On the wide-ranging Hindu, Buddhist, and Jain texts, images, and inscriptions where the sisters of Tumburu can be found, see Teun Goudriaan's introduction to the *Vīṇāśikha Tantra*, 1–62.

93 Goudriaan, "Tumburu and His Sisters," *Wiener Zeitschrift für die Kunde Südasiens* 17 (1973): 76–77.

94 Alexis Sanderson, "History through Textual Criticism in the Study of Śaivism, the Pañcarātra and the Buddhist Yoginītantras," in *Les Sources et le temps/Sources and Time: A Colloquium, Pondicherry 11–12 January 1997*, ed. Nicolas Grimal (Pondicherry, Institut Français de Pondichéry, 2001), 8n5.

95 Elizabeth ten Grotenhuis, *Japanese Mandalas: Representations of Sacred Geography* (Honolulu: University of Hawai'i Press, 1999).

96 Ohira assigns this text to the early fifth canonical stage, or the second half of the fourth century CE. Ohira, *A Study of the Bhagavatīsūtra*, 98.

97 For a discussion of this section of the *Jīvājīvābhigamasūtra*, see Cort, *Framing the Jina*, 93.

98 U. P. Shah, *Studies in Jaina Art*, 87, translation emended.

99 Schubring, *Mahāvīra's Words*, 1.

100 *Arthaśāstra* of Kauṭilya, trans. Olivelle as *King, Governance, and Law in Ancient India*, 106.

101 *Arthaśāstra* of Kauṭilya, trans. Olivelle as *King, Governance, and Law in Ancient India*, 106.

102 In Gough, "Shades of Enlightenment," 6, 24–27, I also suggest that the sections of the *Sthānāṅgasūtra* and the *Āvaśyakaniryukti* that discuss the coloring of the *tīrthṅkaras* may have been influenced by the medieval development of the *ṛṣimaṇḍala* ritual diagram.

103 John E. Cort, "Art, Religion, and Material Culture: Some Reflections on Method," *Journal of the American Academy of Religion*, 64, 3 (1996): 615.

104 S. Mehta, *Maximum City*, 517.

CONCLUSION

1 A Jain layman in Delhi interestingly told me that he skips the recitation of this section of the prayer because he does not believe in superhuman powers. I cannot say how common this practice is.

2 For this portion of the Digambara *pratikramaṇa*, which the text says should only be recited by an *ācārya*, see Ācārya Candrasāgara, ed., *Yatikartavya Prabodh Saṅgrah* (Madhya Pradesh: Śrī Bundelkhaṇḍ Syādvād Pariṣad, 1997), 126–27. Modern Digambaras recite four types of *pratikramaṇa*: the ones (1) performed every morning and night, (2) performed every half-month (*pākṣika*), (3) performed every four months (*cāturmāsika*), and (4) performed yearly (*vārṣika*). The *ṛddhi-maṅgala* is only part of the *pākṣika*. Āryikā Akampamatī, pers. comm., Nagpur, July 2016.

3 For a performance of an *abhiṣeka* in which the Digambara nun Paurṇamatī Mātā, a disciple of Ācārya Vidyāsāgara, recites the *bṛhadśāntimantra*, see "Jain Shanti dhara voice by Shri Purnmati mataji Shishya Acharya shri Vidhya Sagarji Maharaj," https://www.youtube.com/watch?v=Ih6_K5fnGI0.

4 See ritual manual *Cauṃsaṭh Ṛddhi Vidhān*, ed. Āryikā Jñānamatī (Hastinapur: Digambar Jain Trilok Śodh Saṃsthān, 2010). Madhu Khanna has also published a version of the Ring of Disciples, with the *apraticakrā*-mantra at the center, from the nineteenth century. She calls the diagram the "Kalyāṇa Chakra, the Wheel of Fortune," because *kalyāṇa* is written in the center of the diagram. Khanna, *Yantra: The Tantric Symbol of Cosmic Unity* (London: Thames and Hudson, 1981). I thank Nandighoṣasūri for directing me to this. The *Kalyāṇamandirastotra* also has forty-eight *ṛddhi*s associated with it, but few of these *ṛddhi*s are found in the *ṛddhi-maṅgala*. See Sārābhāī Maṇilāl Navāb, ed. *Mahāprābhāvika [sic] Navasmaraṇa* (Ahmedabad: Sārābhāī Maṇilāl Navāb, 1938), 489–502.

5 Manju Jain, pers. comm., Nagpur, July 2016.

6 For Mehtalia's story of how he met Manju Jain, see "Jigar Mehta Shares His Story on Bhaktamar," https://www.youtube.com/watch?v=elpuurl8dZQ.

7 Goodall and Isaacson, "Shared 'Ritual Syntax.'"

8 Madhusūdan Ḍhāṅkī and Jitendra Śāh conclude that Mānatuṅga was not a court poet, as the hagiographies assume, but a Śvetāmbara devotional poet who lived at the end of the sixth century or beginning of the seventh century CE. Ḍhāṅkī and Śāh, *Māntuṅgācārya aur unke Stotra*, 2nd ed. (Ahmedabad: Śāradāben Cimanbhāī Educational Research Centre, 1999), 94–110.

9 Ḍhāṅkī and Śāh, *Māntuṅgācārya aur unke Stotra*, 2.

10 This has been published as *Bhaktāmara, Kalyāṇamandira and Namiuṇa*, ed. and trans.

Hirālāl Rasikdās Kāpadīā with a foreword by Hermann Jacobi (Surat: Sheth Devehand Lalbhai Jain Dharmashala, 1932).

11 For a helpful chart summarizing these stories, see Nalini Balbir, "Bhaktāmara-stotra," *Jainpedia*, n.d., http://www.jainpedia.org/themes/principles/sacred-writings/highlights-of-jainpedia/bhaktamara-stotra. For a full translation of story no. 13, see Rosalind Lefeber, "Jain Stories of Miraculous Power," in *Religions of India in Practice*, ed. Donald S. Lopez Jr. (Princeton, NJ: Princeton University Press, 1995), 429–30. See also Phyllis Granoff, "Cures and Karma: Healing and Being Healed in Jain Religious Literature," in *Self, Soul and Body in Religious Experience*, ed. Albert I. Baumgarten (Leiden: Brill, 1998), 225–30.

12 Because the editor of this text from 1932, Kāpadīā, does not know this mantra's association with the Ring of Disciples diagram, he is confused about this term *vicakra* and wants it to be feminine so that it can refer to a goddess.

13 For different versions of the eleven *pratimās*, see Wiley, *A to Z of Jainism*, 245; and Williams, *Jaina Yoga*, 172–81.

14 On these two scriptures that have now been lost but are listed as *kālika āgamas* in the *Nandīsūtra*, see Kapadia, *History of the Canonical Literature of the Jainas*, 75.

15 To my knowledge, this text has not been published. For a list of Digambara commentaries and *pūjās* on the *Bhaktāmarastotra*, see Ḍhāṅkī and Śāh, *Māntuṅgācārya aur unke Stotra*, 11; and Cort, "Devotional Culture in Jainism," 112–11n10.

16 For the attribution of this *pūjā* to Somasena in the text of the *pūjā* itself, see *Bhaktāmara Mahāmaṇḍala Pūjā*, ed. Paṇḍit Mohanlāl Śāstrī (Bhāratvarṣīya Anekānt Vidvat Pariṣad, n.d.), 97. It is not inconceivable that this is the same Somasena who composed a text on the *Bhaktāmarastotra* in 1484 (see Cort, "Devotional Culture in Jainism, 111–12n10), though much more research needs to be done on Digambara texts on the *Bhaktāmarastotra*.

17 *Bhaktāmara Mahāmaṇḍala Pūjā*, 34–66.

18 For a Hindi translation of Rāyamalla's stories, see Udaylāl Kāslīvāl, *Bhaktāmar-Kathā kā Hindī-Rūpāntar* (Mumbai: Jainsāhityaprasārak Kāryālay, 1930). At the end of his book, Kāslīvāl also provides a list of each mantra and *ṛddhi* associated with each verse and representations of the forty-eight *yantras*.

19 For a good summary of many of the scholarly debates over the length of the *stotra*, see Ḍhāṅkī and Śāh, *Māntuṅgācārya aur unke Stotra*, 23–69; for a helpful chart on the number of *prātihāryas* in some important Śvetāmbara and Digambara texts, see 66–69. See also Vinod Kapashi, *Nine Sacred Recitations of the Jain Religion (a Study of the Nine Smaranas and All Aspects Associated with Them)* (Mumbai: Hindi Granth Kāryālay, 2007), 91–94.

20 The Bharuch temple displays both Haribhadrasūri's forty-four *yantras* and the more commonly found set of forty-eight.

21 Navāb, *Mahāprābhāvika* [*sic*], *citra* 173–268.

22 Tomoko Masuzawa, *The Invention of World Religions: Or, How Universalism Was Preserved in the Language of Pluralism* (Chicago: Chicago University Press, 2005), 260.

23 Max Müller, *The Upanishads*, pt. 1, *Sacred Books of the East*, vol. 1 (Oxford: Clarendon

Press, 1884), xi–xii. On the formative role Müller played in the establishment of the field of comparative religion, see Arie L. Molendijk, *Friedrich Max Müller & the Sacred Books of the East* (Oxford: Oxford University Press, 2016), 122–37.

24 Müller, *The Upanishads*, xli.

25 Molendijk, *Friedrich Max Müller*, 66–67.

26 Friedrich Max Müller, *Natural Religion*, 539, cited in Molendijk, *Friedrich Max Müller*, 92.

27 Folkert, *Scripture and Community*, 44–45.

28 For this passage from the *Uttarādhyayanasūtra*, see Balbir, "The Jain Tradition on Protection," 254–55.

29 R. C. Zaehner to Spicer, December 4, 1958, cited in Molendijk, *Friedrich Max Müller*, 88n209.

30 Jacobi, foreword to Kāpadīā, *Bhaktāmara*, i.

31 Wiley, *A–Z of Jainism*, 62.

BIBLIOGRAPHY

PRIMARY SOURCES

If more than one edition of a text is listed, an asterisk signifies the edition used for citations.

Ādipurāṇa of Jinasena. Pts. 1 and 2. Edited and translated into Hindi by Pannalāl Jain. 10th ed. Delhi: Bhāratīya Jñānpīṭh, 2004.

**Ācārāṅgasūtra*. Edited by Muni Jambūvijaya as *Āyāraṅga-Suttam* (*Ācārāṅgasūtram*). Bombay: Shri Mahāvīra Jaina Vidyālaya, 1977.

Ācārāṅgasūtra. In *Jaina Sūtras I: Sacred Books of the East*, translated by Hermann Jacobi, 22:1–213. Oxford: Clarendon Press, 1884.

Aṅgavidyā. Edited by Muni Shri Punyavijyaya as *Aṅgavijjā: Science of Divination through Physical Signs & Symbols*. Banaras: Prakrit Text Society, 1957.

Arthaśāstra of Kauṭilya. Translated by Patrick Olivelle as *King, Governance, and Law in Ancient India: Kauṭilya's Arthaśāstra*. Oxford: Oxford University Press, 2013.

Aupapātikasūtra. Edited by Upapravarttaka Amaramuni and Shrichand "Saras" Surana, translated by Surendra Bothara as *Illustrated Aupapatik Sutra*. Delhi: Padma Prakashan, 2003.

Bhāgavatapurāṇa. Translated into English by J. L. Shastri and G. V. Tagare as *The Bhāgavata Purāṇa*, 1955. Reprinted, Delhi: Motilal Banarsidass, 2003.

Bhagavatī Ārādhanā. Edited and Translated into Hindi by Kailāścandra Siddhāntśāstrī, 1978. Reprinted, Solapur: Jain Saṃskṛti Samraksak Saṅgh, 2004.

Bhagavatīsūtra. Edited by Upapravarttaka Amaramuni, Shrichand Surana "Saras," and Varuṇamuni. Translated into English by Surendra Bothara as *Illustrated Bhagawati Sutra*. 3 pts. Delhi: Padma Prakashan, 2005–2008.

Bhaktāmara, Kalyāṇamandira and Namiuṇa. Edited and translated by Hīrālāl Rasikdās Kāpadīā with a foreword by Hermann Jacobi. Surat: Sheth Devehand Lalbhai Jain Dharmashala, 1932.

Bhaktāmara Mahāmaṇḍala Pūjā of Somasena. Edited by Paṇḍit Mohanlāl Śāstrī. Bhāratvarṣīya Anekānt Vidvat Pariṣad, n.d.

Bhāvasaṅgraha of Devasena. Hindi commentary by Lālārām Śāstrī. Solapur: Āryikā Sumatimatī Digambar Jain Granthmālā, 1987.

Bhāvasaṅgraha. In *Śrāvakācār Saṅgrah*, pt. 3, edited and translated into Hindi by Hīrālāl Śāstrī, 440–64. Solapur: Jain Saṃskṛti Saṃrakṣak Saṅgh, 1998.

Brahmasiddhāntasamuccaya of Haribhadrasūri. In *Yogaśatakaṃ*, edited by Muni Puṇyavijaya, 47–76. Ahmedabad: Lālbhāī Dalpatbhāī Bhāratīya Saṃskṛti Vidyāmandir, 1965.

Bṛhad Gaṇdhar Valay Vidhān of Āryikā Rājaśrī. Edited by Ācārya Guptinandī. Jaipur: Śārdā Prakāśan, 2003.

Bṛhad Yog Vidhi. Compiled by Ācārya Pūrṇacandrasāgarasūri. Surat: Āgamoddārak Caityavandanamahābhāaṣya of Śāntisūri., n.d.

Cauṃsaṭh Ṛddhi Vidhān. Edited by Āryikā Jñānamatī. Hastinapur: Digambar Jain Trilok Śodh Saṃsthān, 2010.

Dhavalā of Vīrasena. In *Ṣaṭkhaṇḍāgamaḥ. khaṇḍa* 1, *bhāga* 1, *pustaka* 1, and *khaṇḍa* 4, *bhāga* 1, *pustaka* 9, edited and translated into Hindi by Hīrālāl Jain, Phūlcandra Siddhāntśāstrī, and Bālcandra Siddhāntśāstrī. Amaravati: Jain Sāhityoddhārak Fund, 1939–59. Reprinted, Solapur: Jain Saṃskṛti Saṃrakṣak Saṅgh, 2000 & 2005.

Dhyānaśataka of Jinabhadrasūri. Edited and translated into Hindi by Kanhaiyālāl Loḍhā and Suṣmā Siṅghvī. Jaipur: Prākṛt Bhāratī Academy, 2007.

Dhyānastavaḥ. Edited and translated into English by Suzuko Ohira. Delhi: Bhāratīya Jñānpīṭh Prakāśan, 1973.

The Early Upaniṣads: Annotated Text and Translation. Translated by Patrick Olivelle. New York and Oxford: Oxford University Press, 1998.

Gaṇdharvalay Vidhān. Edited by Āryikā Jñānamatī. Hastinapur: Digambar Jain Trilok Śodh Saṃsthān, 2008.

Jambūdvīpaprajñapti. Edited by A. N. Upādhye and Hīrālāl Jain, translated into Hindi by Bālcandra Siddhāntśāstrī as *Jaṃbūdīva-paṇatti-saṃgaho*. Solapur: Jain Saṃskṛti Saṃrakṣak Saṅgh, 1958.

Jñānārṇava of Śubhacandra. 3rd ed. Edited and translated into Hindi by Bālcandra Śāstrī. Solapur: Jain Saṃskṛti Saṃrakṣak Saṅgh, 2006.

Jñānasāra of Padmasiṃha. Edited and translated into Hindi by Kailāścandra Siddhāntśāstrī. Varanasi: Vīr-Sevā-Mandir-Trust Prakāśan, 1984.

Kalpdrum Vidhān. 14th ed. Edited by Āryikā Jñānamatī. Hastinapur: Digambar Jain Trilok Śodh Saṃsthān, 2008.

Kalpasūtra. In *Jaina Sūtras I: Sacred Books of the East*, translated into English by Hermann Jacobi, 22:214–311. Oxford: Clarendon Press, 1884.

Kāmikāgamaḥ Pūrvabhāgaḥ Tantrāvatārapaṭalaḥ. Madras: South Indian Archakar Association, 1975.

Labdhinidhān Śrī Gautam Svāmī. Edited by Muni Harṣabodhivijaya. Mumbai: Śrī Andherī Jain Saṅgh, n.d.

Laghuvidyānuvād. Edited by Gaṇadharācārya Kunthusāgara. Jaipur: Śrī Digambar Jain Kunthuvijay Granthmālā Samiti, 1986.

Mahābandha of Bhūtabali. *Pustak* 1, 3rd ed. Edited and translated into Hindi by Sumerucandra Divākar as *Mahābaṃdho*. Delhi: Bhāratīya Jñānpīṭh, 1998.

Mahāniśīthasūtra. In *Studien zum Mahānisīha, Kapitel 1–5*, edited and translated into English by Jozef Deleu and Walther Schubring. Hamburg: Cram, de Gruyter, 1963.

Mahāvairocanatantra. Translated into English by Stephen Hodge as *The Mahā-Vairocana-Abhisambodhi Tantra with Buddhaguhya's Commentary.* New York: Routledge Curzon, 2003.

Mantradvātriṃśikākalpa. In *Vidyāratna Mahānidhiḥ*, edited by S. K Kotecha. Bombay: Mahāvīr Jain Granthmālā, 1935.

**Mantrarājarahasya* of Simhatilakasūri. In *Sūrimantrakalpasamuccaya*, edited by Muni Jambūvijaya, pt. 1, 1–74. Mumbai: Jain Sāhitya Vikās Maṇḍal, 1969.

Mantrarājarahasya of Simhatilakasūri. Edited by Ācārya Jinavijaya as *Mantrarāja Rahasyam of Śrī Simhatilakasūri.* Bombay: Bharatiya Vidya Bhavan, 1980.

Mūlācāra. 5th ed. 2 pts. Edited by Kailāścandra Śāstrī, Jaganmohanlāl Śāstrī, and Pannālāl Jain, translated into Hindi by Āryikā Jñānamatī. Delhi: Bhāratīya Jñānpīṭh, 2004.

Namaskāra Svādhyāya. Saṃskṛta Vibhāga. Compiled by Dhurandharavijaya Gaṇi, Muni Jambūvijaya, and Muni Tattvānandavijaya. Edited and translated into Gujarati by Tattvānandavijaya. Bombay: Jain Sāhitya Vikās Maṇḍal, 1962.

Niśvāsatattvasaṃhitā. Edited and translated into English by Dominic Goodall, in collaboration with Alexis Sanderson and Harunaga Isaacson, as *The Niśvāsatattvasaṃhitā: The Earliest Surviving Śaiva Tantra.* Pondicherry: Institut Français de Pondichéry, 2015.

Nitya Ārādhanāvidhi of Somacandrasūri. Surat: Śrī Rānder Road Jain Saṅgh, 2013.

Pañcāśakaprakaraṇa of Haribhadrasūri. Edited by Sāgarmal Jain and Kamleśkumār Jain. Translated into Hindi by Dīnānāth Śarmā. Varanasi: Pārśvanāth Vidyāpīṭh, 1997.

Praśnavyākaraṇasūtra. Edited by Pravarttaka Amaramuni and Varuṇamuni, translated by Rajkumar Jain as *Illustrated Prasnavyakaran Sutra.* Delhi: Padma Prakashan, 2008.

Pratiṣṭhāpāṭha of Jayasena. Edited by Hīrācand Nemcand Dośī. Solapur: Śeṭh Hīrācand Nemcand Dośī, 1925.

Pratiṣṭhā Ratnākar. Edited by Darbārī Lāl Koṭhiyā and Jaykumār "Niśānt." Delhi: Prati Vihār Jain Samāj, n.d.

Pratiṣṭhāsāroddhāra of Āśādhara. Edited by Paṇḍit Manoharlāl Śāstrī. Bombay: Jaingranth Uddhārak Kāryālay, 1917.

Pratiṣṭhātilaka of Nemicandra. 2nd ed. Edited by Āryikā Jñānamatī. Hastinapur: Digambar Jain Trilok Śodh Saṃsthān, 2012.

Pratiṣṭhā Vidhi Darpaṇ. Compiled by Ācārya Kunthusāgara. Jaipur: Śrī Digambar Jain Kunthu Vijay Granthmālā Samiti, 1992.

Pravacanasāra of Kundakunda. Edited and translated by A. N. Upadhye as *Pravacanasāra (Pavayaṇasāra): A Pro-canonical Text of the Jainas.* Bombay: Parama-Śruta-Prabhāvaka-Maṇḍala, 1964.

Ṛṣimaṇḍalastotra. Edited by Sārābhāī Maṇilāl Navāb in *Mahāprābhāvika* [*sic*] *Navasmaraṇa*, 509–19. Ahmedabad: Sārābhāī Maṇilāl Navāb, 1938.

Ṛṣimaṇḍalastavayantralekhanam of Siṃhatilakasūri. Edited by Muni Tattvānandavijaya, translated into Gujarati by Muni Dhurandharavijaya. Mumbai: Śrī Navīncandra Aṃbālāl Śāh, 1961.

Puṣpikāḥ. In *Nirayāvaliyā-Suyakkhandha Uvaṅgas 8–12 of the Jain Canon*, translated from Jozef Deleu's Dutch translation by J. W. de Jong and Royce Wiles, 75–96. Tokyo: Chuo Research Foundation, 1996.

Ṣaṭkhaṇḍāgama. Khaṇḍa 1, *bhāga* 1, *pustaka* 1, and *khaṇḍa* 4, *bhāga* 1, *pustaka* 9. Edited and translated into Hindi by Hīrālāl Jain, Phūlcandra Siddhāntśāstrī, and Bālcandra Siddhāntśāstrī. Amaravati: Jain Sāhityoddhārak Fund, 1939–59. Reprinted, Solapur: Jain Saṃskṛti Saṃrakṣak Saṅgh, 2000 & 2005.

Siddhacakra Maṇḍala Vidhāna (*Saṃskṛta*). Edited by Rameścandra Jain and Aśok Kumār Jain. Compiled by Ācārya Vimalasāgara. Lalitpur: Pārśvajyoti Mañc, 1990.

Ṣoḍaśaprakaraṇa of Haribhadrasūri. Edited by Ācārya Vijayarāmacandrasūri. Sisodra, Gujarat: Śrī Jain Śvetāmbar Mūrtipūjak Saṅgh, n.d.

Śrāvakācār Saṅgrah. 5 pts. Edited and translated into Hindi by Hīrālāl Śāstrī. Solapur: Jain Saṃskṛti Saṃrakṣak Saṅgh, 1998.

Śrāvakācāra of Vasunandin. Edited by Bhāgcandra "Bhāskar" Jain and Paṇḍit Vimalkumār Sauṃrayā Jain as *Vasunandi-Śrāvakācāra*. Mumbai: Hindī Granth Kāryālay, 2006.

Śrīgaṇdharvalay Pūjan Saṅgrah. Compiled by Muni Ajitasāgara. Udaipur: Śrī Paṇḍit Guljārī Lāl Caudhrī, 1967.

Śrīkuśalacandrasūripaṭṭapraśastiḥ of Paṇḍit Maṇicandra. Kāśī: Jainmandir, Rāmghāṭ, 1951.

Śrī Pravrajyā-Yogādi Vidhi Saṅgrah. Edited by Gaṇi Nityānanda. Dabhoi, Vadodara: Ārya Śrī Jambūsvāmī Jain Muktābhāī Āgam Mandir, 1975.

Śrī Siddhcakra Mahāpūjan Vidhi. Edited by Ācārya Pradyumnasūri. Ahmedabad: Śrī Aruṇoday Foundation, 2000.

Śrī Siddhcakra Vidhān. Edited by Sanat Kumār Vinod Kumār. Delhi: Jain Sāhitya Sadan, Śrī Digambar Jain Lāl Mandirjī, n.d.

Śrīsubodhāsamācārī [*sic*] of Candrasūri. Bombay: Sheth Devchand Lalabhai Jain Pustakoddhar Fund, 1924.

Śrī Sūrimantra Mahāpūjan evaṃ Vardhamān Vidyā Mahāpūjan. Edited by Gaṇi Somasundaravijaya. N.p., 2007–8.

Śrīsūrimantrapañcaprasthānaprārambhavidhi, Nitya Ārādhanāvidhi, 21 Divasīya Ārādhanāvidhi & Pañcaprasthānapūrṇāhutipūjāvidhi. Edited by Ācārya Somacandrasūri. Surat: Śrī Rānder Road Jain Saṅgh, 2013. *Śrīsūrimantrapañcaprasthānaprārambhavidhi* of Somacandrasūri. Surat: Śrī Rānder Road Jain Saṅgh, 2013

Sthānāṅgasūtra. Edited by Pravarttaka Amaramuni and Shrichand Surana Saras, translated by Surendra Bothra as *Illustrated Shri Sthaananga Sutra*. 2 pts. Delhi: Padma Prakashan, 2004.

Sūrimantrakalpasamuccayaḥ. Pts. 1 and 2. Edited by Muni Jambūvijaya. Mumbai: Jain Sāhitya Vikās Maṇḍal, 1969, 1977.

**Sūtrakṛtāṅgasūtra.* Edited by Muni Jambūvijaya as *Sūyagaḍaṁgasuttaṁ* (*Sūtrakṛtāṅgasūtraṁ*). Bombay: Shrī Mahāvīra Jaina Vidyālaya, 1978.

Sūtrakṛtāṅgasūtra. In *Jaina Sūtras II: Sacred Books of the East*, translated into by Hermann Jacobi, 45:233–435. Oxford: Clarendon Press, 1895.

Tattvānuśāsana. Edited and translated into Hindi by Jugalkiśor "Yugvīr" Mukhtār. Delhi: Vīrsevāmandir Trust Prakāśan, 1963.

Tattvārthasūtra. Translated by Nathmal Tatia as *That Which Is.* San Francisco: HarperCollins, 1994.

Trilokaprajñapti. 2 pts. Edited by A. N. Upadhye and Hiralal Jain, Hindi paraphrase by Balchandra Siddhantasastri as *Tiloya-paṇṇatti.* Sholapur: Jaina Samskriti Samraksaka Samgha, 1951.

Triṣaṣtiśalākāpuruṣacarita of Hemacandra. Translated by Helen Johnson as *Triṣaṣtiśalākāpuruṣacarita, or The Lives of Sixty-Three Illustrious Persons*. Vol. 1. Baroda: Oriental Institute, 1931.

Vardhamāna Vidyā Kalpaḥ. Edited by Nayacandrasāgara. Ahmedabad: Śrī Pūrṇānanda Prakāśanaḥ, 2005.

Vidyānuśāsana. Edited by Muni Guṇadharanandī as *Vidyānuśāsana of Bhaṭṭāraka Matisāgara*. Jaipur: Śrī Jain Divyadhvani Prakāśan, 1990.

Vimal Bhakti Saṅgrah. Compiled by Āryikā Syādvādamatī. Varanasi: Bhāratvarṣīya Anekānt Vidvat Pariṣad, 2000.

Vidhimārgaprapā of Jinaprabhasūri. Edited by Mahopādhyāya Vinayasāgara. Jaipur: Prākṛt Bhāratī Academy, 2000.

Vidhimārgaprapā of Jinaprabhasūri. Translated into Hindi by Sādhvī Saumyaguṇā as *Vidhi Mārg Prapā*. Mumbai: Śrī Mahāvīr Svāmī Jain Derāsar Trust, 2005.

Vīṇāśikhatantra. Translated by Teun Goudriaan as *Vīṇāśikha Tantra: A Śaiva Tantra of the Left Current*. Delhi: Motilal Banarsidass, 1985.

* *Yogaśāstra* of Hemacandrasūri. Translated by Olle Qvarnström as *The Yogaśāstra of Hemacandra: A Twelfth Century Handbook on Śvetāmbara Jainism*. Cambridge, MA: Harvard University Press, 2002.

Yogaśāstra of Hemacandrasūri. Edited by Muni Jambūvijaya as *Yogaśāstram (Sampūrṇam)*. 3 vols. Bombay: Jain Sāhitya Vikās Maṇḍal, 1986.

Yogasūtra of Patañjali. Translated by Barbara Stoler Miller as *Yoga: Discipline of Freedom: The Yoga Sutra Attributed to Patanjali*. New York: Bantam, 1998.

Yogaviṃśikā of Haribhadrasūri. Translated by K. K. Dixit in *Yogadṛṣṭisamuccaya and Yogaviṃśikā of Ācārya Haribhadrasūri*, 109–22. Ahmedabad: Lalbhai Dalpatbhai Bharatiya Sanskriti Vidyamandira, 1970.

SECONDARY SOURCES

Abé, Ryūichi. *The Weaving of Mantra: Kukai and the Construction of Esoteric Buddhist Discourse*. New York: Columbia University Press, 2000.

Acharya, Diwakar. "The Original *Paṇhavāyaraṇa / Praśnavyākaraṇa* Discovered." *International Journal of Jaina Studies (Online)* 3, no. 6 (2007): 1–10.

Altekar, Anant Sadashiv. *The Rāshṭrakūṭas and Their Times*. Poona: Oriental Book Agency, 1934.

Andhare, Shridhar, and Pandit Laxmanbhai Bhojak, *Jain Vastrapatas: Jain Paintings on Cloth*. Ahmedabad: Lalbhai Dalpatbhai Institute of Indology, 2015.

Babb, Lawrence A. *Absent Lord: Ascetics and Kings in a Jain Ritual Culture*. Berkeley: University of California Press, 1996.

Balbir, Nalini. *Āvaśyaka-Studien 1: Introduction générale et traductions*. Stuttgart: Franz Steiner, 1993.

———. "Functions of Multiple-Text Manuscripts in India: The Jain Case." In *The Emergence of Multiple-Text Manuscripts*, edited by Alessandro Bausi, Michael Friedrich, and Marilena Maniaci, 2–30. Berlin: De Gruyter, 2019.

———. "An Investigation of Textual Sources on the *samavasaraṇa* (The Holy Assembly of the Jina')." In *Festschrift Klaus Bruhn*, edited by Nalini Balbir and J. K. Bautze, 67–104. Reinbek: Verlag für Orientalische Fachpublikationen, 1994.

———. "The Jain Tradition on Protection and Its Means." In *Katā me rakkhā, kata me parittā: Protecting the Protective Texts and Manuscripts*, edited by Claudio Cicuzza, 237–304. Bangkok/ Lumbini: Fragile Palm Leaver Foundation/Lumbini International Research Institute, 2018.

———. "Stories from the Āvaśyaka Commentaries." In *The Clever Adultress and Other Stories*, edited by Phyllis Granoff, 17–74. Oakville: Mosaic Press, 1990.

Barodia, U. D. *History and Literature of Jainism*. Bombay: Jain Graduates' Association, 1909.

Bell, Catherine. *Ritual Theory, Ritual Practice*. Oxford: Oxford University Press, 1992.

Bennett, Judith. *Sex Signs: Every Woman's Astrological and Psychological Guide to Love, Men, Sex, Anger, and Personal Power*. New York: St. Martin's Press, 1980.

Bhatt, Bansidhar. *The Canonical Nikṣepa: Studies in Jaina Dialectics*. Leiden: E. J. Brill, 1978.

Bhatt, N. R. Introduction to *Mataṅgapārameśvarāgama (Vidyāpāda) avec le commentaire de Bhaṭṭa Rāmakaṇṭha*, edited by N.R. Bhatt, vii–xxxvii. Pondicherry: Institut Français d'Indologie, 1977.

Bronkhorst, Johannes. "Divine Sound or Monotone? Divyadhvani between Jaina, Buddhist and Brahmanical Epistemology." In *Sanmati: Essays Felicitating Professor Hampa Nagarajaiah on the Occasion of His 80th Birthday*, edited by Luitgard Soni and Jayandra Soni, 83–96. Bengaluru: Sapna Book House, 2015.

———. "Remarks on the History of Jaina Meditation." In *Jain Studies in Honour of Jozef Deleu*, edited by Rudy Smet and Kenji Watanabe, 151–62. Tokyo: Hon-no-Tomosha, 1993.

———. *The Two Traditions of Meditation in Ancient India*. Delhi: Motilal Banarsidass, 1993.

Brooks, Douglas Renfrew. *The Secret of the Three Cities: An Introduction to Hindu Śākta Tantra*. Chicago: University of Chicago Press, 1990.

Brown, Robert L. Introduction to *The Roots of Tantra*, edited by Katherine Anne Harper and Brown. Albany: State University of New York Press, 2002.

Brunner, Hélène "Ātmārthapūjā versus Parārthapūjā in the Śaiva tradition." In *The Sanskrit Tradition and Tantrism*, edited by Teun Goudriaan, 4–23. Leiden: E. J. Brill, 1990.

———. "Le sādhaka: Personage oublié du Śivaisme du sud." *Journal Asiatique* 263 (1975): 411–43.

———. *Mṛgendrāgama, section des rites et section du comportement, traduction, introduction et notes*. Pondicherry: Institut Français d'Indologie Pondichéry, 1985.

———, ed. and trans. *Somaśambhupaddhati, Première Partie: Le rituel quotidien dans la tradition śivaïte de l'Inde du Sud selon Somaśambhu*. Pondicherry: Institut Français d'Indologie, 1963.

———. *Somaśambhupaddhati, Troisième Partie: Rituels occasionnels dans la tradition śivaïte de l'Inde du Sud selon Somaśambhu*. Pondicherry: Institut Français d'Indologie, 1977.

Brunner, Hélène, Gerhard Oberhammer, and André Padoux, eds. *Tāntrikābhidhānakośa I: Dictionnaire des termes techniques de la littérature hindoue tantrique / A Dictionary of Technical Terms from Hindu Tantric Literature / Wörterbuch zur Terminologie hin-*

duistischer Tantren. Vienna: Verlag de Österreichischen Akademie der Wissenschaften, 2000.

Burchett, Patton E. *A Genealogy of Devotion: Bhakti, Tantra, Yoga, and Sufism in North India*. New York: Columbia University Press, 2019.

Burgess, James. "Papers on Shatrunjaya and the Jainas" *Indian Antiquary* 7, no. 13 (1884): 191–96.

Burnouf, Eugène. *Introduction to the History of Indian Buddhism*. Translated by Katia Buffetrille and Donald S. Lopez Jr. Chicago: University of Chicago Press, 2010.

Bühler, Johan Georg. *The Indian Sect of the Jainas*. Translated by James Burgess. 1903. Reprinted, Calcutta: Sisil Gupta, 1963.

Bühnemann, Gudrun. "Maṇḍala, Yantra and Cakra: Some Observations." In *Maṇḍalas and Yantras in the Hindu Traditions*, edited by Bühnemann, 13–56. Leiden: E. J. Brill, 2003.

———. "Maṇḍalas and Yantras in Smārta Ritual." In *Maṇḍalas and Yantras in the Hindu Traditions*, edited by Bühnemann, 57–118. Leiden: E. J. Brill, 2003.

Caillat, Colette. "Le Sādhaka Śaiva à Lumiere de la discipline Jaina." In *Studien zum Jainismus und Buddhismus: Gedenkschrift Für Ludwig Alsdorf*, edited by Klaus Bruhn and Albrecht Wezler, 51–59. Viesbaden: Franz Steiner, 1981.

Candrasāgara, Ācārya, ed. *Yatikartavya Prabodh Saṅgrah*. Madhya Pradesh: Śrī Bundelkhaṇḍ Syādvād Pariṣad, 1997.

Carrithers, Michael. "Jainism and Buddhism as Enduring Historical Streams." *Journal of the Anthropological Society of Oxford* 21, no. 2 (1990): 141–63.

Chapple, Christopher Key. *Reconciling Yogas: Haribhadrasūri's Collection of View on Yoga*. Albany: State University of New York Press, 2003.

———. "Tantric Yoga in the *Mārkaṇḍeya Purāṇa* of Hinduism and the *Jñānārṇava* of Jainism." *Religions* 8, no. 11 (2017): 235–57.

Chaturvedi, Aditya. "Of Revelation and Sādhanā: The Gāyatrī Mantra in the Gāyatrī Tantra." Unpublished manuscript, 2018.

Chaudhuri, Nirad C., Madeleine Biardeau, D. F. Pocock, and T. N. Madad. *The Hinduism Omnibus*. New Delhi: Oxford University Press, 2003.

Childs, Brevard S. *The New Testament as Canon: An Introduction*. Philadelphia: Fortress Press, 1984.

Cohen, Richard J. "The Art of Jain Meditation." In *Glimpses of Jainism*, edited by Surender K. Jain, 127–38. Delhi: Motilal Banarsidass, 1997.

Cort, John E. "Art, Religion, and Material Culture: Some Reflections on Method." *Journal of the American Academy of Religion*, 64, no. 3 (1996): 613–32.

———. "Bhakti in the Early Jain Tradition: Understanding Devotional Religion in South Asia," *History of Religions*, 42, no. 1 (2002): 59–86.

———. "Contemporary Jain Maṇḍala Rituals." In *Victorious Ones: Jain Images of Perfection*, edited by Phyllis Granoff, 140–57. New York: Rubin Museum of Art, 2009.

———. "Devotional Culture in Jainism: Mānatuṅga and His Bhaktāmara Stotra." In *Incompatible Visions: South Asian Religions in History and Culture: Essays in Honor of David M. Knipe*, edited by James Blumenthal, 93–115. Madison: University of Wisconsin Center for South Asia, 2005.

———. "Dios como rey o asceta." In *La Escultura en los Templos Indios: El Arte de la Devo-*

ción, edited by John Guy, translated by Carlos Mayor, 171–79. Barcelona: Fundación "la Caixa," 2007,

———. "Doing It for Others: Merit Transfer and Karma Mobility in Jainism." In *Jainism and Early Buddhism: Essays in Honor of Padmanabh S. Jaini*, edited by Olle Qvarnström, 129–50. Freemont, CA: Asian Humanities Press, 2003.

———. *Framing the Jina: Narratives of Icons and Idols in Jain History*. New York: Oxford University Press, 2010.

———. "The Intellectual Formation of a Jain Monk." *Journal of Indian Philosophy* 29 (2001): 327–49.

———. *Jains in the World: Religious Values and Ideology in India*. New York: Oxford University Press, 2001.

———. "The Jina as King or the Jina as Renouncer: Seeing and Ornamenting Temple Images in Jainism." Mohini Jain Presidential Chair in Jain Studies, inaugural lecture series. University of California, Davis, February 1, 2018.

———. "Medieval Jaina Goddess Traditions." *Numen* 34, no. 2 (1987): 235–55.

———. "Models of and for the Study of the Jains." *Method & Theory in the Study of Religion* 2, no. 1 (1990): 42–71.

———. "A Spell against Snakes and Other Calamities: The Uvasaggaharaṁ Stotra Attributed to Bhadrabāhu Svāmī." *Jinamañjari*, 34, no. 2 (2006): 34–43.

———. "Śvetāmbar Mūrtipūjak Jain Scripture in a Performative Context." In *Texts in Context: Traditional Hermeneutics in South Asia*, edited by J. R. Timm, 171–94. Albany: State University of New York Press, 1991.

———. "World Renouncing Monks and World Celebrating Temples and Icons: The Ritual Culture of Temples and Icons in Jainism." In *Archaeology and Text: The Temple in South Asia*, edited by Himanshu Prabha Ray, 267–95. Oxford: Oxford University Press, 2010.

———. "Worship of Bell-Ears the Great Hero." In *Tantra in Practice*, edited by David Gordon White, 417–33. Princeton, NJ: Princeton University Press, 2000.

Creismeas, Jean-Michel. "Le yoga du Mataṅgapārameśvaratantra à la lumière du commentaire de Bhaṭṭa Rāmakaṇṭha." PhD diss., Sorbonne Université, 2015.

Cunningham, Alexander. *Inscriptions of Asoka*. Calcutta: Office of the Superintendent of Government Printing, 1877.

Dalton, Jacob. "A Crisis of Doxography: How Tibetans Organized Tantra during the 8th–12th Centuries." *Journal of the International Association of Buddhist Studies* 28, no. 1 (2005): 115–81.

Davidson, Ronald M. "Abhiṣeka." In *Esoteric Buddhism and the Tantras in East Asia*, edited by Charles D. Orzech, Henrik H. Sørensen, and Richard K. Payne, 71–75. Leiden: Brill, 2011.

———. *Indian Esoteric Buddhism: A Social History of the Tantric Movement*. New York: Columbia University Press, 2002.

———. "Some Observations on an Uṣṇīṣa Abhiṣeka Rite in Atikūṭa's *Dhāraṇīsaṅgraha*." In *Transformations and Transfer of Tantra in Asia and Beyond*, edited by István Keul, 77–97. Berlin: De Gruyter, 2012.

Davis, Richard H. "Aghoraśiva's Background." *Journal of Oriental Research, Madras* 56–62 (1986–92): 367–78.

———. "Becoming Śiva, and Acting as One, in Śaiva Worship." In *Ritual and Speculation in Early Tantrism: Studies in Honor of André Padoux*, edited by Teun Goudriaan, 107–19. Albany: State University of New York Press, 1992.

———. *Ritual in an Oscillating Universe: Worshiping Śiva in Medieval India*. Princeton, NJ: Princeton University Press, 1986.

Deleu, Jozef. "A Preliminary Note on the Mahānisīha." In *Mahāniśīthasūtra*, in *Studien zum Mahānisīha, Kapitel 1–5*, edited and translated into English by Jozef Deleu and Walther Schubring. Hamburg: Cram, de Gruyter, 1963.

Deo, Shantaram Bhalchandra. *History of Jaina Monachism from Inscriptions and Literature*. Poona: Deccan College Postgraduate and Research Institute, 1956.

———. *Jaina Monastic Jurisprudence*. Banaras: Jaina Cultural Research Society, 1960.

Detige, Tillo. "Digambara Renouncers in Western and Central India." In *Brill's Encyclopedia of Jainism*, edited by Knut A. Jacobsen, John E. Cort, Paul Dundas, and Kristi L. Wiley, 182–215. Leiden: Brill, 2020.

———. "'*Guṇa kahuṃ śrī guru*': *Bhaṭṭāraka Gītas* and the Early Modern Digambara Jaina Saṅgha." In *Early Modern India: Literature and Images, Texts and Languages*, edited by Maya Burger and Nadia Cattoni, 271–85. Heidelberg: CrossAsia-eBooks, 2019.

———. "'*Tataḥ Śrī-Gurus-Tasmai Sūrimantraṃ Dadyāt*,' 'Then the Venerable Guru Ought to Give Him the *Sūrimantra*': Early Modern Digambara Jaina *Bhaṭṭāraka* Consecrations," *Religions* 10, no. 369 (2019): 1–31.

Dhaky, M. A. "The Date of Kundakundācārya." In *Pt. Dalsukhbhai Malvania Felicitation*, Vol. 1, edited by M. A. Dhaky and Sagarmal Jain, 187–206. Varanasi: P. V. Research Institute, 1991.

Ḍhāṅkī, Madhusūsan, and Jitendra Śāh. *Māntuṅgācārya aur unke Stotra*, 2nd ed. Ahmedabad: Śārdāben Cimanbhāī Educational Research Centre, 1997.

Dīkṣit, Rājeś. *Jain Tantra-Śāstra*. Agra: Dīp Publication, 1984.

Divyaratnavijaya, Muni, ed. *Māro Svādhyāy*. N.p: n.p., n.d.

Dundas, Paul. "Becoming Gautama: Mantra and History in Śvetāmbara Jainism." In *Open Boundaries: Jain Communities and Cultures in Indian History*, edited by John E. Cort, 31–52. Albany: State University of New York Press, 1998.

———. "A Digambara Jain Description of the Yogic Path to Deliverance." In *Yoga in Practice*, edited by David Gordon White, 143–61. Princeton, NJ: Princeton University Press, 2012.

———. "A Digambara Jain Saṃskāra in the Early Seventeenth Century: Lay Funerary Ritual according to Somasenabhaṭṭāraka's *Traivarṇikācāra*." *Indo-Iranian Journal* 54 (2011): 99–147.

———. "Haribhadra on Giving." *Journal of Indian Philosophy* 30 (2002): 1–44.

———. *History, Scripture and Controversy in a Medieval Jain Sect*. New York: Routledge, 2007.

———. "How Not to Install an Image of the Jina: An Early Anti-Paurṇamīyaka Diatribe." *International Journal of Jaina Studies (Online)* 5, no. 3 (2009): 1–23.

———. "Jain Attitudes towards the Sanskrit Language." In *Ideology and Status of Sanskrit*, edited by J. E. M. Houben, 137–56. Leiden: E. J. Brill, 1996.

———. "The Jain Monk Jinapati Sūri Gets the Better of a Nāth Yogi," in *Tantra in Practice*, edited by David Gordon White, 231–38. Princeton, NJ: Princeton University Press, 2000.

———. *The Jains*. 2nd ed. London: Routledge, 2002.

———. "A Non-imperial Religion? Jainism in Its 'Dark Age.'" In *Between the Empires: Society in India 300 BCE to 400 CE*, edited by Patrick Olivelle, 383–414. New York: Oxford University Press, 2006.

———. "Shutting Kumudacandra's Mouth: Yaśaścandra's *Mudritakumudacandra* as a Source for the Intra-Jain Debate at Aṇahillapaṭṭana in 1125." Lecture, World Sanskrit Conference, Vancouver, Canada, July 10, 2018.

———. "Textual Authority in Ritual Procedure: The Śvetāmbara Jain Controversy Concerning *Īryāpathikīpratikramaṇa*." *Journal of Indian Philosophy* 39 (2011): 327–50.

Dviveda, Vrajavallabha. "Having Become a God, He Should Sacrifice to the Gods." In *Ritual and Speculation in Early Tantrism: Studies in Honour of André Padoux*, edited by Teun Goudriaan, 121–38. Albany: State University of New York Press, 1992.

Einoo, Shingo. "The Formation of Hindu Ritual." In *From Material to Deity: Indian Rituals of Consecration*, edited by Einoo and Jun Takashima, 24–33. New Delhi: Manohar, 2005.

———. "From *kāmas* to *siddhis*—Tendencies in the Development of Ritual towards Tantrism." In *Genesis and Development of Tantrism*, edited by Einoo, 17–40. Tokyo: Institute of Oriental Culture, University of Tokyo, 2009.

Eltschinger, Vincent. "Dharmakīrti on Mantras and Their Efficiency." In *Esoteric Buddhist Studies: Identity in Diversity. Proceedings of the International Conference on Esoteric Buddhist Studies, Koyasan University, 5 Sept.–8 Sept. 2006*, edited by ICEBS Editorial Board, 273–89. Koyasan: Koyasan University, 2008.

Filliozat, Jean. "Introduction: Les Āgama Çivaïtes." In *Rauravāgama*, edited by N. R. Bhatt, 1:v–xv. Pondicherry: Institut Français d'Indologie, 1961.

Fiordalis, David V. "Miracles and Superhuman Powers in South Asian Buddhist Literature." PhD diss., University of Michigan, 2008.

Flood, Gavin. *The Ascetic Self: Subjectivity, Memory and Tradition*. Cambridge: Cambridge University Press, 2003.

———. *An Introduction to Hinduism*. Cambridge: Cambridge University Press, 1996.

———. "The Purification of the Body in Tantric Ritual Representation." *Indo-Iranian Journal* 45 (2002): 25–43.

———. *The Tantric Body: The Secret Tradition of Hindu Tradition*. London: I. B. Tauris, 2006.

Flügel, Peter. "Demographic Trends in Jaina Monasticism." In *Studies in Jain History and Culture*, edited by Flügel, 312–98. London: Routledge, 2006.

———. "Jainism and the Western World: Jinmuktisūri and Georg Bühler and Other Early Encounters." *Jinamañjari* 18, no. 2 (1998): 36–47.

———. "The Invention of Jainism: A Short History of Jaina Studies." *International Journal of Jaina Studies (Online)* 1, no. 1 (2005): 1–14.

———. "Life and Work of Johannes Klatt." In *Jaina-Onomasticon*, edited by Flügel and Kornelius Krümpelmann, 13–164. Wiesbaden: Harrassowitz Verlag, 2016.

———. "The *Nikkhamaṇa* of Mahāvīra according to the Old Biographies." In *Cāruśrī: Essays in Honour of Svastiśrī Cārukīrti Bhaṭṭāraka Paṭṭācārya*, edited by Jayandra Soni and Hampa Nagarajaiah, 67–80. Bengaluru: Sapna Book House, 2019.

———. "The Power of Death: The Politics of Relic Worship amongst the Jainas." Unpublished manuscript, 2008.

———. "Sacred Matter: Reflections on the Relationship of Karmic and Natural Causality in Jaina Philosophy." *Journal of Indian Philosophy* 40, no. 2 (2012): 119–76.

———. "The Unknown Loṅkā: Tradition and the Cultural Unconscious." In *Jaina Studies*, edited by Colette Caillat and Nalini Balbir, 181–278. Delhi: Motilal Banarsidass, 2008.

Folkert, Kendall W. *Scripture and Community: Collected Essays on the Jains*. Edited by John E. Cort. Atlanta: Scholars Press, 1993.

Gerety, Finnian. "This Whole World Is OM: Song, Soteriology, and the Emergence of the Sacred Syllable." PhD diss., Harvard University, 2015.

Germano, David. "The Funerary Transformation of the Great Perfection (*Rdzogs chen*)." *Journal of the International Association of Tibetan Studies* 1 (2005): 1–54.

———. "The Shifting Terrain of the Tantric Bodies of Buddhas and Buddhists from an Atiyoga Perspective." In *The Pandita and the Siddha: Tibetan Studies in Honour of E. Gene Smith*, edited by Ramon N. Prats, 50–84. Dharamshala: Amnye Machen Institute, 2007.

Geslani, Marko. *Rites of the God-King: Śānti and Ritual Change in Early Hinduism*. New York: Oxford University Press, 2018.

Gethin, Rupert. *The Foundations of Buddhism*. Oxford: Oxford University Press, 1998.

Glasenapp, Helmuth von. *The Doctrine of Karman in Jain Philosophy*. Translated by Barry Gifford. Bombay: Bai Vijibai Jivanlal Panalal Charity Fund, 1942.

———. *Jainism: An Indian Religion of Salvation*. Translated by Shridhar B. Shroti. Delhi: Motilal Banarsidass, 1998.

Glincka, Małgorzata. "Materiality of Language in Jain Philosophy: Introductory Matters." *Internetowy Magazyn Filozoficzny Hybris* 35 (2016): 156–76.

Goodall, Dominic, and Harunaga Isaacson. "On the Shared 'Ritual Syntax' of the Early Tantric Traditions." In *Tantric Studies: Fruits of a Franco-German Collaboration on Early Tantra*, edited by Goodall and Isaacson, 1–76. Pondicherry: Institut Français de Pondichéry, 2016.

Goodall, Dominic, and Harunaga Isaacson. "Tantric Traditions." In *The Continuum Companion to Hindu Studies*, edited by Jessica Frazier, 122–37, 189–91. London: Continuum, 2011.

Goodall, Dominic, and Marion Rastelli, eds. *Tāntrikābhidhānakośa III: Dictionnaire des termes techniques de la littérature hindoue tantrique / A Dictionary of Technical Terms from Hindu Tantric Literature / Wörterbuch zur Terminologie hinduistischer Tantren*. Vienna: Verlag de Österreichischen Akademie der Wissenschaften, 2013.

Goudriaan, Teun. "Tumburu and His Sisters." *Wiener Zeitschrift für die Kunde Südasiens* 17 (1973): 49–95.

Goudriaan, Teun, and Sanjukta Gupta. *Hindu Tantric and Śākta Literature*. Wiesbaden: Otto Harrassowitz, 1981.

Gough, Ellen. "The Digambara *Sūrimantra* and the Tantricization of Jain Image Consecration." In *Consecration Rituals in South Asia*, edited by István Keul, 265–308. Leiden: Brill, 2017.

———. "Jain *Maṇḍalas* and *Yantras*." In *Brill's Encyclopedia of Jainism*, edited by Knut A. Jacobsen, John E. Cort, Paul Dundas, and Kristi L. Wiley. Leiden: Brill, 2020.

———. "When Sound Becomes an Image: Picturing Oṃ in Jainism." *Material Religion*, forthcoming.

———. "Shades of Enlightenment: A Jain Tantric Diagram and the Colours of the Tīrthaṅkaras." *International Journal of Jaina Studies (Online)* 8, no. 1 (2012): 1–47.

———. "Tantric Ritual Elements in the Initiation of a Digambara." In *Tantric Communities in Context*, edited by Nina Mirnig, Marion Rastelli, and Vincent Eltschinger, 233–73. Vienna: Austrian Academy of Sciences, 2019.

———. "Wheel of the Liberated: Jain *Siddhacakras*, Past and Present." In *Objects of Worship in the South Asian Religions: Forms, Practices, and Meanings*, edited by Knut Jacobsen, 85–108. London: Routledge, 2015.

Granoff, Phyllis. "Buddhaghoṣa's Penance and Siddhasena's Crime: Remarks on Some Buddhist and Jain Attitudes towards the Language of Religious Texts." In *From Benares to Beijing: Essays on Buddhism and Chinese Religion*, edited by Koichi Shinohara and Gregory Schopen, 17–33. Oakville, ON: Mosaic Press, 1991.

———. "Cures and Karma: Healing and Being Healed in Jain Religious Literature." In *Self, Soul and Body in Religious Experience*, edited by Albert I. Baumgarten, 218–30. Leiden: Brill, 1998.

———. "Jain Lives of Haribhadrasūri: An Inquiry into the Sources and Logic of the Legends." *Journal of Indian Philosophy* 17 (1989): 105–28.

———. "The Jina Bleeds: Threats to the Faith and the Rescue of the Faithful in Medieval Jain Stories." in *Images, Miracles, and Authority in Asian Religious Traditions*, edited by Richard H. Davis, 121–41. Boulder, CO: Westview Press, 1998.

———. "Jinaprabhasūri and Jinadattasūri: Two Studies from the Śvetāmbara Jain Tradition." In *Speaking of Monks: Religious Biography in India and China*, edited by Granoff and Koichi Shinohara, 1–96. Oakville, Ontario: Mosaic Press, 1992.

———. "The Miracle of a Hagiography without Miracles: Some Comments on the Jain Lives of the Pratyekabuddha Karakaṇḍa." *Journal of Indian Philosophy* 14 (1986): 389–403.

———. "The Place of Ritual: Geographic Boundaries and Sectarian Identity in Medieval Indian Religions." In *Territory, Soil, and Society in South Asia*, edited Daniela Berti and Gilles Tarabout, 143–76. Delhi: Manohar, 2009.

———. "Religious Biography and Clan History among the Śvetāmbara Jains in North India." *East and West* 39, nos. 1–4 (1989): 195–215.

———. "My Rituals and My Gods: Ritual Exclusiveness in Medieval India," *Journal of Indian Philosophy* 29, nos. 1–2 (2001): 109–34.

———. "Unspoken Rules of Debate in Medieval India and the Boundaries of Knowledge." Lecture, Scholasticisms' Practice, and Practices' Scholasticism, CNRS, Paris, April 2015.

Guenther, Herbert. *The Tantric View of Life*. Berkeley: Shambala Publications, 1972.

Gupta, Sanjukta. "The Changing Pattern of Pāñcarātra Initiation: A Case Study in the Reinterpretation of Ritual." In *Selected Studies on Ritual in the Indian Religions: Essays to D. J. Hoens*, edited by Ria Kloppenborg, 69–91. Leiden: E. J. Brill, 1983.

———. "The Worship of Kālī according to the *Toḍala Tantra*." In *Tantra in Practice*, edited by David Gordon White, 463–88. Princeton, NJ: Princeton University Press, 2000.

Gupta, Sanjukta, Dirk Jan Hoens, and Teun Goudriaan. *Hindu Tantrism*. Leiden: E. J. Brill, 1979.

Harvey, Peter. *Introduction to Buddhism: Teachings, History and Practices*. 2nd ed. Cambridge: Cambridge University Press, 2013.

Hastīmala, Ācārya. *Jain Dharm kā Maulik Itihās*. 4th ed. Pt. 1. Jaipur: Samyagjñān Pracārak Maṇḍal, 1999.

Hatley, Shaman. "Erotic Asceticism: The Knife's Edge Observance (*asidhārāvrata*) and the Early History of Tantric Coital Ritual." *Bulletin of the School of Oriental and African Studies* 79, no. 2 (2016): 329–45.

Hegewald, Julia A. B. "Visual and Conceptual Links between Jaina Cosmological, Mythological and Ritual Instruments." *Journal of Jaina Studies (Online)* 6, no. 1 (2010): 1–20.

Hikita, Hiromichi. "Consecration of Divine Images in a Temple." In *From Material to Deity: Indian Rituals of Consecration*, edited by Shingo Einoo and Jun Takashima, 143–97. New Delhi: Manohar, 2005.

Hoernle, Rudolf A. F. "Three Further Pattavalis of the Digambaras." *Indian Antiquary* 21 (1892): 57–84.

———. "Two Pattavalis of the Sarasvati Gachchha of the Digambara Jains." *Indian Antiquary* 20 (1891): 341–61.

Holmstrom, S. "Towards a Politics of Renunciation: Jain Women and Asceticism in Rajasthan." PhD diss., University of Edinburgh, 1988.

Hopkins, Jeffrey. "The Ultimate Deity in Action Tantra and Jung's Warning against Identifying with the Deity," *Buddhist-Christian Studies* 5 (1985): 158–72.

Issitt, Micah, and Carlyn Main. *Hidden Religion: The Greatest Mysteries and Symbols of the World's Religious Beliefs*. Santa Barbara, CA: ABC-CLIO, 2014.

Indrasenasūri, Ācārya, ed. *Anānupūrvī*. N.p., 1997.

Jacobi, Hermann. "Kalpasūtra of Bhadrabāhu." *Abhandlungen für die Kunde des Morgenlandes* 7, no. 1 (1879).

Jacobsen, Knut A., ed. *Yoga Powers: Extraordinary Capacities Attained through Meditation and Concentration*. Leiden: E. J. Brill, 2012.

Jain, Bābūlāl "Ujjval," comp. *Samagra Jain Cāturmās Sūcī*. Mumbai: Gajendra Sandeś Kāryālay, 2019.

Jain, Brahmacārī Maināբāī, comp. *Ācārya Śrī Ādisāgar (Aṅkalikar) kī Jhalak*. Delhi: Ācārya Śri Sanmati Sāgarjī Saṅgh, 1996.

Jain, Jagdish Chandra. *Life in Ancient India as Depicted in the Jain Canons*. Bombay: New Book Company, 1947.

Jain, Jyoti Prasad. *The Jaina Sources of the History of Ancient India (100 B.C.–A.D. 900)*. Delhi: Munshi Ram Manohar Lal, 1964.

Jain, Jyotindra, and Eberhard Fischer. *Jaina Iconography, Part Two: Objects of Meditation and the Pantheon*. Leiden: E. J. Brill, 1978.

Jain, Kailash Chandra. *Malwa through the Ages*. Delhi: Motilal Banarsidass, 1972.

Jain, Kastūrcandra "Suman." *Amer ke Digambar Jain Mandir Sāṃvlājī Nemināth ke Yantralekh*. Digambar Jain Atiśay Kṣetra Śrī Mahāvīrjī, Rajasthan: Jain Vidyā Saṃsthān, 2012.

Jain, Manju. *Jaina Method of Curing*. Nagpur: Metalfab High Tech, 2011.

Jain, Ratancandra. *Jainparamparā aur Yāpnīyasaṅgh*. Pt. 2. Agra: Sarvoday Jain Vidyāpīṭh, 2009.

Jain, S. C. *Structure and Functions of Soul in Jainism*. Delhi: Bharatiya Jnanpith, 1978.

Jain, Sagarmal. *Jaindharm aur Tāntrik Sādhnā*. Varanasi: Pārśvanāth Vidyāpīṭh, 1997.

———, ed. *Samaṇ Suttaṁ*. 2nd ed. Compiled by Jinendra Varni. New Delhi: Bhagwan Mahavir Memorial Samiti, 1999.

———. "Tantra-Sādhnā aur Jain Jīvan Dṛṣṭi." In *Śvetāmbar Sthānakvāsī Jain Sabhā Hīrak Jayanti Granth*, edited by Jain and Ashok Kumar Singh, 481–87. Varanasi: Pārśvanāth Śodhpīṭh, 1994.

Jain Tīrthvandanā: Bhāratvarṣīya Digambar Jain Tīrthkṣetra Kameṭī kā Mukhpatra 2, no. 11 (May 2012).

Jain, Sudhā. *Jain evaṃ Baudh Yog: Ek Tulnātmak Adhyayan*. Varanasi: Pārśvanāth Vidyāpīṭh, 2001.

Jaini, Jagmanderlal. *Outlines of Jainism*. Cambridge: Cambridge University Press, 1916.

Jaini, Padmanabh S. "Bhavyatva and Abhavyatva: A Jaina Doctrine of 'Predestination.'" In *Mahāvīra and His Teachings*, edited by A. N. Upadhye, N. Tatia, D. Malvania, M. Mehta, N. Shastri and K. Shastri, 95–111. Bombay: Mahāvīra Nirvāṇa Mahotsava Samiti, 1977.

———. "*Cātuyāma-saṁvara* in the Pālī Canon." In *Essays in Jaina Philosophy and Religion*, edited by Piotr Balcerowicz, 119–36. Delhi: Motilal Banarsidass, 2003.

———. *Gender and Salvation: Jaina Debates on the Spiritual Liberation of Women*. Berkeley: University of California Press, 1991.

———. "Is There a Popular Jainism?" In *The Assembly of Listeners: Jains in Society*, edited by Michael Carrithers and Caroline Humphrey, 187–200. Cambridge: Cambridge University Press, 1991.

———. *The Jaina Path of Purification*. Berkeley: University of California Press, 1979.

———. "The Jainas and the Western Scholar." *Sambodhi* 5, nos. 2–3 (1976): 121–31.

Jambūvijaya, Muni, ed. *Catalogue of the Manuscripts of the Pāṭaṇa Jain Bhaṇḍāras*. Pt. 3. Compiled by Muni Puṇyavijaya. Ahmedabad: Sharadaben Chimanbhai Educational Research Centre, 1991.

Jhavery, Mohanlal Bhagwandas. *Comparative and Critical Study of Mantrashastra (with Special Treatment of Jain Mantravada)*. Ahmedabad: Sarabhai Manilal Nawab, 1944.

Johnson, W. J. *Harmless Souls: Karmic Bondage and Religious Change in Early Jainism with Special Reference to Umāsvāti and Kundakunda*. Delhi: Motilal Banarsidass, 1995.

Johrāpurkar, Vidyādhar P. *Bhaṭṭārak Sampradāy*. Sholapur: Jain Saṃskṛti Saṃrakṣak Saṅgh, 1958.

Kafle, Nirajan. "The Niśvāsamukha, the Introductory Book of the Niśvāsatattvasaṃhitā: Critical Edition, with an Introduction and Annotated Translation Appended by Śivadharmasaṅgraha 5–9." PhD diss., University of Leiden, 2015.

Kapadia, Hiralal Rasikdas. *A History of the Canonical Literature of the Jainas*. 1941. Reprinted, Ahmedabad: Sharadaben Chimanbhai Educational Research Centre, 2000.

Kapashi, Vinod. *Nine Sacred Recitations of the Jain Religion (a Study of the Nine Smaranas and All Aspects Associated with Them)*. Mumbai: Hindī Granth Kāryālay, 2007.

Kāslīvāl, Kastūrcand. *Rājasthān ke Jain Sant: Vyaktitva evaṃ Kṛtitva*. Jaipur: Śrī Digambar Jain Atiśay Kṣetra Śrī Mahāvīrjī, 1967.

Kaslīvāl, Udaylāl. *Bhaktāmar-Kathā kā Hindī-Rūpāntar*. Mumbai: Jainsāhityaprasārak Kāryālay, 1930.

Khanna, Madhu. *Yantra: The Tantric Symbol of Cosmic Unity*. London: Thames and Hudson, 1981.

Koch, Rolf Heinrich. "Āvaśyaka-Tales from the Namaskāra-Vyākhyā." *Indologica Taurinensia* XVII–XVIII (1991–92): 221–71.

Kopytoff, Igor. "The Cultural Biography of Things: Commoditization as Process." In *The Social Life of Things: Commodities in Cultural Perspective*, edited by Arjun Appadurai, 64–94. Cambridge: Cambridge University Press, 1986.

Kragh, Ulrich Timm. "Localized Literary History: Sub-text and Cultural Heritage in the Āmer Śāstrabhaṇḍār, a Digambara Manuscript Repository in Jaipur." *International Journal of Jaina Studies (Online)* 9, no. 3 (2013): 1–53.

Kuśalakīrtivijaya, Muni, comp. *Jinśāsan Adhiṣṭhāyak Sampuṭ*. 2 pts. Ahmedabad: Gītārth Gaṅgā, 2018.

Laidlaw, James. *Riches and Renunciation: Religion, Economy, and Society among the Jains*. Oxford: Clarendon Press, 1995.

Larson, Gerald James. "Differentiating the Concepts of 'yoga' and 'tantra' in Sanskrit Literary History." *Journal of the American Oriental Society* 129, no. 3 (2009): 487–98.

Latthe, A. B. *An Introduction to Jainism*. 1905. Reprinted, Delhi: Jain Mittra Mandal, 1964.

Lefeber, Rosalind. "Jain Stories of Miraculous Power." In *Religions of India in Practice*, ed. Donald S. Lopez Jr., 426–33. Princeton, NJ: Princeton University Press, 1995.

Leumann, Ernst. *An Outline of the Āvaśyaka Literature*. Translated by George Baumann. Ahmedabad: L. D. Institute of Indology, 2010.

Long, Jeffery D. *Jainism: An Introduction*. London: I. B. Tauris, 2009.

Lopez, Donald S. Jr. *Elaborations on Emptiness: Uses of the Heart Sūtra*. Princeton, NJ: Princeton University Press, 1996.

Mallinson, James, and Mark Singleton. *Roots of Yoga*. London: Penguin Classics, 2017.

Malvani, Dalsukh, Jayandra Soni, and Karl H. Potter, eds. *Encyclopedia of Indian Philosophies, Vol. X: Jain Philosophy*. Pt. 1. Delhi: Motilal Banarsidass, 2007.

Masuzawa, Tomoko. *The Invention of World Religions: Or, How Universalism Was Preserved in the Language of Pluralism*. Chicago: Chicago University Press, 2005.

McBride, Richard D. II. "Is There Really 'Esoteric' Buddhism?" *Journal of the International Association of Buddhist Studies* 27, 2 (2004): 329–56.

McCarter, Simone. "The Body Divine: Tantric Śaivite Ritual Practices in the *Svacchandatantra* and Its Commentary." *Religions* 5 (2014): 738–50.

Mehta, Gita. *A River Sutra*. New York: Vintage Books, 1993.

Mehta, Suketu. *Maximum City: Bombay Lost and Found*. New York: Vintage Books, 2004.

Minkowski, Christopher. "Why Should We Read the Maṅgala Verses?" In *Śāstrārambha: Inquiries into the Preamble in Sanskrit*, edited by Walter Slaje, 1–24. Wiesbaden: Harrassowitz Verlag, 2008.

Mitra, Kalipada. "Magic and Miracle in Jaina Literature." *Indian Historical Quarterly* XV, no. 2 (1939): 175–82.

Molendijk, Arie L. *Friedrich Max Müller & the "Sacred Books of the East."* Oxford: Oxford University Press, 2016.

Monier-Williams, Monier. *Hinduism*. London: Society for Promoting Christian Knowledge, 1877.

Müller, Max, trans. *The Upanishads: Sacred Books of the East*. Vol. 1. Oxford: Clarendon Press, 1884.

Mukhtar, Jugal Kishore "Yugvir," ed. and comp. *Puratana-Jainvakya-Suchi*. Pt. 1. Saharanpur, UP: Vir-Sewa-Mandir, 1950.

Nagarajaiah, Hampa. *A History of the Rāṣṭrakūṭas of Maḷkhēḍ and Jainism*. Bangalore: Ankita Pustaka, 2000.

Nāgendra. *Mahopādhyāy Vinaysāgar: Jīvan, Sāhitya aur Vicār*. Jaipur: Prākṛt Bhāratī Academy, 1999.

Nandighoṣasūri, Ācārya. *Labdhi: Ek Vaijñānik Viśleṣaṇ (Labdhi: A Scientific Analysis)*. Ahmedabad: Research Institute of Scientific Secrets from Indian Oriental Scriptures, 2017.

Navāb, Sārābhāī Maṇilāl, ed. *Mahāprābhāvika* [*sic*] *Navasmaraṇa*. Ahmedabad: Sārābhāī Maṇilāl Navāb, 1961.

Numark, Mitch. "The Scottish 'Discovery' of Jainism in Nineteenth-Century Bombay." *Journal of Scottish Historical Studies* 33, no. 1 (2013): 20–51.

Ohira, Suzuko. *A Study of the Bhagavatīsūtra: A Chronological Analysis*. Ahmedabad: Prakrit Text Society, 1994.

———. "Treatment of Dhyāna in the *Tattvārthādhigamasūtra*." *Indian Philosophical Quarterly* 3, no. 1 (1975): 51–64.

Olivelle, Patrick. "Celibacy in Classical Hinduism." In *Celibacy and Religious Traditions*, edited by Carl Olson, 151–64. Oxford: Oxford University Press, 2008.

Orr, Leslie C. "Orientalists, Missionaries, and Jains: The South Indian Story." In *The Madras School of Orientalism: Producing Knowledge in Colonial South India*, edited by Thomas R. Trautman, 263–87. New York: Oxford University Press, 2009.

Orzech, Charles D. "The 'Great Teachings of Yoga,' the Chinese Appropriation of the Tantras, and the Question of Esoteric Buddhism." *Journal of Chinese Religions* 34 (2006): 29–77.

———. "Ritual Subjects: Homa in Chinese Translations and Manuals from the Sixth through Eighth Centuries." In Payne and Witzel, *Homa Variations*, 266–90.

———. "Tantric Subjects: Liturgy and Vision in Chinese Esoteric Ritual Manuals." In *Chinese and Tibetan Esoteric Buddhism*, edited by Yael Bentor and Meir Shahar, 18–40. Leiden: Brill, 2017.

Orzech, Charles D., Richard K. Payne, and Henrik H. Sørensen. "Introduction: Esoteric Buddhism and the Tantras in East Asia: Some Methodological Considerations." In *Esoteric Buddhism and the Tantras in East Asia*, ed. Orzech, Payne, and Sørensen (Leiden: Brill, 2011), 3–18.

Padoux, André. "Hindu Tantrism." In *The Encyclopedia of Religion*, edited by Mircea Eliade, 14:272–76. New York: Macmillan, 1986.

———. "Mantras—What Are They?" In *Understanding Mantras*, edited by Harvey P. Alper, 295–318. Albany, NY: State University of New York Press, 1989.

———. *The Hindu Tantric World*. Chicago: Chicago University Press, 2017.

Padoux, André, and Roger-Orphé Jeanty, trans. *The Heart of the Yogini: The Yoginīhṛdaya, a Sanskrit Tantric Treatise*. Oxford: Oxford University Press, 2013.

Pal, Pratapaditya. *The Peaceful Liberators: Jaina Art from India*. Los Angeles: Los Angeles County Museum of Art, 1994.

———. "Two Jain Yantras of the Fifteenth Century." In *Studies in Jaina Art and Iconography and Allied Subjects in Honour of Dr. U. P. Shah*, edited by R. T. Vyas, 23–26. Vadodara: Oriental Institute, 1995.

Payne, Richard K., and Michael Witzel, eds. *Homa Variations: The Study of Ritual Change across the Longue Durée*. New York: Oxford University Press, 2016.

Petrocchi, Alessandra. *The Gaṇitatilaka and Its Commentary: Two Medieval Sanskrit Mathematical Texts*. New York: Routledge, 2019.

Pingree, David. *Jyotiḥśāstra: Astral and Mathematical Literature*. Wiesbaden: Otto Harrassowitz, 1981.

Pollock, Sheldon. "The Languages of Science in India." In *Forms of Knowledge in Early Modern Asia: Explorations in the Intellectual History of India and Tibet, 1500–1800*, edited by Pollock, 19–48. Durham, NC: Duke University Press, 2011.

Prārthanāsāgara, Muni. *Mantra Yantra aur Tantra*. 4th ed. N.p: Muni Śrī Prārthnā Sāgar Foundation, 2011.

Pratibha Pragya, Samani. "Prekṣā Meditation: History and Methods." PhD diss., SOAS, University of London, 2017.

Quintanilla, Sonya Rhie. *History of Early Stone Sculpture at Mathura, ca. 150 BCE–100 CE*. Leiden: Brill, 2007.

Qvarnström, Olle. "Stability and Adaptability: A Jain Strategy for Survival and Growth." *Indo-Iranian Journal* 41 (1998): 33–55.

Rastelli, Marion. "Maṇḍalas and Yantras in the Pāñcarātra Tradition." In *Maṇḍalas and Yantras in the Hindu Tradition*, edited by Gudrun Bühnemann, 119–52. Leiden: E. J. Brill, 2003.

———. "The Religious Practice of the 'Sādhaka' according to the Jayākhyasaṃhitā." *Indo-Iranian Journal* 43, no. 4 (2000): 319–95.

Rao, S. K. Ramachandra. *Śrī-Chakra: Its Yantra, Mantra and Tantra*. Bangalore: Kalpatharu Research Academy, 1982.

Richards, John F. "Early Modern India and World History." *Journal of World History* 8, no. 2 (1997): 197–209.

Rodrigues, Hillary P. *Introducing Hinduism*. New York: Routledge, 2006.

Roth, Gustav. "Notes on Pamca-Namokkāra Parama-Maṅgala." In *Indian Studies: Selected Papers* by Roth, ed. Heinz Bechert and Petra Kieffer-Pülz, 129–46. Delhi: Sri Satguru Publications, 1986.

Śāh, Ambālāl Premcand, ed. *Śrīsūrimantrakalpasandoha*. Ahmedabad: Sarabhai Manilal Nawab, 1948.

Śāh, Dhīrajlāl Ṭokarśī. *Jap-Dhyān-Rahasya*. Mumbai: Ārādhnā Vastu Bhaṇḍār, 1974.

———. *Mantracintāmaṇi*. Mumbai: Prajñā Prakāśan Mandir, 1967.

———. *Mantradivākar*. Mumbai: Prajñā Prakāśan Mandir, 1975.

———. *Mantravijñān*. Mumbai: Prajñā Prakāśan Mandir, 1975.

———. *Namaskār-Mantrasiddhi*. Mumbai: Narendrakumār Dhīrajlāl Śāh, 1968.

———. *Tantronuṃ Tāraṇ*. Mumbai: Jain Sāhitya Prakāśan Mandir, 1961.

Salomon, Richard. *Indian Epigraphy: A Guide to the Study of Inscriptions in Sanskrit, Prakrit, and the Other Indo-Aryan Languages*. New York: Oxford University Press, 1998.

Samuel, Geoffrey. *The Origins of Yoga and Tantra: Indic Religions to the Thirteenth Century*. Cambridge: Cambridge University Press, 2008.

Sanderson, Alexis. "The Doctrine of the Mālinīvijayottaratantra." In *Ritual and Speculation in Early Tantrism: Studies in Honour of André Padoux*, edited by Teun Goudriaan, 281–312. Albany: State University of New York Press, 1992.

———. "History through Textual Criticism in the Study of Śaivism, the Pañcarātra and the Buddhist Yoginītantras." In *Les Sources et le temps/Sources and Time: A Colloquium, Pondicherry 11–12 January 1997*, edited by Nicolas Grimal, 1–47. Pondicherry, Institut Français de Pondichéry, 2001.

———. "Keynote Lecture: The Śākta Transformation of Śaivism." Lecture handout, World Sanskrit Conference, Vancouver, July 10, 2018.

———. "The Lākulas: New Evidence of a System Intermediate between Pāñcārthika Pāsupatism and Āgamic Śaivism." *Indian Philosophical Annual* 24 (2006): 143–217.

———. "Maṇḍala and Āgamic Identity in the Trika of Kashmir." In *Mantras et Diagrammes Rituelles dans l'Hindouisme*, edited by André Padoux, 169–207. Paris: Centre National de la Recherche Scientifique, 1986.

———. "The Śaiva Age—the Rise and Dominance of Śaivism during the Early Medieval Period." In *Genesis and Development of Tantrism*, edited by Shingo Einoo, 41–349. Tokyo: Institute of Oriental Culture, University of Tokyo, 2009.

———. "The Śaiva Literature." *Journal of Indological Studies* 24 and 25 (2012–2013): 1–113.

———. "Śaivism and the Tantric Traditions." In *The World's Religions*, edited by S. Sutherland, L. Houlden, P. Clarke, and F. Hardy, 660–704. London: Routledge, 1988.

———. "Vajrayāna: Origin and Function." In *Buddhism into the Year 2000: International Conference Proceedings*, 87–102. Bangkok: Dhammakāya Foundation, 1995.

Saumyaguṇā, Sādhvī. *Jain Muni ke Vratāropaṇ kī Traikālik Upyogitā Navyayug ke Sandarbh meṃ*. Ladnun: Jain Viśva Bhāratī Viśvavidyālay, 2014.

———. *Jain Vidhi-Vidhān Sambandhī Sāhitya kā Bṛhad Itihās*. Pt. 1. Shajapur: Prācya Vidyāpīṭh, 2006.

Schubring, Walther. *The Doctrine of the Jainas Described after the Old Sources*. Rev. ed. Translated by Wolfgang Beurlen. Delhi: Motilal Banarsidass, 2000.

———. *Mahāvīra's Words*. Translated by Willem Bollée and Jayandra Soni. Ahmedabad: L. D. Institute, 2004.

Shah, Priyabala, ed. *Mudrāvicāraprakaraṇam and Mudrāvidhiḥ*. Baroda: Oriental Institute, 1956.

Shah, Umakant P. "Iconography of the Sixteen Jaina Mahāvidyās." *Journal of the Indian Society of Oriental Art* 15 (1947): 114–77.

———. *Jaina-Rūpa-Maṇḍana (Jaina Iconography)*. New Delhi: Abhinav, 1987.

———. "A Peep into the Early History of Tantra in Jain Literature." In *Bhārata-Kaumudī: Studies in Indology in Honor of Dr. Radha Kumud Mookerji*, part 2, edited by N. K. Sidhanta, B. C. Law, C. D. Chatterjee, and V. S. Agrawala, 839–54. Allahabad: Indian Press, 1946.

———. *Studies in Jaina Art*. 1955. Reprinted, Varanasi: Parsvanatha Vidyapitha, 1998.

———. "Supernatural Beings in the Jain Tantras." In *Acharya Dhruva Smaraka Grantha*. Ahmedabad: Gujarat Vidya Sabha, 1946.

———. "Varddhamāna [*sic*] -Vidyā-Paṭa." *Journal of the Indian Society of Oriental Arts* IX (1941): 42–51.

Shāntā, N. *The Unknown Pilgrims: The Voice of the Sādhvīs: The History, Spirituality and Life of the Jaina Women Ascetics*. Translated by M. Rogers. Delhi: Sri Satguru Publications, 1997.

Sharf, Robert H. *Coming to Terms with Chinese Buddhism: A Reading of the Treasure Store Treatise*. Honolulu: University of Hawai'i Press, 2002.

———. "Thinking through Shingon Ritual." *Journal of the International Association of Buddhist Studies* 26, no. 1 (2003): 51–96.

———. "Visualization and Mandala in Shingon Buddhism." In *Living Images: Japanese Buddhist Icons in Context*, edited by Sharf and Elizabeth Horton Sharf, 151–97. Stanford, CA: Stanford University Press, 2001.

Shinohara, Koichi. *Spells, Images, and Maṇḍalas: Tracing the Evolution of Esoteric Buddhist Rituals*. New York: Columbia University Press, 2014.

Shastri, Devendra Muni. *Source Book in Jaina Philosophy*. Udaipur: Sri Tarak Guru Jain Granthalaya, 1983.

Śīlacandravijaya, Muni. *Śāsan Samrāṭ*. Ahmedabad: Tapagācchīya Śeṭhśrī Jindās Dharmdās Dhārmik Trust, Kadambgiri Vāṭī, 1973.

Soni, Jayandra. "Dravya, Guṇa and Paryāya in Jaina Thought." *Journal of Indian Philosophy* 19 (1991): 75–88.

Stephen, Michele. "Sūrya-Sevana: A Balinese Tantric Practice." *Archipel* 89 (2015): 95–124.

Strong, John S. *The Experience of Buddhism: Sources and Interpretations*. 2nd ed. Belmont, CA: Wadsworth Thompson Learning, 2002.

Surdam, Wayne Edward. "South Indian Śaiva Rites of Initiation: The Dīkṣāvidhi of Aghoraśivācārya's Kriyākramadyotikā." PhD diss., University of California, Berkeley, 1984.

Takashima, Jun. "Pratiṣṭhā in the Śaiva Āgamas." In *From Material to Deity: Indian Rituals of Consecration*, edited by Shingo Einoo and Takashima, 115–42. New Delhi: Manohar, 2005.

Tatia, Nathmal. *Studies in Jaina Philosophy*. Banaras: Jain Cultural Research Society, 1951.

Taylor, Sarah Pierce. "Aesthetics of Sovereignty: The Poetic and Material Worlds of Medieval Jainism." PhD diss., University of Pennsylvania, 2016.

Ten Grotenhuis, Elizabeth. *Japanese Mandalas: Representations of Sacred Geography*. Honolulu: University of Hawai'i Press, 1999.

Törzsök, Judit. "How Śāktism Began." Lecture handout, 17th World Sanskrit Conference. Vancouver, July 13, 2018.

———. "The Search in Śaiva Scriptures for Meaning in Tantric Ritual." In *Mélanges tantriques à la mémoire d'Hélène Brunner / Tantric Studies in Memory of Hélène Brunner*, edited by Dominic Goodall and André Padoux, 449–79. Pondicherry: Ecole Française d'Extrême Orient, 2007.

Tsong-kha-pa, H.H. the Dalai Lama, and Jeffrey Hopkins. *Deity Yoga*. Ithaca, NY: Snow Lion Publications, 1987.

———. *Tantra in Tibet: The Great Exposition of Secret Mantra, Vol. 1*. Delhi: Motilal Banarsidass, 1987.

Tubb, Gary A. "Hemacandra and Sanskrit Poetics." In *Open Boundaries: Jain Communities and Cultures in Indian History*, edited by John E. Cort, 53–66. Albany: State University of New York Press, 1998.

Urban, Hugh B. "The Extreme Orient: The Construction of 'Tantrism' as a Category in the Orientalist Imagination," *Religion* 29 (1999): 123–46.

———. *Tantra: Sex, Secrecy, Politics and Power in the Study of Religions*.Berkeley: University of California Press, 2003.

Varṇī, Jinendra, ed. *Jainendra Siddhānt Koś*. 6th ed. 6 pts. Delhi: Bhāratīya Jñānpīṭh, 2002.

Vinayasāgara, Upādhyāya. *Gautam Rās: Ek Pariśīlan*. Jaipur: Prākṛt Bhārtī Academy, 1987.

———. "Upādhyāy Sakalcandrakaṇi [*sic*] Racit Dhyānadīpikā (Saṃskṛt) Saṅgrah Granth hai." *Anusandhān* 47 (March 2009): 76–80.

Vose, Steven M. "The Making of a Medieval Jain Monk: Language, Power and Authority in the Works of Jinaprabhasūri (c. 1261–1333)." PhD diss., University of Pennsylvania, 2013.

Wallis, Christopher. *Tantra Illuminated: The Philosophy, History, and Practice of a Timeless Tradition*. Petulama, CA: Mattamayūra Press, 2012.

Weber, Max. *The Religion of India: The Sociology of Hinduism and Buddhism*. Translated by Hans H. Gerth and Don Martindale. Glencoe, IL: Free Press, 1958.

Wedemeyer, Christian K. "Antinomianism and Gradualism: The Contextualization of the Practices of Sensual Enjoyment (*Caryā*) in the Guhyasamāja Ārya Tradition." *International Journal of Buddhist Studies* 3 (2002): 181–95.

———. *Making Sense of Tantric Buddhism: History, Semiology, and Transgression in the Indian Traditions*. New York: Columbia University Press, 2013.

———. "Tropes, Typologies, and Turnarounds: A Brief Genealogy of the Historiography of Tantric Buddhism." *History of Religions* 40, no. 3 (February 2001): 223–59.

White, David Gordon. *The Alchemical Body: Siddha Traditions in Medieval India*. Chicago: University of Chicago Press, 1996.

———. "Introduction: Tantra in Practice: Mapping a Tradition." In *Tantra in Practice*, edited by White, 3–38. Princeton, NJ: Princeton University Press, 2000.

———. *Kiss of the Yoginī: "Tantric Sex" in Its South Asian Contexts*. Chicago: University of Chicago Press, 2003.

Wiles, Royce. "The Dating of the Jaina Councils: Do Scholarly Presentations Reflect the Traditional Sources?" In *Studies in Jaina History and Culture: Disputes and Dialogues*, edited by Peter Flügel, 61–85. London: Routledge, 2006.

Wiley, Kristi L. *The A to Z of Jainism*. Lanham: Scarecrow Press, 2009.

———. "Early Śvetāmbara and Digambara Karma Literature: A Comparison." In *Jaina Stud-*

ies: Papers of the 12th World Sanskrit Conference, edited by Colette Caillat and Nalini Balbir, 43–60. Delhi: Motilal Banarsidass, 2008.

———. "Extrasensory Perception and Knowledge in Jainism." In *Essays in Jaina Philosophy and Religion*, edited by Piotr Balcerowicz, 89–109. Delhi: Motilal Banarsidass, 2003.

———. "Supernatural Powers and Their Attainment in Jainism." In *Yoga Powers: Extraordinary Capacities Attained through Meditation and Concentration*, edited by Knut A. Jacobsen, 145–94. Leiden: E. J. Brill, 2012.

Williams, Robert. "Haribhadra." *Bulletin of the School of Oriental and African Studies, University of London* 28, no. 1 (1965): 101–11.

———. *Jaina Yoga: A Survey of the Mediaeval Śrāvakācāras.* 1963. Reprinted, Delhi: Motilal Banarsidass, 1991.

Woodroffe, Sir John. *Shakti and Shâkta: Essays and Addresses on the Shâkta Tantrashâstra.* 3rd ed. London: Luzac, 1929.

Yadava, Ganga Prasad. *Dhanapāla and His Times: A Socio-cultural Study Based upon His Works.* New Delhi: Naurang Rai, 1982.

INDEX

Page numbers followed by *f* and *t* indicate figures and tables, respectively. Numbers followed by n indicate endnotes.

abhavya jīvas, 237n77
Abhidhānacintāmaṇi (Hemacandrasūri), 250n83
Abhinavagupta, 131–32, 242n43
abhiṣeka (ritual ablution), 12, 76–77, 90, 197, 223n33, 270n3
A(ñ)cala Gaccha or Vidhi Pakṣa, 246n31
ācāmāmla fasts, 83–84, 235n60
Ācāradinakara (Vardhamānasūri), 151
Ācārāṅgasūtra, 46–47, 56, 64–66, 116, 154*t*, 155, 211–13, 238n6, 240n21, 247n47, 247n50
ācāryamantra, 72
ācāryas (mendicant leaders), 244n12, 244n18, 249n69; becoming Gautama, 185–90, 189*f*; Digambara, 93–94, 94*f*, 97, 97*t*, 105; five types of proper conduct (*pañcācāra*), 249n69; lineage, 67–68; modern rites, 148–49, 151, 177, 197; promotion ceremonies, 72–77, 81, 85*t*, 86–90, 97, 97*t*, 253n115; Śvetāmbara, 93, 148–49; temple images, 95; Worship Ceremony of the Five Sections (*pañcaprasthānavidhi*), 177–90, 179*t*, 180*f*, 183*f*, 187*f*. *See also specific ācāryas by name*
Acharya Shri Kailasasagarsuri Gyanmandir (Koba, Gujarat), 220n6
Ādipurāṇa of Jinasena, 65–67, 118, 203, 254n23
āgamas (canonical texts or scriptures), 15–16, 80–81, 151–53, 192–93, 211, 244n20, 263n25, 264n26, 264n28, 264n32. *See also specific texts*
Āgamika Gaccha, 246n31
aghorabrahmacāritva, 234n47
Aghoraśiva, 128–29
Agni, 184
Agrawal, B. C., 238n3
Agrāyaṇīya, 34
ahiṃsā (nonviolence), 7, 54
Ahimsa: Non-violence (Tobias), 238n3
āhvāhanamudrā (invitation gesture), 165, 166*f*, 168
Ājīvikas, 25
Akalaṅka, 120
ālambana (support of meditation), 117, 254n22
All-Gathering Maṇḍala, 61–62, 242n40
Ambikā, 268n74
Amitagati, 135–36, 139, 142–43, 203, 259n79, 259n82
Amoghavajra, 12
Amoghavarṣa, 33, 65
Amṛtacandra, 22, 253n2
Anagāradharmāmṛta (Āśādhara), 243n6, 255n31
anālambana (meditation without support), 117–18, 121
Anandasāgarasūri, 239n13
Ānandjī Kalyāṇjī, 147
anānupūrvī ("No Fixed Sequence"), 141
Añcala Gaccha, 160, 169, 246n31

Andhare, Shridhar, 263n12
aṅga (limb or main texts), 85, 151–52, 154*t*
*aṅgamantra*s, 257n60
aṅganyāsa, 164
aṅgaśuddhi, 253n3
Aṅgavidyā ("Knowledge of the Parts of the Body"), 29–31, 264n28
aṅgulīnyāsa, 163
añjalimudrā (salutation gesture), 163, 166*f*, 167, 167*f*
Aṅkalīkara, Ādisāgara, 104–5, 239n10, 253n109
antevāsin, 75
Anti-superstition and Black Magic Act (Maharashtra), 4
anuttarayoga (supreme yoga), 13
anuvrata (minor vows), 255n32
anuyoga (examination), 80–81
Anuyogadvārasūtra, 80–81, 85, 154*t*
Aparājitā, 64, 86, 158, 171*f*, 172, 191–93
appendices (*cūlikā*), 80–81, 151–53, 154*t*
Apraticakrā, 102, 203, 205, 207
apraticakrā-mantra, 70–71, 96*f*, 98–102, 252nn101–2, 260n100, 270n4
Ārādhanāpatākā, 264n28
arhaṃ (mantra for an omniscient being), 101–2, 112, 123, 200
arhat (omniscient being, enlightened soul), 22, 96, 120, 123–24, 127–29, 133–34, 143, 182, 203, 238n85
Arthaśāstra, 193
Aruṇavijaya, Pannyāsa, 73*f*
Āśādhara, Paṇḍita, 92, 126, 243n6, 249n75, 250n88, 254n9, 255n31
asceticism, 3–16, 114–15, 224nn45–46, 225n51, 228n72, 233n37, 261n115; initiation traditions, 67–68, 84, 97, 97*t*; Jain ritual syntax, 201, 213–14; modern, 144–45, 148–49
aśivopaśamanī (Spell That Pacifies Dangerous Things), 206–7
Aśokacandrasūri, Ācārya, 175
Aśokan rock edicts, 32
Aśokasāgarasūri, 49–51
Āṣṭādhyāyī (Pāṇini), 152
Aṣṭāhnikaparva (Festival of Eight Days), 111–15, 112*f*
astramudrā (weapon gesture), 166*f*, 167–69
astrology, 31, 235n63
Atharvaveda, 228n73
Atikūṭa, 61–62
Atimārga (ascetic Śaiva sects), 9–14, 63, 221n18, 222n19, 222nn24–25, 228n72
*atiśaya*s (fourteen miraculous signs), 94, 250n83
Ātmārāmajī (Vijayānandasūri), 149
Āturapratyākhyāna, 264n28
Aupapātikasūtra, 25, 117, 154*t*, 254n21, 261n115
auspicious pots (*kumbha*), 182
avadhi (clairvoyance), 5, 26, 213, 232n27, 234n43, 237n82
avaguṇṭhanamudrā (hiding gesture), 165, 166*f*, 168–69, 266n49
Avalon, Arthur. *See* Woodroffe, John
āvaśyaka (six essential duties of a mendicant), 33, 54, 240n19, 247n45
Āvaśyakacūrṇi (Jinadāsa), 40, 57–58, 237n83
Āvaśyakaniryukti, 32, 56–57, 59, 192, 236n68, 255n27, 269n102
Āvaśyakasūtra, 80, 82, 85, 153–54, 154*t*, 155, 246n38
Āvaśyakaṭīkā (Haribhadrasūri), 58, 237n83
āyagapaṭa, 58
āyambil, 179*t*, 186, 235n60

Babb, Lawrence A., 144–45, 256n41
Bāhubali, 99, 100*t*, 251n97, 267n59
bāhubalividyā (Spell of Bāhubali), 99, 100*t*, 173, 179*t*
Bālacandrasūri, 259n86
Balātkāra Gaṇa, 89, 98, 250–51n91
Balbir, Nalini, 57–58, 230n13, 236n68, 240n26, 255n27, 262n12, 264n28, 271n11
bandhamokṣiṇī (Spell That Frees One from Bonds), 206
Bell, Catherine, 17
Bhadrabāhu I, 117, 232n33, 237n73, 244n11
Bhadraguptācārya, 260n100
Bhāgavatapurāṇa, 18–19
Bhagavatī Ārādhanā, 117
Bhagavatīsūtra, 25, 55, 84, 117, 153–54, 154*t*, 240n21, 261n115, 264n32

Bhairavapadmāvatīkalpa, 227n66, 231n23
bhajana, 253n5
Bhaktāmarastotra ("Hymn of the Devoted Gods"), 3–5, 16, 152, 198–200, 227n65, 271n15; length, 208–10; *ṛddhi-maṅgala* association, 204–13; *yantras*, 208–11, 209f
Bhaktaparijñā, 246n40, 264n28
Bharata, 65
Bhāskaranandi, 260n93
Bhatt, Bansidhar, 237n78
Bhatt, N. R., 244n20
bhaṭṭārakas, 89–91, 97, 97*t*, 102–5, 248n63, 249n67, 251n92, 253n110
bhāvamaṅgala, 237n79
bhāvanās (reflective meditations), 137
Bhāvasaṅgraha (Devasena), 119–26, 129–30, 132–33, 254n24, 255n33
bhavya jīvas, 237n77
Bhavyamārgopadeśa Upāsakādhyayana of Jinadeva, 134
Bhoja, 135
Bhojak, Pandit Laxmanbhai, 263n12
Bhomīyājī, 268n74
bhūmaṇḍalas, 257n52
bhūmiśuddhi (purification of the space), 163
Bhūtabali, 26–29, 34–35, 232n25
bhūtaśuddhi, 122, 168, 223n27, 256n38
Bīsapantha, 92, 239n10, 253n4
bliss (*sukha*), 58, 139, 143, 201, 230n6
brahmamantras, 129, 222n26, 257n60
Brahmasiddhāntasamuccaya of Haribhadrasūri, 64, 242–43nn50–51
bṛhadśāntimantra, 197, 270n3
Bṛhad Yog Vidhi, 151, 155, 239n13, 263n20
bṛhatsiddhacakra (Expanded Wheel of the Liberated Soul), 123–24
Bronkhorst, Johannes, 130–31, 240n27, 254n15
Brown, Robert, 8
Brunner, Hélène, 77, 244n20, 248n56, 256n39
Buddhi, 203
buddhiṛddhi (power of the intellect), 237n82
Buddhism, 11–15, 224n47, 242n45, 266n55; All-Gathering Maṇḍala, 61–62; initiation ceremonies, 11–12, 46, 61–62; initiation levels, 77–78; South Asian, 231n18; Tantric, 11–14, 122, 225n52, 245n25; Tibetan, 188–89; Vajrayāna, 9
Bühler, Georg, 16, 152, 211–12
Bühnemann, Gudrun, 9
Burgess, James, 262n3
Burnouf, Eugène, 15

Caillat, Collette, 248n55
caityavandana, 242n47, 255–56n35
Caityavandanamahābhāṣyā (Śāntisūri), 136–37
cakra (wheel), 220n5
Cakreśvarī, 102, 171*f*, 268n74
Cāksū Digambara Jain Temple (Jaipur, Rajasthan), 111–12, 112*f*
Cāmuṇḍarāya, 243n6, 255n31
Candanākumārī, Sādhvī, 229n76
Candra Gaccha, 151
Candraprabha, 178
Candrasāgara, Ācārya, 270n2
Candrasūri, Ācārya, 151
Candravedhyaka, 264n28
Canon I, 263n26
Canon II, 263n26
Canon-far, 263n26
Canon-near, 263n26
cāraṇas, 233n36
Cāritrasāra (Cāmuṇḍarāya), 243n6, 255n31
Carrithers, Michael, 45–46
caryātantra, 13
cattārimaṅgala (Fourfold Maṅgala), 237n85
Catuḥśaraṇa, 264n28
Cauṃsaṭh Ṛddhi Vidhān, 270n4
celestial cow gesture (*surabhimudrā*), 165, 166*f*
celibacy (*brahmacarya*), xv, 7, 12, 14, 18, 28, 46, 48, 54, 68, 228n72, 234n47
chadmastha, 137
Chāndogya Upaniṣad, 20
Chandra, Moti, 235n58
Chandranāth Digambar Mandir (Karanja, Maharashtra), 89
Chapple, Christopher Key, 241n31, 259n89
Chaturvedi, Aditya, 242n46
chedasūtra (canonical text on mendicant disciple), 30, 80, 85, 151–53, 154*t*
Christianity, 211, 225n53

clairvoyance (*avadhi*), 5, 39, 100, 172, 213, 232n27, 237n82, 265n40
cloth diagram (*paṭa*), xv, 71–72, 74, 81, 85*t*, 101, 156, 160–61, 220n5, 265n40, 267n63. See also *sūrimantrapaṭa; vardhamānavidyāpaṭa*
Cloth Diagram of the Mantra of the Mendicant Leader (*sūrimantrapaṭa*), 51, 70–71, 74, 85*t*, 87, 98–102, 139, 146–7, 197, 243n3, 262–63n12, 265n37; condensed (*saṅkṣipta*) version, 156; expanded (*bṛhat*) version, 156; in modern worship, 146–7, 149, 160–91, 166*f*, 179*t*; Nandighoṣasūri's, 169–74, 170*f*, 171*f*
Cloth Diagram of the Spell of Mahāvīra (*vardhamānavidyāpaṭa*), 85*t*, 86, 146, 197, 248n52; in modern worship, 146–69, 157*f*, 161*f*, 166*f*, 191; shrines for, 160–61, 161*f*
clothes: for *pūjā*, 267n70; purification of (*vastraśuddhi*), 163, 253n3; removal of, 55–56, 93, 104–5
Cohen, Richard, 261n110
consciousness (*caitanya*), 230n6
Cort, John E., 142, 145–46, 152, 194, 220n8, 225n52, 225n54, 227n65, 230n13, 238n3, 240n23, 243n5, 250n83, 259n85
cosmic energy, 146, 169
Council of Valabhi, 151–52, 193
cūlikā (appendix), 51, 83, 151–52, 154*t*
cult of Gautama, 266n58
Cunningham, Alexander, 236n67
curative powers, 234n52

Dabholkar, Narendra, 219n2
daily worship practices, xvi, 11, 109–95, 266n45, 269n87; *Nitya Ārādhanā Vidhi* ("Ritual for Daily Worship") (Somacandrasūri), 175–77; with *sūrimantrapaṭa* (Cloth Diagram of the Mantra of the Mendicant Leader), 160–69, 166*f*, 175–77; with *vardhamānavidyāpaṭa* (Cloth Diagram of the Spell of Mahāvīra), 160–69, 161*f*, 166*f*
Dalai Lama, 188–89
Darśanasāra of Devasena, 119, 254n24
Daśāśrutaskandha: Kalpasūtra (eighth chapter), 14, 153–54, 154*t*, 238n6, 240n24
Daśavaikālikasūtra, 80–82, 85, 152–55, 154*t*, 246n38
Daulatarāma, Paṇḍita, 260n102
Davidson, Ronald, 229n73
Davis, Richard H., 255n25, 256n38
deity yoga (*devatāyoga*), 12–13, 188–90, 223n37, 268n84
Deleu, Jozef, 235n59
Deo, Shantaram Bhalchandra, 240n20
detachment, xvii, 186
Detige, Tillo, 89
Devacandra, 260n101
Devānandā, 240n21
Devasena, 142–43; *Bhāvasaṅgraha*, 119–26, 129–30, 132–33, 254n24, 255n33; *Darśanasāra*, 119, 254n24
Devasūri, 137, 176
devatāyoga (deity yoga), 12–13, 188–90, 223n37, 268n84
Devendrakīrti, 91
Devendrastava, 264n28
Dhaky, M. A. (Ḍhāṅkī, Madhusūdan), 210, 239n15
Dhanapāla, 255n25
Dhārā, Madhya Pradesh, 119
dhāraṇās, 138, 259n89, 260n91
Dhāraṇīsaṅgraha, 61–62
Dharasena, 34
dharmadhyāna (*dharmyadhyāna*), 116, 135, 255n31
Dharmakīrti, 21–22
Dharmindar, 265n37
Dhavalā of Vīrasena, 24, 33–40, 202–3
dhenumudrā, 168–69, 266n49
Dhṛti, 101, 139, 203
dhyāna, 116–17, 130–31, 254nn15–16, 255n31, 261n115
Dhyānadīpikā of Devacandra, 260n101
Dhyānadīpikā of Sakalacandragaṇin, 260n101
Dhyānaśataka of Jinabhadrasūri, 117–19, 254n18, 254n22
Dhyānastava of Bhāskaranandi, 260n93
Dhyānavicāra, 260n101

dhyeya (object of meditation), 114–15, 125–27, 130, 139, 142, 261n110
diagrams: cloth (*paṭa*), 85*t*, 156, 160–61, 220n5, 265n40, 267n63 (see also *sūrimantrapaṭa; vardhamānavidyāpaṭa*); of initiation, 45–68, 85*t*, 97–103; *nandyāvarta* (extended *svastika*), 182, 268n72, 268n74; that contain mantras (see *yantras*)
Digambara Jainism, 220n5, 230n5, 232n33, 236n69; *ācāryas*, 93–94, 94*f*, 105; *aṣṭakapūjā*, 253n4; *Bhaktāmarastotra* length, 208–10; Cāksū Temple (Jaipur), 111–12, 112*f*; *cāraṇas*, 233n36; *dhyāna*, 254n15; early, 24–26, 75–76; early modern, 88–91; essential duties, 247n45; Festival of Eight Days (Aṣṭāhnikaparva), 111; fire *maṇḍalas* (*hutāśana*), 256n36; *gaṇadharavalayamantra*, 243n3, 251n97; Gaṇadhara Valaya ritual, 243n5hand gestures, 256n37; image consecration ceremonies, 73–74, 91–97, 94*f*; influence on Hemacandrasūri's *Yogaśāstra*, 137–41; *īryāpathaśuddhi*, 255n35; Jina's Preaching Assembly, 56; *maṇḍalas*, 97, 97*t*, 243n5; mantras of promotion, 88–94; meditation practices, 117–26, 130–41; mendicant initiation, 45–56, 49*f*, 50*f*, 64–68, 72–74, 88–99, 94*f*, 97*t*, 203, 239nn9–11; mendicant ranks, 75–76; modern practices, 103–7, 141, 197–200, 213; Paras TV, 142; path to liberation, 118; *prātihāryas*, 271n19; *pratikramaṇa*, 270n2; Ring of Disciples (*gaṅadharavalaya*), 39–40, 69–70, 70*f*, 73*f*, 102–3, 252n103, 252n108, 270n4; ritual diagrams, 97–99, 141; *sakalīkaraṇa* (unification) rites, 257n53, 257n59; *saṅghas*, 89; superhuman powers, 24–25; *sūrimantra* (Mantra of the Mendicant Leader), 70–71, 104–7, 251n97, 253n112; *Tattvārthasūtra*, 254n17; Terāpanthī, xv, xvii, 19, 30, 92, 111–13, 236n69; texts, 24–25, 102–4, 119–20, 152, 263n25; *Trilokaprajñapti*, 24–25; *vardhamānavidyā* (Spell of Mahāvīra), 104; *vidhānas*, 142, 239n12, 256n40; *yantras*, 141–42, 257n46, 261n106
digbandhana, 253n3
Dikpāla Deva, 171*f*
dīkṣā (renunciation), 45–47, 238n3
Dīkṣit, Rājeś, 227n70
dīpaka (lamp): establishment of, 182
dīptatapas, 233n41
dismissing gesture (*visarjanamudrā*), 166*f*, 168
Dīvālī, 185–90, 268n83
divinization, 9, 12–13, 189–90
doṣanirnāśinī (Spell That Destroys Faults), 206
Drāviḍa *saṅgha*, 89
dravyamaṅgala, 237n79
Dundas, Paul, 78–79, 229n4, 231n17, 241n32, 254n10, 257n48, 259n84, 260n100, 265n42
Dvīpasāgaraprajñapti, 264n28
Dviveda, Vrajavallabha, 229n73

early literature, 53–58
early modern India, 228n71
earth (*pṛthvī*) *maṇḍala*, 256n42
Einoo, Shingo, 228n73
energy (*vīrya*), 230n6
esoteric Buddhism, 13
esotericization, 17
essential duties (*āvaśyaka*), 54, 82, 84, 178, 201, 427n45, 254n22
establishing gesture (*sthāpanāmudrā*), 165, 166*f*, 168
Expanded Wheel of the Liberated Soul (*bṛhat-siddhacakra*), 123–24
extended *svastika* (*nandyāvarta*), 182, 268n72
extraordinary powers (*labdhi*, *ṛddhi*, *siddhi*), 3, 5, 10, 12, 24–31, 39, 41, 69, 74, 99, 103, 136, 148, 159, 173, 190, 197, 201–202, 231n18, 232–235nn28–57, 237nn81–82, 251n97, 259n83, 269n89, 270n1
eyes (painted), 170–71, 266n55

fasts and fasting, 7, 66, 201, 233n41, 247n46; *ācāmāmla*, 83–84, 235n60; *āyambil*, 186; *nirvikṛtika*, 83–84; *nīvi*, 247n48; *ugratapas*, 233n40; *upvās*, 178, 234n43; in Worship of the Five Sections (*pañcaprasthānavidhi*), 177–78, 179*t*

female mendicants: leaders (*mahattarā/pravartinī*), 81, 85*t*, 86, 155, 248n53, 265n35, 266n52; nuns, 69–70, 70*f*, 155; ranks, 75, 155
Festival of Eight Days (Aṣṭāhnikaparva), 111–15, 112*f*
festivals, 141
fire *maṇḍala*, 256n36
fire offerings (*homa*, *havana*), 17, 49, 184–85, 229n73, 239n12, 242n46, 268nn74–75, 268n78
firepits, 268n74
Fischer, Eberhard, 250n87, 261n110
five auspicious events (*pañcakalyāṇaka*), 92–93
five eternal syllables, 122
Fivefold Praise (*pañcanamaskāra*), xvi, 22–24, 75, 236n71, 258n60, 266n53; commentary on, 33–40; ritual use of, 51–53, 52*f*, 85*t*
Five Sections (*pañcaprasthāna*), 149. *See also* Worship Ceremony of the Five Sections (*pañcaprasthānavidhi*)
Five Supreme Beings (*pañcaparameṣṭin*), 22, 34, 48, 51, 121–25, 127, 130, 132–35, 140–42, 162, 164, 168, 176, 214, 256n44, 257n53
Five Supreme Beings gesture (*parameṣṭhimudrā*), 167–69, 167*f*, 256n37
Flood, Gavin, 8, 11, 228n72
flower-throwing rites, 58–62, 84, 241n32, 242n45
Flügel, Peter, 224n47, 231n16, 231n21, 238n6, 239n13, 246n31, 247n41
Folkert, Kendall, 152
Fourfold Maṅgala (*cattārimaṅgala*), 237n85
fourteen miraculous signs (*atiśaya*), 94
Frontiers of Peace, 238n3
fruition acts (*kartranvayakriyā*), 118

gacchas (mendicant lineages), 89, 148–49; six extant, 246n31
Gaṇadhara Valaya, 243n5
gaṇadhara (disciples of the *tīrthaṅkaras*), 25, 75–76
gaṇadharavalaya (Ring of Disciples), 39–40, 90, 115, 197, 252n103, 252n108, 270n4; as diagram of initiation and promotion, 48–49, 50*f*, 69–70, 70*f*, 73*f*, 95–97, 96*f*, 97*t*, 103, 136; Digambara sources on, 102–3; early descriptions, 203
gaṇadharavalayamantra, 207–8, 251n97, 252n103
gaṇadharavalayayantra, 243n3, 252n108
gaṇadharavidyā, 101–2
Gaṇakārikā, 222n26
gaṇas (mendicant groups), 89
gaṇins (mendicant group leaders), 75–76, 151–53, 154*t*, 169
Gaṇipiṭaka (*yakṣa* personification of the scriptures), 100*t*, 171*f*, 174, 178–81, 180*f*, 185
Gaṇividyā, 264n28
Gautama, 34, 63, 100*t*, 174, 178, 266n58; becoming, for Dīvālī, 185–90, 189*f*; in the shrine for Worship of the Five Sections (*pañcaprasthānavidhi*), 180, 180*f*; in *sūrimantrapaṭa* (Cloth Diagram of the Mantra of the Mendicant Leader), 173–74
gāyatrīmantra, 242n46
Gāyatrītantra, 242n46
Geertz, Clifford, 263n26
Genzu, 191
Gerety, Finnian, 229n1
Germano, David, 16–17
Geslani, Marko, 228n73, 229n73
gesture of the Five Supreme Beings (*parameṣṭhimudrā*), 167, 167*f*, 256n37
gesture of well-being (*saubhāgyamudrā*), 167, 167*f*, 179*t*
gestures. See *mudrās* (hand gestures)
Ghaṇṭākarṇa, 268n74
ghoraguṇa, 251n97
ghoraparākramarddhi, 234nn45–46
Glasenapp, Helmuth von, 226n62, 255n27, 266n56
Glincka, Małgorzata, 230n5
Gomukha, 171*f*
Goodall, Dominic, 201–2, 222n26, 241n34, 260n90
Gorāṭika monastery, 119
Gośāla, 25
Goudriaan, Teun, 269n92
Gough, Ellen, 250n86, 256n44

Granoff, Phyllis, 21–22, 229n2, 241n31, 246n32, 246n35, 250n90, 271n11
guardians of the area (*kṣetrapālas*), 182
Guhyasamājatantra, 13
Guhyatantra, 242n45
Gulābcandra, Pandit, 92
guṇa (qualities of the soul), 24, 94, 112, 184, 202, 230n6, 231n21, 253n2
Guṇākarasūri, 204–7, 213
guṇasthānas (stages of purification), 119, 120*t*, 125, 255n27
guṇavratas, 255n32
Guṇodayasāgarasūri, Ācārya, 247n44
Gupta, Sanjukta, 244n21, 266n47
guptis, 234n47
guruparamparā (guru's tradition), 248n54
gurupūjā (worship of the guru), 262n4
gurus, 18, 48–51, 54, 67–68, 81–84, 104–5, 160, 174–75, 182
guru's footprints (*pādukā*), 157*f*, 171*f*, 172, 182

hair, pulling out (*muṃḍāvaṇa*), 47–48, 54–56, 59, 66, 93
hand gestures. See *mudrās*
Haribhadrasūri, 58–59, 115, 210–11, 237n83, 241nn32–33, 271n20; *Brahmasiddhāntasamuccaya*, 64; *Pañcāśakaprakaraṇa*, 59–62, 203, 241n32; *Ṣoḍaśaprakaraṇa*, 117–18; *Yogaviṃśikā*, 117–18
Hatley, Shaman, 228n72
havana, 268n74
healing practices, 3–5, 198–201
Hegewald, Julie A. B., 240n23
Hemacandrasāgarasūri, 49–51
Hemacandrasūri, 132, 142–43, 259nn87–88, 260n92; *Abhidhānacintāmaṇi*, 250n83; *Triṣaṣṭiśalākapuruṣacarita*, 192–93; *Yogaśāstra*, 131, 137–41, 260n101
hiding gesture (*avaguṇṭhanamudrā*), 168–69
Hinduism, 9–11, 15, 46, 224n47, 225nn52–53
Hoernle, Rudolf A. F., 232n25
Holmstrom, S., 238n3
homa (fire offerings), 184–85, 229n73, 239n12, 242n46, 268n75
Hopkins, Jeffrey, 188–89, 268n84
hṛdayaśuddhi (purification of heart), 163
Hrī, 203
hutāśana (fire *maṇḍalas*), 256n36
"Hymn of the Devoted Gods" (*Bhaktāmarastotra*), 3

Iḍar Śākhā, 98
image consecration ceremonies, 73–74, 91–97, 94*f*, 245n23, 250n85, 258–59n60
image-worshiping Jains, 19, 145–55, 204, 213–14, 236n69, 246n31, 262n4
India, early modern, 228n71
indra (a king of the gods), 46, 112*f*, 113, 122–24, 128, 171*f*, 179*t*, 181
Indranandin, 227n66
Indrāṇī Devī, 171*f*
indras and *indrāṇīs*, 122–23, 256nn40–41, 265n38
Indrasenasūri, 143
initiation ceremonies, 45–107, 49*f*, 50*f*, 238n3, 239n13, 244n20; *abhiṣeka*, 12, 228n73; Digambara, 45–56, 49*f*, 50*f*, 64–67, 239nn9–11; flower-throwing rites, 58–62, 84, 241n32, 242n45; Pāñcarātra, 244n21; Śaiva, 244nn20–21; Śvetāmbara, 49–64, 52*f*, 239n9
initiation diagrams: Digambara, 97–103; *maṇḍalas*, 45–68, 242n43; Ring of Disciples (*gaṇadharavalaya*), 69–70, 70*f*, 73*f*, 95–97, 96*f*, 97*t*, 103, 136; Śvetāmbara, 97–103
initiatory gurus, 104–5
invitation gesture (*āhvāhanamudrā*), 165, 166*f*, 168
īryāpatha (Path of One's Movement), 122
īryāpathaśuddhi, 255n35
īryāpathikīsūtra (Sūtra of the Path of One's Movement), 161–62, 255n35
Isaacson, Harunaga, 201–2
Island of Rejoicing (Nandīśvaradvīpa), 111
Issitt, Micah, 266n55
Īśvarasaṃhitā, 242n45

Jacobi, Hermann, 14, 211–14
Jagatuṅga, 236n70

Jain, Hīrālāl, 236n70
Jain, Jyotindra, 250n87
Jain, Jyoti Prasad, 231n22, 261n110
Jain, Kastūrcandra "Suman," 261n106
Jain, Manju, 3–5, 199–201, 211, 270n6
Jain, Ratancandra, 89
Jain, Sagarmal, xvi, 227n70
Jain, S. C., 230n6, 253n2
Jain Studies, 225n48, 226n60, 228n72
Jain Tantra, 225n52, 227n66
Jaina Method of Curing (Manju Jain), 3–5, 199–200
Jaina Yoga (Williams), 115, 254n10
Jaini, Padmanabh S., 14, 114, 230n6, 237n77, 254n19, 255n27, 255n32, 256n44
Jainism, xvi–xvii, 21, 220n5, 224n47; as ascetic, 14–16, 114–15; canon, 15–16, 151–52, 211; councils, 263n24; early, 41; early literature, 53–58; meditation with Śaiva terms, 130–41; mendicant initiation, 45–107, 49*f*, 50*f*; mendicant ranks, 75–88, 105, 155; modern lay, 141–43; modern scholarship on, 211–14; path to liberation, 7; ritual syntax of asceticism, 201, 213–14; tantric practices, 4–5, 16, 41; true, 5, 15
Jamāli, Prince, 240n20
Jambū, 67–68
Jambūdvīpa, 192–93
Jambudweep, 72
Jambūvijaya, Muni, 150, 175, 252n102, 252n104, 259n87, 260n100
Jayā Devī, 171*f*, 191–93
jayādevīs, 179*t*, 191–93, 265n38
Jayākhyasaṃhitā, 61, 245n23, 256n38, 266n46
Jayantā, 86, 158, 171*f*, 172, 193
Jayantī, 64, 191
Jayasena (pseud. Vasubindu), 92–94, 96*f*, 239n16, 250n85
Jeanty, Roger-Orphé, 261n104
Jhavery, Mohanlal Bhagwandas, 227n70
Jinabhadrasūri, 117–19, 254n18, 254n22
Jinacandra, 200
Jinacandrasāgarasūri, 49–51
Jinadāsa, 40
Jinadeva, Bhaṭṭāraka, 134
jina icons, 95
jina images, 95
Jinamaṇisāgara, 265n39
Jinamuktisūri, Śrīpūjya, 152, 211–12
Jinapatisūri, 79–80
Jinaprabhasūri, Ācārya, xvi, 79–80, 175, 246n34, 251n97, 252n103, 253n115, 258n60; *Sūrimantrabṛhatkalpavivaraṇa*, 98, 101–2, 105–7, 181, 188, 204; *Vidhimārgaprapā*, 79–88, 85*t*, 150–53, 160, 246n38, 247n50, 248n53, 264n28
Jinaprajñā, Sādhvī, 265n35
jinas, 5, 25–26, 62, 92–93, 240n21
Jina's Preaching Assembly (*samavasaraṇa*), 240nn23–27, 264n31; early descriptions, 192; as initiation diagram, 45–68, 84, 85*t*, 104; in modern worship, 203; *nandīracanā*, 81, 83, 246n41
Jinasena, Ācārya, 65–67, 78, 118, 203, 251n97, 254n23
Jītakalpa, 264n28
Jīvājīvābhigamasūtra, 154*t*, 192–93, 269n97
Jñānamatī, Āryikā, 69–72, 92, 95, 270n4
Jñānārṇava of Śubhacandra, 137–39, 251n97, 259n89
Jñānasāgara, Ācārya, 198–99
Jñānasāra of Padmasiṃha, 133–35
Jñātādharmakathā, 55–56
Johrāpurkar, Vidyādhar P., 251n91
Jvālāmālinī, 268n74
Jvālāmālinīkalpa, 227n66
Jyotiṣakaraṇḍaka, 264n28

kālagrahaṇa, 83–84, 153–54
kālamaṅgala, 237n79
Kalānidhi, Pravartinī Sādhvī, 154, 266n52
Kalāprabhasāgarasūri, Ācārya, 145*f*
Kālī: invocations of, 173–74
Kalinga caves, 32
kalmaṣadahana (burning away of impurities), 163
Kālodāyī, 240n21
Kalpadrumavidhāna, 256n40
Kalpasūtra, 14, 153–54, 154*t*, 185–86, 211–14, 238n6, 240n24

"Kalyāṇa Chakra, the Wheel of Fortune" (Khanna), 270n4
Kalyāṇamandirastotra, 212–13, 270n4
Kāmakumāranandī, 199
Kāmikāgama, xvi, 16, 219n3, 222n19
Kāpadīā, Hirālāl Rasikdās (Hiralal Rasikdas Kapadia), 247n47, 271n12
Kapashi, Vinod, 271n19
Kapiñjalasaṃhitā, 245n23
karma, 230n5, 255n27; destruction of, 6–7, 10, 143, 213–14, 236n69, 237n79; laws of, 62
Karnataka, 89
kartranvaya (fruition acts), 65, 118
Kārttika, 111, 185
Kashmirian Śaiva tradition, 131
Kāslīvāl, Kastūrcand, 251n92
Kāslīvāl, Udaylāl, 271n18
Kāṣṭhā *saṅgha*, 89
Kastūrasūri, 174
Kaṭha Upaniṣad, 20
Kaula, 228n72
Kauṇḍinya, 222n26
Kāvya kā Kariśmā, 199
kāyabalaṛddhi, 235n55
Keśi, 213–14
Khanna, Madhu, 270n4
Kharatara Gaccha, 79–80, 147–52, 156–57, 169, 246n31, 246n35
Khāravela, 32
Kīrti, 203
Kishore, Jugal, 254n24
Koch, Rolf Heinrich, 237n83
Kopytoff, Igor, 227n68
koṣṭhabuddhiṛddhi, 232n28
Kragh, Ulrich Timm, 226n63
Kriyākoṣa of Daulatrām, 260n103
Kriyākramadyotikā of Aghoraśiva, 128–29
kriyātantra, 13
Kṛṣṇa, 18–19
kṣetramaṅgala, 237n79
kṣetrapālas (guardians of the area), 176, 182
Kubjikāmata, 131–32
Kukai, 191
Kumārapāla, 131, 137
kumbha (auspicious pots), 182
Kumudacandra, 137
Kundakunda, 53–56, 90–91, 126, 239n15
kuṇḍas, 268n74
Kunthusāgara, Ācārya, 239n10
Kuśāgranandī, Ācārya, 73*f*
Kuśalacandrasūri, Ācārya, 149

labdhipadas, 99–102, 252nn101–3
labdhis (special powers), 5, 24, 220n4, 231n23
Laghu Śākhā, 80
Laidlaw, James, 268n83
Lakṣmī, 100*t*, 171*f*, 173–74, 180, 180*f*, 203; fire offerings to, 184–85; worship of the fourth section of the *sūrimantra* dedicated to, 181–85, 183*f*
Lākula Śaivas, 222n25
Lalitavistarā, 241n33
lamp (*dīpaka*): establishment of, 182
language, 21, 229n2
laukāntika gods, 267n68
Lecher antenna, 146
Lefeber, Rosalind, 271n11
Leumann, Ernst, 236n68
Liberation: path to, xv–xvi, 7–9, 111–43, 254n18; stages on (*guṇasthānas*), 119, 120*t*, 125, 255n27
liberation-granting mantras, 63–64. *See also* mantras
Long, Jeffery D., 14
Loṅkāgaccha, 229n76
Loṅkā Śāh, 229n76, 247n41
Lopez, Donald, 8
Lotus Gesture (*padmamudrā*), 182
lotus motif, 256n43

Mace, Sonya Rhie, 24
Mādhavasena, 135, 259n79
Madhumatī, 255n25
magic, 16–17
magical spells, 29–30
Mahābandha of Bhūtabali, 26–29, 34
Mahākarmaprakṛtiprābhṛta, 34
mahāmantras, 269n89
Mahāniśīthasūtra, 30–31, 63, 80–81, 85*t*, 153–54, 154*t*, 190, 235n59, 236n69

Mahāprajña, Ācārya, xvi–xvii
Mahāpratyākhyāna, 264n28
mahāpūjanas (great worship ceremonies), 142, 220n5
Mahārāja, Paṇḍita (Ācārya Yugabhūṣaṇasūri), 155, 265n35, 266n52
mahattarās (female mendicant leaders), 265n35; promotion ceremony, 81, 85*t*, 86, 155, 248n53, 266n52; required study, 155
Mahāvairocana, 13, 242n45, 256n39
Mahāvairocanābhisambodhitantra (*Mahāvairocanatantra*), 12–13, 223n34, 223n36, 223n39
Mahāvīra, 4, 25, 46–47, 63–64, 116, 178, 238n6, 240n21; death of, 185–86; *ṇamo vaḍḍhamāṇaṃ* (Praise to the Mahāvīra), 96–97; in *pañcaprasthānavidhi*, 180, 180*f*; in *sūrimantrapaṭa*, 171*f*, 174; *vardhamānamantra* (mantra of Mahāvīra), 48, 93, 97*t*, 249n81; *vardhamānavidyā* (Spell of Mahāvīra), 64, 84–88, 85*t*, 104, 159; *vardhamānavidyāpaṭa* (Cloth Diagram of the Spell of Mahāvīra), 85*t*, 86, 146–69, 157*f*, 161*f*, 166*f*, 191, 197, 248n52
Mahāvīrakīrti, 239n10
mahāvrata (five mendicant vows), 7, 47–48, 54, 63, 80, 83–84, 90–91, 153, 201, 213
mahāyogatantras, 13
Main, Carlyn, 266n55
Mālava, 92, 119, 135, 255n25
Mālinīvijayottaratantra, 141
Mallī, 240n21
Mallinson, James, 224n46
Malliṣeṇa, 227n66
Mānatuṅga, 204, 270n8
maṇḍalas, 9, 220n5, 228n73; All-Gathering Maṇḍala, 61–62, 242n40; *bhūmaṇḍalas*, 257n52; Buddhist, 12; Digambara, 97, 97*t*; earth, 256n42; fire, 256n36; Genzu, 191; of initiation, 45–68, 81, 85*t*, 97, 97*t*, 242n43; with *jayādevīs*, 191; lotus motif, 256n43; modern use, 243n5; ritual use, 15; *ṛṣimaṇḍala*, 269n102; in tantric traditions, 142, 201–2; throwing flowers onto, 58–62; *yāgamaṇḍalas*, 95, 250n87
maṅgalas, 19–24, 31–40. See also *ṛddhi-maṅgala*
Maṇibhadra, 268n74
Maṇiprabhasāgara, Upādhyāya, 160–61, 161*f*, 198–99
Mañjuśriyamūlakalpa, 13, 191
Manthānabhairava, 131–32
"mantra bath" (*mantrasnāna*), 163
Mantradvātriṃśikākalpa, 260n100
mantramārga (path of mantras), 9–11, 13, 17, 222n19
mantrarāja, 253n115
Mantrarājarahasya of Siṃhatilakasūri, 98–101, 100*t*, 147, 160, 190–91, 204, 266n57
mantras, 3–8, 20–24, 227n68, 230n8; *ācāryamantra*, 72; *aṅgamantras*, 257n60; *apraticakrā-mantra*, 70–71, 96*f*, 98–99, 102, 252nn101–2, 260n100; *brahmamantras*, 257n60; *bṛhadśāntimantra*, 197, 270n3; Buddhist, 12; daily use, xvi; diagrams that contain (see *yantras*); Digambara, 69–76, 88–91, 97, 97*t*; *gaṇadharavalayamantra*, 207–8, 251n97, 252n103; imposition on body (*nyāsa*), 11, 17, 114, 121–23, 163–64, 190, 257n53, 269n87; of initiation, 45–68, 69–107, 85*t*, 97*t*; of liberation, 63–64; *mahāmantras*, 269n89; modern use, 197–214; numbered, 259n77; *padasthadhyāna*, 133–34; *pañcanamaskāra* ("Fivefold Praise"), xvi, 22–24, 33–40, 75, 236n71, 258n60, 266n53; path of (*mantramārga*), 9–10; Prakrit, 229n4; *ṛddhimantras*, 69; repetition (*japa*), 13, 179*t*, 202; ritual use, 9–13, 48–49, 49*f*, 84–85, 126–29, 142, 223n36, 226n63, 242n46; Sanskrit, 229n4; *sūrimantra* (Mantra of the Mendicant Leader), 70–71, 84–88, 85*t*, 90, 97, 97*t*, 104–5, 172–73, 198, 250n85, 251n97, 253n112, 262n5; Śvetāmbara, 69–76, 79–88, 85*t*; tantric traditions, xvi–xvii, 143, 201–2; *vardhamānamantra* (mantra of Mahāvīra), 48, 93, 97*t*, 249n81; *vicakrāya svāhā*, 102
mantraśāstra, 3–7, 16, 21–22, 89, 107, 226n62
Manusmṛti, 244n18
Maraṇasamādhi, 264n28
Mathura, 262n2
Māthura *saṅgha*, 89

Mattamayūras, 255n25
meditation, 261n115; Amitagati's text on, 135–36; categories of, 260n101; components of, 116–18; definition of, 116, 132; Devasena's development of, 119–26; Devasena's texts on, 132–33; *dharmadhyāna*, 135, 255n31; *dhyāna*, 116–17, 130, 254nn15–16, 255n31, 261n115; on diagrams, 115, 119, 129–30; Digambara practices, 130–41; Jain, 130–41; on mantras, 121, 129; as a means of liberation, 111–43, 254n18; objects of (*dhyeya*), 114–15, 125–27, 130, 139, 142, 261n110; *padastha*, 130–41, 259n85; Padmasiṃha's text on, 133–35; *piṇḍastha*, 130–41, 258n76, 259n85; pure (*śukla*), 38, 116–17, 125, 129–30, 133, 136, 259n88; Rāmasena's development of, 126–30; Rāmasena's texts on, 132–33; reflective (*bhāvanās*), 137; ritual use of *yantras* as, 142–43; *rūpastha*, 130–41; *rūpātīta*, 130–41; *rūpavarjita*, 132–33, 138–39, 260n93; *stha*, 130–41, 259n72, 260n101; *śukladhyāna*, 116; with support (*ālambana*), 117–18, 121, 130, 141; without support (*anālambana*, *nirālambana*), 117–18, 121, 132–33; tantric, 111–43, 268n84; *tattvabhū dhāraṇā*, 260n92; *tattvarūpavatī dhāraṇā*, 260n92; types of, 116–17, 132–36; virtuous (*dharma/dharmya*), 117–19, 135–36, 142–43, 255n31
Megha, Prince, 55, 240n20
Mehta, Gita, 238n3
Mehta, Suketu, 45
Mehtalia, Jigar, 200–201, 270n6
mendicants: Digambara, 88–97, 94*f*, 105; female, 75, 155, 265n35; female leader (*mahattarā*, *pravartinī*), 75, 81, 85*t*, 86, 155, 248n53, 265n35, 266n52; group (*gacćha*, *gaṇa*), 78–79, 89, 148–150; group leader (*gaṇadhara*, *gaṇin*), 75–76, 151–53, 154*t*, 169; higher levels, 75, 84–88; initiation, 45–107, 49*f*, 50*f*, 85*t*, 94*f*, 97*t*, 203; itinerant, 148–49; leader (*ācārya*, *sūri*), 49–51, 52*f*, 75–76, 81, 85*t*, 86–90, 97, 97*t*, 105, 151; *mūrtipūjaka*, 149; novice (*śaikṣa*, *antevāsin*), 75; ordinary (*sādhu*), 75; ordination (*upasthāpanā*), 83–84, 85*t*; *pravartin*, 75–76; preacher (*vācaka*, *vācanācārya*), 75, 80, 85–87, 85*t*, 265n40; promotion ceremonies, 150–51, 155, 248n53; ranks, 75–88, 105, 155; renunciation (*pravrajyā*), 81–84; required study, 155; respecting (*vinaya*), 144–45; scholar (*pannyāsa*, *paṇḍita*), 151; serving (*vaiyāvṛttya*), 144–45; *sthavira*, 75; Śvetāmbara, 79–88, 91; tantric ritual history, 190–95; teacher (*upādhyāya*), 49–51, 75–76, 85*t*, 86, 89–90, 97, 97*t*, 151, 155, 248n53; temple images of, 95
Merutuṅgasūri, 98, 160, 175, 245n28
Mīnarāja, 31
mind-reading, 93, 237n82
Minkowski, Christopher, 23
minor vows (*anuvrata*), 255n32
missionaries, 224n47
modernity, 16–17
modern mantras, 197–214
modern monks, 103–7, 144–95, 213–14
modern scholarship, 211–14
modern *yantras*, 141–43
mokṣa-mārg ideology, 220n8
Molendijk, Arie L., 272n23
monasteries (*maṭha*), 89
monastic orders, 75–79
monks: daily practices, 266n45; Digambara, 103–7; initiation ceremonies, 72–74, 81, 85*t*, 91–97, 94*f*, 97*t*; initiation levels, 104; lineages, 78–79; modern, 103–7, 144–95, 213–14; *mūrtipūjaka*, 49, 148–53, 154*t*, 169, 211; naked, 104–5; ordinary (*muni*), 151; ranks, 75–79, 151; Śvetāmbara, 103–7; tantric rituals, 144–95
Mount Meru, 192
Mṛgendrāgama, 168
mudrās (hand gestures), xv, 9, 247n43, 266n47, 266n51, 267n65; Buddhist, 12; opened oyster shell (*muktāśukti*), 59, 81; tantric traditions, 142, 168–69, 201–2; teaching gesture (*pravacanamudrā*), 188, 189*f*; for Worship Ceremony of the Five Sections (*pañcaprasthānavidhi*), 177–78, 179*t*

Muḥammad bīn Tughluq, 79
Mukhtār, Jugalkiśor, 126
muktāśuktimudrā, 59, 81
Mūlācāra, 32–33, 48, 55, 68, 75–76, 212, 236n68
Mūlamadhyakakārikā of Nāgārjuna, 32
Mūla Saṅgha, 89
Mūlasūtra, 10, 61, 222n26
mūlasūtras (root scriptures), 151–54, 154*t*, 246n38
Müller, Friedrich Max, 211, 271n23
muṃḍāvaṇa (pulling out of one's hair), 55–56, 93
Munisundarasūri, 181
mūrtipūjaka, 19, 49, 148–51, 154*t*, 169, 211, 268n74

Nāgacandra, 207–8
Nāgārjuna, 32
naimittikas (types of divination), 233n34
Nākoḍābhairava, 268n74
Nāmamaṅgala, 237n79
namaskāras, 38
Ṇamokār, 22
ṇamo vaḍḍhamāṇaṃ (Praise to the Mahāvīra), 96–97
nandī, *nandīkriyā*, or *nandīvidhi*, 82–83, 153–54, 264nn31–32
Nandi, Ramendra Nath, 255n25
Nandighoṣasūri, Ācārya, 146–48, 154–55, 166*f*, 174; *sūrimantrapaṭa* (Cloth Diagram of the Mantra of the Mendicant Leader), 169–74, 170*f*, 171*f*; worship of the Cloth Diagram of the Mantra of the Mendicant Leader (*sūrimantrapaṭa*), 176; worship of the Five Sections (*pañcaprasthānavidhi*), 178–90, 180*f*, 183*f*, 187*f*, 189*f*
nandīracanā, 81, 83, 246n41
Nandīsūtra, 80–85, 154*t*, 247n47, 264n28, 271n14
Nandīśvaradvīpa (Island of Rejoicing), 111, 122–23
nandyāvarta (extended *svastika*), 182, 268n72, 268n74
Narakavibhakti, 264n28
navanidhi (nine treasures), 171*f*, 172, 266n56
Navkār, 22
Nayacandrasāgara, 50–51, 52*f*, 160–68, 239n13
Nemacanda, 91
Nemicandra, 92–95, 103, 139, 252n108
Nemisūri, Ācārya, 148–49, 174–75, 177
Nepal, 266n55
nikṣepa, 36–37, 127, 237nn78–79
nine treasures (*navanidhi*), 171*f*, 172, 266n56
nirālambana (meditation without support), 132–33
Nirvāṇakalikā, 245n26
nirvikṛtika fasts, 83–84
Niśvāsamukha, 9–10, 222n19
Niśvāsatattvasaṃhitā, 10, 61, 222n26, 245n25
nitthāragapāragāhoha ("May you pass beyond the cycle of rebirth"), 146
Nitya Ārādhanā Vidhi ("Ritual for Daily Worship") of Somacandrasūri, 175–77
Nityānanda, Gaṇin, 264n28
nityāpūjā, 255n34
nīvi, 247n48
"No Fixed Sequence" (*anānupūrvī*), 141
Nokār, 22
non-Saiddhāntika Mantramārga, 223n29
novice mendicants (*śaikṣa*), 75
nudity, 104–5
Numark, Mitch, 224n47
numbered mantras, 259n77
nuns, 69–70, 70*f*, 155
nyāsa, 11, 17, 114, 121–23, 163–64, 190, 257n53, 269n87

objects of meditation (*dhyeya*), 114–15, 125–27, 130, 139, 142, 261n110
Oghaniryuktisūtra, 152, 155, 246n38
Ohira, Suzuko, 24, 231n19, 254n16, 255n27, 269n96
Olivelle, Patrick, 68
oṃ, 20, 35, 229n1, 256n44
omniscience, 93–94
ordination (*upasthāpanā*), 83–84
Orientalism, 224n47
Orzech, Charles, 67, 185

pacification (*śānti*) rites, 228n73
padastha, 130–41, 259n85

padasthadhyāna, 132–34, 136
padasthadhyeya, 139
padmamudrā (Lotus Gesture), 182
Padmanandin, 98, 251n92, 252n108
Padmasiṃha, 133–35, 142–43
Padmāvatī, 268n74
Padoux, André, 9, 15, 21–22, 261n104
painted eyes, 170–71, 266n55
pākṣikapratikramaṇa, 197, 270n2
Pal, Pratapaditya, 243n3
Pali Canon, 11–12
Palitana, 175, 198
Pañcagulī, 268n74
Pañcakalpa, 264n28
pañcakalyāṇaka (five auspicious events), 92–93
pañcanamaskāra (Fivefold Praise), xvi, 22–24, 75, 236n71, 258n60, 266n53; commentary on, 33–40; ritual use of, 51–53, 52*f*, 85*t*
pañcaparameṣṭimudrā, 122, 179*t*
pañcaparameṣṭin (Five Supreme Beings), 22, 34, 48, 51, 121–25, 127, 130, 132–35, 140–42, 162, 164, 168, 176, 214, 256n44, 257n53
pañcaprasthāna ("Five Sections"), 149
pañcaprasthānavidhi (Worship Ceremony of the Five Sections): becoming Gautama for Dīvālī, 185–90; concluding fire offerings for Lakṣmī Devī, 181–85; required rites, 177–78, 179*t*; shrines for, 178–86, 180*f*, 183*f*, 187*f*, 194–95
Pāñcarātra, 9–11, 223n29, 225n52, 242n45, 244n20, 256n38; daily rites, 11, 266n45; flower-throwing rites, 61; initiation rites, 11, 61, 77, 222n26, 244n21
Pañcāśakaprakaraṇa of Haribhadrasūri, 59–60, 62, 203, 241n32
pañcavaktramudrā, 168–69
Pandit, Piyush, 199
paṇḍitas (mendicant scholars), 151
Pāṇini, 152
pannyāsa (mendicant scholar), 151, 155–56, 160, 263n20
Paramāra kings, 135
parameṣṭhimudrā (Five Supreme Beings gesture), 167–69, 167*f*, 256n37
parameṣṭhinyāsa, 164
Paras TV, 142
paravidyocchedinī (Spell That Neutralizes Other Spells), 206
Pārśvacandra Gaccha, 246n31
Paryuṣaṇa, 213
Pāśupatas, 10, 222n21
Pāśupatasūtra, 222n21, 222n26, 257n60
paṭa (cloth diagram), 85*t*, 156, 160–61, 220n5, 265n40, 267n63. See also *sūrimantrapaṭa*; *vardhamānavidyāpaṭa*
Patañjali, 132, 259n73
Path of One's Movement (*īryāpatha*), 122
Pāṭil, Śivgouḍā, 104–5
Paumacariya of Vimalasūri, 230n8
Paurṇamatī Mātā, 270n3
pauṣṭikavidhāna ceremony, 268n74
piṇḍa, 132, 141
Piṇḍaniryuktisūtra, 155, 246n38
piṇḍastha, 130–41, 259n85
piṇḍasthadhyāna, 132–33, 138, 258n76
Pingree, David, 235n63
power of the intellect (*buddhiṛddhi*), 237n82
powers of austerities, 251n97
Prabandhacintāmaṇi of Merutuṅgasūri, 245n28
Prabhācandrasūri, 21–22, 98, 204, 251n92
Prabhāvakacarita of Prabhācandrasūri, 204
Pradyumnasūri, Ācārya, 261n113
pragmatic texts, 226n63
Pragya, Samani Pratibha, 254n18
praise(s): Fivefold Praise (*pañcanamaskāra*), xvi, 22–24, 33–40, 51–53, 52*f*, 75, 85*t*, 236n71, 258n60, 266n53; litany to practitioners with superhuman powers, 26; litany to the Digambara tradition (*digambarāmnaya*), 105–6; to the Mahāvīra (*ṇamo vaḍḍhamāṇaṃ*), 96–97; power of, 40–41; Prakrit, 5, 17–18, 22
Prajñāpanāsūtra, 21, 154*t*, 255n27
prakīrṇakas (miscellaneous scriptures), 29, 80, 85, 151–53, 246n40, 264n28, 264–65n34
Prakrit litany, 5, 17–18, 22
Prakrit mantras, 229n4
Pramukhasāgara, 72
Praṇāmasāgara, 72

Prārthanāsāgara, Muni, 227n70
Praśnavyākaraṇasūtra, 23, 231n14
prasthānas, 252n98
prātihāryas, 259n85, 271n19
pratikramaṇa, 54, 80, 161, 197, 236n71, 265n42, 270n2
pratimās, 271n13
pratiṣṭhācārya (ritual specialists), 92
Pratiṣṭhāpāṭha of Jayasena, 92–94, 96*f*, 250n85
Pratiṣṭhāpāṭha of Vasunandin, 92–94, 249n73
Pratiṣṭhā Ratnākar, 92
Pratiṣṭhāsāroddhāra of Āśādhara, 92
Pratiṣṭhātilaka of Nemicandra, 92–95, 139
pratyekabuddhas, 250n90
pravacanamudrā (teaching gesture), 167, 167*f*, 188, 189*f*
Pravacanasāra of Kundakunda, 53–56, 90–91
pravartinīs (female mendicant leaders), 265n35; promotion ceremony, 81, 85*t*, 86, 155, 248n53, 266n52; required study, 155
pravartins, 75–76
pravrajyā (renunciation), 81–84
preaching assemblies. *See* Jina's Preaching Assembly (*samavasaraṇa*)
preserving gesture (*sannidhānamudrā*), 165, 166*f*, 168
Priyadarśanā, Sādhvī, 261n103
promotion ceremonies. *See* initiation ceremonies
proper conduct (*ācāra*), 249n69
prosperity ceremony (*pauṣṭikavidhāna*), 268n74
protective *vajras*, 257n46
Protestants, 152, 224n47
pṛthvīmaṇḍalas, 256n42
pūjā: Bīsapanthī, 253n4; clothes for, 267n70; communal, 256n41; eightfold (*aṣṭaka*), 112*f*, 113, 253n4; *gurupūjā* (worship of the guru), 262n4; *nityāpūjā*, 255n34; tantric, 255n34; Terāpanthī, 113
Pūjyapāda, Ācārya, 116, 119–20, 254n16
Pulakasāgara, 72
pulling out of one's hair (*muṃḍāvaṇa*), 55–56, 93
Puṇḍarīka, 178
Purandara, 255n25
pure meditation (*śukladhyāna*), 38, 116–17, 125, 129–30, 133, 136, 259n88
purification of one's heart (*hṛdayaśuddhi*), 163
purification of the space (*bhūmiśuddhi*), 163
purification rituals, 256n38
purification stages (*guṇasthānas*), 119, 120*t*, 125, 255n27
Pūrṇacandrasāgarasūri, 50–51, 151, 155, 239n13, 264n28
Pūrṇimā Gaccha, 160
Puruṣārthānuśāsanagata Śrāvakācāra, 260n103
pūrvas, 27, 30, 34–35, 232n33
Pushpagiri, 72
Puṣpadanta, 34, 236n71
Puṣpadantasāgara, Ācārya, 72
putraka, 76–77

qualities of the soul (*guṇa*), 24, 94, 112, 202, 184, 230n6, 231n21, 253n2
Qvarnström, Olle, 131

Rājapraśnīyasūtra, 154*t*
Rājaśekharasūri, Ācārya, 98, 175, 181, 252n98, 267n62
Rājayaśasūri, Ācārya, 198–99
Rāmacandrasūri, Ācārya, 154, 198–99
Rāmasena, 126–30, 132–33, 142–43
Rastelli, Marion, 241n34, 260n90
Ratnaśekharasūri, 261n107
Rawson, Philip S., 262n12
Rāyamalla, Brahmacārin, 207–8, 271n18
ṛddhi-maṅgala, 5, 17–18, 23–41; *Bhaktāmarastotra* association, 204–13; evolution, 201–4; modern scholarship, 211–14; modern use, 197–201; ritual use, 29–31, 48–49, 71–72, 98–99, 136. *See also* Ring of Disciples (*gaṇadharavalaya*)
ṛddhimantra, 69
ṛddhis (extraordinary powers), 24, 173, 220n4, 270n4
reflective meditations (*bhāvanās*), 137
renunciation: *dīkṣā*, 45–47, 238n3; *muṃḍāvaṇa* (pulling out of one's hair), 55–56, 93; *pravrajyā*, 81–84

respecting mendicants (*vinaya*), 144–45
retaining gesture (*sannirodhamudrā*), 165, 166*f*, 168
Ṛgvedasaṃhitā, 20
Right Conduct (*sāmācārī*), 151
Ring of Disciples (*gaṇadharavalaya*), 39–40, 90, 115, 197, 252n103, 252n108, 270n4; as diagram of initiation and promotion, 69–70, 70*f*, 73*f*, 95–97, 96*f*, 97*t*, 103, 136; Digambara sources on, 102–3; early descriptions, 203
ritual diagrams: Digambara, 141; early, 203; *maṇḍala*-like, 203; meditation on, 115; of mendicant promotion, 97–103; Śvetāmbara, 169–70, 170*f*, 171*f*
ritualized sex, 7–8, 228n72
ritual language, 229n2
ritual objects, 261n110
rituals, 144–45, 247n46, 267n67; ablution (*abhiṣeka*), 12, 76–77, 90, 197, 223n33, 270n3; *bhūtaśuddhi* rites, 122; daily practices, 109–95, 266n45, 269n87; fire-offering rites, 229n73; flower-throwing rites, 58–62, 84, 241n32, 242n45; great worship ceremonies (*mahāpūjanas*), 142, 220n5; Jain syntax of asceticism, 201, 213–14; of liberation, 9; mantra-based, 9, 13, 84–85, 223n36, 226n63, 242n46; of modern monks, 144–95; pacification (*śānti*), 228n73; tantric, xv, 19, 144–95, 225n52; unification (*sakalīkaraṇa*), 122–28, 142, 165, 168, 253n3, 256n39, 256n41, 257n53, 257–58nn59–60, 266n46, 269n87; worship ceremonies (*vidhānas*), 114, 142, 220n5, 239n12, 256n40. *See also specific rites*
ṛjumati, 232n32
rogāpahāriṇī (Spell That Rids One of Illness), 205
Rohiṇī Devī, 171*f*
Roth, Gustav, 231n17
Royal Asiatic Society, 262n12
Ṛṣabha, 25, 99, 178, 203, 236n71
Ṛṣabhadatta, 240n21
Ṛṣibhāṣita ("Sayings of Seers"), 80–81, 85
ṛṣimaṇḍala, 269n102
Rsimandalastotra, 220n5
Rudrapallīya Gaccha, 204
rūpa (form), 117–18, 121, 130, 141
rūparahita, 137, 259n85
rūpasthadhyāna, 130–41
rūpātīta, 130–41
rūpavarjita, 132–33, 138

sādhaka, 76–77, 244n20
sādhu (ordinary mendicant), 22, 75, 238n85
sādhvī (ordinary nun), 155, 247n44, 265n35
Sāgara Śākhā (Tapā Gaccha), 239n13
Śāh, Ambālāl Premcand, 263n12
Śāh, Dhīrajlāl Ṭokarśī, 16, 226n64
Saiddhāntika Śaivism, 119
śaikṣa (novice mendicant), 75
Śailaka, King, 240n20
Śaiva Age, 78, 225n52, 225n55
Śaiva Atimārga, 9–14, 63–64, 221n18, 222n19, 222nn24–5, 228n72
Śaiva Kūlamārga, 11, 131–32, 266n45
Śaiva Mantramārga, 9–14, 20–21, 63–64, 221n18, 228n72; initiation ceremonies, 77–78; initiation levels, 76–77, 244n20; non-Saiddhāntika, 223n29
Śaiva Siddhānta, 223n29, 245n29; initiation ceremonies, 77; meditation practices, 128–29; monastery Gorāṭika, 119; *Mṛgendrāgama*, 168; *sādhyamantra*, 248n56
Śaivism, 9–10, 220n18, 225n52, 244n20; initiation ceremonies, 77–78; initiation levels, 76–77; meditation practices, 128–29; meditation terms, 130–41; Tantric, 9–10; unification rites (*sakalīkaraṇa*), 122
Sakalacandra, 207–8, 260n101
Sakalakīrti, 98, 251n92
sakalīkaraṇa (unification) rites, 122–28, 142, 165, 168, 253n3, 256n39, 256n41, 257–58nn59–60, 257n53, 266n46, 269n87
Śakti, 223n29
salutation gesture (*añjalimudrā*), 163, 166*f*, 167, 167*f*
salvation, 225n51
sāmācārī texts, 151, 263n19
Samagra Jain Cāturmās Sūcī, 147

Samaṇ Suttaṁ, 72
samavasaraṇa (Jina's Preaching Assembly), 240nn23–27, 264n31; early descriptions, 192; as an initiation diagram, 45–68, 84, 85*t*, 104; in modern worship, 203; *nandīracanā*, 81, 83, 246n41
Samavāyāṅgasūtra, 154*t*
samayin, 76–77
samitis, 234n47, 240n18
Saṃstāraka, 264n28
samyaktva, 82, 112, 120, 135
Sanderson, Alexis, 9–10, 131–32, 191, 220n18, 222n19, 225n52, 225n55, 228n72, 242n43
Saṅghadāsa, 240n24
Sanmatisāgara, Muni, 105
sannidhānamudrā (proximity gesture), 165, 166*f*, 168
sannirodhamudrā (restraining gesture), 165, 166*f*, 168
Sanskrit, ix, 20, 229n4
Santalāla, Paṇḍit, 111–12
śāntidhārā, 197
Śāntisūri, Ācārya, 136–37
Sarasvatī, 31, 100*t*, 171*f*, 172–74, 180, 180*f*
sarasvatīvidyā (Spell of Sarasvatī), 205
Sarvākṣarasannipātin, 232n33
Sarvārthasiddha, 67
Sarvārthasiddhi of Pūjyapāda, 116, 119–20, 254n16
Sarvatathāgatatattvasaṅgraha, 12–13, 67
śāsanadevatā (deities of the teachings), 102
Śāstrī, Devendrakumār, 236n71
Śāstrī, Lālārām, 256n36
Ṣaṭkhaṇḍāgama ("Scripture of Six Parts"), 19, 22, 212, 232nn25–26, 255n27; *ṛddhi-maṅgala*, 23–31, 38, 198, 202–3
Sātvatasaṃhitā, 61
saubhāgyamudrā (gesture of well-being), 167, 167*f*, 179*t*
saubhāgyavidyā, 99
Saumyaguṇā, Sādhvī, 245n26, 246n41
savaiyā, 106
"Sayings of Seers" (*Ṛṣibhāṣita*), 80–81
Śayyambhava, Ārya, 82
Schubring, Walther, 235n59, 263n21
Scripture of the Mantra of Amoghapāśa's Miraculous Transformations (Bodhiruci), 185
Scriptures: appendices (*cūlikā*), 151–52, 154*t*; canonical texts (*āgamas*), 15–16, 80–81, 151–53, 211, 244n20, 263n25, 264n26, 264n28, 264n32; Digambara, 152, 263n25; Jain Canon, 151–53, 211; limb or main texts (*aṅga*), 85, 151–52, 154*t*; miscellaneous scriptures (*prakīrṇakas*), 85, 151–53, 246n40, 264n28, 264–65n34; pragmatic texts, 226n63; *pūrvas*, 34, 232n33; required study for female mendicants, 155; required study for modern monks, 152–53, 154*t*; root scriptures (*mūlasūtras*), 151–54, 154*t*, 246n38; rule books (*chedasūtra*), 85, 151–53, 154*t*; *sāmācārī* texts, 263n19; sub-limbs or subsidiary texts (*upāṅga*), 151–52, 154*t*; Śvetāmbara, 152–53; of *yogavidhi*, 85, 151–53. *See also specific texts*
secrecy, 87, 105, 142, 147–48
sedentary ascetics, 148–49
Sena Gaṇa, 89
serving mendicants (*vaiyāvṛttya*), 144–45
sex, ritualized, 228n72
Shah, Jitendra, 210
Shah, Priyabala, 247n43, 256n37
Shah, Umakant P., 227n70, 228n72, 231n17, 240n26, 248n52, 257n45
Shāntā, N., 238n3
Sharf, Robert, 18–19, 142
Sharma, Mangal, 156
Shinohara, Koichi, 228n73
shrines, 29; for worship of the Cloth Diagram of the Spell of Mahāvīra (*vardhamānavidyāpaṭa*), 160–61, 161*f*; for Worship of the Five Sections (*pañcaprasthānavidhi*), 178–86, 180*f*, 183*f*, 187*f*, 194–95
siddha (liberated, or pure soul), 22, 32, 53, 66–67, 112, 114, 122, 132, 135, 138, 186, 190, 222n21, 238n85
Siddhabhakti, 251n97
siddhacakra (Wheel of the Liberated Soul), 127, 197, 250n89, 259n82, 261n107, 261n113; *bṛhatsiddhacakra* (Expanded Wheel

of the Liberated Soul), 123–24; *siddha-cakravidhāna* (Worship Ceremony of the Wheel of the Liberated Soul), 111–15, 112*f*, 121–26
Siddhacakrapūjā of Śubhacandra, 111–12
siddhacakravidhāna (Worship Ceremony of the Wheel of the Liberated Soul), 111–15, 112*f*, 121–26
Siddhacakra Vidhān of Santalāla, 111–12
Siddhaprābhṛta, 264n28
siddhapratimā, 250n89
siddhis (superhuman powers), 5, 10, 12–13, 24–31, 41, 173, 201, 220n4, 222n24, 228n73, 231n16, 231n18
śikhimaṇḍalas (fire *maṇḍalas*), 256n36
śikṣāvratas, 255n32
Siṃhatilakasūri, 98–101, 103, 175, 251n95; *Mantrarājarahasya*, 147, 160, 190–91, 204; *Vardhamānavidyākalpa*, 190–91
Sindhurāja, 135
Singleton, Mark, 224n46
Sirivālacariya of Ratnaśekharasūri, 261n107
Sisters of Tumburu, 191, 269n92
Sīyaka II, 119
Skandaka, 240n21
social traditions, 67–68
Ṣoḍaśaprakaraṇa of Haribhadrasūri, 117–18
Somacandrasūri, Ācārya, xvi, 175, 267nn62–63; *Nitya Ārādhanā Vidhi* ("Ritual for Daily Worship"), 175–77; *Śrīsūrimantrapañcaprasthānaprārambhavidhi*, 177–78, 181
Somadevasūri, 132
Somasena, 207–8, 213, 271n16
Sonagiri, Madhya Pradesh, 89
Soni, Jayandra, 237n76
soul (*jīva*), 6–7, 20–21, 24, 35–36, 127, 129, 147, 171; disembodied, 136, 139; liberated, pure, or purified (*siddha*), 22, 32, 53, 66–67, 112, 114, 122, 132, 135, 138, 186, 190, 222n21, 238n85; meditation on, 116, 127–29, 133, 143, 202; omniscient, or enlightened (*arhat*), 22, 96, 120, 123–24, 127–29, 133–34, 143, 182, 203, 238n85; qualities of (*guṇa*), 24, 94, 112, 202, 184, 230n6, 231n21, 253n2
South Asian Buddhism, 231n18
spell goddesses (*vidyādevī*), 124, 180*t*, 257n45, 265n38
Spell of Bāhubali (*bāhubalividyā*), 99–100, 173, 179*t*
Spell of Mahāvīra (*vardhamānavidyā*), 64; Cloth Diagram of the Spell of Mahāvīra (*vardhamānavidyāpaṭa*), 85*t*, 86, 146–69, 157*f*, 161*f*, 166*f*, 191, 197, 248n52; imparting, 84–88, 85*t*; second *vardhamānavidyā*, 159; texts on, 104
Spell of Sarasvatī (*sarasvatīvidyā*), 205
Spell of Śrutadevatā (*Mahāniśīthasūtra*), 30
Spell of Tribhuvanasvāminī, Giver of All Desires, 206
spells, 235n62; of the *Aṅgavidyā* ("Knowledge of the Parts of the Body"), 29–30; *vidyās*, 21–22, 230n8, 267n64
Spell That Bestows Wealth (*śrīsampādinī*), 206
Spell That Destroys Faults (*doṣanirnāśinī*), 206
Spell That Frees One from Bonds (*bandhamokṣiṇī*), 206
Spell That Gets Rid of Poison (*viṣāpahāriṇī*), 206
Spell That Neutralizes Other Spells (*paravidyocchedinī*), 206
Spell That Pacifies Dangerous Things (*aśivopaśamanī*), 206–7
Spell That Rids One of Illness (*rogāpahāriṇī*), 205
spiritual development (*guṇasthāna*), 119, 120*t*, 125, 255n27
Śrāvakācāra of Amitagati, 135–36, 139, 203
Śrāvakācāra of Vasunandin, 134
Śrāvakācār Saṅgrah, 255n33, 260n102
Śrī, 100*t*, 203
Śrī Atiśay Kṣetra, 89
śrīcakra, 160, 259n83
Śrī Digambar Jain Candraprabhujī Mandir (Aṅkroṃ kā Rāstā, Kiśanpol Bāzār, Jaipur), 106
śrīpūjyas, 148–49
śrīsampādinī (Spell That Bestows Wealth), 206
Śrīsūrimantrapañcaprasthānaprārambhavidhi, 177–78, 181
Śrī Vardhmānvidyā Nitya Ārādhanā Vidhi, 160

Śrīvidyā tradition, 259n83
Śrutadevatā, 30–31, 173, 235n61
Śrutakevalin, 232n33
Stephen, Michele, 255n34
stha meditations, 130, 259n72, 260n101
Sthānakavāsī Jainism, 19, 30, 236n69
Sthānāṅgasūtra, 75, 117, 154*t*, 231n23, 244n12, 247n50, 269n102
sthāpanācārya, 51, 83–84, 176, 239n14
Sthāpanāmaṅgala, 237n79
sthāpanāmudrā (establishing gesture), 165, 166*f*, 168
sthavira, 75–76, 265n40
sthavirī, 75
Sthūlabhadra, 232n33
stūpas, 266n55
Subāhuparipṛcchaśāstra, 231n18
Śubhacandra, 137, 259n87, 260n92; *Jñānārṇava*, 137–39, 251n87
Śubhacandra, Bhaṭṭāraka, 98, 103, 142–43, 251n92, 252n108; *Siddhacakrapūjā*, 111–12
Subhadrā, 240n21
Śubhakarasiṃha, 12–13, 77
Śubhaṅkarasūri, 12, 174
Subodhāsāmācārī of Candrasūri, 151
Sudharman Svāmin, 173, 251
śukladhyāna (abstract or pure meditation), 38, 116–17, 125, 129–30, 133, 136, 259n88
superhuman powers (*labdhi*, *ṛddhi*, *siddhi*), 3, 5, 10, 12, 24–31, 39, 41, 69, 74, 99, 103, 136, 148, 159, 173, 190, 197, 201–202, 231n18, 232–235nn28–57, 237nn81–82, 251n97, 259n83, 269n89, 270n1
supreme yoga (*anuttarayoga*), 13
surabhimudrā (celestial cow gesture), 165, 166*f*
Surendrasūri, Ācārya, 198–99
Sūri Mahāmantra Mandir, 175
sūrimantra (Mantra of the Mendicant Leader), 70–71, 90, 104–5, 250n85, 251n97, 253n112, 262n5; components, 99, 100*t*, 266n57; imparting, 84–88, 85*t*, 93–94, 97, 97*t*, 105; *lakṣmīpīṭha* ("Section of Lakṣmī"), 173; *mahāvidyāpīṭha* ("Section of the Great Spell"), 100*t*, 173; *mantrapīṭha*, 100*t*, 174; *mantrarājapīṭha*/*mantrādhirājapīṭha* ("Section of the King of Mantras"), 100*t*, 174; modern use, 198; *pañcaprasthāna* ("Five Sections"), 149; *pañcaprasthānavidhi* ("Worship Ceremony of the Five Sections"), 177–90, 179*t*, 180*f*, 183*f*, 187*f*; popularity of, 149–50; premodern description of, 105–7; ritual use, 149–50; texts on, 99–101, 104–7; *upavidyāpīṭha* ("Section of the Secondary Spell"), 100*t*, 173; *vidyāpīṭha* ("Section of Knowledge"), 172–73
Sūrimantrabṛhatkalpavivaraṇa of Jinaprabhasūri, 98, 101–2, 105–7, 181, 188, 204
Sūrimantrakalpasamuccayaḥ, 150, 175
sūrimantrapaṭa (Cloth Diagram of the Mantra of the Mendicant Leader), 243n3, 262–63n12, 265n37; *bṛhat* (expanded) version, 156; daily worship of, 139, 146, 149, 160–91, 166*f*; modern use, 197, 203–4; Nandighoṣasūri's, 169–74, 170*f*, 171*f*; premodern use, 170; in promotion ceremonies, 70–71, 74, 85*t*, 99–102; ritual use, 149, 203–4; *saṅkṣipta* (condensed) version, 156
Sūrimukhyamantrakalpa of Merutuṅgasūri, 160
sūris (mendicant leaders), 151
Sūrya, 171*f*
Sūryodayasūri, Ācārya, 174, 176
sūtra (thread), 8
Sūtra of the Path of One's Movement (*īryāpathikīsūtra*), 161–62, 255n35
Sūtrakṛtāṅgasūtra, 22–23, 154*t*, 211–13, 238n8, 247n50
svastika symbol, 32
Svāyambhuvasūtrasaṅgraha, 61, 76–77
Śvetāmbara Jainism, 220n5, 230n5, 232n31; *ācāryas*, 93, 148–49; anti-iconic sects, 236n69; *anuyoga* (examination) or *yogavidhi*, 80–81; art, 240nn23–24; auspicious images, 266n55; auspicious symbols, 267n71; *Bhaktāmarastotra* length, 208–10; canonical texts (*āgamas*), 15–16, 80–81, 152–53, 192–93, 211, 220n8, 230n8, 263n25; *cāraṇas*, 233n36; Cloth Diagram of the Mantra of the Mendicant Leader

(*sūrimantrapaṭa*), 70–71, 74, 85*t*, 99–102, 243n3, 262–63n12, 265n37; *dhyāna*, 254n15; Dīvālī celebrations, 268n83; early, 24–26, 75–76; essential duties, 247n45; *gacchas*, 148–49; hand gestures, 256n37; *havanas*, 268n74; image-worshiping, 19, 145–55, 204, 213–14, 236n69, 246n31, 262n4; *īryāpathikīsūtra*, 255n35; Jina's Preaching Assembly, 56; Kharatara Gaccha, 79; litanies to practitioners with superhuman powers, 26; *Mahāniśīthasūtra*, 30–31, 63, 235n59, 236n69; *maṇḍalas*, 243n5; meditation, 117–19, 260n101; mendicant community, 149–50; mendicant groups (*gaccha*, *gaṇa*), 78–79; mendicant initiation, 49–64, 52*f*, 67–68, 72–74, 77–78, 91, 97–99, 150–51, 239n9; mendicant ranks, 75–76, 79–88; modern lay worshipers, 141, 145–46, 197–200, 213; modern monks, 103–7, 213–14; *mūrtipūjaka*, 19, 49, 148–51, 154*t*, 169, 268n74; path to liberation, 118; *prātihāryas*, 271n19; ritual diagrams, 97–99, 170–71, 266n55; scriptures, 152; superhuman powers, 24–25, *sūrimantra* (Mantra of the Mendicant Leader), 99–100, 100*t*, 104, 106–7, 245n25, 251n97, 266n57; *sūrimantrapaṭas* (Cloth Diagram of the Mantra of the Mendicant Leader), 70–71, 74, 243n3; tantric rituals, 58–64, 146–47; Tapā Gaccha, 79; *Tattvārthasūtra*, 16, 254n17; texts, 24–25, 99–100, 104, 119, 136–41, 236n68; *vardhamānavidyā* (Spell of Mahāvīra), 104; *vāsakṣepa* (throw of scent), 144–46; *yantras*, 141

Svopajñabhāṣya, 231n23

Syādvādamatī, Aryika, 239n10

symbols, 32, 241n30, 267n71

Taṇḍulavaitālika, 264n28

Tantra, xvi, 8–9

tantra (term), xvi, 221n10

tantra(s), 3–8, 13

Tantrāloka of Abhinavagupta, 242n43

tantric (*tāntrika*) (term), xv–xvii, 8–9, 17–19

Tantric Age, 78, 245n27

Tantric Buddhism, 11–14, 122, 225n52, 245n25

Tantric Śaivism, 9–10

Tantric Studies, xv

tantric traditions, xv, xvi–xvii, 7–19, 241n33; deity yoga, 268n84; early, 41, 46; *maṇḍalas*, 201–2; *mantras*, 201–2; meditation, 111–43, 268n84; mendicant initiations, 45–107; mendicant rituals, 190–95; *mudrās*, 201–2; yoga, 224n45, 268n84

Tantrism, 8, 225n52, 245n25

Tapā Gaccha, 79, 148–55, 169, 175, 239n13, 246n31

tapas (asceticism, austerities), 7, 15, 23, 25, 40, 46, 51, 74, 76, 115–16, 143, 178, 201, 221n8

tapasvī (ascetic) yoga, 224n45

Tathāgatas, 67

Tatia, Nathmal, 254n15

tattvabhū dhāraṇā, 260n92

Tattvānuśāsana, 126–30, 132

Tattvārthasāra, 253n2

Tattvārthasūtra, 6–7, 16, 74, 76, 80, 84, 115–17, 144–45, 201, 254nn16–17, 261n115

tattvarūpavatī dhāraṇā, 260n92

Taylor, Sarah Pierce, 254n23

teaching gesture (*pravacanamudrā*), 167, 167*f*, 177, 179*t*, 188, 189*f*

temple icons, 93

temples, 72

Terāpantha, xvii, 19, 30, 92, 111–13, 236n69

Tibetan Buddhism, 188–89

Tilakācārya, 263n19

Tilakamañjarī of Dhanapāla, 255n25

tīrthaṅkaras, 25, 39, 49, 56, 66, 74, 92–93, 95–96, 102–3, 125, 136, 160, 173, 178, 202, 213, 234–35nn53–54, 269n97

Tīrthodgālī, 264n28

Tobias, Michael, 238n13

Toḍalatantra, 266n49

Toliya, Pratapkumar, 260n103

Törzsök, Judit, 228n72

transliteration, ix

Tribhuvanasvāminī, 100*t*, 159, 171*f*, 173–74, 180, 180*f*, 206, 267n59

Trika tradition, 242n43

Trilokaprajñapti, 24–25, 33, 192, 231n22, 233n35

triratna (three jewels), 241n30
Triṣaṣṭiśalākapuruṣacarita of Hemacandra, 192–93
Tristuti Gaccha, 246n31
Tsong-kha-pa, 188–89, 268n84
Tubb, Gary A., 259n68
Tumburu, 191–93

ugratapas, 27, 105, 233n40
Umāsvāti, 231n23
unification (sakalīkaraṇa) rites, 122–28, 142, 165, 168, 253n3, 256n39, 256n41, 257n53, 257–58nn59–60, 266n46, 269n87
upādhyāyas (mendicant teachers): promotion ceremonies, 50–51, 75–76, 81, 85t, 86, 89–90, 97, 97t, 248n53; modern, 151, 155
Upadhye, A. N., 239n15
upāṅga (sub-limb or subsidiary text), 80, 85, 151–52, 154t
Upāsakādhyayana, 260n103
upasthāpanā (ordination), 83–84
upvās (complete fast), 178, 179t, 234n43
Uttarādhyayanasūtra, 80–81, 85, 153–55, 154t, 211–14, 246n38, 272n28
Uttara Śākhā (Balātkāra Gaṇa), 98

vācakas (mendicant preachers), 75, 151, 265n40
vacanabalaṛddhi, 234n54
vācanācāryas (mendicant preachers), 80, 85–86, 85t, 248n53, 265n40
Vaijayanta, 193
Vairāgyanandī, Ācārya, 47–49, 49f, 105, 239n10
Vaiṣṇavas, 122, 245n23
vaiyāvṛttya (serving mendicants), 144–45
Vajra, 233n33
Vajrabodhi, 12
Vajrapañjarastotra, 162–63, 265nn43–44
vajras, 124, 162–63, 257n46
Vajrayāna Buddhism, 9, 12, 17, 226n58
Vākpati Muñja, 135
valaya (ring), 220n5
Vanarāja, 245n28
vardhamānamantra (mantra of Mahāvīra), 48, 93, 97t, 249n81
Vardhamānasūri, 151
vardhamānavidyā (Spell of Mahāvīra), 64; imparting, 51, 84–88, 85t, 151, 154–55; second, 159; texts on, 104, 190–91
Vardhamāna Vidyā Kalpaḥ, 160–68
Vardhamānavidyākalpa of Siṃhatilakasūri, 190–91
vardhamānavidyāpaṭa (Cloth Diagram of the Spell of Mahāvīra), 85t, 86, 146–69, 157f, 191, 197, 248n52; daily worship of, 160–69, 161f, 166f; shrines for, 160–61, 161f
vardhamānayantra, 249–50n82
vargaṇās, 21, 230n5
Varṇī, Jinendra, 230n5
vāsakṣepa (throw of scent), 144–46, 145f, 160–61, 165, 166f, 169, 194–95, 262nn3–4, 266n53
vastraśuddhi (purification of clothes), 163, 253n3
Vasubindu. See Jayasena
Vasunandin, 92–94, 134, 249n73, 258n76
Vaṭṭakera, 32
Vedic traditions, 9, 228n73, 242n46
Vibhavasāgara, Ācārya, 92–93, 94f
vicakrāya svāhā mantra, 102, 136, 203
vidhānas (worship ceremonies), 114, 142, 220n5, 239n12, 256n40
Vidhimārgaprapā of Jinaprabhasūri, 79–88, 85t, 150–53, 160, 246n38, 247n50, 248n53, 264n28
Vidhi Pakṣa, 246n31
Vidyānuśāsana, 243n6, 256n36, 256n42
vidyās, 21–22, 230n8, 267n64. See also spells
Vijayā Devī, 171f, 172, 191–93
Vijayānandasūri (Ātmārāmajī), 149
Vijñānasūri, 174
vikriyāṛddhi, 233n35
Vimala Gaccha, 246n31
Vimalasāgara, Ācārya, 198–99, 239n10
Vimala Saṅgha, 239n10
Vimalasūri, 230n8
Vīṇāśikhatantra, 191
Vinaya (Pali Canon), 11–12
vinaya (respecting mendicants), 7, 23, 144–45
Vinayasāgara, Upādhyāya, 147–48, 156–59, 157f, 260n101

vipulamati, 232n32
Vīrasena, 24, 33–40, 202–3, 237n81, 255n31
virtuous meditation (*dharma/dharmyadhyāna*), 117–19, 135–36, 142–43, 255n31
viṣāpahāriṇī (Spell That Gets Rid of Poison), 206
visarjanamudrā (dismissing gesture), 166*f*, 168
Viṣṇu, 172, 266n46
Vṛddhayavanajātaka of Mīnarāja, 31
Vyākhyāprajñapti ("Proclamation of Explanations [of Mahāvīra]"), 153–54
Vyavahārasūtra (Bhadrabāhu), 75, 153, 244n11

weapon gesture (*astramudrā*), 166*f*, 167–69
Weber, Albrecht, 16, 152
Weber, Max, 225n51
Wedemeyer, Christian, 228n72
welcoming gesture (*añjalimudrā*), 163, 166*f*
Western Transmission, 131–32
Wheel of the Liberated Soul (*siddhacakra*), 127, 197, 250n89, 259n82, 261n107, 261n113; Expanded Wheel of the Liberated Soul (*bṛhatsiddhacakra*), 123–24; Worship Ceremony of the Wheel of the Liberated Soul (*siddhacakravidhāna*), 111–15, 112*f*, 121–26
Wiles, Royce, 263n24
Wiley, Kristi L., 231n16, 232nn26–27, 251n97, 255n27
Williams, Robert, 115, 240nn18–19, 241n32, 254n10
wisdom, 233n37
Woodroffe, John (pseud. Arthur Avalon), xvi
worship ceremonies: *gurupūjā* (worship of the guru), 262n4; *mahāpūjanas* (great worship ceremonies), 142, 220n5; *vidhānas*, 114, 142, 220n5, 239n12, 256n40
Worship Ceremony of the Five Sections (*pañcaprasthānavidhi*): becoming Gautama for Dīvālī, 185–90; concluding fire offerings for Lakṣmī, 181–85; required rites, 177–78, 179*t*; shrines for, 178–86, 180*f*, 183*f*, 187*f*, 194–95
Worship Ceremony of the Wheel of the Liberated Soul (*siddhacakravidhāna*), 111–15, 112*f*, 121–26

Yadava, Ganga Prasad, 255n25
yāgamaṇḍalas, 95, 250n87
yantras (diagrams that contain mantras), xvi, 71, 220n5, 271n20; of *Bhaktāmarastotra*, 208–11, 209*f*; Digambara, 141–42, 198–99, 207–8, 257n46, 261n106; *Jaina Method of Curing* (Jain), 3; modern use, 141–43, 198–99, 207–11; as objects of meditation (*dhyeya*), 114–15, 125–26, 130, 139, 142, 261n110; ritual use, 142–43, 203; Śvetāmbara, 141, 198–99, 220n5
Yāpanīya *saṅgha*, 89
Yaśastilaka of Somadevasūri, 132
Yaśobhadrasūri, 174
yatis, 262n9
Yixing, 12
yoga: action, 21, 54; monastic practices, 151
yoga, 224n45, 241n33, 258n73, 268n84; *anuttarayoga* (supreme), 13; *devatāyoga* (deity yoga), 12–13, 188–90, 223n37, 268n84; *tapasvī* (ascetic), 224n45
Yogadṛṣṭisamuccaya, 241n33
yoganikṣepa (permission to study scriptures), 82
Yogasāra (Yogīndu), 259n72
Yogaśāstra of Hemacandrasūri, 131, 137–41, 260n101
Yogasūtra of Patañjali, 132, 259n73
Yogasūtrabhāṣya, 231n18
yogatantras, 13
yogavidhi, 80–81, 85, 151–53, 155
Yogaviṃśikā of Haribhadrasūri, 117–18
Yogīndu, 259n72
Yoginīhṛdayatantra, 141, 261n104
YouTube, 142
Yugabhūṣaṇasūri, Ācārya (Paṇḍit Mahārāj), 155, 265n34, 266n52

Zaehner, R. C., 212

www.ingramcontent.com/pod-product-compliance
Lightning Source LLC
Chambersburg PA
CBHW051349290426
44108CB00015B/1947
* 9 7 8 0 2 2 6 7 6 7 0 6 2 *